Science, Morality
& Feminist Theory

Canadian Journal of Philosophy
Other Supplementary Volumes

New Essays in the History of Philosophy
Edited by Terence Penelhum and Roger A. Shiner

New Essays in the Philosophy of Mind
Edited by Terence Penelhum and Roger A. Shiner

New Essays on Plato and the Pre-Socratics
Edited by Roger A. Shiner and John King-Farlow

New Essays on Contract Theory
Edited by Kai Nielsen and Roger A. Shiner

New Essays on Rationalism and Empiricism
Edited by Charles E. Jarrett, John King-Farlow and F.J. Pelletier

New Essays on John Stuart Mill and Utilitarianism
Edited by Wesley E. Cooper, Kai Nielsen and Steven C. Patten

New Essays in Philosophy of Language
Edited by Francis Jeffry Pelletier and Calvin G. Normore

Marx and Morality
Edited by Kai Nielsen and Steven C. Patten

New Essays in Ethics and Public Policy
Edited by Kai Nielsen and Steven C. Patten

New Essays on Plato
Edited by Francis Jeffry Pelletier and John King-Farlow

New Essays on Aristotle
Edited by Francis Jeffry Pelletier and John King-Farlow

New Essays in Philosophy of Mind, Series II
Edited by David Copp and J.J. MacIntosh

Nuclear Weapons, Deterrence, and Disarmament
Edited by David Copp

The University of Calgary Press
Calgary, Alberta, Canada

Science, Morality
& Feminist Theory

Edited by
Marsha Hanen & Kai Nielsen

©1987 Canadian Journal of Philosophy

The University of Calgary Press
Calgary, Alberta, Canada

ISSN 0229-7051   ISBN 0-919491-13-8

For Amy, Sharon and Anne

Table of Contents

III — Some Applications

IV — Selves and Integration

Acknowledgements

Many people have helped immeasurably in preparing this volume. We wish especially to thank Carol Evans for her efficient and careful organizational and administrative work; Margaret Walker and Dianne Potter for help with that organization; and Arlene Thomas and Maggie Kohl for typing and related help.

Edrie Sobstyl prepared the bibliography, did the proofreading and organized the design work and Carol Sheehan provided advice on design.

Original art work for the cover was done by Alice Mansell and the cover design was done by Kris Twyman. Brenda Baker has provided support in a number of ways.

Finally, we wish to thank all of the contributors both for their excellent articles and for their help and advice along the way.

Introduction: Toward Integration

MARSHA HANEN
General Studies
University of Calgary
Calgary, AB
Canada T2N 1N4

> The desire for integration is so central to philosophy, I think, that no philosophical tendency will long endure without it. On the other hand, every attempt at integration which has been too grand has collapsed. — Hilary Putnam (*Realism and Reason*, 303)

Feminist theory, whether specifically philosophical or not, has been integrative in a number of ways. In epistemology and metaphysics it has attacked dualisms and dichotomies and tried to show that mind and body, reason and emotion, civilization and nature are neither separate nor separable; in ethics, we have agreed that rules, principles and justice must be tempered with a sense of caring and community; and, more generally, we have been at pains not to draw too sharp lines between philosophy and psychology, history and anthropology, literary theory and sociology. Nevertheless, we are all to some extent creatures of our backgrounds, and we find it hard to step out of our areas of certified expertise, so that even feminist philosophy, despite its integrative ideology, has usually remained confined within fairly traditional headings. This volume grew out of two convictions: first, that a collection of essays in feminist theory to be published by the *Canadian Journal of Philosophy* was long overdue; and second, that the field had attained sufficient maturity that it should be possible to exhibit in such a collection the connections and integration that we have so long espoused.

Feminist thought has tended to concentrate on one or the other of two areas: ethics and political theory on the one hand, epistemology and philosophy of science on the other. These have usually been seen as two (or more) quite separate subjects, just as in mainstream philosophy, and they have generally attracted quite different people to work in them: moral philosophers rarely write about epistemology, and philosophers of science do not usually write about ethics.

The ethics/politics stream has had two main foci: the elaboration of alternative feminist political theories such as liberalism, Marxism, radical feminism, socialism[1] and the development of a specifically feminist ethics. None of the papers in this volume specifically addresses either the development of these theories or the choice among them, though several of the papers can be said to begin by assuming one or other of these views — typically some form of liberal or socialist feminism. The reasons for the turning away from this approach not only in this collection but in the feminist literature generally may be quite straightforward: there may be little more to be said at this stage, for we have seen that the various theories overlap and that our feminist practice often falls under more than one political theory at any given time. I shall say a little more about this at the end of this essay.

In ethics we have seen a move away from an almost exclusive concentration on justice and hierarchies of rules toward a more dynamic ethics of care and a stress on the wholeness of persons.[2] Still, the focus has been primarily on questions of ethics, with little attempt to integrate the insights gained with those of feminist epistemology. The latter has also had two main strains: the critique of science and especially of bias both in the scientific establishment and in scientific research, and the broader critique of our understanding of rationality in terms of dichotomous thinking and the separation

---

1 See, for example, Alison M. Jaggar, *Feminist Politics and Human Nature* (Totowa, NJ: Rowman and Allanheld 1983).

2 Carol Gilligan, *In a Different Voice* (Cambridge, MA: Harvard University Press 1982); Nel Noddings, *Caring* (Berkeley, CA: University of California Press 1984)

of male and female with its concomitant denigration of the female.[3] One well-known attempt to cope with both strains can be found in Sandra Harding's *The Science Question in Feminism*[4] where we find the elaboration of several theories of science — feminist empiricism, feminist standpoint theories and feminist postmodernism — all of which (but perhaps especially the latter two) provide something of a new approach to epistemology. Still, there has been no more attempt from this side than from the side of ethics to integrate insights from the two areas.

Even on the face of it, however, integration is implied in that the recognition of alternative standpoints and of the impossibility of a truly neutral point of view is related to a recognition of the interconnections among human beings and caring for others. But one way to see the possibilities for integration in greater depth is to look at the structure of the present volume.

We begin with two essays which set the stage for the discussion by describing in very clear terms part of the feminist program for science and for ethics. Alison Jaggar points out that the now widespread recognition that science always embodies certain values or biases opens an important avenue for systematic philosophical reflection on these values and biases and the extent to which they are warranted. She quite explicitly speaks of warrant and desirability 'in the political and moral as well as epistemological senses of those terms.'[5] Her argument parallels, in some respects, that of Sandra Harding mentioned earlier. In particular, she is claiming that bias against women in scientific research is not merely a matter of surface methodological flaws that can be easily corrected; rather, it results from an incorrect and overly simple conceptualization

---

3 Ruth Bleier, *Science and Gender: A Critique of Biology and Its Theories on Women* (Elmsford, NY: Pergamon Press 1984); Genevieve Lloyd, *The Man of Reason* (Minneapolis, MN: University of Minnesota Press 1984)

4 Sandra Harding, *The Science Question in Feminism* (Ithaca, NY: Cornell University Press 1986)

5 All quotations from this point on are from papers in the present volume, unless otherwise indicated. Specific page references are not given.

which fails to take sufficient account of women's social inequality. This social inequality, she claims, is as much a determinant of sexual difference as our views of the latter are about inequality: research into sexual sameness and difference no more represents an area of value-neutral 'fact' than does any other area of social science. Put another way, 'sex differences are constructed as much as they are discovered, and ... sex inequality is a primary determinant of their construction.'

The argument that nature and culture should not be seen as opposed but rather as mutually constitutive also suggests that epistemology and morality are but two sides of one coin. No longer can we think of morality either as a separate sphere or moral prescriptions as arising from incontrovertible scientific facts discovered by means of neutral research methods. The facts are themselves as much constructed by the surrounding social realities as are the moral prescriptions. Jaggar's exhibition of the dialectical interrelatedness of sexual sameness and difference with sexual equality and inequality seem to me to suggest a similar interrelatedness between ethics and epistemology.

Annette Baier develops the fundamental point in the area of ethics — that justice, which has received pride of place in mainstream writing in recent years, is but one virtue among many, and not necessarily the pre-eminent one. The emphasis that used to be missing but that has now entered the sphere of moral theory is on caring, concern for others and community with them. Her discussion is especially helpful in that she is careful to make clear that the 'new' perspective is as much a difference of emphasis as it is a deep difference in content and in that she points out some of the connections between this perspective and certain parts of the philosophical tradition (e.g. that stemming from Hegel) that have been less central in recent Anglo-American philosophy than the justice perspective that derives from Kant. Nevertheless, the difference in emphasis, or in 'voice,' as Gilligan puts it, gives rise to a far-reaching critique of liberal morality arising from its questionable record in relation to women and minorities, its pretense of equality in the face of facts of inequality and its lack of attention to relations, such as certain family relations, that are not freely chosen. But perhaps most important for our purposes is the critique that arises from the overemphasis on rational, intellectual control of the emotions. It is here that Baier's essay makes contact with our integrative theme through her stress on the importance of cultivating desirable forms of emotion, as exemplified in parental love of children as opposed to the mere rational control of undesirable emotions. And the upshot of this revision of morality will be a true integration − not only of male and female moral wisdom, but also of the moral skills that flow from each.

The central section of the book is devoted to a collection of papers that point to new directions that emerge from critiques of various stages in the philosophical dialectic in both epistemology and ethics. But although some of these papers appear on the surface to fit fairly clearly into one or the other of these areas, most draw on both, and thereby illustrate the naturalness of the connections between them.

Alison Wylie's insightful discussion of Sandra Harding's *The Science Question in Feminism* provides not only a careful summary of some of the main arguments of that book, but also a useful clarification of and challenge to some of Harding's suggestions about the dangers of overstressing the values of comprehensive and coherent theories. Wylie points to an ambivalence she finds in Harding's way of dealing with the tensions created by the appeal of three quite different and inconsistent feminist views of science − empiricism, standpoint theories and postmodernism. On the one hand, there is the turning away from the search for coherence at all costs and a certain embracing of tolerance as exemplified in postmodernist rejection of the ideal of 'one true story' about reality. On the other hand, there is the importance of recognizing the tensions in our social realities that give rise to and are reflected in the tensions in our thought; and this appears to be a coherentist move toward an overarching explanatory theory that will account for the dissonances both in our lives and in our theories. Of course, we will not achieve such a theory, but this strain in Harding's thought suggests it is as much a desirable ideal as it is for other coherentists who are nevertheless more limited in not giving voice to what has been learned in the last twenty years from feminist critics of science and epistemology.

Wylie thus takes Harding to be recommending only a 'qualified tolerance of incoherence' and to be reacting not against 'coherence as such, but coherence arbitrarily constructed and inappropriately imposed.' And Wylie sees the 'evolution of increasingly coherent and comprehensive theories,' so long as coherence is appropriate, as 'a core regulative ideal.'

Harding's response does not make it clear whether she accepts this characterization of the ambivalence expressed in *The Science Question in Feminism* as pulling in two opposite directions; but she does reaffirm her view that both the feminist science critiques and postmoderism have much to offer and we should not even try to choose between them. Indeed, Harding wants to claim that a full appreciation of the tensions and contradictions is needed in order to transform the very context of inquiry from one that has already been inadequate to the feminist projects toward one that will accommodate them. One of the most interesting points she makes is that the standard opposition between truth-grounded epistemologies and relativism is an inadequate representation of our experience. Different and apparently incompatible accounts may both be true, and a claim may be false in innumerable ways. Moreover, science without moral, political and historical self-consciousness is inadequate, and yet this is the paradigm of science to which we have all adhered until recently. And it is only with integration of the moral and political that we can expect to produce a science that is conceptually adequate to a feminist outlook.

Marilyn Friedman's paper, like Annette Baier's, concentrates on moral philosophy, and specifically on some questions that emerge from the work of Carol Gilligan,[6] whose discussions of two moral 'voices' in terms of the contrast between an ethic of justice and universality and an ethic of care and relatedness are well known. Friedman argues, first, that whether or not there are clear empirical differences between the moral reasoning of men and women, the genders are 'moralized' in different ways, resulting in a 'division of moral labor' between the genders. Second, she argues that the two categories of care and justice overlap and indeed that the former, if it is to be morally adequate, involves the latter. Third, she tries

---

6 Gilligan, *In A Different Voice*

to develop some of the differences between care and justice in relation to their different treatment of individuals. Friedman's claim is thus that, in Western society at least, men and women are conceived of in relation to different moral expectations: it is more a question of the different moral concerns we attribute to men and women than it is of actual statistical difference.

Furthermore, in the sense in which justice is a matter of giving people their due, personal relationships of caring involve justice. Neither care nor justice by itself defines an appropriate moral standpoint. Still, this does not mean that the thesis about the existence of different moral voices is incorrect. This can best be seen if we attend to the difference between a moral commitment whose primary focus is on particular persons and one whose primary focus is on general rules and abstract principles. It is here that Friedman's discussion transcends moral philosophy, for the notion of caring for others in their particularity implies a concern for the respects in which different human beings are distinguishable and therefore not interchangeable. Developed further, this might help us to understand why individual human lives are important and why an emphasis on numbers alone fails somehow to capture that sense of importance. Friedman's paper thus has important implications not only for our views of a more adequate moral life, but also points toward a new emphasis in our conceptions of human nature.

A related set of issues is discussed by Virginia Held. She asks the question: What would social relations look like if, instead of thinking of them 'as contractual, we thought of them as *like* relations between mothers and children'? As a contrast with the usual models of 'economic man' and 'rational contractors,' Held develops the notion of a 'mothering person' where mothering is free of patriarchal domination and may be carried on by either women or men. The suggestion is that we consider what it would mean to extend features such as caring, concern, openness and trust, whose normal home is within the private domain, to the public domain. 'The relation between mothering person and child, hardly understandable in contractual terms, may be a more fundamental human relation, and a more promising one on which to build our recommendations for the future, than is any relation between rational contractors.'

This sort of idea has very broad implications for virtually all aspects of human relations: for the extent to which they are voluntary, self-interested, permanent and non-replaceable, for the meaning of equal respect and concern, the limited nature of rights to non-interference, the relation between privacy and social interdependency, and our views of power. Moral theory has always been based on particular conceptions of human nature, but what recent feminist work makes clear is that we need to rethink our conception of both morality and human nature in a more social form, that any conception embodies an ideology and that it behooves us to examine ideologies and to consider which ones are likely to provide the best vision of moral and intellectual life.

Sybil Schwartzenbach pursues some of these questions in a more specific vein – in relation to Rawls's notion of ownership. In particular, she argues that Rawls's analysis, 'supplemented by an account of ... "reproductive labor" ... tends to a form of democratic socialism.' Like Virginia Held and a number of other authors represented in this volume, Schwartzenbach sees the conflict between different notions of the self – in her terms, a private 'acquisitive' one and a moral 'purposeful' one as requiring resolution. She sees these, and two corresponding theories of ownership as both present in Rawls's difference principle, without the tensions between them having been resolved. But once we add a third conception of labor and ownership – that of women's distinctive labor as caretaker – we are pushed toward a reading of the difference principle that requires a socialist politics.

The model of child (and husband and aged) care is not here being used in quite the way that Held uses it; nor is it meant to be confined to traditional women's activity. Rather, it encompasses various forms of friendship and can be found in varying degrees in activities such as 'teaching, ministering, artistic performances, etc.' 'Female ownership' is shared and non-exclusive, non-economic, and emphasizes responsibility, guardianship and the notion of gift. It is a form which has been overlooked, not only by the liberal tradition but by the Marxist one as well. Schwartzenbach's claim is that, as women progressively enter the public labor market, it is at least possible that the workplace *and* private family relations will be transformed into a form of socialist, collective decision-making and labor-sharing. Whether this will happen is to some extent up to us; but note that the conception of the morally and politically ideal is again bound up with a conception of selfhood, or personality and motivation.

All of the essays in this volume are to some extent concerned with morality and to some extent with modes of knowing and theories of human nature. As well, they move back and forth between theory and example or application. John Exdell's paper is an interesting case in point. Exdell uses the case of the modern debate over the ethical status of 'feminine virtue' as a basis for assessing whether 'MacIntyre's[7] doctrine of virtue ... lays the foundation for genuinely non-ideological ethical judgments.' The particular examples he chooses include the views of Aristotle, Mary Wollstonecraft and Virginia Woolf in *To the Lighthouse*, and Exdell argues that MacIntyre's theory in *After Virtue* does allow us to 'set boundaries which exclude conceptions of virtue that function to justify relations of domination and subordination,' albeit 'not in the way that MacIntyre himself suggests.' The kind of society that would be compatible with MacIntyre's non-ideological conception of virtue would be one very much in keeping with the feminist transformative vision – a society in which both men and women 'share the responsibilities of household and public life without inhabiting discordant worlds with separate virtues,' a world in which 'the "womanly" values of caring and mutuality ... [are] extended outward as the organizing principles of the larger community.' It is the entire human world that requires transformation – not only our conceptions of appropriate social relations but our very conceptions of appropriate human behaviour and virtue itself. Interestingly enough, all of our authors in this group – Exdell, Schwartzenbach, Held and Friedman – agree with Baier in recommending a transformation of our conception of human flourishing so as to include features of both the current masculine and feminine worlds, but suitably integrated and without the negative aggression and competition of the former or the inappropri-

---

7 Alasdair MacIntyre, *After Virtue* (Notre Dame, IN: University of Notre Dame Press 1981)

ate subservience of the latter. The aim is integration, though of course the stress in these writing is, quite properly, on the value of those qualities that have traditionally been trivialized in male-dominated society.

Patriarchal culture has devalued women's voices not only in direct ways, by claiming women to be incapable of true morality, but also in less direct ways, by providing such mixed messages as to lead women into 'confusion and a kind of moral madness.' Kathryn Morgan explores four ways in which this happens and all of them, not surprisingly, involve an intertwining of epistemological and moral features. Women are denied full moral agency by denying them features which are claimed to be essential to such agency or by attributing to them features which make it impossible for them fully to exercise such agency. On these theories, men's and women's natures are taken to be significantly different, this difference giving rise to women's moral inferiority. Alternatively, women are relegated to the realm of private morality, told that this is all they are capable of, but that real morality involves the public domain and such features as rational impartiality, and then women are blamed for not possessing the qualities that exemplify genuine morality.

Another madness-inducing ploy is to turn virtues into vices and the other way round. Thus features which are thought praiseworthy in a man are treated as blameworthy in a woman; and there are the moral double-binds that arise from our socialization to romantic love and the use of manipulative power. As well, there is the moral invisibility of domestic labor and mothering, so that women often feel morally worthless when doing these things.

The recipe for change, not surprisingly, involves, among other things, a careful feminist critique both of theories of human nature and of previously accepted moral paradigms. 'We can expect new models of the self, perhaps pluralistic in nature, to emerge ... it may be that a looser, more open-textured notion of human consciousness will be necessary and that our epistemic paradigms will be similarly challenged in this process.' So again we see a way in which feminist theory not only issues in but almost presupposes a parallel reworking both of epistemology and morals, and an intertwining of the two into a kind of equilibrium where neither has primacy.

Moral madness is seen by Morgan as imposed on women; but Steven Burns argues that it is too easy here to be led yet again into false dichotomies: the autonomy ideal is no more sane than the heteronomy one. Moral sanity, he tells us, is the product of a 'dialectical understanding of the moral self. Both the heteronomous and the autonomous self are caricatures, warped beings whose sanity is at best only apparent, who are double-bound by the myths in which they have come to believe.' Moral sanity requires, among other things, that we come to see ourselves not only through our own eyes, but also through the eyes of the appropriate (rather than victimizing or destructive) others.

Barbara Houston reminds us of the danger inherent in reclaiming women's moral virtues without at the same time being aware of women's relative powerlessness and the extent to which adoption of the 'womanly' virtues of caring, nurturing, conciliating and the like may serve only to further entrench our devaluation and subordination. Once again, the necessity of avoiding gender essentialism, whether biological or cultural, comes to the fore, for if the virtues in question are thought to be virtues which only women can have, then the possibility for moral and political change of the appropriate kind will be too easily foreclosed.

Houston makes another very interesting point that ties her work, for all its concern with morality, more closely with the epistemological concerns of Harding and Wylie. Her suggestion is that there appear to be at least two distinct feminist standpoints with regard to morality — the one focussing mainly on women's distinctive moral experience and women's moral agency, and the other on the political struggle necessary 'to alter the condition of women's subordination.' There are difficulties with both perspectives, and also difficulties with giving up either one; yet they are to some extent in tension. The challenge is to develop a coherent theory that does not turn away from the insights of either of the two standpoints; and this challenge has much in common with the one articulated by Harding with respect to the possibility of constructing a coherent feminist account of science.

Only two papers in this collection take as their main focus the application of feminist theory to a particular problem. Susan Sherwin undertakes to show the difference it makes in assessing the propriety of developing in vitro fertilization if we adopt a feminist approach to ethics as opposed to one of the more traditional theological, or utilitarian, or deontological approaches. Issues of autonomy and control, for example, are seen in a different light by feminist theorists from that provided by utilitarianism or deontologism; and these extend not only to problems of ensuring freedom of choice in an environment controlled by persons other than the 'choosers,' but also to more overtly political questions. 'We find that the capitalism, racism, sexism, and elitism of our culture have combined to create a set of attitudes which view children as commodities whose value is derived from their possession of parental chromosomes.' The ideas of children as property and women as unfulfilled if they do not have children reflect cultural values which are both unrealistic and stultifying for many, and raise real questions about the pressure to have children reflected in the sometimes almost frantic pursuit of IVF.

A feminist ethics, for Sherwin as for many others, stresses relations among persons, concrete situations and the interconnectedness of economic, social and political considerations. Though not always explicit in Sherwin's paper, her rethinking of ethics requires a concomitant rethinking not only of our moral, social and political principles, but also of our notions of personhood, of what we know and can know, of how we know it and of what we should endeavor to find out.

A similar problem is addressed by Christine Overall in her paper 'Surrogate Motherhood.' Focussing on the questions of reproductive choice, Overall suggests that traditional conceptualizations of the notion of such choice may be faulty. 'The problem is that there is a real moral danger in the sort of conceptual framework which presents surrogate motherhood as even a *possible* freely chosen alternative for women.' The model of free market choice and surrogate motherhood as a freely chosen 'job' is unrealistic for a number of reasons having to do with our traditional ideologically-tainted ideas of what constitutes choice or coercion. Overall's pointing up of the connection between certain moral conclusions and the conceptual framework within which they are situated helps us again to see that pronouncements about human well-being are inadequate if they are made to depend solely upon traditional contractual principles, standard rules, or even consequences for the majority.

The remaining three papers attend more explicitly to some of the notions of connection and integration that I have been stressing. In particular, they try to provide a more encompassing view of the self, persons and morality than traditional philosophy has allowed; and in so doing, they point the way to an integration of various branches of philosophy that have more often been treated in isolation from one another.

Sheila Mullett focusses on self-knowledge in relation to moral life. She describes 'four forms of self-knowledge which emerge in a caring relation and which enhance the moral aspect of the self-in-relation.' The first involves what Iris Murdoch calls 'unselfing' — the sort of shift in perspective that allows us to focus attention away from the self in order to achieve some detachment and avoid preoccupation with oneself and a distorted or unbalanced view of the importance of things. We achieve better balance by focussing our care and concern elsewhere — on others. The second form of self-knowledge, which Mullett labels 'edification,' comes about when we come to appreciate, admire and emulate desirable qualities in others. The third is 'regret' — 'the genuine dismay we feel when we have harmed someone we care for' — and must be distinguished from the guilt and unworthiness we may feel in such situations. The latter focusses unproductively on the self, whereas the former attends to the other. A fourth form of self-knowledge — 'introspection' — is achieved when we become aware of our motives in particular relationships and 'gain insight into, and detachment from some of our baser motives.' All four of these modes of self-knowledge involve both an essential connection between self and other and the integration of thought and emotion.

Using as an example the case of a bulimic student, Mullett shows how a moral theory (such as Richard Brandt's) that focusses entirely on rational decision-making without attending to caring attitudes cannot possibly be an adequate theory. Reason and emotion must be integrated if the theory is to work. Even Charles Taylor's theory, though close to what Mullett is advocating, fails to pay sufficient attention to ways in which changes in our relations to others can change our experience and thus our perception of the moral life.

Marsha Hanen

One of the recurring themes in this volume is that of the importance of an adequate theory of human nature, of personhood and
of the self. Ann Ferguson argues that two prominent theories of the
self — the rational maximizer theory of classical liberalism and the
difference theory, according to which women are essentially different from men, are both inadequate. Both are too atomistic, static
and essentialist. A better view is an aspect theory, according to which
the self is a changing and not necessarily unified thing, and 'conscious selfhood is an ongoing process in which both unique individual
priorities and social constraints vie in limiting and defining one's
self-identity.' It is important to this view not only that our selves
have many aspects, but also that these are sometimes in conflict with
one another. None of these aspects can be determined to be more
fundamental or more authentic, nor can we expect always to be in
harmony, since opposing forces are pulling at us; but there is correspondingly no fixed content to masculinity and feminity — these
vary with social and other situations. Each person must do the integration for herself and, as this will vary with our different personalities and contexts, the result must be a form of ethical pluralism.
Nevertheless, Ferguson believes that an emphasis on friendships
among women will be empowering for all aspects of the self,
whether they be primarily of the rational maximizer kind or primarily
of the nurturing and supportive kind.

The idea that different aspects of the self may be in conflict with
one another connects with Sandra Harding's concerns about too-
quick attempts to achieve coherent, totalizing theories. It may be
that the conflict generated by one's nurturing role within the family and the need to operate on impersonal rules in one's job is just
not resolvable in any straightforward way; and for all our talk of
the need for men to learn more relational ways of being, the world
of work outside the home is, for most women, still very far from
giving any genuine voice to that sort of perception.

The emphasis that I have been placing on the integration of ethics
and epistemology is perhaps best exemplified in Lorraine Code's
paper 'Second Persons.' It will be clear by now that I do not mean
by this emphasis drawing together for its own sake, without regard
for genuine conflict which may or may not be resolvable at a particular time. Rather, my concern has been that philosophical thinking

has been carried out in compartmentalized ways without apparent realization that one cannot think adequately about morality, or knowledge, or personhood in isolation from any of the others. I shall have more to say in a moment about the kind of academic specialization that has, I think, engendered this sort of attitude.

Lorraine Code tries to show what is wrong with the conception of 'autonomous man' that has been taken to be 'an exemplar of what is best in human nature.' Autonomous man has much in common with Ferguson's rational maximizer, and with characters assumed in the papers of, for example, Baier, Friedman, Held, Schwartzenbach and Mullett. The concept is clearly an abstraction, not applicable to all men and applicable to some women; and not all of the salient features — self-sufficiency, independence, self-reliance, individualism, emphasis on expedience and efficiency — are applicable to all persons to whom the label applies. Code thinks that traditional views in this area amount to 'autonomy-obsession,' which can be corrected by concentrating on the primacy of interdependence and community and recognizing that we are, in Baier's phrase, 'second persons,' whose uniqueness, individuality, creativity and self-awareness 'grow out of interdependence, and continually turn back to it for affirmation and continuation.'

Code agrees with Ferguson that persons are not 'unified, wholly self-conscious selves': their being often involves 'contradiction, ambiguity, and gaps in self-awareness.' As well, she agrees with many of our authors about the centrality of responsibility, care and trust, especially in early development. But, she argues, 'these insights do not warrant granting "maternal thinking" or its close analogues (for example, family living) paradigmatic status.' On this point she appears to be in disagreement with Held. The usual picture of 'maternal thinking' is inclined to suppress the ambivalence we often feel toward those in our care, and also unjustifiably to posit wholeness in the caregiver when she may well be fragmented in various ways. Although it might be possible to introduce enough disclaimers and corrections into our conception of mothering to accommodate both these difficulties and also men and women who do not mother, Code believes that a more suitable candidate for paradigmatic status would be intimate personal friendships. Such relationships exhibit some of the features of family relationshps such as non-interchangeability of persons, and are perhaps better models for some, such as reciprocity and trust. Indeed, certain features of friendship might serve as models for other kinds of human relationship. It may even be that our more formal, 'public' selves can in some respects behave more like our more personal 'private' selves so that we and those to whom we relate will experience greater integration and less fragmentation.

Code points out that there are clear epistemic analogues to autonomy-obsession in the moral sphere.

> In the "autonomy of knowledge" view, it is taken for granted that knowledge is the *product* of enquiry, and that it can stand alone in the sense that the details of the process that has gone into its production are irrelevant to its shape, content, and/or evaluation. Knowledge judged worthy of that name is commonly assumed to be timelessly and placelessly true, and its objects are assumed to be independent of knowing subjects .... And although *individual*, autonomous knowees are depicted as the producers of knowledge, these are clearly the same abstract individuals who are the heroes of moral discourse. Their specificity, and their cognitive "location" count for nothing: indeed, should these threaten to intrude into epistemological discussion, such intrusion must be suppressed.

Knowledge is as much interpersonal as is morality, and equally requires a notion of trust and trustworthiness. Very little of what we know comes directly from our own observation, despite the centrality of the observation model in Western epistemology. We learn from others in myriad ways, and one of the things we try to teach our students is how to evaluate claims to knowledge. Lying, secrecy and witholding of information do not in general conduce to either morally or epistemically healthy communities. If communication were really the end-in-view, as it is often alleged to be, it is hard to see how the defensiveness and territoriality of the intellectual life could have become so prevalent. As well, the idea of a focus on understanding rather than on prediction and control might take us some way toward breaking down the old ideas of objectivity and the presumed boundary between subject and object that have been such an important part of cognitive autonomy-obsession.

These last two points have, I think, profound implications well beyond the confines of the problem of working out better theories of ethics and epistemology, important though that is. One problem with our theories and our understanding of the world, not only in philosophy but more generally, is the extreme territoriality and specialization of the academy. Knowledge is viewed not only as a product, but also as the exclusive property of particular individuals and groups. History is to be taught and written about only by historians and persons who are not specialists in the art of the Italian Renaissance should not speak about Leonardo da Vinci. We are all uneasy about making pronouncements outside our narrow areas of specialization, and no doubt this is wise up to a point. But it is also stultifying and quite impossible to stick to, given the explosion of information and the changing boundaries of knowledge of the past few decades.

Happily, feminist studies have been in the forefront of the effort to break down some of these barriers and to adopt a more integrative view of knowledge. Not only have feminists stressed interdisciplinarity and connections of knowledge, so that we have come to expect ourselves to know the feminist literature in anthropology and economics, psychology and literature as well as in our own field, but we have also, at least some of the time, tried to use that knowledge to gain more comprehensive understanding of our material.

In a way, this is all very congenial for philosophers who have for some time thought philosophy *of* to be at least respectable. To do philosophy of science, one must have a reasonable grasp of some sciences, and the same applies, mutatis mutandis, to philosophy of art or philosophy of law. Still, philosophers have typically thought that no one else is capable of doing philosophy, and, worse, that feminist theorizing is not philosophy. It seems to me that this protectionist attitude has been one of the main causes of intellectual stagnation in a number of areas. Recognition of connectedness, not only among people but also of knowledge, is essential to achieving any reasonably whole pictures; and focus on narrow specialisms will necessarily yield only partial insights.

To see the philosophical enterprise too narrowly is to distort it. This is true both of the tendency to treat philosophy in abstraction from other areas such as science or art, and also of the tendency to focus narrowly on particular problems in philosophy without seeing their interconnections. Views of human nature, knowing, morality and politics must inform and be informed by one another; and this is something that feminist philosophers know, even if they do not always make the point explicit. Of course, some non-feminist philosophers know it as well, and we can in some respects find kindred approaches in the work of Goodman, Putnam and Rorty,[8] as well as that of some continental philosophers. Still, much as we find important and congenial themes in this work such as anti-foundationalism and anti-essentialism, the problems of gender are hardly even considered, much less worked out. Feminist visions are thus much more comprehensive.

Still, as Code points out, the tendency in philosophy represented by contemporary pragmatism and related views can hardly be claimed to be mainstream. And it seems to me patent that one of the things that militates against its becoming so is the academic protectionism and narrowness that makes any crossing of boundaries suspect. Controlling one's subject matter is paramount. This is a difficult attitude to counter, and in trying to counter it, we must be careful to avoid the reverse pitfall — that of ranging too widely over topics we have not mastered. Still, some intellectual risk-taking fits well with the integrative and interdependent approach of feminism.

The matter of interdisciplinary integration, though a clear ideological tenet in most feminist academic work, is less well worked out than other integrative themes. This is not surprising, given the problems of expertise and territoriality to which I have alluded. Still, feminist studies have tried, and there are some attempts in this volume, expecially in the discussions of social scientific material by Jaggar, Wylie and Harding, the many references to the work of Gilligan, the literary examples of Exdell and Burns, and the widespread attention to psychological theory by Mullett and others.

---

8 Nelson Goodman, *Ways of Worldmaking* (Indianapolis: Hackett Publishing Company 1978) and *Of Mind and Other Matters* (Cambridge, MA: Harvard University Press 1984); Hilary Putnam, *Realism and Reason* (Cambridge, UK: Cambridge University Press 1983); Richard Rorty, *Philosophy and the Mirror of Nature* (Princeton, NJ: Princeton University Press 1979) and *Consequences of Pragmatism* (Minneapolis, MN: Universtiy of Minnesota Press 1982)

Another interesting attempt along these lines occurs in *Women's Ways of Knowing* by four psychologists.[9] The very spirit in which the book was written — as a collective enterprise rather than as four separate pieces — illustrates the feminist ideal of co-operative work. As well, the authors attempt to integrate philosophical, literary and educational material with the psychology which is their main focus. The work is based on intensive interviews with 135 women from diverse racial, class, ethnic and educational backgrounds, which makes it much more encompassing than traditional psychological studies. The women interviewed were also different ages, some from rural backgrounds and others from urban ones. The authors are investigating different ways in which women view reality and gain knowledge as well as how these are intertwined with our self-concepts. Their work can thus be seen as the other side of Carol Gilligan's coin — a focus on views of reality and knowledge rather than on morality.

Both studies make prominent use of the metaphor of voice, but the knowledge research develops the metaphor much further and contrasts it with visual metaphors which are so common in traditional approaches to science and morality. 'We found that women repeatedly used the metaphor of voice to depict their intellectual and ethical development; and that the development of a sense of voice, mind, and self were intricately intertwined.'[10] Unusual among works on knowing, this one is very moving, for it details in very concrete, individual terms the struggles involved in gaining a voice, in overcoming the sense of powerlessness that comes from growing up disadvantaged in various ways. Integrative thinking, connectedness, complexity, tolerance of ambiguity, avoidance of compartmentalization are all exhibited here in the actual experience of women, and we find an intertwining of theory with experience that is extremely rare in academic research and writing. The work is thus a model and a working out of a number of feminist ap-

---

9 M.F. Belenky, B.M. Clinchy, N.R. Goldberger and J.M. Tarule, *Women's Ways of Knowing* (New York: Basic Books 1986)

10 Ibid., 18

proaches that have until recently remained largely in the realm of theory. And however much we may disagree with various points (I think, for example, that the interpretation of and emphasis on relativism is a mistake)[11] the model of an integrative approach to knowledge is rightly destined to be extremely influential.

These reflections bring me back to the quotation from Putnam with which I began. I shall not attempt to answer the question of why the pressure to integrate is so strong in philosophy, why intellectual and artistic life seems so often to exhibit repeating cycles (e.g. classicism and romanticism) or why the integration itself is so unstable. What is interesting is that, whatever may be the 'mainstream,' attention to integration, to context, to historical embeddedness, are part of the intellectual and moral *zeitgeist*, and this is evident not just in feminist writing. Much that is best in the philosophical tradition is informed by these values, as is the work of some European philosophers, of Putnam, Goodman and Rorty, and of many of the male moral philosophers cited in the essays in this volume. But in these works the gender aspect is usually absent with the consequent distortions that feminists have pointed out.

The centrality to feminism of an integrative approach seems to me well documented. But there is still a gap between theory and practice which needs to be closed. We need to be able to see traditionally separate branches of philosophy as informing one another without one being dominant, and philosophy itself as not separate from other disciplines, from lived experience, or from efforts to create a better society. It is in this sense that all feminist theorizing is political, for one of its aims is change, even if we do not all agree about just what change is desirable or what are the best means for achieving it. None of the essays in this collection is explicitly an essay in political philosophy. It is still widely believed that feminist theory is political theory — conservative or liberal or Marxist or radical, and that feminist work in whatever discipline is only to be

---

11 See Marsha Hanen, 'Feminism, Reason and Philosophical Method,' in W. Tomm, ed., *Effects of Feminist Approaches on Research Methodology* (Waterloo, ON: Wilfrid Laurier University Press forthcoming).

counted as feminist theory to the extent that it explicitly develops one or other of these approaches. These essays make it clear that that is not so. The political agenda is no more amenable to traditional compartmentalization than is the rest of the agenda, and it is one of the collective strengths of these essays that they get on with the business of working out the detailed integration of theory with women's experiences without an overemphasis on political categorization. The extent to which these essays build on existing feminist work, posing new questions and developing new themes testifies to the field's ongoing intellectual, moral, and political vitality.

I

Two Aspects: Science and Morality

CANADIAN JOURNAL OF PHILOSOPHY
Supplementary Volume 13

Sex Inequality and Bias in Sex Differences Research*

ALISON M. JAGGAR
University of Cincinnati
Cincinnati, OH 45221
U.S.A.

I Science and Philosophy

The relationship of philosophy to science is a matter of long historical dispute. Philosophy has been described variously as the mother, the queen or the handmaiden of science, depending on whether the philosopher's role was perceived as that of giving birth to science, of regulating and legitimating scientific discourse or of clearing the conceptual underbrush in the way of scientific advance. This essay, by contrast, is grounded on a conception of philosophy and science as partners or sisters, perhaps even as Siamese twin sisters, both proceeding from the same impulse to understand ourselves and the world and to change both for the better. Occasionally relations between philosophy and science have been marred by sibling rivalry, with each sister claiming the right to control and limit the pretensions of the other. In fact, however, philosophy and science are in-

---

* This paper was prepared for a symposium on Bias in Sex Differences Research, held at the Annual Meeting of the American Association for the Advancement of Science, Chicago, 14-18 February, 1987.

terdependent and ultimately inseparable. To borrow a famous slogan from another context: science without philosophy is blind; philosophy without science is empty.

The contemporary prestige of scientific knowledge makes the dependence of philosophy on science quite evident. For instance, it is easy to see how social and political philosophy requires information from such sciences as psychology, economics, political science, sociology, anthropology and even biology and the various technologies. A knowledge of many sciences is necessary to give substance to philosophical ideals of human well-being and fulfillment, to add trenchancy to philosophical critiques of oppression, and to avoid idle speculation or utopianism by identifying the limits (even if only historically contingent limits) of social and political possibility.

Less readily recognized today is the dependence of science on philosophy. This lack of recognition is a result of the fact that, for much of the twentieth century, positivism has shaped the conceptions of science that have been held by philosophers, by scientists and even by the general public. Positivism portrayed science as a purely empirical enquiry, based entirely on observation and guided solely by the nature of reality, independent of human interests or desires. The intrusion of any element of interest or desire into the supposedly value neutral enterprise of science was viewed by positivism as contamination and damaging bias.

Positivism finally is dying, though it remains powerful in its death throes, and it is now generally admitted that values inevitably enter into science on many levels: in the selection and definition of the problems undertaken for investigation; in the choice of the method used to investigate those problems; and in the interpretation as well as the application of the results. It is now hardly controversial to note that research programmes always incline in a certain direction insofar as they always are oriented towards certain findings and always rest on certain methodological and other presuppositions. This inclination may be described as a bias, but such bias no longer is seen as necessarily deleterious. It is now acknowledged that some biases may enhance rather than diminish both the reliability and the social value of the research findings.

Especially since the scientific revolution of the seventeenth century, philosophers have been fascinated by science, reflecting on its goals and consequences and exploring the conceptual and other relations between different scientific enquires. Philosophers have been interested particularly in issues of scientific method, such as the basis of scientific claims to objectivity, the nature of scientific rationality and the avoidance of distortion and damaging bias. The contemporary recognition that scientific research always embodies certain values or biases opens up new ways in which philosophers may contribute to science. In addition to studying scientific method and the conceptual connections between various scientific enquiries, philosophers may contribute to science by reflecting systematically on the values that it incorporates. If all science necessarily has a certain bias, philosophers can discuss which biases are warranted and which are undesirable — in the political and moral as well as epistemological senses of those terms.

In this essay, I want to identify an invidious bias that is embedded in much research into sex differences. I shall argue that bias against women is endemic in any such research programme that fails to take account at every stage of women's social inequality. It is primarily because its view of the relation between sexual difference and sexual inequality is too simplistic that much sex differences research rationalizes and so perpetuates women's subordination.

II Sex Differences and Sex Inequality

Western society has always been organized around the assumption that the differences between the sexes go far beyond a simple difference in procreative function. Almost all human activities have been classified as more appropriate to one sex or the other (although these classifications have changed historically) and, where both sexes have engaged nevertheless in the same activity, such as driving a car, they have been expected to do so in ways that our culture defines as distinctively masculine or distinctively feminine. The prevailing sexual division of labour always has been buttressed by a mass of philosophical, scientific and popular claims about the different needs and capacities of women and men. Contemporary society differs from classical Greek society more in the content of its claims about sex differences than in the firmess of its convictions about inherent sex polarity. Today, these include claims that women differ from men not only in physiological functioning but in their cognitive abilities, their emotional predispositions and their aptitude for various skills.

Western society historically has claimed not only that women were different from men but also that they were inferior to men. For example, Aristotle defined women as infertile, imperfect and deformed men and associated them with matter, passivity and irrationality. Men, by contrast, were identified with form, with activity and with rationality. Given these contrasts, it is hardly surprising that Aristotle defined women's virtue as obedience and men's as ruling. Contemporary society is much less blatant in its claims about women's inferiority, but the contemporary inequality between women and men is only somewhat less than existed in classical Athens. Certainly it is true that western women today can vote and are no longer confined to the household, but men still occupy most positions of power and authority in politics, the economy, education, the arts and religion. Waged or salaried women working full time still are paid substantially less than men (and the gap widens at the lower educational levels); a much larger proportion of single parent families headed by women than men subsists below the poverty line; women are subjected constantly to male harassment, rape and physical violence. Male dominance is implicit in all the encounters of daily life: for instance, men typically arrange their bodies so as to occupy more physical space than women of the same race or class; they tend to speak louder than women, to interrupt women more frequently than men and to touch women's bodies in familiar or disrespectful ways.

It is the pervasive existence of sex inequality that always has motivated research into sex differences. Investigation into sexual difference has seemed to promise answers to the urgent questions of why women everywhere are subordinated and whether and how that subordination can be ended. Invariably, anti-feminists have justified women's subordination in terms of perceived differences between the sexes, and feminists have responded to their claims in a variety of ways. Some feminists have challenged the existence of

28

certain alleged sex differences; others have accepted that some sex differences do exist but have denied either that these differences are innate or that they have the social implications drawn by anti-feminists. I shall argue that the traditional association between questions of sex difference and questions of sex equality is far more than simply historical. I believe that what appear to be two different issues (a scientific and a philosophical one) in reality are aspects of a single issue: that science and philosophy, here as elsewhere, in principle are inseparable.

When I first started thinking about sexual equality, back in the early 1970s I accepted without question the widely shared assumption that assertions of similarity and difference, on the one hand, and assertions of equality and inequality, on the other, each had a different logical status. I thought of assertions of similarity and difference as empirical claims, justified ultimately by reference to observation. They described the way the world was, independently of the way we would like it to be. By contrast, I thought of assertions about social equality and inequality as being recommendations, value judgments, prescriptions rather than descriptions, incapable in principle of being justified by reference to empirical observation. They prescribed the way the world should be, independently of how it actually was.

Of course, I recognized that there was some relation between assertions about similarity or difference, on the one hand, and assertions about equality or inequality, on the other. Since equality ordinarily is taken to require treating people with similar needs and capacities alike, and treating people with different needs and capacities differently, it was natural to suppose that, in figuring out how to treat people equally, one should start by investigating their similarities and differences. I did not believe that the results of those investigations would logically imply anything about how people *ought* to be treated (to suppose that, I thought, would be committing the naturalistic fallacy of deducing values from facts, 'ought' from 'is'). However, I believed that the findings of science would still be indispensable bases for making informed recommendations about social policy. In this sense, therefore, I thought of the scientific investigation of sexual similarity or difference as something that should be logically prior to a philosophical consideration of sexual equality.

I now think that this conception of the relation between sexual difference and sexual equality was hopelessly naive. I no longer view investigations into sexual similarity and difference as value neutral scientific research, as resulting in *discoveries* that logically precede or constitute the basis in some way for philosophical *decisions* about sexual equality. On the contrary, I now believe that our decisions about sexual equality are at least as much the basis for our supposed discoveries about similarity and difference. Indeed, on both the practical and the symbolic level, I now think that social equality or inequality may be the major determinant of our scientific conclusions about sexual similarity or sexual difference. In what follows, I shall argue that women's social inequality often translates directly into scientific claims that women are 'naturally' different from or inferior to men. These claims, in turn, reinforce and so perpetuate women's subordination.

III How Sex Inequality Shapes Sex Differences Research

Every human individual is different from every other individual and, the more we know about a person, the more here special differences and uniqueness emerge. Every individual is also similar in some ways to every other individual and, the more we know about a person, the more we come to perceive what we have in common with her. Whether we emphasize or even whether we notice differences or commonalities depends on a variety of factors including our expectations, our interests and even the conceptual and linguistic resources available to us.

Contemporary society is organized in such a way as to emphasize commonalities between individuals of the same sex and differences between individuals of opposite sexes. It does this through the institution of gender, which is a set of social norms that regulates the activity of individuals according to their sex. Unlike some other cultures, western culture recognizes only two genders, the masculine and the feminine. Male individuals are expected to act in ways that are defined by the culture as masculine, and females are supposed to act in ways that are defined as feminine. In contemporary western society, practically every aspect of life, from the most trivial to the most profound, is governed by a set of gendered expectations. The ways we move and speak, the ways we work, play and make love, even the ways we laugh, hold our cigarettes and blow our noses, all are regulated by norms that reflect, reinforce and occasionally modify prevailing understandings of gender.

Science is concerned with the uncovering and explanation of regularities, both similarities and differences. It begins with perceived patterns and goes on to investigate whether those patterns are a manifestation of deeper underlying regularities. Within a gendered society, it is impossible to ignore patterns of intra-sex similarity and inter-sex difference. Such patterns are given so much emphasis that, when science develops, it is inevitable that they should become the object of scientific scrutiny. Moreover, in a society where the sexes are unequal, it is inevitable that scientists should be assigned to discover whether this inequality is grounded in some inherent difference between the sexes — a difference that is construed, equally inevitably, as a defect characteristic of the subordinate sex.

The existence of sexual inequality not only provides the original inspiration for sex differences research; it also makes certain hypotheses about the causes of that inequality initially more plausible than others, encouraging scientists to pose their questions in a way that orients the enquiry in a particular direction or gives it a certain bias. That bias is towards uncovering ways in which women are inherently different from and even inferior to men. This is not to assert that any scientific investigation into sex differences that is undertaken in a context of sex inequality necessarily will emerge with findings of female inferiority or even sex differences; the prevailing social values are not irresistible and research may be undertaken whose bias runs counter to the mainstream. But it is to say that the research context of sex inequality makes it more likely that research programmes that promise to confirm existing sex prejudice will be funded, that sex differences rather than sex similarities will be discovered, that those differences will be interpreted as female deficiencies rather than as women's strengths, and that research results that reinforce existing sex hierarchies will receive a warmer welcome than results that challenge the sexual status quo.

If sex difference researchers fail to remain constantly mindful of the social inequality of the sexes, their research is likely to be biased against women at several levels. First of all, this inequality is likely to condition their expectations in a way that influences or biases their initial observation of the extent of sexual difference. For instance, they may perceive men as generally taller than women, a perception encouraged by the norms of heterosexual coupling, even though the mean difference in height between western women and men is only a few inches, whereas the normal distribution of height within each sex is over two feet.

In addition, the context of sex inequality may well condition the values assigned to sexual difference. One example that has received much attention in recent years is the reported finding by Lawrence Kohlberg and his associates that women are less likely than men to attain the highest levels of moral development. This finding resulted from testing women's development on a scale derived from the study of male subjects, a test instrument that defined women's allegedly different approach to moral thinking as a deficiency in moral rationality (Kohlberg 1981).

The fact that sex differences research occurs in a context of sex inequality biases not only the direction of the research but also the ways in which its results are received, and sometimes even forces revision of those results. Failure to discover sex differences is not news, but the announcement of differences meets with all kinds of media attention, expecially if the supposed differences can be interpreted as giving males a genetic superiority. One example is the wide exposure given in 1980 to the alleged discovery of a male 'math gene.'[1] In the midst of this excitement, the media generally ignore methodological criticisms made by feminists, especially if these are at all subtle. If a finding of sex difference appears as female superiori-

---

[1] Anne Fausto-Sterling (1985, 54d) describes the presentation of the story in the *New York Times*, *Time* and *Newsweek*, following the original research article by Benbow and Stanley (1980). Fausto-Sterling goes on to summarize flaws in the reasoning for Benbow's and Stanley's conclusion, that women are inherently weaker than men in mathematical ability. None of these flaws, however, has been noted, much less headlined, in the popular media.

ty, however, the 'discovery' may be hastily reinterpreted or defined away. The early development of I.Q. tests provides a clear example of this. When females performed better on the tests, this was taken as an indicator of the tests' invalidity and the tests were revised until the males performed up to the female standard. One doubts that the tests would have been revised if females had performed worse than males. Certainly the generally lower performance of people of colour on I.Q. tests went unquestioned for decades and it has taken considerable political agitation to begin any move towards overhauling the tests for cultural bias.

Bias against women is not a new phenomenon in the history of sex differences research. The nineteenth century science of craniology, for instance, claimed that women were less intelligent than men because they had smaller brains, quite disregarding the fact that, if brain size was important at all, it had to be the size of the brain relative to the size of the body. In the 1870s and 1880s, Dr. Edward Clarke of Harvard University opposed the admission of women to higher education on the grounds that strenuous thinking would cause too much blood to flow into women's brains and result in the atrophy of their reproductive organs (Rosenberg 1982, 5). These examples are always good for a laugh at women's studies meetings, but they are not so funny when one starts to notice how much of present investigation into sex differences still is infected by assumptions that are biased towards finding women inferior.

In the next section, I want to draw attention to a particularly fundamental assumption, one that is prevalent in many sex difference research programmes and that is especially significant in biasing the research against women. This is the assumption that sex differences exist prior to and independent of sexual inequality. Such an assumption obscures the feminist recognition that sex differences are constructed as much as they are discovered, and that sex inequality is a primary determinant of their construction.

IV How Sex Inequality Shapes Sex Differences

On the most obvious level, it is easy to see how the cognitive and emotional capacities of men and women are likely to be influenced substantially by the unequal social experiences of boys and girls. Feminists from the earliest days have bemoaned the ways in which women's lack of access to education has prevented them from developing their moral and intellectual capacities. We are now able to identify more subtle discouragements to certain types of intellectual achievement, both in the infant experience of boys and girls and in the schooling process itself. Such discouragement may continue to a very advanced state of education: one of my professors in graduate school used to claim that women PhDs were incapable of orgasm.

It is also easy to see how certain physical differences between women and men are affected by social inequalities. These differences may sometimes be quite gross, as in the case of Chinese footbinding or as in the contemporary deformation of women's feet, tendons and backs by high heeled shoes. Different forms of exercise also encourage different muscular development in males and females, with males tending toward greater development of the upper body. Even differences in height are affected by such social factors as diet and exercise. When the diet of girls is less adequate nutritionally than that of boys, it is predictable that girls will remain smaller. But even in societies where both boys and girls receive an adequate diet, the physical training of girls influences their adult height. The onset of puberty in girls, unlike its onset in boys, dramatically slows female growth. However, since the onset of puberty depends in part on the ratio of fat to body weight, it tends to occur later in girls who are more athletic and so have less body fat. Other things being equal, athletic girls thus tend to grow taller than girls who are less athletic — and how athletic girls are encouraged to be of course is generally a function of social attitudes (Lowe 1983, 48).

No one doubts that sex differences are influenced to some extent by social inequalities, though few people other than feminists recognize how great is that extent. But most people also assume that there are certain fundamental differences which underlie those that are socially imposed, differences that constitute the physiological basis for the social elaboration of gender. This is certainly the assumption grounding much sex differences research, which is commonly conceived as the project of investigating how much of the observed differences between males and females is due to genetic and how much to social factors; in more traditional terms, how much to nature and how much to nurture. This question, however, is incapable of being answered, and it is incapable in principle as well as in practice.

We have seen already that our genetic inheritance (our genotype) operates always in a particular environment that profoundly shapes not only our behaviour and our cognitive and emotional capacities but also affects our physical structure (our phenotype). This is as true of sexual differences as it is of any other features of our biological constitution, such as our dexterous hands with their opposable thumbs. Even such a so-called fact of life as that women give birth to helpless infants, which require a long period of post-natal care, appears to have been a social achievement in at least two ways. First of all, this evolutionary development was a response to a cultural innovation, the invention of tools, which gave a survival advantage to tool users and so encouraged biological selection not only for the hand but also simultaneously for larger brains and for the narrower pelvises appropriate for walking on two legs, thus leaving the hands free for tool use. These later two evolutionary trends generated what anthropologist Sherwood Washburn (1960) has called the 'obstetrical dilemma': increasingly large-headed infants had to be born through increasingly narrow birth cannals.[2] Not only was the so-called obstetrical dilemma generated by the social invention of tools: the solution of this dilemma, too, was a social achievement. For the solution lay in infants being born at an earlier stage of development and this solution was possible only because our forebears lived in relatively co-operative social groups and did not leave each mother alone to care for her infant. If the latter had happened, rates of

---

2 Washburn's observation and its implications are discussed by Dorothy Dinnerstein (1976, ch.2).

reproduction would have slowed so much that, with high mortality, the species could not have survived.

The general point is not just that our genetic inheritance is socially malleable and capable of being expressed in the present in a wide variety of ways; more fundamentally, what we have inherited itself is partly the product of earlier social developments. For this reason, the whole nature/nurture distinction is fundamentally misleading when applied to human beings: we simply cannot identify any social phenomena that are independent of biological influence, nor any human 'natural' or biological features that are independent of social influence. Because of this, it is impossible in principle to distinguish the innate from the social components in the constitution of human beings. As far as human beings are concerned, the relation between nature and culture is mutually constitutive or dialectical: to oppose one to the other is incomprehensible. Everything that we are and do is simultaneously natural and social.

V How Sex Differences Research Promotes Sex Inequality

Given the impossibility in principle of identifying differences between the sexes that are unaffected by social inequalities, one might ask why so much money and energy continue to be poured into pursuing this will of the wisp. What is the explanation for the seemingly endless preoccupation with seeking inherent, typically physiological causes for sex differences in the face of the overwhelming perceptible similarities between women and men as groups, in the face of the plausibility of the social explanations for the differences that do exist, and in the face of the logical impossibility of identifying non-social genetic determinants for these? Part of the answer is surely that such research helps to rationalize and justify the continuation of sex inequality.

First of all, the very existence of so much research lends credence to the belief that indeed there must be significant mental and physical differences between the sexes, a belief that persists despite the common sense observation, noted a decade ago by Gayle Rubin (1975, 179), that, although men and women are, of course, different ... they are not as different as day and night, earth and sky, yin and yang, life and death. In fact, from the standpoint of nature, men and women are closer to each other than either is to anything else — for instance, mountains, kangaroos, or coconut palms.

Even where there are differences between groups of people, it is often far from clear that sex is the most salient variable. Even within a culture, the range of variations in ability between the average man and the average women typically is much less than the range of variations in ability between individuals of the same sex. But when the belief that indeed there are deep differences between the sexes is coupled with the evaluation of those differences as female deficiencies, then two necessary premises are established for a plausible argument that sex inequality is rooted in female inferiority.

The next essential step in this argument is a demonstration that women's alleged deficiencies are rooted in women's nature. This step is supplied by research that purports to link supposedly observed differences between the sexes with underlying physiological structures that are taken to be relatively impervious to social manipulation. Research that purports to establish these links fulfils the function of reifying or naturalizing existing sex differences.

Of course, even an irrefutable demonstration of women's innate inferiority would not establish conclusively that women should not enjoy social equality with men. Feminists could argue alternatively that women should be subjected to remedial education or even to surgical 'correction.' (The arguments advanced here would depend in part on whether the equality sought was formal or substantive, a complication that must be ignored for now.) Since any such special interventions would be open to challenge as unfair, unnatural or just too expensive, however, it is clear that any sex differences research that claims to establish some physiologically based female incapacity in practice encourages general acceptance of sex inequality as both natural and (therefore) as desirable.

My conclusion is not, of course, that sex differences research should be abandoned. It is rather that, in a social context of male dominance, such research should be approached with suspicion — the same suspicion with which we might approach race difference research in a racist society or gentile/Jew difference research in an anti-semitic one. In a social context of inequality, there will always be a tendency for this kind of research to have an undesirable bias towards rationalizing rather than challenging existing inequality.

In a sexually egalitarian society, I suspect there might be little interest in the scientific investigation of sex differences, perhaps because there would be so few to investigate. In our own society, however, sex inequality is so deep and its legitimation by science is so widespread that feminists cannot afford to abandon our own research into sex differences. Feminist research avoids the mainstream bias against women because it is undertaken with an explicit consciousness of the ways in which sex inequality shapes both the subject and the process of sex differences research.

Feminist research is not predicated on the assumption that currently there exist no real differences between women and men. Obviously, some do exist. But feminist researchers refuse to assume that these differences are eternal and that their significance is unchanging. Feminist researchers note that perceived differences between women and men are socially constructed on many levels and that their meaning is assigned by the social context of male dominance. For this reason, feminist research cannot take the existence of differences between the sexes as a scientific, factual, value free basis for normative policy decisions regarding sexual equality or inequality. For feminists recognize that the differences we observe are the results of inequality as much as the causes of or justifications for inequality. Male dominance exaggerates and may even create most sexual differences. The abolition of male dominance would transform and minimize sex differences in ways and to an extent that we cannot foresee. Thus recommendations about sexual equality and inequality that are based on claims about sexual similarity or difference are partially self-fulfilling predictions. Sexual differences are more created than discovered. Sexual sameness and difference and sexual equality and inequality are reciprocally interactive and mutually dependent. Rather than being logically and methodologically separable, they are dialectically interrelated.

References

Benbow, Camilla P., and Julian C. Stanley. 'Sex Differences in Mathematical Ability: Fact or Artifact,' *Science* **210** (1980), 1262-4.

Dinnerstein, Dorothy. *The Mermaid and the Minotaur: Sexual Arrangements and Human Malaise*. New York: Harper and Row 1976.

Fausto-Sterling, Anne. *Myths of Gender: Biological Theories About Women and Men*. New York: Basic Books 1985.

Kohlberg, Lawrence. *The Philosophy of Moral Development*. San Francisco: Harper and Row 1981.

Lowe, Marion. 'The Dialectic of Biology and Culture,' in Marion Lowe and Ruth Hubbard, eds., *Woman's Nature: Rationalizations of Inequality*. New York: Pergamon Press 1983.

Rosenberg, Rosalind. *Beyond Separate Spheres: Intellectual Roots of Modern Feminism*. New Haven, CT: Yale University Press 1982.

Rubin, Gayle. 'The Traffic in Women: Notes on the "Political Economy" of Sex,' in Rayna R. Reiter, ed., *Toward an Anthropology of Women*. New York: Monthly Review Press 1975, 157-210.

Washburn, Sherwood. 'Tools and Human Evolution,' *Scientific American* (1960).

CANADIAN JOURNAL OF PHILOSOPHY
Supplementary Volume 13

The Need for More than Justice

ANNETTE C. BAIER
University of Pittsburgh
Pittsburgh, PA 15213
U.S.A.

In recent decades in North American social and moral philosophy, alongside the development and discussion of widely influential theories of justice, taken as Rawls takes it as the 'first virtue of social institutions,'[1] there has been a counter-movement gathering strength, one coming from some interesting sources. For some of the most outspoken of the diverse group who have in a variety of ways been challenging the assumed supremacy of justice among the moral and social virtues are members of those sections of society whom one might have expected to be especially aware of the supreme importance of justice, namely blacks and women. Those who have only recently won recognition of their equal rights, who have only recently seen the correction or partial correction of long-standing racist and sexist injustices to their race and sex, are among the philosophers now suggesting that justice is only one virtue among many, and one that may need the presence of the others in order to deliver its own undenied value. Among these philosophers of the philosophical counterculture, as it were — but an increasingly large counterculture — I include Alasdair MacIntyre,[2]

---

1 John Rawls, *A Theory of Justice* (Harvard University Press)

2 Alasdair MacIntyre, *After Virtue* (Notre Dame: Notre Dame University Press)

Michael Stocker,[3] Lawrence Blum,[4] Michael Slote,[5] Laurence Thomas,[6] Claudia Card,[7] Alison Jaggar,[8] Susan Wolf[9] and a whole group of men and women, myself included, who have been influenced by the writings of Harvard educational psychologist Carol Gilligan, whose book *In a Different Voice* (Harvard 1982; hereafter D.V.) caused a considerable stir both in the popular press and, more slowly, in the philosophical journals.[10]

Let me say quite clearly at this early point that there is little disagreement that justice is *a* social value of very great importance, and injustice an evil. Nor would those who have worked on theories of justice want to deny that other things matter besides justice. Rawls, for example, incorporates the value of freedom into his account of justice, so that denial of basic freedoms counts as injustice. Rawls also leaves room for a wider theory of the right, of which the theory of justice is just a part. Still, he does claim that justice is the 'first' virtue of social institutions, and it is only that claim about priority that I think has been challenged. It is easy to exaggerate the dif-

---

3 Michael Stocker, 'The Schizophrenia of Modern Ethical Theories,' *Journal of Philosophy* **73**, 14, 453-66, and 'Agent and Other: Against Ethical Universalism,' *Australasian Journal of Philosophy* **54**, 206-20

4 Lawrence Blum, *Friendship, Altruism and Morality* (London: Routledge & Kegan Paul 1980)

5 Michael Slote, *Goods and Virtues* (Oxford: Oxford University Press 1983)

6 Laurence Thomas, 'Love and Morality,' in *Epistemology and Sociobiology*, James Fetzer, ed. (1985); and 'Justice, Happiness and Self Knowledge,' *Canadian Journal of Philosophy* (March, 1986). Also 'Beliefs and the Motivation to be Just,' *American Philosophical Quarterly* **22** (4), 347-52

7 Claudia Card, 'Mercy,' *Philosophical Review* **81**, 1, and 'Gender and Moral Luck,' forthcoming.

8 Alison Jaggar, *Feminist Politics and Human Nature* (London: Rowman and Allenheld 1983)

9 Susan Wolf, 'Moral Saints,' *Journal of Philosophy* **79** (August, 1982), 419-39

10 For a helpful survey article see Owen Flanagan and Kathryn Jackson, 'Justice, Care & Gender: The Kohlberg-Gilligan Debate Revisited,' *Ethics*

ferences of view that exist, and I want to avoid that. The differences are as much in emphasis as in substance, or we can say that they are differences in tone of voice. But these differences do tend to make a difference in approaches to a wide range of topics not just in moral theory but in areas like medical ethics, where the discussion used to be conducted in terms of patients' rights, of informed consent, and so on, but now tends to get conducted in an enlarged moral vocabulary, which draws on what Gilligan calls the ethics of *care* as well as that of *justice*.

For 'care' is the new buzz-word. It is not, as Shakespeare's Portia demanded, mercy that is to season justice, but a less authoritarian humanitarian supplement, a felt concern for the good of others and for community with them. The 'cold jealous virtue of justice' (Hume) is found to be too cold, and it is 'warmer' more communitarian virtues and social ideals that are being called in to supplement it. One might say that liberty and equality are being found inadequate without fraternity, except that 'fraternity' will be quite the wrong word, if as Gilligan initially suggested, it is *women* who perceive this value most easily. ('Sorority' will do no better, since it is too exclusive, and English has no gender-neuter word for the mutual concern of siblings.) She has since modified this claim, allowing that there are two perspectives on moral and social issues that we all tend to alternate between, and which are not always easy to combine, one of them what she called the justice perspective, the other the care perspective. It is increasingly obvious that there are many male philosophical spokespersons for the care perspective (Laurence Thomas, Lawrence Blum, Michael Stocker) so that it cannot be the prerogative of women. Nevertheless Gilligan still wants to claim that women are most unlikely to take *only* the justice perspective, as some men are claimed to, at least until some mid-life crisis jolts them into 'bifocal' moral vision (see D.V., ch. 6).

Gilligan in her book did not offer any explanatory theory of why there should be any difference between female and male moral outlook, but she did tend to link the naturalness to women of the care perspective with their role as primary care-takers of young children, that is with their parental and specifically maternal role. She avoided the question of whether it is their biological or their social parental role that is relevant, and some of those who dislike her book are worried precisely by this uncertainty. Some find it retrograde to hail as a special sort of moral wisdom an outlook that may be the product of the socially enforced restriction of women to domestic roles (and the reservation of such roles for them alone). For that might seem to play into the hands of those who still favor such restriction. (Marxists, presumably, will not find it so surprising that moral truths might depend for their initial clear voicing on the social oppression, and memory of it, of those who voice the truths.) Gilligan did in the first chapter of D.V. cite the theory of Nancy Chodorow (as presented in *The Reproduction of Mothering* [Berkeley 1978]) which traces what appears as gender differences in personality to early social development, in particular to the effects of the child's primary caretaker being or not being of the same gender as the child. Later, both in 'The Conquistador and the Dark Continent: Reflections on the Nature of Love' (*Daedalus* [Summer 1984]), and 'The Origins of Morality in Early Childhood' (in press), she develops this explanation. She postulates two evils that any infant may become aware of, the evil of detachment or isolation from others whose love one needs, and the evil of relative powerlessness and weakness. Two dimensions of moral development are thereby set − one aimed at achieving satisfying community with others, the other aiming at autonomy or equality of power. The relative predominance of one over the other development will depend both upon the relative salience of the two evils in early childhood, and on early and later reinforcement or discouragement in attempts made to guard against these two evils. This provides the germs of a theory about *why*, given current customs of childrearing, it should be mainly women who are not content with only the moral outlook that she calls the justice perspective, necessary though that was and is seen by them to have been to their hard won liberation from sexist oppression. They, like the blacks, used the language of rights and justice to change their own social position, but nevertheless see limitations in that language, according to Gilligan's findings as a moral psychologist. She reports their discontent with the individualist more or less Kantian moral framework that dominates Western moral theory and which influenced moral psychologists such as Lawrence

Kohlberg,[11] to whose conception of moral maturity she seeks an alternative. Since the target of Gilligan's criticism is the dominant Kantian tradition, and since that has been the target also of moral philosophers as diverse in their own views as Bernard Williams,[12] Alasdair MacIntyre, Philippa Foot,[13] Susan Wolf, Claudia Card, her book is of interest as much for its attempt to articulate an alternative to the Kantian justice perspective as for its implicit raising of the question of male bias in Western moral theory, especially liberal-democratic theory. For whether the supposed blind spots of that outlook are due to male bias, or to non-parental bias, or to early traumas of powerlessness or to early resignation to 'detachment' from others, we need first to be persuaded that they *are* blind spots before we will have any interest in their cause and cure. Is justice blind to important social values, or at least only one-eyed? What is it that comes into view from the 'care perspective' that is not seen from the 'justice perspective'?

Gilligan's position here is most easily described by contrasting it with that of Kohlberg, against which she developed it. Kohlberg, influenced by Piaget and the Kantian philosophical tradition as developed by John Rawls, developed a theory about typical moral development which saw it to progress from a pre-conventional level, where what is seen to matter is pleasing or not offending parental authority-figures, through a conventional level in which the child tries to fit in with a group, such as a school community, and conform to its standards and rules, to a post-conventional critical level, in which such conventional rules are subjected to tests, and where those tests are of a Utilitarian, or, eventually, a Kantian sort — namely ones that require respect for each person's individual rational will, or autonomy, and conformity to any implicit social contract such

---

11 Lawrence Kohlberg, *Essays in Moral Development*, vols. I & II (New York: Harper and Row 1981, 1984)

12 Bernard Williams, *Ethics and the Limits of Philosophy* (Cambridge: Cambridge University Press 1985)

13 Philippa Foot, *Virtues and Vices* (Berkeley: University of California Press 1978)

wills are deemed to have made, or to any hypothetical ones they would make if thinking clearly. What was found when Kohlberg's questionnaires (mostly by verbal response to verbally sketched moral dilemmas) were applied to female as well as male subjects, Gilligan reports, is that the girls and women not only scored generally lower than the boys and men, but tended to *revert* to the lower stage of the conventional level even after briefly (usually in adolescence) attaining the post conventional level. Piaget's finding that girls were deficient in 'the legal sense' was confirmed.

These results led Gilligan to wonder if there might not be a quite different pattern of development to be discerned, at least in female subjects. She therefore conducted interviews designed to elicit not just how far advanced the subjects were towards an appreciation of the nature and importance of Kantian autonomy, but also to find out what the subjects themselves saw as progress or lack of it, what conceptions of moral maturity they came to possess by the time they were adults. She found that although the Kohlberg version of moral maturity as respect for fellow persons, and for their rights as equals (rights including that of free association), did seem shared by many young men, the women tended to speak in a different voice about morality itself and about moral maturity. To quote Gilligan, 'Since the reality of interconnexion is experienced by women as given rather than freely contracted, they arrive at an understanding of life that reflects the limits of autonomy and control. As a result, women's development delineates the path not only to a less violent life but also to a maturity realized by interdependence and taking care' (D.V., 172). She writes that there is evidence that 'women perceive and construe social reality differently from men, and that these differences center around experiences of attachment and separation … because women's sense of integrity appears to be intertwined with an ethics of care, so that to see themselves as women is to see themselves in a relationship of connexion, the major changes in women's lives would seem to involve changes in the understanding and activities of care' (D.V., 171). She contrasts this progressive understanding of care, from merely pleasing others to helping and nurturing, with the sort of progression that is involved in Kohlberg's stages, a progression in the understanding, not of mutual care, but of mutual *respect*, where this has its Kantian overtones of distance, even of some fear for the respected, and where personal autonomy and *in*dependence, rather than more satisfactory interdependence, are the paramount values.

This contrast, one cannot but feel, is one which Gilligan might have used the Marxist language of alienation to make. For the main complaint about the Kantian version of a society with its first virtue justice, construed as respect for equal rights to formal goods such as having contracts kept, due process, equal opportunity including opportunity to participate in political activities leading to policy and law-making, to basic liberties of speech, free association and assembly, religious worship, is that none of these goods do much to ensure that the people who have and mutually respect such rights will have any other relationships to one another than the minimal relationship needed to keep such a 'civil society' going. They may well be lonely, driven to suicide, apathetic about their work and about participation in political processes, find their lives meaningless and have no wish to leave offspring to face the same meaningless existence. Their rights, and respect for rights, are quite compatible with very great misery, and misery whose causes are not just individual misfortunes and psychic sickness, but social and moral impoverishment.

What Gilligan's older male subjects complain of is precisely this sort of alienation from some dimly glimpsed better possibility for human beings, some richer sort of network of relationships. As one of Gilligan's male subjects put it, 'People have real emotional needs to be attached to something, and equality does not give you attachment. Equality fractures society and places on every person the burden of standing on his own two feet' (D.V., 167). It is not just the difficulty of self reliance which is complained of, but its socially 'fracturing' effect. Whereas the younger men, in their college years, had seen morality as a matter of reciprocal non-interference, this older man begins to see it as reciprocal attachment. 'Morality is ... essential ... for creating the kind of environment, interaction between people, that is a prerequisite to the fulfillment of individual goals. If you want other people not to interfere with your pursuit of whatever you are into, you have to play the game,' says the spokesman for traditional liberalism (D.V. 98). But if what one is 'into' is interconnexion, interdependence rather than an individual autonomy that may involve 'detachment,' such a version of morality will come to seem inadequate. And Gilligan stresses that the interconnexion that her mature women subjects, and some men, wanted to sustain was not merely freely chosen interconnexion, nor interconnexion between equals, but also the sort of interconnexion that can obtain between a child and her unchosen mother and father, or between a child and her unchosen older and younger siblings, or indeed between most workers and their unchosen fellow workers, or most citizens and their unchosen fellow citizens.

A model of a decent community different from the liberal one is involved in the version of moral maturity that Gilligan voices. It has in many ways more in common with the older religion-linked versions of morality and a good society than with the modern Western liberal ideal. That perhaps is why some find it so dangerous and retrograde. Yet it seems clear that it also has much in common with what we can call Hegelian versions of moral maturity and of social health and malaise, both with Marxist versions and with so-called right-Hegelian views.

Let me try to summarize the main differences, as I see them, between on the one hand Gilligan's version of moral maturity and the sort of social structures that would encourage, express and protect it, and on the other the orthodoxy she sees herself to be challenging. I shall from now on be giving my own interpretation of the significance of her challenges, not merely reporting them.[14] The most obvious point is the challenge to the individualism of the Western tradition, to the fairly entrenched belief in the possibility and desirability of each person pursuing his own good in his own way, constrained only by a minimal formal common good, namely a working legal apparatus that enforces contracts and protects individuals from undue interference by others. Gilligan reminds us that noninterference can, especially for the relatively powerless, such as the very

---

14 I have previously written about the significance of her findings for moral philosophy in 'What Do Women Want in a Moral Theory?' *Nous* **19** (March 1985), 'Trust and Antitrust,' *Ethics* **96** (1986), and in 'Hume the Women's Moral Theorist?' in *Women and Moral Theory*, Kittay and Meyers, ed., forthcoming.

young, amount to neglect, and even between equals can be isolating and alienating. On her less individualist version of individuality, it becomes defined by responses to dependency and to patterns of interconnexion, both chosen and unchosen. It is not something a person *has*, and which she then chooses relationships to suit, but something that develops out of a series of dependencies and interdependencies, and responses to them. This conception of individuality is not flatly at odds with, say, Rawls' Kantian one, but there is at least a difference of tone of voice between speaking as Rawls does of each of us having our own rational life plan, which a just society's moral traffic rules will allow us to follow, and which may or may not include close association with other persons, and speaking as Gilligan does of a satisfactory life as involving 'progress of affiliative relationship' (D.V., 170) where 'the concept of identity expands to include the experience of interconnexion' (D.V., 173). Rawls can allow that progress to Gilligan-style moral maturity may be *a* rational life plan, but not a moral constraint on every life-pattern. The trouble is that it will not do just to say 'let this version of morality be an optional extra. Let us agree on the essential minimum, that is on justice and rights, and let whoever wants to go further and cultivate this more demanding ideal of responsibility and care.' For, first, it cannot be satisfactorily cultivated without closer cooperation from others than respect for rights and justice will ensure, and, second, the encouragement of some to cultivate it while others do not could easily lead to exploitation of those who do. It obviously *has* suited some in most societies well enough that others take on the responsibilities of care (for the sick, the helpless, the young) leaving them free to pursue their own less altruistic goods. Volunteer forces of those who accept an ethic of care, operating within a society where the power is exercised and the institutions designed, redesigned, or maintained by those who accept a less communal ethic of minimally constrained self-advancement, will not be the solution. The liberal individualists may be able to 'tolerate' the more communally minded, if they keep the liberals' rules, but it is not so clear that the more communally minded can be content with just those rules, nor be content to be tolerated and possibly exploited.

For the moral tradition which developed the concept of rights, autonomy and justice is the same tradition that provided 'justifications' of the oppression of those whom the primary right-holders depended on to do the sort of work they themselves preferred not to do. The domestic work was left to women and slaves, and the liberal morality for right-holders was surreptitiously supplemented by a different set of demands made on domestic workers. As long as women could be got to assume responsibility for the care of home and children, and to train their children to continue the sexist system, the liberal morality could continue to be the official morality, by turning its eyes away from the contribution made by those it excluded. The long unnoticed moral proletariat were the domestic workers, mostly female. Rights have usually been for the privileged. Talking about laws, and the rights those laws recognize and protect, does not in itself ensure that the group of legislators and rights-holders will not be restricted to some elite. Bills of rights have usually been proclamations of the rights of some in-group, barons, land-owners, males, whites, non-foreigners. The 'justice perspective,' and the legal sense that goes with it, are shadowed by their patriarchal past. What did Kant, the great prophet of autonomy, say in his moral theory about women? He said they were incapable of legislation, not fit to vote, that they needed the guidance of more 'rational' males.[15] Autonomy was not for them, only for first class, really rational, persons. It is ironic that Gilligan's original findings in a way confirm Kant's views – it seems that autonomy really may not be for women. Many of them reject that ideal (D.V., 48), and have been found not as good at making rules as are men. But where Kant concludes – 'so much the worse for women,' we can conclude – 'so much the worse for the male fixation on the special skill of drafting legislation, for the bureaucratic mentality of rule worship, and for the male exaggeration of the importance of independence over mutual interdependence.'

It is however also true that the moral theories that made the concept of a person's rights central were not just the instruments for excluding some persons, but also the instruments used by those who demanded that more and more persons be included in the favored

---

15 Immanuel Kant, *Metaphysics of Morals*, sec. 46

group. Abolitionists, reformers, women, used the language of rights to assert their claims to inclusion in the group of full members of a community. The tradition of liberal moral theory has in fact developed so as to include the women it had for so long excluded, to include the poor as well as rich, blacks and whites, and so on. Women like Mary Wollstonecraft used the male moral theories to good purpose. So we should not be wholly ungrateful for those male moral theories, for all their objectionable earlier content. They were undoubtedly patriarchal, but they also contained the seeds of the challenge, or antidote, to this patriarchal poison.

But when we transcend the values of the Kantians, we should not forget the facts of history – that those values were the values of the oppressors of women. The Christian church, whose version of the moral law Aquinas codified, in his very legalistic moral theory, still insists on the maleness of the God it worships, and jealously reserves for males all the most powerful positions in its hierarchy. Its patriarchical prejudice is open and avowed. In the secular moral theories of men, the sexist patriarchal prejudice is today often less open, not as blatant as it is in Aquinas, in the later natural law tradition, and in Kant and Hegel, but is often still there. No moral theorist today would say that women are unfit to vote, to make laws, or to rule a nation without powerful male advisors (as most queens had), but the old doctrines die hard. In one of the best male theories we have, John Rawls's theory, a key role is played by the idea of the 'head of a household.' It is heads of households who are to deliberate behind a 'veil of ignorance' of historical details, and of details of their own special situation, to arrive at the 'just' constitution for a society. Now of course Rawls does not think or say that these 'heads' are fathers rather than mothers. But if we have really given up the age-old myth of women needing, as Grotius put it, to be under the 'eye' of a more 'rational' male protector and master, then how do families come to have any one 'head,' except by the death or desertion of one parent? They will either be two-headed, or headless. Traces of the old patriarchal poison still remain in even the best contemporary moral theorizing. Few may actually say that women's place is in the home, but there is much muttering, when unemployment figures rise, about how the relatively recent flood of women into the work force complicates the problem, as if it would be a good thing if women just went back home whenever unemployment rises, to leave the available jobs for the men. We still do not really have a wide acceptance of the equal right of women to employment outside the home. Nor do we have wide acceptance of the equal duty of men to perform those domestic tasks which in no way depend on special female anatomy, namely cooking, cleaning, and the care of weaned children. All sorts of stories (maybe true stories), about children's need for one 'primary' parent, who must be the mother if the mother breast feeds the child, shore up the unequal division of domestic responsibility between mothers and fathers, wives and husbands. If we are really to transvalue the values of our patriarchal past, we need to rethink all of those assumptions, really test those psychological theories. And how will men ever develop an understanding of the 'ethics of care' if they continue to be shielded or kept from that experience of caring for a dependent child, which complements the experience we all have had of being cared for as dependent children? These experiences form the natural background for the development of moral maturity as Gilligan's women saw it.

Exploitation aside, why would women, once liberated, not be content to have their version of morality merely tolerated? Why should they not see themselves as voluntarily, for their own reasons, taking on *more* than the liberal rules demand, while having no quarrel with the content of those rules themselves, nor with their remaining the only ones that are expected to be generally obeyed? To see why, we need to move on to three more differences between the Kantian liberals (usually contractarians) and their critics. These concern the relative weight put on relationships between equals, and the relative weight put on freedom of choice, and on the authority of intellect over emotions. It is a typical feature of the dominant moral theories and traditions, since Kant, or perhaps since Hobbes, that relationships between equals or those who are deemed equal in some important sense, have been the relations that morality is concerned primarily to regulate. Relationships between those who are clearly unequal in power, such as parents and children, earlier and later generations in relation to one another, states and citizens, doctors and patients, the well and the ill, large states and small states, have had to be shunted to the bottom of the agenda, and then dealt with by some sort of 'promotion' of the weaker so that an appearance of virtual equality is achieved. Citizens collectively become equal to states, children are treated as adults-to-be, the ill and dying are treated as continuers of their earlier more potent selves, so that their 'rights' could be seen as the rights of equals. This pretence of an equality that is in fact absent may often lead to desirable protection of the weaker, or more dependent. But it somewhat masks the question of what our moral relationships *are* to those who are our superiors or our inferiors in power. A more realistic acceptance of the fact that we begin as helpless children, that at almost every point of our lives we deal with both the more and the less helpless, that equality of power and interdependency, between two persons or groups, is rare and hard to recognize when it does occur, might lead us to a more direct approach to questions concerning the design of institutions structuring these relationships between unequals (families, schools, hospitals, armies) and of the morality of our dealings with the more and the less powerful. One reason why those who agree with the Gilligan version of what morality is about will not want to agree that the liberals' rules are a good minimal set, the only ones we need pressure *everyone* to obey, is that these rules do little to protect the young or the dying or the starving or any of the relatively powerless against neglect, or to ensure an education that will form persons to be *capable* of conforming to an ethics of care and responsibility. Put baldly, and in a way Gilligan certainly has not put it, the liberal morality, if unsupplemented, may *unfit* people to be anything other than what its justifying theories suppose them to be, ones who have no interest in each others' interests. Yet some must take an interest in the next generation's interests. Women's traditional work, of caring for the less powerful, especially for the young, is obviously socially vital. One cannot regard any version of morality that does not ensure that it gets well done as an adequate 'minimal morality,' any more than we could so regard one that left any concern for more distant future generations an optional extra. A moral theory, it can plausibly be claimed, cannot regard concern for new and future persons as an optional charity left for those with a taste for it. If the morality the theory endorses is to sustain itself, it must provide for its own continuers, not just take out a loan on a carefully encouraged maternal instinct or on the enthusiasm of a self-selected group of environmentalists, who make it their business or hobby to be concerned with what we are doing to mother earth. The recognition of the importance for all parties of relations between those who are and cannot but be unequal, both of these relations in themselves and for their effect on personality formation and so on other relationships, goes along with a recognition of the plain fact that not all morally important relationships can or should be freely chosen. So far I have discussed three reasons women have not to be content to pursue their own values within the framework of the liberal morality. The first was its dubious record. The second was its inattention to relations of inequality or its pretence of equality. The third reason is its exaggeration of the scope of choice, or its inattention to unchosen relations. Showing up the partial myth of equality among actual members of a community, and of the undesirability of trying to pretend that we are treating all of them as equals, tends to go along with an exposure of the companion myth that moral obligations arise from freely *chosen* associations between such equals. Vulnerable future generations do not choose their dependence on earlier generations. The unequal infant does not choose its place in a family or nation, nor is it treated as free to do as it likes until some association is freely entered into. Nor do its parents always choose their parental role, or freely assume their parental responsibilities any more than we choose our power to affect the conditions in which later generations will live. Gilligan's attention to the version of morality and moral maturity found in women, many of whom had faced a choice of whether or not to have an abortion, and who had at some point become mothers, is attention to the perceived inadequacy of the language of rights to help in such choices or to guide them in their parental role. It would not be much of an exaggeration to call the Gilligan 'different voice' the voice of the potential parents. The emphasis on care goes with a recognition of the often unchosen nature of the responsibilities of those who give care, both of children who care for their aged or infirm parents, and of parents who care for the children they in fact have. Contract soon ceases to seem the paradigm source of moral obligation once we attend to parental responsibility, and justice as a virtue of social institutions will come to seem at best only first equal with the virtue, whatever its name, that ensures that each new generation is made appropriately welcome and prepared for their adult lives.

This all constitutes a belated reminder to Western moral theorists of a fact they have always known, that as Adam Ferguson, and David Hume before him emphasized, we are born into families, and the first society we belong to, one that fits or misfits us for later ones, is the small society of parents (or some sort of child-attendants) and children, exhibiting as it may both relationships of near equality and of inequality in power. This simple reminder, with the fairly considerable implications it can have for the plausibility of contractarian moral theory, is at the same time a reminder of the role of human emotions as much as human reason and will in moral development as it actually comes about. The fourth feature of the Gilligan challenge to liberal orthodoxy is a challenge to its typical *rationalism*, or intellectualism, to its assumption that we need not worry what passions persons have, as long as their rational wills can control them. This Kantian picture of a controlling reason dictating to possibly unruly passions also tends to seem less useful when we are led to consider what sort of person we need to fill the role of parent, or indeed want in any close relationship. It might be important for father figures to have rational control over their violent urges to beat to death the children whose screams enrage them, but more than control of such nasty passions seems needed in the mother or primary parent, or parent-substitute, by most psychological theories. They need to love their children, not just to control their irritation. So the emphasis in Kantian theories on rational control of emotions, rather than on cultivating desirable forms of emotion, is challenged by Gilligan, along with the challenge to the assumption of the centrality of autonomy, or relations between equals, and of freely chosen relations.

The same set of challenges to 'orthodox' liberal moral theory has come not just from Gilligan and other women, who are reminding other moral theorists of the role of the family as a social institution and as an influence on the other relationships people want to or are capable of sustaining, but also, as I noted at the start, from an otherwise fairly diverse group of men, ranging from those influenced by both Hegelian and Christian traditions (MacIntyre) to all varieties of other backgrounds. From this group I want to draw attention to the work of one philosopher in particular, namely Laurence Thomas, the author of a fairly remarkable article[16] in which he finds sexism to be a more intractable social evil than racism. In a series of articles, and a forthcoming book,[17] Thomas makes a strong case for the importance of supplementing a concern for justice and respect for rights with an emphasis on equally needed virtues, and on virtues seen as appropriate *emotional* as well as rational capacities. Like Gilligan (and unlike MacIntyre) Thomas gives a lot of attention to the childhood beginnings of moral and social capacities, to the role of parental love in making that possible, and to the emotional as well as the cognitive development we have reason to think both possible and desirable in human persons.

It is clear, I think, that the best moral theory has to be a cooperative product of women and men, has to harmonize justice and care. The morality it theorizes about is after all for all persons, for men and for women, and will need their combined insights. As Gilligan said (D.V., 174), what we need now is a 'marriage' of the old male and the newly articulated female insights. If she is right about the special moral aptitudes of women, it will most likely be the women who propose the marriage, since they are the ones with more natural empathy, with the better diplomatic skills, the ones more likely to shoulder responsibility and take moral initiative, and the ones who find it easiest to empathize and care about how the other party feels. Then, once there is this union of male and female moral wisdom, we maybe can teach each other the moral skills each gender currently lacks, so that the gender difference in moral outlook that Gilligan found will slowly become less marked.

---

16 Laurence Thomas, 'Sexism and Racism: Some Conceptual Differences,' *Ethics* **90** (1980), 239-50; republished in *Philosophy, Sex and Language*, Vetterling-Braggin, ed. (Totowa, NJ: Littlefield Adams 1980)

17 See articles listed in note 6, above. The forthcoming book has the title *A Psychology of Moral Character*.

II

Critiques:
Science, Ethics and Method

CANADIAN JOURNAL OF PHILOSOPHY
Supplementary Volume 13

The Philosophy of Ambivalence: Sandra Harding on The Science Question in Feminism

ALISON WYLIE
University of Western Ontario
London, ON
Canada N6G 1G7

I Feminist Critiques of Science

In the past three decades scholars in virtually every humanistic and social scientific research discipline, and in some natural sciences (especially the life sciences), have drawn attention to quite striking instances of gender bias in the modes of practice and theorizing typical of traditional fields of research. They generally begin by identifying explicit androcentric biases in definitions of the subject domains appropriate to specific scientific fields. Their primary targets, in this connection, have been research that leaves women out altogether (e.g., anthropological research that has arbitrarily and, as it turns out, falsely characterized subsistence systems and political structures exclusively in terms of male activities; [see Slocum 1975]), research that ignores women's contributions or victimization (e.g., in the definition of literary or artistic canons and historical traditions), and research that conceptualizes its subject, male or female, human or non-human, in explicitly gender biased terms (e.g., models of animal behaviour that project onto it the gender-specific attributes of particular human societies and models of human psychological develop-

59

ment that take exclusively male patterns of development as the norm and characterize distinctive female patterns as 'deviant'; see Harraway 1978 and Gilligan 1982, respectively).

Attempts to rectify these most evident errors and limitations initially yielded various forms of 'remedial' research which take women's activities, experiences, contributions, and perspectives as their primary subject. Despite redressing an evident imbalance, this tradition of interest in 'women worthies,' 'women victims,' and 'women's contributions' (as Harding describes it) very quickly proved limited in its own right. It became evident that domain-definition bias is frequently rooted in underlying, essentially sexist and mistaken assumptions about the nature of the subject. Consequently, broadening the field of inquiry to consider women very often simply moved the reproduction of sexist theory to a new level; the results were sexist theories about women, or about a domain newly recognized to include female subjects. Dale Spender (1980) makes just such a critique of the early research on female-specific patterns of language use, directing attention to underlying sources of gender bias that had persisted despite a concern to consider women (see Ringelheim 1985 for a comparable critique of studies of women as victims).

Even with the corrective of critical analyses like Spender's, discipline-specific critiques typically preserve, at their core, the conviction that the errors they expose have arisen simply through a misuse or misapplication of scientific method; they are critiques of what is taken to be 'bad science,' not science as such. In this they leave unchallenged standard empiricist assumptions about the self-corrective, objective nature of science and presume that, properly practiced, scientific method can be expected to root out even the most pervasive errors due to gender bias.

Challenges to these assumptions have begun to emerge through what amounts to second-order philosophical reflection on the import of the original, discipline-specific critiques. Where, in many cases, highly competent and conscientious empirical research (i.e., good science, 'science as usual') consistently failed to expose sexist bias — it only became apparent when feminist researchers brought a new critical perspective to bear — questions arise about the capacity of science to counter the bias introduced by social and political (non-cognitive) factors. In addition, some theorists have come to suspect that extant research methods may not merely allow androcentric bias to enter and persist but may actually generate it. With this, what began as a worry about specific errors in analysis and the application of scientific method has converged on and, in fact, significantly extended, the radical critiques of science developed by those sociologists, philosophers, and historians of science who conceive science as an irreducibly social enterprise. The initial feminist critiques have become the basis for raising questions about the nature and status of the scientific enterprise itself.

Harding's project is very broad in conception, considered in light of these developments. She first characterizes and situates the interconnections holding among the whole range of feminist critiques of science that have appeared in recent years, beginning with the discipline-specific critiques due to feminist practitioners active in particular fields. She then moves to consider the increasingly comprehensive and radical challenges to science that these critiques have generated in the context of general feminist theory and philosophy. As Harding portrays it, the movement between specific and general critiques is dialectical. Their combined effect has been to show that gender-specific biases pervade what we have traditionally thought of as 'humanly inclusive problematics' (15); questions are raised about whether such an ideal is possible, or even desirable. In what follows I will concentrate on Harding's account of the way in which the specific, 'feminist empiricist' critiques yield this more profound challenge, and then assess some of the broader implications of her response to the emerging critical options.

II The 'Science Question in Feminism'

Harding takes, as her point of departure, the 'least threatening' discipline-specific critiques of science: critiques that focus on the role of women as practitioners in science (their exclusion or marginalization, historically) and on androcentric bias in the 'soft' social sciences. She adopts a two-pronged strategy here. In the first instance she is concerned to show how these critiques 'undermine their parental [empiricist] discourse,' forcing the conclusion that it is not just bad science but virtually all forms of scientific practice that are liable to gender bias. The argument here is as described above; in the sciences where feminist critiques have been most successful, mainly the social and life sciences, scientific method has not only failed to eliminate but has systematically reproduced gender bias. In addition, Harding is concerned to demonstrate that these most effective critiques can be extended to fields that have been thought immune to them, specifically, the natural sciences.

In connection with this second strategy, Harding draws on general sociological critiques of mathematics (due to Kline 1980 and Bloor 1977) and on textual analyses of the role of metaphor in the natural sciences (e.g., Merchant 1980) to establish that feminist critiques might plausibly apply to these areas. Her argument is not that such feminist critiques have been successfully developed, indeed, she raises some important questions about the efforts that have been made in this direction. It is, rather, that there is good prima facia reason to suspect that they could be, given the inroads made by general sociological analyses of these fields. Harding's further argument for extending feminist critiques to the 'hard' sciences is that even if the project of direct criticism should not succeed, feminist analyses that establish inherent bias in the 'soft' sciences may well have much broader significance than is recognized by those who presume that these fields are, at best, idiosyncratic and peripheral. She argues that, in fact, compared with the breadth of subject matter covered by the social sciences, the natural sciences are really very limited in scope. There are, moreover, strong indications that the methods and standards of practice successful in this narrow field may not prove very widely applicable outside of it. The status of the natural sciences and mathematics as arbiters of what shall count as science is therefore open to question; in the end, perhaps the 'hard' sciences, not the social sciences, should be considered anomalous and peripheral. In this case, feminist critiques of science cannot be dismissed because they succeed in establishing gender bias 'only' in the social sciences; success here may be the crucial part of a general argument for considering science inherently gender-biased.

These generalizations of the discipline-specific critiques dramatically broaden the scope of feminist analyses of sexism in science;

they now extend, potentially at least, to all branches of science rather than to a few suspect sub-fields, and to methods and standards of practice that exemplify 'science as usual,' not just bad science. The question this raises is whether or in what sense science is an androcentric enterprise as a whole. With this, Harding argues, the original 'woman question in science' is reformulated as the much more radical 'science question in feminism.'

III Feminist Standpoint Theories

Recast in these terms, feminist critiques of science converge on the extensive body of non-feminist critiques developed by historians, sociologists, and philosophers of science who argue that science is through and through a social enterprise. The general point on which these critics agree, despite wide divergence in the detail of their analyses, is that 'received view' ideals of objectivity and the conviction that scientific method is self-cleansing are simply untenable; the products of science are marked by the identities of its practitioners, the social conditions under which they operate, and the cultural projects in which they engage.

Despite these common themes, however, there is an important point at which feminist critiques of science, indeed any self-consciously political critique of science (e.g., the Marxist standpoint critiques), diverge quite sharply from apolitical traditions of criticism (e.g., the epistemological and sociological critiques initiated by Kuhn, Hanson, Feyerabend, and to some extent by the Strong School sociologists such as Barnes and Bloor). It comes when feminist critics undertake to propose alternatives to the androcentric theories and forms of practice that they reject. They, and standpoint theorists generally, are deeply concerned to establish an understanding of how things actually stand in a given subject domain; above all, they seek to determine what possibilities exist for constructive action that might improve the conditions of life. They are therefore unwilling to give up the conviction that some conceptions of reality are privileged and, in fact, insist that the social identity or standpoint of scientific observers makes a positive difference epistemically.

The justification that standpoint theorists give for assuming that some standpoints assure greater breadth and accuracy of understanding than others (described in detail by Harding in ch. 6) is that members of oppressed or disenfranchised groups will often be painfully aware of institutions and 'standing conditions' (implicit social conventions and power structures) that put them at a disadvantage, while the beneficiaries of this disadvantage frequently deny or fail to acknowledge that any such constraints exist. This argument has been extended to women and the awareness of gender structures by a number of feminist theorists. Harding cites, in particular, Dorothy Smith (1979, see also 1974) who argues that women occupy a 'standpoint' from which the gendered nature of social reality will be uniquely visible because they typically engage in the activities of maintaining physical and domestic well-being that create the conditions of privilege enjoyed by most men. The advantage of standpoint theory for feminist critics, Harding argues, is that it allows them to move decisively beyond the contradictions inherent in the discourse of feminist empiricism that so often informs discipline-specific critiques of sexism in science. Such a position takes it as a central tenet that social context and one's position in it are relevant to all science, good, bad, usual or abnormal. It is thus unexceptional that feminist critics should have found that their standpoint as women afforded them special insights about the nature and existence of gender bias. By contrast, feminist empiricists are caught in the awkward poisition of exploiting the epistemic advantages of their standpoint as women while endorsing the ideal that scientific inquiry is objective in that an inquirer's social, political standpoint is irrelevant.

This move away from entrenched ideals of objectivity is distinct from the turn typically taken by non-politicized critics of science. Feminist projects that are conceived in terms of a 'stand-point' epistemology are dedicated to achieving a fuller, more accurate understanding of women's experience and of women's status and roles within encompassing social contexts. As Harding observes, 'there is nothing relativistic about such ... project[s]' (138). Their proponents assume throughout that there are facts of the matter to be comprehended more and less accurately and that these can be effectively used to set the received record straight, to expose the fallacies and errors of patriarchal thinking about social and natural reality. In short, they accord special epistemic privilege to the observations, conceptual categories, and explanatory theories produced by women; these are meant to displace patriarchal versions, not merely to stand as an alternative to them. In endorsing what amount to 'successor science' projects, standpoint theorists directly counter those politically unaligned and post-modernist positions according to which pluralistic relativism is an unavoidable consequence of recognizing the social political nature of science. They thus remain committed to a variant of the enlightenment ideal of producing a unitary, authoritative conception of reality.

IV Standpoint Theory vs. Post-Modernism

The central objection to feminist 'successor science' projects and the standpoint theory they presuppose is that they assume a unity of experience among women that is, on many accounts, quite implausible. Challenges to this thesis of unity have been prominent in a more general context of debate where the target is the emphasis that radical feminists have placed on cross-cultural, historical commonalities in women's experience (see, for example, the discussion of Rich by Ferguson, Zita and Addelson, 1981). Perhaps the most telling criticisms have come from women of colour who object that their own experience and perspectives differ profoundly from those taken as standard by the predominantly middle class, white, educated women who have dominated feminist politics. They charge that the cost of building solidarity among women has been a loss of appreciation of the diversity of standpoints occupied by women, considered as individuals whose lives are also shaped by determinants of race and class. Once this is reclaimed and made central to feminist analysis, characteristically post-modernist themes emerge. The recognition of diversity in the concrete experience to which we recur in evaluating knowledge claims raises the possibility that divergent conceptual, theoretical frameworks may not be reducible to one another or to a common ground. With this, the possibility of adjudicating between knowledge claims originating in different contexts or of establishing a unitary theory that is valid across contexts is decisively undermined. The feminist critique of science thus becomes a critique not just of particular instances of bad (sexist) science, nor even of science conducted from an androcentric standpoint, but of all science insofar as it is committed to foundationalist projects of commensuration and unification.

Harding develops an intriguing comparison between Africanist and feminist politics to drive home her objections to the notion that women occupy a distinctive standpoint. She observes that the world views presumed distinctive of women and of African cultures are both characterized by a sense of continuity with the natural world and an absorption of individuals into their communities, by sharp contrast with the individualism and objectivism of patriarchal and Euroamerican world views. The point is obvious; if some men, including men socialized in strongly gender differentiated contexts, develop the same world view as that which distinguishes the standpoint of women, then any claim that women share a unique standpoint (qua, world view) is highly suspect. Harding adds the observation that, given the manifest differences among African cultures, the commonality attributed to their world view begins to look rather arbitrary itself. She suggests that it may be an artifact of colonial politics; diversity is submerged where, in the eyes of a dominant, colonial culture, a range of very different cultures are identified together as 'other' and exploitable. The question arises whether the situation is not, perhaps, similar for women. More specifically, the suspicion arises that appeals to a distinctive women's standpoint take over, uncritically, a definition imposed by those who control and dominate, a definition that systematically obscures diversity as part of the project of defining women as 'other,' as exhibiting a narrow range of capabilities and interests, and as appropriate objects of exploitation. Presumably such conceptual categories threaten immanent betrayal of feminist projects wherever they are central to them.

It is perhaps significant that when Harding considers the example of Africanist world views she does not directly counter the unity claims of radical feminism or feminist standpoint theories − the argument that women share important features of experience by virtue of being systematically oppressed − even though this is the argument she discusses when initially characterizing standpoint theories. Rather, she challenges the claims of object relations theory, an independent, psychoanalytic justification for the thesis of commonality according to which systematic gender differences in what Harding calls a world view are considered a product of gender-related differences in early childhood experience (see the title essay in Keller 1985 for a discussion of the relevance of this to science). Where the primary caretaker of children is typically a woman, the processes of differentiation of self from others and the development of personal identity and of capacities for relating to others are found to proceed quite differently for female than male children. Females are said to develop a sense of identity defined by continued connection with their mothers while males separate themselves from their mothers much earlier and more decisively, developing a strongly autonomous identity and sense of disconnection from others. The appeal to Africanist world views seems decisive as a counter-example here insofar as woman are the primary care-takers of children in African contexts; if the same psychological processes of development can be presumed to unfold, the anomaly is that in these contexts they produce males whose world view replicate many features of that which is supposed to distinguish women.

Harding's own reservations about the presumed unity of the African world view raises several questions about the efficacy of this comparison. But this aside, it should be evident that the Africanist comparison undermines only the specific thesis that early childhood experience produces gender-distinctive world views; it does not necessarily undermine formulations of the thesis that appeal to other sources of commonality in women's experience. It might still be the case that significant similarities exist in women's experience simply because, whatever the context, they find themselves disadvantaged relative to their male counterparts; they are channelled into a disproportionately narrower range of roles and activities than men, whatever their talent, and these roles and activities are systematically devalued relative to those associated with men. Where, in addition, women have primarily to do with domestic and reproductive labour, it might be expected that substantive, as well as relational, commonalities exist as well. Variability along a number of other dimensions — economic, cultural, socio-political — may produce dramatic differences in how this labour is organized and experienced.

Nonetheless, the insight of radical feminists like Rich, and of standpoint theorists like Smith, still holds; women find themselves in 'subdominant' gender-defined positions within each of these contexts and, from these positions, they participate in activities that support the privileges of men. Despite considerable variability in what this means for particular women, this general feature of women's experience is sufficiently universal, by all anthropological and historical accounts, that it would seem to support at least a qualified conception of a distinctive women's standpoint, one which takes into account the fact that gender is by no means the only factor shaping women's lives.

Although Harding does not take up the possibility of reformulating and defending a standpoint theory that appeals to the dynamics of oppression rather than of the unconscious as its foundation, it would seem that she must be sympathetic to something of this sort. Immediately after developing the Africanist critique she makes a series of suggestions about concepts and analytic categories that might be useful in building a unifying theory, what she calls a 'unified field theory,' which take account of diversity and incorporate the categories central to analyses of both racism and sexism. Such a theory would comprehend the ways in which the lives and identities of all who are not in dominant positions are systematically 'fractured.' Harding thus proposes a politics of solidarity based on what she calls an 'oppositional consciousness,' a consciousness of personal identity and commonality with others that is defined by a contrast with the interests and identities of dominant classes of various kinds. Although this would seem intended to support the sort of qualified conception of a distinctive 'women's' standpoint described above, I remain unclear just what its status and content is to be. Harding does not elaborate on the details of the proposed unifying theory, or indicate how it relates to extant standpoint theories. In fact, she seems to undermine the whole enterprise of seeking such a theory when she subsequently endorses the insights of post-modernism – 'there is no "woman" to whose social experiences the feminist and standpoint justificatory strategies can appeal; there are, instead, *women*' (192) – and insists that we must be tolerant of disjunctions and inconsistencies in the theories we produce.

In what seems an acknowledgement that her position is an uneasy one, Harding argues that feminists 'cannot afford' to give up either the successor science projects defined by empiricist and standpoint theorists, or the 'vision' of post-modernism introduced by critics of these projects. Research in the standpoint and empiricist mode can claim to demonstrate, in terms respected within patriarchal institutions, the patent falsity of sexist assumptions about the capabilities, interests, and needs of women, and about their role in and contributions to society. This is absolutely essential from the point of view of feminist political interests in effecting a change in oppressive power relations when, given these relations, 'neither feminist politics nor feminist theory stands in a relationship of reciprocity to patriarchal theory and politics' (195). Harding therefore insists that feminists should not 'cut themselves off' from the possibility of making such counter claims and, thus, of benefitting from 'humanism's perversions' (196). She also insists, however, that the insights of post-modernism are indispensable as a source of inspiration concerning the possibilities that lie beyond existing structures and institutions; they articulate a vision of the desired future that the successor science projects strive to realize. Harding thus concludes that perhaps 'we should [simply] learn to live with [the inconsistencies and tensions]' created by the appreciation that both post-modernist and successor science perspectives are indispensable (196). More exuberantly, she urges that we engage in 'enthusiastic violation of the founding taboos of Western humanism' (193). I turn now to consider some questions that this position raises.

V Ambivalence

The general lesson that Harding draws from these observations for epistemology and science is that 'stable and coherent theories are not always the ones to be desired' (243); ambivalence and, more specifically, a reticence to seek coherence at all costs, may often be appropriate given the state of our understanding both of a given subject domain and of the scientific enterprise. Harding's endorsement of ambivalence is, however, ambivalent in itself. On the side of post-modernism and tolerant ambivalence, she makes the principled claim that the search for a stable, coherent 'master theory' is misguided. She argues this on two grounds. First, the search for 'one true story' about reality, indeed, the presumption that there is *a* reality with a unitary structure about which the scientific enterprise theorizes, represents a vain attempt to return to some non-existent 'original unity' of consciousness (193). It contravenes both the political ideals of feminism and feminist insights about the social, political nature of science. Quoting Flax, Harding observes that such a project is, perhaps, only meaningful to those working from within a privileged standpoint; 'Only to the extent that one person or group can dominate the whole, can "reality" appear to be governed by one set of rules or be constituted by one privileged set of social relationships' (193, from Flax 1986). In addition, Harding argues that because the social context about which and in which we theorize is itself constantly undergoing transformation, it is unavoidable that our theories will be internally dissonant. A determination to root out incoherence and ambivalence is, then, both politically pernicious and futile.

The ambivalence inherent in Harding's endorsement of ambivalence becomes evident when, by contrast with the foregoing arguments, she suggests that we should tolerate tensions and incoherences in our theories because they provide valuable clues to the dissonances in the lived social reality from which they derive. There are, she observes, 'important understandings to be gained in seeking the social origins of instabilities and incoherences in our thoughts and practices — understandings that we cannot arrive at if we repress recognition of instabilities and tensions in our thought' (244). This is a very different rationale for eschewing 'totalizing' theories than the first mentioned. Significantly, perhaps ironically, it embodies a clear commitment to seek a unitary or univeralizing theory, however (contingently) limited our efforts in this direction may be. Even more ambitiously, it suggests that a properly reconstructed, emancipatory science should seek to understand not only the complexities and contradictions of our social experience, but should also explain reflexively why our theories tend to be fractured, dissonant, and incomplete given this experience; it should provide a unitary understanding of social life both as we live it and as we theorize it.

This ambivalence in rejecting 'totalizing' theory surfaces at several other points in Harding's discussion. One is the proposal mentioned earlier that feminists should respond to post-modern critics by developing a 'unified field theory' which comprehends the contradictory experiences of individuals occupying a variety of different standpoints. Another is Harding's observation that, in granting primacy to 'fractured identities' (i.e. in refusing to obscure dissonance by imposing an artificial unity), she grants primacy *only* to those fractured identities that are based on a 'solid and nondefensive core identity, and only within a unified opposition, a solidarity against culturally dominant forces for unitarianism' (247). The suggestion seems to be that, however elusive it may be, some form of fundamental or primary unity underlies the contradictions that surface in individual experience and collective action.

On balance, it is unavoidable that Harding recommends, at best, a qualified tolerance of incoherence in our theories. Coherent theories are not desirable at any cost, specifically not at the cost of submerging the insights and understandings of diversely situated inquirers; we should not ignore or deny contradictions in our experience and in our theories. Nevertheless, it is a persistent theme in *The Science Question in Feminism* that we should not complacently accept such incoherence. Perhaps we should not, in fact, '[simply] learn to live with it,' as Harding sometimes suggests. On pain of inappropriately imposing coherence on Harding's own text, I suggest that her acknowledgement of incoherence figures primarily as a goad to seek more broadly integrative categories and explanatory schemas, ones that move beyond existing theories in grasping more completely the reality in which we all participate, that we all maintain and create, despite fundamental differences among us. Moreover, I would argue that her endorsement of this ideal is more than a merely strategic concession. What Harding rejects in reacting against 'falsely universalizing' theory is not coherence as such, but coherence arbitrarily constructed and inappropriately imposed.

The primary value of Harding's analysis of science is, I suggest, her clear identification of the constructive tensions that emerge in feminist critiques of science. She establishes beyond doubt that scientific theorizing of all kinds, especially social scientific theorizing, must incorporate a reflexive component that is sensitive to the constitutive role of gender; it must acknowledge and account for the standpoint it embodies. This, however, need not and should not end with a celebration of inchoate difference but should rather stand as an impetus and source of directives for transcending the limitations of existing standpoint-specific theories. Whether we can ever achieve an overarching unity of understanding is beside the point. The evolution of increasingly coherent and comprehensive theories remains a core regulative ideal that emerges out of the very projects of criticism and empancipation that call 'totalizing' theories into question.

Acknowledgment

The support provided by SSHRC for research on 'Feminist Critiques of Science' (a grant held jointly by the author and Kathleen Okruhlik) is gratefully acknowledged.

References

Barry Barnes. *Scientific Knowledge and Sociological Theory*. London: Routledge & Kegan Paul 1974.

_____. *Interests and the Growth of Knowledge*. London: Routledge & Kegan Paul 1977.

David Bloor. *Knowledge and Social Imagery*. London: Routledge & Kegan Paul 1977.

Mary Daly. *Gyn/Ecology: The Metaethics of Radical Feminism*. Boston: Beacon Press 1978.

Ann Ferguson, Jacquelyn N. Zita and Kathryn Pyne Addelson. 'On "Compulsory Heterosexuality and Lesbian Existence": Defining the Issues,' in Nannerl O. Keohane, Michelle Z. Rosaldo, and Barbara C. Gelpi, eds. *Feminist Theory: A Critique of Ideology*. Chicago: University of Chicago Press 1982, 147-88.

Paul Feyerabend. *Against Method*. London: New Left Books 1975.

Jane Flax. 'Gender as a Social Problem: In and for Feminist Theory,' *American Studies/Amerika Studien* (1986; as cited by Harding, 264).

Carol Gilligan. *In a Different Voice: Psychological Theory and Women's Development*. Cambridge, MA: Harvard University Press 1982.

Norwood Russell Hanson. *Patterns of Discovery*. Cambridge: Cambridge University Press 1958.

Evelyn Fox Keller. *Reflections on Gender and Science*. New Haven: Yale University Press 1985.

Morris Kline. *Mathematics: The Loss of Certainty*. New York: Oxford University Press 1980.

Robin Lakoff. *Language and Woman's Place*. New York: Harper and Row 1975.

Carolyn Merchant. *The Death of Nature: Women, Ecology, and the Scientific Revolution*. New York: Harper and Row 1980.

Evelyn Reed. *Sexism and Science*. New York: Pathfinder 1978.

Adrienne Rich. 'Compulsory Heterosexuality and Lesbian Existence,' *Signs* 5 (1980), 631-60.

Joan Ringelheim. 'Women and the Holocaust: A Reconsideration of Research,' *Signs* 10 (1985), 741-91.

Sally Slocum. 'Woman the Gatherer: Male Bias in Anthropology,' reprinted in Rayna Reiter, ed. *Toward an Anthropology of Women*. New York: Monthly Review Press 1975.

Dorothy E. Smith. 'The Social Construction of Documentary Reality,' *Sociological Inquiry* 44 (1974), 258-67.

_____. 'A Sociology for Women' in J. Sherman and E. T. Beck, eds. *The Prism of Sex: Essays in the Sociology of Knowledge*. Madison, WI: University of Wisconsin Press 1979.

Dale Spender. *Man Made Language*. Boston: Routledge & Kegan Paul 1980.

CANADIAN JOURNAL OF PHILOSOPHY
Supplementary Volume 13

Ascetic Intellectual Opportunities: Reply to Alison Wylie

SANDRA HARDING
University of Delaware
Newark, DE 19711
U.S.A.

A broad spectrum of challenges to traditional epistemologies has been generated by feminist inquiry in biology and the social sciences, on the one hand, and by what are called the postmodern critiques, on the other hand. However, in fundamental ways the two sets of critiques are opposed to each other. The feminist science critiques challenge the legitimacy of any position that fails to recognize the salience to knowledge-seeking of close-to-universal male dominance, and to acknowledge the value of research generated from women's perspectives. It is this last claim that puts the two sets of critiques in opposition. The postmoderns think it reveals regressive political and intellectual tendencies on the part of feminists; they question the viability of the enlightenment projects on which the feminist science critiques depend.

Should one try to incorporate the most valuable insights of each tendency into a single, consistent 'position'? This project is probably doomed to fail given the tensions between the two tendencies. Moreover, the very attempt surely will dull the valuable critical edges of each. Or should we try to nourish the most valuable aspects of each critique, acknowledging that there are fundamental tensions between the two projects? From the perspective of traditional assumptions about what counts as 'good theory,' this second approach doesn't. But is the problem here with the proposal that we should be able to tolerate certain kinds of overt ambiguity and ambivalence in our theorizing, or with traditional notions of 'good theory'? Here are several of the central problems that I raised in *The Science Question in Feminism*, and ones that Alison Wylie discusses in a way I find illuminating in 'The Philosophy of Ambivalence.'

I do not intend to try to solve these problems. I think they should remain frustratingly unresolvable exactly because both the feminist science critiques and the postmodern tendencies have a great deal to offer for our future feminist theories and practices – indeed for all theory and practice. Full appreciation of the tensions and contradictions between the two projects creates possibilities for transforming the intellectual and political practices within which the projects remain incompatible. Instead, I want to stress here how impoverished are the resources traditional epistemology has offered for the feminist science projects. I conclude by pointing to three opportunities – ascetic ones – that the postmodern critiques offer for the science projects, though I do not suggest that seizing these opportunities would succeed in dissolving the tensions between the projects. They would, however, improve the science projects, in my view.

I Impoverished Resources

In *The Science Question in Feminism*, I pointed to two justificatory strategies that have emerged in the last decade: feminist empiricism and the feminist standpoint epistemology. These have been developed to account for the fact that the new feminist inquiry in biology and the social sciences appears to have produced less false (more reliable, better supported by empirical data, etc.) results of research than results that had been produced through purportedly value-free inquiries. That is, from the perspective of the traditional epistemologies of the natural and social sciences, specifically feminist inquiry appears anomolous and in need of explicit and additional justification beyond the routine kind of presentation of evidence that empirical researchers usually make in describing their research procedures.

There are at least three sources of feminist inquiry's anomolous status. In the first place, if scientific method is an effective way to eliminate social biases from the results of scientific research, then questions arise as to why the sexist and androcentric biases shaping virtually every aspect of social science as well as much of biology have not been eliminated. Is scientific method impotent to carry out this project – the very kind of one for which it was designed? Second, to be thought of as the kind of person who can be counted as a 'knower' – an agent or generator of knowledge – is to be thought 'by nature' capable of reason, of dispassionate, impartial judgment, of abstract thought, and of objective analyses that separate one's desires for how the world should be arranged from one's descriptions and explanations of the world. But to be a woman is thought to preclude possession of such traits. Is the idea of 'women knowers' – of 'woman as knower,' or 'woman, the knower,' and of women's experiences providing fruitful origins for scietific problematics and reliable groundings for knowledge claims – a contradiction in terms? (To take an all-too-familiar case here, think of the struggle we have had to get women's testimony about rape, wife battering, sexual harrassment, and incest experiences accepted as reliable by police, the courts, employers, psychiatrists, other men and women, etc.) Finally, the less false picture of the world emerging from feminist inquiry clearly has been created through research guided by the political goals of the women's movement. Yet the main traditional epistemology has insisted on the necessity of keeping politics out of science. ('Think of Lysenkoism! Think of Nazi science!' they say.) How can politically-guided research be increasing the objectivity of inquiry? These problems reveal the inappropriateness of comfort with traditional theories of knowledge.

Nevertheless, in attempting to resolve these problems in as conservative a way as possible, feminists have tried to make the results of feminist inquiry expectable from the perspective of traditional epistemologies. They have turned to earlier attempts to arrive at a satisfactory answer to these kinds of questions when they arose about other social groups claiming the ability and right to define reality. These feminist strategies are by no means uncontroversial, but it is important to recognize that the analyses are intended to 'save the phenomena' – to make the anomolous character of feminist-produced 'better science' disappear by presenting this research as if it were yet one more case of patterns already well understood in the philosophies of science.

Researchers within biology and the social sciences have tried to fit the new research into some of science's own ways of understanding its history and practices. This is what I called 'feminist empiricism.' Liberalism's empiricist epistemology sanctions the activation of politics in scientific inquiry in two places. Politics is supposed to infuse what are taken to be the central constitutive features of science, and it is considered appropriate at the 'periphery' of science, where science 'comes in contact with society.' In the former case, scientific method[1] is supposed to be a moral and political good in itself. As Rudolf Carnap put the point, the central beliefs of the Vienna Circle included

> ...that all deliberate action presupposes knowledge of the world, and that the scientific method is the best method of acquiring knowledge, and that therefore science must be regarded as one of the most valuable instruments for the improvement of life.[2]

(Of course, one can contest the claim that scientific method *in itself* is a moral and political good; one can argue that this claim reflects a politically useful desire to shield scientific practices from critical scrutiny — as many critics of science have argued.) In the latter case, politics *is* sanctioned at science's periphery, at the places where scientists and their projects 'come in contact' with the surrounding 'environment' of funding agencies, congressional investigating committees, public relations activities, scientific scandals, and so forth. Between the constitutive center of scientific method and the

---

1 Whatever that is; for discussion see Chapter 2 of *The Science Question in Feminism* (Ithaca, NY: Cornell University Press 1986), 'The Method Question'; *Hypatia: A Journal of Feminist Philosophy*, forthcoming special issue on feminism and science; and my edited collection *Feminism and Methodology: Social Science Issues* (Bloomington, IN: Indiana University Press 1987).

2 Rudolf Carnap, 'Autobiographical Statement,' in P. A. Schilpp, ed., *The Philosophy of Rudolf Carnap* (La Salle, IL: Open Court 1963), 83

distant periphery of 'society' stretches out in purportedly glisten-
ing purity and pristine transcendence all of scientific practice and
belief, past, present, and future. The achievements of prize-winning
literary fictions pale before such a magnificent creation as this myth.
Researchers attempting to account for the 'puzzling' presence of sexism in science, for the possibility of women's experience generating and legitimating important new kinds of descriptions and
explanations, and for the importance of politics in feminist research
have ingeniously figured out how to fit their epistemological accounts into this procrustean bed with a little trimming here, a little
reinterpretation there, and the constant insistence that skeptics just
'look and see' how the empirical evidence supports the degendered
claims over the traditional gendered ones – as the evidence indeed
does. Their main rhetorical weapon is to claim that the sexist and
androcentric claims are just the consequence of 'bad science'; that
every 'really good scientist' knows, for instance, that it is bad practice to have only men interview only men about both men's and
women's beliefs and behaviors. Of course, few thought to question
this kind of 'bad science' that was, in fact, the norm in anthropology, sociology, some areas of biology, psychology, etc., until the recent women's movement – just one of the problems that appear
for this nevertheless valuable epistemological strategy. In *The Science
Question...* I also pointed to ways in which feminist empiricism in
fact undermines its paternal empiricist philosophy of science.[3]

   To deal with the inadequacies inherent to any feminist attempt
to use the resources of empiricist epistemology, other theorists have
turned for resources to the other great philosophy of science – that
provided by Marxist theory. Starting from a theory, an ontology,
of politically conflicting groups rather than from the assumption of
essentially asocial individuals that is characteristic of Liberalism's
empiricism, the feminist standpoint theorists have had little trouble developing an inherently more coherent and explanatorily
powerful theory of why feminist inquiry has succeeded where so

---

3 See, e.g., 162.

much traditional inquiry has failed.[4] Of course, the theory looks no more Marxist after its feminist transformations than feminist empiricism remains loyal to empiricism, but this is not the main problem here — at least not from the perspective of feminist theory.

II New Projects

More problematic is that a valuable — but at present extremely fragile — tendency in feminist analysis and practice appears threatened with annihilation in the standpoint theories (as well as in their empiricist sister). It is the desire to nourish and preserve from extinction that tendency that generates some of the best of the feminist postmodernist critiques. Thus the agendas of feminists working in the natural and social sciences and those developing the issues for feminism raised by the postmodern discourses are not only different but, apparently, on a collision course. But do we need to choose between these two projects?

The natural and social scientists want to correct the false accounts of women, men, gender relations, and the social and natural worlds infused with such relations that are enshrined in their disciplines. These false accounts are used to direct — or, at least, to justify — public policy that is not only sexist, but virtually always also racist and bourgeois in the sense that it oppresses women differently and worse who are not white and/or not members of the dominating classes. In one way or another, they perceive their scientific projects to be continous with those that have shaped modern science itself at key moments in its history: knowledge is power, and the power of science can be used to improe the lot of the exploited, the powerless, the emiserated. Moreover, belief that is less false comes from looking and seeing the way the world is with the help of theories that are not constructed to justify the condition of those in the dominating groups. The improved belief produced through feminist inquiry enables women and men to begin to arrive at more compre-

---

4 Chapter 6 discusses these standpoint epistemologies.

hensive and deeper understandings of the forces that shape our lives, and to change the world in ways that reduce women's exploitation, powerlessness and misery.

In contrast, the feminist postmodernists charge that the feminist scientists fail to criticize the desirability not just of *present* mutually supportive relations between knowledge and power, but of *any* such relations. The scientists leave feminism, its concepts of the subject of history and of knowledge/science, still deeply mired in anachronistic and politically damaging Enlightenment assumptions that have been seriously challenged in the non-feminist discourses since the 19th Century, and are also under severe scrutiny in the non-Western discourses. Can these postmodern criticisms be understood as opportunities for feminist transformations? Let me point to three ways in which I think some of the postmodern criticisms can be taken as opportunities, while avoiding certain dangers threatened by some postmodernist agendas. Here is the point where certain intellectual asceticisms become attractive.

III Feminist Theory Without the Feminine

First there are the charges of essentialism and false universalizing. Women of color, lesbians, working class women, and women in other cultures point out that gender has different configurations in their worlds from that assumed universal on the basis of Western women's experience. Moreover, feminism itself laid the groundwork for the demise of 'woman' and 'the feminine' when it argued that there is no 'man' but only men and women.[5]

The challenge for feminism is to reformulate theories of women's oppression without claiming to describe or explain 'woman' or 'the feminine,' and without claiming to speak on the basis of 'woman's

---

5 Two comments: first, in the U.S., though not in France, notions of feminine specificity and essentialism are almost inextricably linked; second, this charge of essentialism is certainly not uniquely made by postmodernist critics, but it is also part of their complaint against feminist theory.

experience' (singular) or 'feminine experience.' However, unmediated postmodernism is not helpful here. Postmodernists tend to lose (or argue against the very desirability of) feminist theory altogether – to lose sight of the widespread existence of male-dominance in all its many historically and culturally specific forms – in their concern for understanding the different ways gender is expressed and for understanding the possibilities in a genderless future. What is needed for feminist science is theory that can explain male dominance in its 'endless variety and monotonous similarity,' in Gayle Rubin's memorable phrase.[6] This seems to me a difficult task, but by no means an impossible one.

IV Feminist Science Without Truth

How can there be 'one true story' about women, men, gender and social life when there is no *woman's* experience to which to appeal in trying to legitimate such a story? While the appeal to notions of truth appears less and less useful for feminism's scientific and epistemological projects, even more unsatisfactory is the fall into relativism – sometimes even the explicit commitment to it – which appears to be the only alternative to truth-grounded epistemologies for the two mainstream philosophies of science. There is little problem in recognizing that Caribbean women of color and Native American women may well provide equally true though different accounts of how male dominance functions in their lives. I can never understand why issues of relativism are raised about such different accounts of different lives at all. Moreover, no feminist will agree to the equal scientific value of men's and women's characteristic accounts of rape, incest, wife battering, the impoverishment of women, and other phenomena where all men benefit from some men's oppression of women.

---

6 Nancy Fraser and Linda Nicholson make this point in 'Social Criticism Without Philosophy: An Encounter Between Feminism and Postmodernism,' presented at the Eastern A.P.A., Boston, December, 1986.

Perhaps a way out of this impasse lies in breaking the symmetry between truth and falsity by exploiting the intuition that while for a claim to be true, every part of it must match or work well in the world (to appeal to the correspondence and pragmatic theories of truth characteristically held by working social scientists and biologists), while a claim can be false in virtually innumerable ways. Partly or in total it can fail to be supported by the available evidence. Or a richer conceptual system can become preferable to the one in which it was embedded. Thus one is not forced into indefensible appeals to no longer plausible notions – such as one true story about, or picture of, 'reality' – when one argues that the results of feminist research in biology and the social sciences are preferable because they are less false than the androcentric claims they replace.[7] While there is not and cannot be one true story of reality, some claims are empirically less defensible than others.

V History and Science Without the Transcendental Subject

Finally, the postmodernist tendencies problematize the notion of the subject of history and science (the subject who would revolutionize history or science) who is outside the historical forces she/he would direct, who is untouched by the causes of (false) belief that clearly shape others' beliefs and behaviors. What is required here is a more robust reflexivity than has been heretofore recommended for scientists. The challenge is to provide the very same kind of account of our own beliefs and behaviors that we recommend to explain the beliefs and behaviors of others. However such an account must not degenerate into the kind of 'hyper-reflexivity' that 'elevates' the history and practices of science right out of the real world and into

---

7 Thomas S. Kuhn prepares for this move in *The Structure of Scientific Revolutions* (Chicago: University of Chicago Press 1970). See also David Bloor, *Knowledge and Social Imagery* (London: Routledge & Kegan Paul 1977).

a mere 'text' of interest only for scholarly analysis.[8] Our robustly reflexive science must be able to generate scientific and political energy and direction, not just intellectual reflection.

Several guides may be helpful here as we face the challenge of developing this kind of theory. For one thing, this requirement not only calls for a kind of moral, political and historical self-consciousness by inquirers that is anathema to empiricist traditions. It also requires that scientists themselves be educated in how to develop this kind of consciousness. Looking in a different direction, we can see that it also sets constraints on the kinds of theories that we should find plausible to explain others' beliefs and behaviors, and on what constitutes the proposal of a theoretical account 'in good conscience.' Let me give three examples here. If I do not recognize how *my* accounts are shaped by race and gender forces, then on what grounds can I claim such causal tendencies for Western men's? Obviously our own accounts are also culturally specific in these ways, and we need to understand these dynamics better. To take another example, if accounts of the sexism of individuals are not sufficient to explain culture-wide aspects of male-dominance, then neither should we regard the ethnocentrism of individual feminist theorists as a sufficient explanation of the ethnocentrism of feminist theory. Finally, if earlier feminist theorists were intellectually talented, industrious, and motivated by emancipatory ends, and yet their theories are woefully inadequate (racist, wrong-headed, intellectually confined by the politics of their day, etc.), then brilliance, hard work and good will are not sufficient to explain the greater adequacy of contemporary feminist accounts. Theories that locate themselves as firmly as possible in history recover in the results of research more of the 'research process' we need to examine in order to better evaluate the research.

---

8 See Hilary Rose, 'Hyper-reflexivity: A New Danger for the Countermovements,' in *Countermovements in the Sciences: Sociology of Science Yearbook*, Helga Nowotny and Hilary Rose, eds. (Dordrecht: Reidel 1979), and Hilary Rose and Steven Rose, 'Radical Science and Its Enemies,' in *Socialist Register*, Ralph Miliband and John Saville, eds. (Atlantic Highlands, NJ: Humanities Press 1979).

VI Conclusion

Most philosophers and feminist researchers in the social sciences and biology already find the standpoint epistemology deeply threatening to the understandings of science into which they have been socialized. Moreover, they find the postmodernist tendencies virtually incomprehensible in their own domains, and unimaginable as a guide to biology and social science research. I still think it important to spend time appreciating the strengths, the powers of these two important contemporary critical tendencies before choosing sides between them. One consequence of this attitude will be to increase our resistance to generating and accepting coherent theories that do not do justice to 'the data,' as Wylie notes. Another consequence will be to direct our attention to the search for more broadly integrative categories and explanatory schemas, as Wylie also points out. But I think that there is yet a third benefit to be gained, and that is the toleration for and interest in those kinds of ambiguities in theorizing that reflect tensions and contradictions in social relations — not just in thought about them. These 'reflected tensions' offer us valuable clues to social practices that may or may not need to be changed — not just to imperfect thought.

CANADIAN JOURNAL OF PHILOSOPHY
Supplementary Volume 13

Beyond Caring:
The De-Moralization of Gender

MARILYN FRIEDMAN
Bowling Green State University
Bowling Green, OH 43403-0222
U.S.A.

Introduction

Carol Gilligan heard a 'distinct moral language' in the voices of women who were subjects in her studies of moral reasoning.[1] Though herself a developmental psychologist, Gilligan has put her mark on contemporary feminist moral philosophy by daring to claim the competence of this voice and the worth of its message. Her book, *In*

---

1 *In a Different Voice* (Cambridge, MA: Harvard University Press 1982), 73. More recently, the following works by Gilligan on related issues have also appeared: 'Do the Social Sciences Have an Adequate Theory of Moral Development?' in Norma Haan, Robert N. Bellah, Paul Rabinow and William M. Sullivan, eds., *Social Science as Moral Inquiry* (New York: Columbia University Press 1983), 33-51; 'Reply,' *Signs* **11** (1986), 324-33; and 'Remapping the Moral Domain: New Images of the Self in Relationship,' in Thomas C. Heller, Morton Sosna and David E. Wellberry, eds., *Reconstructing Individualism* (Stanford, CA: Stanford University Press 1986) 237-52. Throughout this paper, all page references inserted in the text are to *In a Different Voice*.

a Different Voice, which one theorist has aptly described as a best-seller,[2] explored the concern with care and relationships which Gilligan discerned in the moral reasoning of women and contrasted it with the orientation toward justice and rights which she found to typify the moral reasoning of men.

According to Gilligan, the standard (or 'male') moral voice articulated in moral psychology derives moral judgments about particular cases from abstract, universalized moral rules and principles which are substantively concerned with justice and rights. For justice reasoners: the major moral imperative enjoins respect for the rights of others (100); the concept of duty is limited to reciprocal noninterference (147); the motivating vision is one of the equal worth of self and other (63); and one important underlying presupposition is a highly individuated conception of persons.

By contrast, the other (or 'female') moral voice which Gilligan heard in her studies eschews abstract rules and principles. This moral voice derives moral judgments from the contextual detail of situations grasped as specific and unique (100). The substantive concern for this moral voice is care and responsibility, particularly as these arise in the context of interpersonal relationships (19). Moral judgments, for care reasoners, are tied to feelings of empathy and compassion (69); the major moral imperatives center around caring, not hurting others, and avoiding selfishness (90); and the motivating vision of this ethic is 'that everyone will be responded to and included, that no one will be left alone or hurt' (63).

While these two voices are not necessarily contradictory in all respects, they seem, at the very least, to be different in their orientation. Gilligan's writings about the differences have stimulated extensive feminist reconsideration of various ethical themes.[3] In this

---

2 Frigga Haug, 'Morals Also Have Two Genders,' trans. Rodney Livingstone, *New Left Review* **143** (1984), 55.

3 These sources include: Owen J. Flanagan, Jr. and Jonathan E. Adler, 'Impartiality and Particularity,' *Social Research* **50** (1983), 576-96; Nel Noddings, *Caring* (Berkeley: University of California Press 1984); Claudia Card, 'Virtues and Moral Luck' (unpublished paper presented at American Philosophical Association, Western Division Meetings, Chicago, IL, April 1985, and at the Conference

paper, I use Gilligan's work as a springboard for extending certain of those themes in new directions. My discussion has three parts. In the first part, I will address the unresolved question of whether or not a gender difference in moral reasoning is empirically confirmed. I will propose that even if actual statistical differences in the moral reasoning of women and men cannot be confirmed, there is nevertheless a real difference in the moral norms and values culturally associated with each gender. The genders are 'moralized' in distinctive ways. Moral norms about appropriate conduct, characteristic virtues and typical vices are incorporated into our conceptions of femininity and masculinity, female and male. The result is a dichotomy which exemplifies what may be called a 'division of moral labor'[4] between the genders.

In the second part of the paper, I will explore a different reason why actual women and men may not show a divergence of reasoning along the care-justice dichotomy, namely, that the notions of

---

on Virtue Theory, University of San Diego, San Diego, CA, February 1986); Marilyn Friedman, *Care and Context in Moral Reasoning*, MOSAIC Monograph #1 (Bath, England: University of Bath 1985), reprinted in Carol Harding, ed., *Moral Dilemmas* (Chicago: Precedent 1986), 25-42, and in Diana T. Meyers and Eva Feder Kittay, eds., *Women and Moral Theory* (Totowa, NJ: Rowman and Littlefield 1987), 190-204; all the papers in Meyers and Kittay; Linda K. Kerber, 'Some Cautionary Words for Historians,' *Signs* 11 (1986), 304-10; Catherine G. Greeno and Eleanor E. Maccoby, 'How Different is the "Different Voice,"' *Signs* 11 (1986) 310-16; Zella Luria, 'A Methodological Critique,' *Signs* 11 (1986), 316-21; Carol B. Stack, 'The Culture of Gender: Women and Men of Color,' *Signs* 11 (1986), 321-4; Owen Flanagan and Kathryn Jackson, 'Justice, Care, and Gender: The Kohlberg-Gilligan Debate Revisited,' *Ethics* 97 (1987), 622-37. An analysis of this issue from an ambiguously feminist standpoint is to be found in: John M. Broughton, 'Women's Rationality and Men's Virtues,' *Social Research* 50 (1983), 597-642. For a helpful review of some of these issues, cf. Jean Grimshaw, *Philosophy and Feminist Thinking* (Minneapolis: University of Minnesota Press 1986), esp. chs. 7 and 8.

4 This term is used by Virginia Held to refer, in general, to the division of moral labor among the multitude of professions, activities, and practices in culture and society, though not specifically to gender roles. Cf. *Rights and Goods* (New York: The Free Press 1984), ch. 3. Held is aware that gender roles are part of the division of moral labor but she mentions this topic only in passing, p. 29.

care and justice overlap more than Gilligan, among others, has realized. I will suggest, in particular, that morally adequate care involves considerations of justice. Thus, the concerns captured by these two moral categories do not define necessarily distinct moral perspectives, in practice.

Third, and finally, I propose that, even if care and justice do not define distinct moral perspectives, nevertheless, these concepts do point to other important differences in moral orientation. One such difference has to do with the nature of relationship to other selves, and the underlying form of moral commitment which is the central focus of that relationship and of the resulting moral thought. In short, the so-called 'care' perspective emphasizes responsiveness to particular persons, in their uniqueness, and commitment to them as such. By contrast, the so-called 'justice' perspective emphasizes adherence to moral rules, values and principles, and an abstractive treatment of individuals, based on the selected categories which they instantiate.

Let us turn first to the issue of gender difference.

I The Gender Difference Controversy

Gilligan has advanced at least two different positions about the care and the justice perspectives. One is that the care perspective is distinct from the moral perspective which is centered on justice and rights. Following Gilligan,[5] I will call this the 'different voice' hypothesis about moral reasoning. Gilligan's other hypothesis is that the care perspective is typically, or characteristically, a *woman's* moral voice, while the justice perspective is typically, or characteristically a *man's* moral voice. Let's call this the 'gender difference' hypothesis about moral reasoning.

The truth of Gilligan's gender difference hypothesis has been questioned by a number of critics who cite what seems to be disconfirming empirical evidence.[6] This evidence includes studies by

---

5 Gilligan, 'Reply,' 326

6 Research on the 'gender difference' hypothesis is very mixed. The studies which

the psychologist Norma Haan, who has discerned two distinct moral
voices among her research subjects, but has found them to be util-

---

appear to show gender differences in moral reasoning for one or more age
levels include: Norma Haan, M. Brewster-Smith and Jeanne Block, 'Moral
Reasoning of Young Adults: Political-social Behavior, Family Background, and
Personality Correlates,' *Journal of Personality and Social Psychology* **10** (1968),
183-201; James Fishkin, Kenneth Keniston and Catharine MacKinnon, 'Moral
Reasoning and Political Ideology,' *Journal of Personality and Social Psychology*
27 (1973), 109-19; Norma Haan, 'Hypothetical and Actual Moral Reasoning
in a Situation of Civil Disobedience,' *Journal of Personality and Social Psychology*
32 (1975), 255-70; Constance Holstein, 'Development of Moral Judgment: A
Longitudinal Study of Males and Females,' *Child Development* **47** (1976), 51-61
(showing gender differences in middle adulthood but not for other age
categories; see references below); Sharry Langdale, 'Moral Orientations and
Moral Development: The Analysis of Care and Justice Reasoning across Different Dilemmas in Females and Males from Childhood through Adulthood' (Ed.
D. diss., Harvard Graduate School of Education 1983); Kay Johnston, 'Two
Moral Orientations – Two Problem-solving Strategies: Adolescents' Solutions
to Dilemmas in Fables,' (Ed. D. diss., Harvard Graduate School of Education
1985). The last two sources are cited by Gilligan, 'Reply,' p.330.

Among the studies which show no gender differences in moral reasoning
at one or more age levels are: E. Turiel, 'A Comparative Analysis of Moral
Knowledge and Moral Judgment in Males and Females,' *Journal of Personality*
44 (1976), 195-208; C.B. Holstein, 'Irreversible Stepwise Sequence in the Development of Moral Judgment: A Longitudinal Study of Males and Females'
(showing no differences in childhood or adolescence but showing differentiation in middle adulthood; see reference above); N. Haan, et al., 'Family Moral
Patterns,' *Child Development* **47** (1976), 1204-6; M. Berkowitz, et al., 'The Relation of Moral Judgment Stage Disparity to Developmental Effects of Peer Dia-
logues,' *Merrill-Palmer Quarterly* **26** (1980), 341-57; and Mary Brabeck, 'Moral
Judgment: Theory and Research on Differences between Males and Females,'
Developmental Review **3** (1983), 274-91.

Lawrence J. Walker surveyed all the research to date and claimed that rather
than showing a gender-based difference in moral reasoning, it showed differences based on occupation and education: 'Sex Differences in the Development of Moral Reasoning,' *Child Development* **55** (1984), 677-91. This
'meta-analysis' has itself recently been disputed: Norma Haan, 'With Regard
to Walker (1984) on Sex "Differences" in Moral Reasoning' (University of California, Berkeley, Institute of Human Development mimeograph 1985); Diana
Baumrind, 'Sex Differences in Moral Reasoning: Response to Walker's (1984)
Conclusion That There Are None,' *Child Development* (in press). The last two
sources are cited by Gilligan, 'Reply,' p.330.

ized to approximately the same extent by both females and males.[7]
In an attempt to dismiss the research-based objections to her
gender difference hypothesis, Gilligan now asserts that her aim was
not to disclose a statistical gender difference in moral reasoning, but
rather simply to disclose and interpret the differences in the two
perspectives.[8] Psychologist John Broughton has argued that if the
gender difference is not maintained, then Gilligan's whole explanatory framework is undermined.[9] However, Broughton is wrong. The
different voice hypothesis has a significance for moral psychology
and moral philosophy which would survive the demise of the gender
difference hypothesis. At least part of its significance lies in revealing the lopsided obsession of contemporary theories of morality, in
both disciplines, with universal and impartial conceptions of justice
and rights and the relative disregard of *particular*, interpersonal relationships based on partiality and affective ties.[10] (However, the

---

7 Norma Haan, 'Two Moralities in Action Contexts,' *Journal of Personality and
Social Psychology* **36** (1978), 286-305. Also cf. Norma Haan, 'Moral Reasoning
in a Hypothetical and an Actual Situation of Civil Disobedience,' *Journal of
Personality and Social Psychology* **32** (1975), 255-70; and Gertrud Nunner-Winkler,
'Two Moralities? A Critical Discussion of an Ethic of Care and Responsibility
versus an Ethic of Rights and Justice,' in William M. Kurtines and Jacob L.
Gewirtz, *Morality, Moral Behavior, and Moral Development* (New York: John Wiley
& Sons 1984), 348-61.

8 Gilligan, 'Reply,' 326

9 Broughton, 'Women's Rationality and Men's Virtues,' 636

10 Gilligan's work arose largely as a critical reaction to the studies of moral reasoning carried on by Lawrence Kohlberg and his research associates. For the reaction by those scholars to Gilligan's work and their assessment of its importance
to moral psychology, see Lawrence Kohlberg, 'A Reply to Owen Flanagan and
Some Comments on the Puka-Goodpaster Exchange,' *Ethics* **92** (1982), 513-28;
and Lawrence Kohlberg, Charles Levine and Alexandra Hewer, *Moral Stages:
A Current Reformulation and Response to Critics* (Basel: Karger 1983), 20-7, 121-50.
   In philosophy, themes related to Gilligan's concerns have been raised
by, among others: Michael Stocker, 'The Schizophrenia of Modern Ethical
Theories,' *Journal of Philosophy* **63** (1976) 453-66: Bernard Williams, 'Persons,
Character and Morality,' in Amelie O. Rorty, ed., *The Identities of Persons*

different voice hypothisis is itself also suspect if it is made to depend on a dissociation of justice from care, a position which I shall challenge in Part II of this paper.)

But *what about* that supposed empirical disconfirmation of the gender difference hypothesis? Researchers who otherwise accept the disconfirming evidence have nevertheless noticed that many women readers of Gilligan's book find it to 'resonate ... thoroughly with their own experience.'[11] Gilligan notes that it was precisely one of her purposes to expose the gap between women's experience and the findings of psychological research,[12] and, we may suppose, to critique the latter in light of the former.

These unsystematic, anecdotal observations that females and males do differ in ways examined by Gilligan's research should lead us either: (1) to question, and examine carefully, the methods of that empirical research which does not reveal such differences; or (2) to suspect that a gender difference exists but in some form which is not, strictly speaking, a matter of statistical differences in the moral reasoning of women and men. Gilligan has herself expressed the first of these alternatives. I would like to explore the second possibility.

Suppose that there were a gender difference of a sort, but one which was not a simple matter of differences among the form or substance of women's and men's moral reasonings. A plausible ac-

---

(Berkeley: University of California 1976), reprinted in Bernard Williams, *Moral Luck* (New York: Cambridge University Press 1982), 1-19; Lawrence Blum, *Friendship, Altruism and Morality* (London: Routledge & Kegan Paul 1980); Alasdair MacIntyre, *After Virtue* (Notre Dame, IN: University of Notre Dame 1981), esp. Ch. 15; Michael Stocker, 'Values and Purposes: The Limits of Teleology and the Ends of Friendship,' *Journal of Philosophy* **78** (1981), 747-65; Owen Flanagan, 'Virtue, Sex and Gender: Some Philosophical Reflections on the Moral Psychology Debate,' *Ethics* **92** (1982), 499-512; Michael Slote, 'Morality Not a System of Imperatives,' *American Philosophical Quarterly* **19** (1982), 331-40; and Christina Hoff Sommers, 'Filial Morality,' *Journal of Philosophy* **83** (1986), 439-56

11 Greeno and Maccoby, 'How Different is the 'Different' Voice?' 314-15

12 Gilligan, 'Reply,' 325

count might take this form. Among the white middle classes of such western industrial societies as Canada and the United States, women and men are associated with different moral norms and values at the level of the stereotypes, symbols, and myths which contribute to the social construction of gender. One might say that morality is 'gendered' and that the genders are 'moralized.' Our very conceptions of femininity and masculinity, female and male, incorporate norms about appropriate behavior, characteristic virtues, and typical vices.

Morality, I suggest, is fragmented into a 'division of moral labor' along the lines of gender, the rationale for which is rooted in historic developments pertaining to family, state, and economy. The tasks of governing, regulating social order, and managing other 'public' institutions have been monopolized by men as their privileged domain, and the tasks of sustaining privatized personal relationships have been imposed on, or left to, women.[13] The genders have thus been conceived in terms of special and distinctive moral projects. Justice and rights have structured male moral norms, values, and virtues, while care and responsiveness have defined female moral norms, values, and virtues. The division of moral labor has had the dual function both of preparing us each for our respective socially defined domains and of rendering us incompetent to manage the affairs of the realm from which we have been excluded. That justice is symbolized in our culture by the figure of a woman is a remarkable irony; her blindfold hides more than the scales she holds.

To say that the genders are moralized is to say that specific moral ideals, values, virtues, and practices are culturally conceived as the special projects or domains of specific genders. These conceptions would determine which commitments and behaviors were to be considered normal, appropriate, and expected of each gender, which commitments and behaviors were to be considered remarkable or heroic, and which commitments and behaviors were to be con-

---

13 For a discussion of this historical development, cf. Linda Nicholson, 'Women, Morality and History,' *Social Research* **50** (1983) 514-36; and her *Gender and History* (New York: Columbia University Press 1986) esp. chs. 3 and 4.

sidered deviant, improper, outrageous, and intolerable. Men who fail to respond to the cry of a baby, fail to express tender emotions, or fail to show compassion in the face of the grief and sorrow of others, are likely to be tolerated, perhaps even benignly, while women who act similarly can expect to be reproached for their selfish indifference. However, women are seldom required to devote themselves to service to their country or to struggles for human rights. Women are seldom expected to display any of the special virtues associated with national or political life. At the same time, women still carry the burden of an excessively restrictive and oppressive sexual ethic; sexual aggressiveness and promiscuity are vices for which women in all social groups are roundly condemned, even while many of their male counterparts win tributes for such 'virility.'

Social science provides ample literature to show that gender differences are alive and well at the level of popular perception. Both men and women, on average, still conceive women and men in a moralized fashion. For example, expectations and perceptions of women's greater empathy and altruism are expressed by both women and men.[14] The gender stereotypes of women center around qualities which some authors call 'communal.' These include: a concern for the welfare of others; the predominance of caring and nurturant traits; and, to a lesser extent, interpersonal sensitivity, emotional expressiveness, and a gentle personal style.[15]

By contrast, men are stereotyped according to what are referred to as 'agentic' norms.[16] These norms center primarily around asser-

---

14 Cf. Nancy Eisenberg and Roger Lennon, 'Sex Differences in Empathy and Related Capacities,' *Psychological Bulletin* **94** (1983), 100-31.

15 Cf. Alice H. Eagly, 'Sex Differences and Social Roles' (unpublished paper presented at Experimental Social Psychology, Tempe, AZ, October 1986), esp. p.7. Also cf: Alice H. Eagly and Valerie J. Steffen, 'Gender Stereotypes Stem From the Distribution of Women and Men Into Social Roles,' *Journal of Personality and Social Psychology* **46** (1984), 735-54.

16 The stereotypes of men are not obviously connected with justice and rights, but they are connected with the excessive individualism which Gilligan takes

tive and controlling tendencies. The paradigmatic behaviors are self-assertion, including forceful dominance, and independence from other people. Also encompassed by these norms are patterns of self-confidence, personal efficacy, and a direct, adventurous personal style.

If reality failed to accord with myth and symbol, if actual women and men did not fit the traits and dispositions expected of them, this might not necessarily undermine the myths and symbols, since perception could be selective and disconfirming experience reduced to the status of 'occasional exceptions' and 'abnormal, deviant cases.' 'Reality' would be misperceived in the image of cultural myth, as reinforced by the homogenizing tendencies of mass media and mass culture, and the popular imagination would have little foothold for the recognition that women and men were not as they were mythically conceived to be.

If I am right, then Gilligan has discerned the *symbolically* female moral voice, and has disentangled it from the *symbolically* male moral voice. The moralization of gender is more a matter of how we *think* we reason than of how we actually reason, more a matter of the moral concerns we *attribute* to women and men than of true statistical differences between women's and men's moral reasoning. Gilligan's findings resonate with the experiences of many people because those experiences are shaped, in part, by cultural myths and stereotypes of gender which even feminist theorizing may not dispel. Thus, both women and men in our culture *expect* women and men to exhibit this moral dichotomy, and, on my hypothesis, it is this expectation which has shaped both Gilligan's observations and the plausibility which we attribute to them. Or, to put it somewhat differently, *whatever* moral matters men concern themselves with are categorized, estimably, as matters of 'justice and rights,' whereas the moral concerns of women are assigned to the devalued categories of 'care and personal relationships.'

It is important to ask why, if these beliefs are so vividly held, they might, nevertheless, still not produced a reality in conformity with

---

to underlie the justice orientation. Cf. Eagly, 'Sex Differences and Social Roles,' 8.

them.[17] How could those critics who challenge Gilligan's gender hypothesis be right to suggest that women and men show no significant differences in moral reasoning, if women and men are culturally educated, trained, pressured, expected, and perceived to be so radically different?[18]

Philosophy is not, by itself, capable of answering this question adequately. My admittedly *partial* answer to it depends upon showing that the care/justice dichotomy is rationally implausible and that the two concepts are conceptually compatible. This conceptual compatibility creates the empirical possibility that the two moral concerns will be intermingled in practice. That they are actually intermingled in the moral reasonings of real women and men is, of course, not determined simply by their conceptual compatibility, but requires as well the wisdom and insight of those women and men who comprehend the relevance of both concepts to their experiences.[19] Philosophy does not account for the actual emergence

---

17 Eagly argues both that people do show a tendency to conform to shared and known expectations, on the parts of others, about their behavior, and that a division of labor which leads people to develop different skills also contributes to differential development; 'Sex Differences and Social Roles,' *passim.* It follows from Eagly's view that if the genders are stereotypically 'moralized,' they would then be likely to develop so as to conform to those different expectations.

18 Eagly and Steffen have found that stereotypic beliefs that women are more 'communal' and less 'agentic' than men, and that men are more 'agentic' and less 'communal' than women are based more deeply on occupational role stereotypes than on gender stereotypes; 'Gender Stereotypes Stem From the Distribution of Women and Men Into Social Roles,' *passim.* In this respect, Eagly and Steffen force us to question whether the gender categorization which pervades Gilligan's analysis really captures the fundamental differentiation among persons. I do not address this question in this paper.

19 In correspondence, Marcia Baron has suggested that a factor accounting for the actual emergence of 'mixed' perspectives on the parts of women and men may have to do with the instability of the distinction between public and private realms to which the justice/care dichotomy corresponds. Men have always been recognized to participate in both realms and, in practice, many women have participated, out of choice or necessity, in such segments of the public world as that of paid labor. The result is a blurring of the experiential segregation which otherwise might have served to reinforce distinct moral orientations.

of wisdom. That the genders do not, in reality, divide along those moral lines is made *possible*, though not inevitable, by the conceptual limitations of both a concept of care dissociated from considerations of justice and a concept of justice dissociated from considerations of care. Support for this partial explanation requires a reconceptualization of care and justice — the topic of the next part of my discussion.

II Surpassing the Care/Justice Dichotomy

I have suggested that if women and men do not show statistical differences in moral reasoning along the lines of a care/justice dichotomy, this should not be thought surprising since the concepts of care and justice are mutually compatible. People who treat each other justly can also care about each other. Conversely, personal relationships are arenas in which people have rights to certain forms of treatment, and in which fairness can be reflected in ongoing interpersonal mutuality. It is this latter insight — the relevance of justice to close personal relationships — which I will emphasize here.

Justice, at the most general level, is a matter of giving people their due, of treating them appropriately. Justice is relevant to personal relationships and to care precisely to the extent that considerations of justice itself determine appropriate ways to treat friends or intimates. Justice as it bears on relationships among friends or family, or on other close personal ties, might not involve duties which are universalizable, in the sense of being owed to all persons simply in virtue of shared moral personhood. But this does not entail the irrelevance of justice among friends or intimates.

Moral thinking has not always dissociated the domain of justice from that of close personal relationships. The earliest Greek code of justice placed friendship at the forefront of conditions for the realization of justice, and construed the rules of justice as being coextensive with the limits of friendship. The reader will recall that one of the first definitions of justice which Plato sought to contest, in the *Republic*, is that of 'helping one's friends and harming one's enemies.'[20] Although the ancient Greek model of justice among friends reserved that moral privilege for free-born Greek males, the conception is, nevertheless, instructive for its readiness to link the notion of justice to relationships based on affection and loyalty. This provides an important contrast to modern notions of justice which are often deliberately constructed so as to avoid presumptions of mutual concern on the parts of those to whom the conception is to apply.

As is well known, John Rawls, for one, requires that the parties to the original position in which justice is to be negotiated be mutually disinterested.[21] Each party is assumed, first and foremost, to be concerned for the advancement of her own interests, and to care about the interests of others only to the extent that her own interests require it. This postulate of mutual disinterestedness is intended by Rawls to ensure that the principles of justice do not depend on what he calls 'strong assumptions,' such as 'extensive ties of natural sentiment.'[22] Rawls is seeking principles of justice which apply to everyone in all their social interrelationships, *whether or not* characterized by affection and a concern for each other's well-being. While such an account promises to disclose duties of justice owed to all other parties to the social contract, it may fail to uncover *special* duties of justice which arise in close personal relationships the foundation of which is affection or kinship, rather than contract. The methodological device of assuming mutual disinterest might blind us to the role of justice among mutually interested and/or intimate parties.

Gilligan herself has suggested that mature reasoning about care incorporates considerations of justice and rights. But Gilligan's conception of what this means is highly limited. It appears to involve simply the recognition 'that self and other are equal,' a notion which

---

20 Book I, 322-35. A thorough discussion of the Greek conception of justice in the context of friendship can be found in Horst Hutter, *Politics as Friendship* (Waterloo, ON: Wilfrid Laurier University Press 1978).

21 Rawls, *Theory of Justice*, 13 and elsewhere

22 Ibid., 129

serves to override the problematic tendency of the ethic of care to become *self-sacrificing* care in women's practices. However, important as it may be, this notion hardly does justice to justice.

There are several ways in which justice pertains to close personal relationships. The first two ways which I will mention are largely appropriate only among friends, relatives, or intimates who are of comparable development in their realization of moral personhood, for example, who are both mature responsible adults. The third sort of relevance of justice to close relationships, which I will discuss shortly, pertains to families, in which adults often interrelate with children — a more challenging domain for the application of justice. But first the easier task.

One sort of role for justice in close relationships among people of comparable moral personhood may be discerned by considering that a personal relationship is a miniature social system, which provides valued mutual intimacy, support, and concern for those who are involved. The maintenance of a relationship requires effort by the participants. One intimate may bear a much greater burden for sustaining a relationship than the other participant(s) and may derive less support, concern, and so forth than she deserves for her efforts. Justice sets a constraint on such relationships by calling for an appropriate sharing, among the participants, of the benefits and burdens which constitute their relationship.

Marilyn Frye, for example, has discussed what amounts to a pattern of *violation* of this requirement of justice in heterosexual relationships. She has argued that women of all races, social classes, and societies can be defined as a coherent group in terms of a distinctive function which is culturally assigned to them. This function is, in Frye's words, 'the service of men and men's interests as men define them.'[23] This service work includes personal service (satisfaction of routine bodily needs, such as hunger, and other mundane tasks), sexual and reproductive service, and ego service. Says Frye, '... at every race/class level and even across race/class lines

---

23 *The Politics of Reality* (Trumansburg. NY: The Crossing Press 1983) 9

men do not serve women as women serve men.'[24] Frye is, of course, generalizing over society and culture, and the sweep of her generalization encompasses both ongoing close personal relationships as well as other relationships which are not close or are not carried on beyond specific transactions, for example, that of prostitute to client. By excluding those latter cases for the time being, and applying Frye's analysis to familial and other close ties between women and men, we may discern the sort of one-sided relational exploitation, often masquerading in the guise of love or care, which constitutes this first sort of injustice.

Justice is relevant to close personal relationships among comparable moral persons in a second way as well. The trust and intimacy which characterize special relationships create special vulnerabilities to harm. Commonly recognized harms, such as physical injury and sexual assault, become more feasible; and special relationships, in corrupt, abusive, or degenerate forms, make possible certain uncommon emotional harms not even possible in impersonal relationships. When someone is harmed in a personal relationship, she is owed a rectification of some sort, a righting of the wrong which has been done her. The notion of justice emerges, once again, as a relevant moral notion.

Thus, in a close relationship among persons of comparable moral personhood, care may degenerate into the injustices of exploitation, or oppression. Many such problems have been given wide public scrutiny recently as a result of feminist analysis of various aspects of family life and sexual relationships. Woman-battering, acquaintance rape, and sexual harassment are but a few of the many recently publicized injustices of 'personal' life. The notion of distributive or corrective injustice seems almost too mild to capture these indignities, involving, as they do, violation of bodily integrity and an assumption of the right to assault and injure. But to call these harms injustices is certainly not to rule out impassioned moral criticism in other terms as well.

---

24 Ibid., 10

The two requirements of justice which I have just discussed exemplify the standard distinction between distributive and corrective justice. They illustrate the role of justice in personal relationships regarded in abstraction from a social context. Personal relationships may also be regarded in the context of their various institutional settings, such as marriage and family. Here justice emerges again as a relevant ideal, its role being to define appropriate institutions to structure interactions among family members, other household cohabitants, and intimates in general. The family, for example,[25] is a miniature society, exhibiting all the major facets of large-scale social life: decision-making affecting the whole unit; executive action; judgments of guilt and innocence; reward and punishment; allocation of responsibilities and privileges, of burdens and benefits; and monumental influences on the life-chances of both its maturing and its matured members. Any of these features *alone* would invoke the relevance of justice; together, they make the case overwhelming.

Women's historically paradigmatic role of mothering has provided a multitude of insights which can be reconstructed as insights about the importance of justice in family relationships, especially those relationships involving remarkable disparities in maturity, capability, and power.[26] In these familial relationships, one party grows into moral personhood over time, gradually acquiring the capacity to be a responsible moral agent. Considerations of justice pertain to the mothering of children in numerous ways. For one thing, there may be siblings to deal with, whose demands and conflicts create the context for parental arbitration and the need for a

---

25 For an important discussion of the relevance of justice to the family, cf. Susan Moller Okin, 'Justice and Gender,' *Philosophy and Public Affairs* **16** (1987), 42-72.

26 For insightful discussions of the distinctive modes of thought to which mothering gives rise, cf. Sara Ruddick, 'Maternal Thinking,' *Feminist Studies* **6** (1980) 342-67; and her 'Preservative Love and Military Destruction: Some Reflections on Mothering and Peace,' in Joyce Trebilcot, ed., *Mothering: Essays in Feminist Theory* (Totowa, NJ: Rowman & Allanheld 1983) 231-62; also Virginia Held, 'The Obligations of Mothers and Fathers,' in Trebilcot, ed. 7-20.

fair allotment of responsibilities and privileges. Then there are decisions to be made, involving the well-being of all persons in the family unit, whose immature members become increasingly capable
over time of participating in such administrative affairs. Of special
importance in the practice of raising children are the duties to nurture and to promote growth and maturation. These duties may be
seen as counterparts to the welfare rights viewed by many as a matter of social justice.[27] Motherhood continually presents its practitioners with moral problems best seen in terms of a complex framework
which integrates justice with care, even though the politico-legal discourse of justice has not shaped its domestic expression.[28]

I have been discussing the relevance of justice to close personal
relationships. A few words about my companion thesis — the
relevance of care to the public domain — is also in order.[29] In its more
noble manifestation, care in the public realm would show itself,
perhaps, in foreign aid, welfare programs, famine or disaster relief,
or other social programs designed to relieve suffering and attend to
human needs. If untempered by justice in the public domain, care
degenerates precipitously. The infamous 'boss' of Chicago's old-time
Democratic machine, Mayor Richard J. Daley, was legendary for his
nepotism and political partisanship; he cared extravagently for his
relatives, friends, and political cronies.[30]

---

27 This point was suggested to me by L.W. Sumner.

28 John Broughton also discusses the concern for justice and rights which appears in women's moral reasoning as well as the concern for care and relationships featured in men's moral reasoning; 'Women's Rationality and Men's
Virtues,' esp. 603-22. For a historical discussion of male theorists who have
failed to hear the concern for justice in women's voices, cf. Carole Pateman,
'"The Disorder of Women": Women, Love, and the Sense of Justice,' *Ethics*
91 (1980), 20-34.

29 This discussion owes a debt to Francesca M. Cancian's warning that we should
not narrow our conception of love to the recognized ways in which women
love, which researchers find to center around the expression of feelings and
verbal disclosure. Such a conception ignores forms of love which are stereotyped as characteristically male, including instrumental help and the sharing
of activities. Cf. 'The Feminization of Love,' *Signs* **11** (1986), 692-709.

30 Cf. Mike Royko, *Boss: Richard J. Daley of Chicago* (New York: New American
Library 1971).

In recounting the moral reasoning of one of her research subjects, Gilligan once wrote that the 'justice' perspective fails 'to take into account the reality of relationships' (147). What she meant is that the 'justice' perspective emphasizes a self's various rights to noninterference by others. Gilligan worried that if this is all that a concern for justice involved, then such a perspective would disregard the moral value of positive interaction, connection, and commitment among persons.

However, Gilligan's interpretation of justice is far too limited. For one thing, it fails to recognize positive rights, such as welfare rights, which may be endorsed from a 'justice' perspective. But beyond this minor point, a more important problem is Gilligan's failure to acknowledge the potential for *violence and harm* in human interrelationships and human community.[31] The concept of justice, in general, arises out of relational conditions in which most human beings have the capacity, and many have the inclination, to treat each other badly.

Thus, notions of distributive justice are impelled by the realization that people who together comprise a social system may not share fairly in the benefits and burdens of their social cooperation. Conceptions of rectificatory, or corrective, justice are founded on the concern that when harms are done, action should be taken either to restore those harmed as fully as possible to their previous state, or to prevent further similar harm, or both. And the specific rights which people are variously thought to have are just so many manifestations of our interest in identifying ways in which people deserve protection against harm by others. The complex reality of social life encompasses the human potential for helping, caring for, and nurturing others *as well as* the potential for harming, exploiting, and oppressing others. Thus, Gilligan is wrong to think that the justice perspective completely neglects 'the reality of relation-

---

31 Claudia Card has critiqued Gilligan's work for ignoring, in particular, the dismaying harms to which women have historically been subjected in heterosexual relationships, including, but by no means limited to, marriage ('Virtues and Moral Luck,' 15-17).

ships.' Rather, it arises from a more complex, and more realitic, estimate of the nature of human interrelationship.

In light of these reflections, it seems wise both to reconsider the seeming dichotomy of care and justice, and to question the moral adequacy of either orientation dissociated from the other. Our aim would be to advance 'beyond caring,' that is, beyong *mere* caring dissociated from a concern for justice. In addition, we would do well to progress beyond gender stereotypes which assign distinct and different moral roles to women and men. Our ultimate goal should be a non-gendered, non-dichotomized, moral framework in which all moral concerns could be expressed. We might, with intentional irony, call this project, 'de-moralizing the genders.'

III Commitments to Particular Persons

Even though care and justice do not define mutually exclusive moral frameworks, it is still too early to dispose of the 'different voice hypothesis.' I believe that there is something to be said for the thesis that there are different moral orientations, even if the concepts of care and justice do not capture the relevant differences and even if the differences do not correlate statistically with gender differences.

My suggestion is that one important distinction has to do with the nature and focus of what may be called 'primary moral commitments.' Let us begin with the observation that, from the so-called 'care standpoint,' responsiveness to other persons in their wholeness and their particularity is of singular importance. This idea, in turn, points toward a notion of moral commitment which takes *particular persons* as its primary focus.[32] A form of moral commitment which contrasts with this is one which involves a focus on general and abstract rules, values, or principles. It is no mere coincidence, I

---

32 Discussion in part III of my paper draws upon the insights of Claudia Card, 'Virtues and Moral Luck' and Seyla Benhabib, 'The Generalized and the Concrete Other: Visions of the Autonomous Self,' in Meyers and Kittay, eds., *Women and Moral Theory*, 154-77.

believe, that Gilligan found the so-called 'justice' perspective to feature an emphasis on *rules* (e.g., p.73).

In Part II of this paper, I argued that the concepts of justice and care are mutually compatible and, to at least some extent, mutually dependent. Based on my analysis, the 'justice perspective' might be said to rest, at bottom, on the assumption that the best way to *care* for persons is to respect their rights, and to accord them their due, both in distribution of the burdens and benefits of social cooperation, and in the rectification of wrongs done. But to uphold these principles, it is not necessary to respond with emotion, feeling, passion, or compassion to other persons. Upholding justice does not require the full range of mutual responsiveness which is possible between persons.

By contrast, the so-called 'ethic of care' stresses an ongoing responsiveness. This ethic is, after all, the stereotypic moral norm for women in the domestic role of sustaining a family in the face of the harsh realities of a competitive marketplace and an indifferent polis. The domestic realm has been idealized as the realm in which people, as specific individuals, were to have been nurtured, cherished, and succored. The 'care' perspective discussed by Gilligan is a limited one; it is not really about care in all its complexity, for, as I have argued, that notion *includes* just treatment. But it *is* about the nature of relationships to particular persons grasped as such. The key issue is the sensitivity and responsiveness to another person's emotional states, individuating differences, specific uniqueness, and whole particularity. The 'care' orientation focuses on whole persons and de-emphasizes adherence to moral rules.

Thus, the important conception which I am extracting from the so-called 'care' perspective is that of commitment to particular persons. What is the nature of this form of moral commitment? Commitment to a specific person, such as a lover, child, or friend, takes as its primary focus the needs, wants, attitudes, judgments, behavior, and overall way of being of that particular person. It is specific to that individual and is not generalizable to others. We show a commitment to someone whenever we attend to her needs, enjoy her successes, defer to her judgment, and find inspiration in her values and goals, simply because they are *hers*. If it is *who she is*, and not her actions or traits subsumed under general rules, which matters as one's motivating guide, then one's responsiveness to her reflects a person-oriented, rather than a rule-based, moral commitment.

Thus, the different perspectives which Gilligan called 'care' and 'justice' do point toward substantive differences in human interrelationship and commitment. Both orientations take account of relationships in some way; both may legitimately incorporate a concern for justice and for care, and both aim to avoid harm to others and (at the highest stages) to the self. But from the standpoint of 'care,' self and other are conceptualized in their *particularity* rather than as instances for the application of generalized moral notions. This difference ramifies into what appears to be a major difference in the organization and focus of moral thought.

This analysis requires a subtle expansion. Like care and justice, commitments to particular persons and commitments to values, rules, and principles are not mutually exclusive within the entire panorama of one person's moral concerns. Doubtless, they are intermingled in most people's moral outlooks. Pat likes and admires Mary because of Mary's resilience in the face of tragedy, her intelligent courage, and her good-humored audacity. Pat thereby shows a commitment *in general* to resilience, courage, and good-humored audacity as traits of human personality.

However, in Mary, these traits coalesce in a unique manner: perhaps no one will stand by a friend in deep trouble quite so steadfastly as Mary; perhaps no one petitions the university president as effectively as Mary. The traits which Pat likes, in general, converge to make *Mary*, in Pat's eyes, an especially admirable human individual, a sort of moral exemplar. In virtue of Pat's loyalty to her, Mary may come to play a role in Pat's life which exceeds, in its weightiness, the sum total of the values which Pat sees in Mary's virtues, taken individually and in abstraction from any particular human personality.

Pat is someone with commitments both to moral abstractions and to particular persons. Pat is, in short, like most of us. When we reason morally, we can take up a stance which makes either of these forms of commitment the focal point of our attention. The choice of which stance to adopt at a given time is probably, like other moral alternatives, most poignant and difficult in situations of moral ambiguity or uncertainty when we don't know how to proceed. In such situations, one can turn *either* to the guidance of principled commitments to values, forms of conduct, or human virtues, *or* one can turn to the guidance which inheres in the example set by a trusted friend or associate — the example of how *she* interprets those same moral ambiguities, or how *she* resolves those same moral uncertainties.

Of course, the commitment to a particular person is evident in more situations than simply those of moral irresolution. But the experience of moral irresolution may make clearer the different sorts of moral commitment which structure our thinking. Following cherished values will lead one out of one's moral uncertainties in a very different way than following someone else's example.

Thus, the insight that each person needs some others in her life who recognize, respect, and cherish her particularity in its richness and wholeness is the distinctive motivating vision of the 'care' perspective.[33] The sort of respect for persons which grows out of this vision is not the abstract respect which is owed to all persons in virtue of their common humanity, but a respect for individual worth, merit, need, or, even, idiosyncracy. It is a form of respect which involves admiration and cherishing, when the distinctive qualities are valued intrinsically, and which, at the least, involves toleration when the distinctive qualities are not valued intrinsically.

Indeed, there is an apparent irony in the notion of personhood which underlies some philosophers' conceptions of the universalized moral duties owed to all persons. The rational nature which Kant, for example, takes to give each person dignity and to make each of absolute value, and, therefore, irreplaceable,[34] is no more than an abstract rational nature in virtue of which we are all alike. But if we are all alike in this respect, it is hard to understand why we would be irreplaceable. Our common rational nature would seem to make us indistinguishable and, therefore, mutually interchange-

---

33 This part of my discussion owes a debt to Claudia Card.

34 Cf. Immanuel Kant, *Groundwork of the Metaphysics of Morals*, trans. Lewis White Beck (Indianapolis: Bobbs-Merrill 1959), 46-7, 53-4.

able. Specific identity would be a matter of indifference, so far as our absolute value is concerned. Yet it would seem that only in *virtue* of our distinctive particularity could we each be truly irreplaceable.

Of course, our particularity does not *exclude* a common nature, conceptualized at a level of suitable generality. We still deserve equal respect in virtue of our common humanity. But we are also *more* than abstractly and equivalently human. It is this 'more' to which we commit ourselves when we care for others in their particularity.

Thus, as I interpret it, there is at least one important difference in moral reasoning brought to our attention by Gilligan's 'care' and 'justice' frameworks. This difference hinges on the primary form of moral commitment which structures moral thought and the resulting nature of the response to other persons. For so-called 'care' reasoners, recognition of, and commitment to, persons in their particularity is an overriding moral concern.[35]

Unlike the concepts of justice and care, which admit of a mutual integration, it is less clear that these two distinct forms of moral commitment can jointly comprise the focus of one's moral attention, in any single case. Nor can we respond to all other persons equally well in either way. The only integration possible here may be to seek the more intimate, responsive, committed relationships with people who are known closely, or known in contexts in which differential needs are important and can be known with some reliability, and to settle for rule-based equal respect toward that vast number of others whom one cannot know in any particularity.

At any rate, to tie together the varied threads of this discussion, we may conclude that nothing intrinsic to gender demands a division of moral norms which assigns particularized, personalized commitments to women and universalized, rule-based commitments to men. We need nothing less than to 'de-moralize' the genders, ad-

---

35 For a helpful discussion on this topic, cf. Margaret Walker, 'Moral Particularism,' unpublished manuscript presented at the Pacific Division Meetings of the American Philosophical Association, March 1987.

vance beyond the dissociation of justice from care, and enlarge the symbolic access of each gender to all available conceptual and social resources for the sustenance and enrichment of our collective moral life.[36]

---

36 I am grateful to Larry May, L.W. Sumner, Marcia Baron, and Christopher Morris for a helpful comments on previous drafts of this paper. Earlier versions were presented to the Society for Women in Philosophy, Midwestern Division (USA), Madison, WI, October 1986; Society for Value Inquiry, Chicago, IL, April 1987; Seminar on Contemporary Social and Political Thought, University of Chicago, May 1987; Third International Interdisciplinary Congress on Women, Dublin, Ireland, July 1987; and Annual Conference of MOSAIC (Moral and Social Action Interdisciplinary Colloquium), Brighton, England, July 1987.

CANADIAN JOURNAL OF PHILOSOPHY
Supplementary Volume 13

Non-contractual Society: A Feminist View*

VIRGINIA HELD
City University of New York
New York, NY 10036
U.S.A.

Contemporary society is in the grip of contractual thinking. Realities are interpreted in contractual terms, and goals are formulated in terms of rational contracts. The leading current conceptions of rationality begin with assumptions that human beings are independent, self-interested or mutually disinterested, individuals; they then typically argue that it is often rational for human beings to enter into contractual relationships with each other.

On the side of description, assumptions characteristic of a contractual view of human relations underlie the dominant attempts to view social realities through the lenses of the social sciences.[1] They

---

* This paper was first presented at a conference at Loyala University on April 18, 1983. It has also been discussed at philosophy department or women's studies colloquia at Hamilton and Dartmouth, at a conference on feminist theory at the University of Cincinnati, and at a conference on contractarianism at the University of Western Ontario. I am grateful to the many persons who have commented on the paper on these occasions, and also to Elise Boulding, Marsha Hanen, Kai Nielsen, Carole Pateman, Elizabeth Potter, and Sara Ruddick for additional comments.

1 As Carole Pateman writes, 'One of the most striking features of the past two decades is the extent to which the assumptions of liberal individualism have permeated the whole of social life.' Carole Pateman, *The Problem of Political Obligation: A Critique of Liberal Theory* (Berkeley: University of California Press 1985), 182-3. All those fields influenced by rational choice theory — and that

also underlie the principles upon which most persons in contemporary Western society claim their most powerful institutions to be founded. We are told that modern democratic states rest on a social contract,[2] that their economies should be thought of as a free market where producers and consumers, employers and employees make contractual agreements.[3] And we should even, it is suggested, interpret our culture as a free market of ideas.[4]

On the side of prescription, leading theories of justice and equality such as those of Rawls, Nozick, and Dworkin, suggest what social arrangements should be like to more fully reflect the requirements of contractual rationality.[5] And various philosophers claim that even morality itself is best understood in contractual terms.[6] The vast domain of rational choice theory, supposedly ap-

---

includes most of the social sciences — thus 'hark back to classical liberal contract doctrines,' Pateman writes, 'and claims that social order is founded on the interactions of self-interested, utility-maximizing individuals, protecting and enlarging their property in the capitalist market' (183).

2 E.g. Thomas Hobbes, *Leviathan*, C.B. Macpherson, ed. (Baltimore: Penguin 1971); John Locke, *Two Treatises of Government*, Peter Laslett, ed. (New York: Mentor 1965); Jean-Jacques Rousseau, *The Social Contract*, Charles Frankel, ed. (New York: Hafner 1947); The U. S. Declaration of Independence; and of course a literature too vast to mention. As Carole Pateman writes of this tradition, 'a corollary of the liberal view ... is that social contract theory is central to liberalism. Paradigmatically, contract is the act through which two free and equal individuals create social bonds, or a collection of such individuals creates the state' (180).

3 E.g. Adam Smith, *The Wealth of Nations*, M. Lerner, ed. (New York: Random House 1937) and virtually the whole of classical and neo-classical economics.

4 The phrase has been entrenched in judicial and social discussion since Oliver Wendell Holmes used it in *Abrams v. United States* (250 U.S. 616, 630 [1919]).

5 E.g. John Rawls, *A Theory of Justice* (Cambridge, MA: Harvard University Press 1971); Robert Nozick, *Anarchy, State, and Utopia* (New York: Basic Books 1974); and Ronald Dworkin, *Taking Rights Seriously* (Cambridge, MA: Harvard University Press 1977).

6 E.g. David A. J. Richards, *A Theory of Reasons for Action* (New York: Oxford University Press 1971); and David Gauthier, *Morals By Agreement* (New York: Oxford University Press 1986).

plicable to the whole range of human activity and experience, makes the same basic assumptions about individuals, contractual relations, and rationality, as are by now familiar in the social contract tradition.[7] And contractual solutions are increasingly suggested for problems which arise in areas not hitherto thought of in contractual terms, such as in dealing with unruly patients in treatment contexts, in controlling inmates in prisons, and even in bringing up children.

When subjected to examination, the assumptions and conceptions of contractual thinking seem highly questionable. As descriptions of reality they can be seriously misleading. Actual societies are the results of war, exploitation, racism, and patriarchy far more than of social contracts. Economic and political realities are the outcomes of economic strength triumphing over economic weakness more than of a free market. And rather than a free market of ideas, we have a culture in which the loudspeakers that are the mass media drown out the soft voices of free expression. As expressions of normative concern, moreover, contractual theories hold out an impoverished view of human aspiration.

To see contractual relations between self-interested or mutually disinterested individuals as constituting a paradigm of human relations is to take a certain historically specific conception of 'economic man' as representative of humanity. And it is, many feminists are beginning to agree, to overlook or to discount in very fundamental ways the experience of women.

I shall try in this paper to look at society from a thoroughly different point of view than that of economic man. I shall take the point of view of women, and especially of mothers, as the basis for trying to rethink society and its possible goals. Certainly there is no single point of view of women; the perspectives of women are potentially as diverse as those of men. But since the perspectives of women have all been to a large extent discounted, across the spectrum, I

---

7 For a recent sample, see the symposium 'Explanation and Justification in Social Theory,' in *Ethics* **97**, 1.

shall not try to deal here with diversity among such views, but rather to give voice to one possible feminist outlook.

The social contract tradition and bourgeois conceptions of rationality have already been criticized for some time from Marxian and other continental perspectives. These perspectives, however, usually leave out the perspective of mothers as fully as do those they criticize, so I shall not try to deal here with these alternatives either. I shall try instead to imagine what society would look like, for both descriptive and prescriptive purposes, if we replaced the paradigm of 'economic man' and substituted for it the paradigm of mother and child. I shall try to explore how society and our goals for it might appear if, instead of thinking of human relations as contractual, we thought of them as *like* relations between mothers and children. What would social relations look like? What would society look like if we would take the relation between mother and child as not just one relation among many, but as the *primary* social relation? And what sorts of aspirations might we have for such a society?

On the face of it, it seems plausible to take the relation between mother and child as *the* primary social relation, since before there could have been any self-sufficient, independent men in a hypothetical state of nature, there would have had to have been mothers, and the children these men would have had to have been. And the argument could be developed in terms of a conceptual as well as a causal primacy. However, let me anticipate a likely reaction and say before I begin this exploration that I doubt that the view I am going to present is the one we should end up with. I doubt that we should take any one relation as paradigmatic for all the others. And I doubt that morality should be based on any one type of human relation. In my recent book *Rights and Goods* I argue for different moral approaches for different contexts, and try to map out which approaches are suitable for which contexts.[8] Perhaps this book will turn out to be a mere stage in my thinking, and I will eventually suppose that relations between mothers and children should

---

8 Virginia Held, *Rights and Goods. Justifying Social Action* (New York: Free Press/Macmillan 1984)

be thought of as primary, and as the sort of human relation all other human relations should resemble or reflect. But I am inclined at this point to think that we will continue to need conceptions of different types of relations for different domains, such as the domains of law, of economic activity, and of the family.

To think of relations between mothers and children as paradigmatic, however, may be an important stage to go through in reconstructing a view of human relationships that will be adequate from a feminist point of view. Since the image of rational economic man in contractual relations is pervasive in this society, and expanding constantly, it may be a useful endeavor to try to see everything in this different way, as if the primary social relation is that between mother and child, and as if all the others could and should be made over in the image of this one, or be embedded in a framework of such relations. In any case, if we pay attention to this neglected relation between mother and child, perhaps we can put a stop to the imperialism of the model of economic man, and assert with conviction that at least there are some or perhaps many domains where this model is definitely not appropriate. And perhaps we can show that morality must be as relevant to, and moral theory as appropriately based on, the context of mothering as the context of contracting. To the extent that some of our relations should be seen as contractual, we should recognize how essentially limited rather than general such relations are. And to the extent that some of morality should be understood in terms of what rational contractors would agree to, we should recognize that such a morality can only be suitable for a particular domain of human relations, and should not be supposed to be a model for morality in general.

Rational choice theorists point out that their theories are formulated for just those situations where individuals do seek to maximize their own interests and are uninterested in each others' interests. Their theories, they suggest, are not intended to deal with people in love. But the questions I am trying to raise in this paper have to do with how we ought to treat, conceptually, a great variety of human relations. Of course we *can*, theoretically, treat them *as* contractual, but *should* we do so? Is it plausible to do so? And when we ask these questions we can see that of course it is not only in special cases that persons can be and perhaps should be and often are bound together in social ties of a non-contractual kind.

To see society in terms of family rather than marketplace relationships is not new. Feudal conceptions, for instance, drew analogies between monarchs and the heads of households. But these were views based on relations between patriarchal fathers and their wives and children, not views of society seen in terms of mothering. To explore the latter is not to suggest a return to pre-contractual society, but to consider what further progress is needed.

Since it is the practice of mothering with which I shall be concerned in what follows, rather than with women in the biological sense, I shall use the term 'mothering person' rather than 'mother.' A 'mothering person' can be male or female. So I shall speak of 'mothering persons' in the same gender-neutral way that various writers now try to speak of 'rational contractors.' If men feel uncomfortable being referred to as, or even more so in being, 'mothering persons,' this may possibly mirror the discomfort many mothers feel adapting to the norms and practices, and language, of 'economic man.'

It is important to emphasize that I shall look at the practice of mothering not as it has in fact existed in any patriarchal society, but in terms of what the characteristic features of this practice would be without patriarchal domination. In method this may be comparable to what has been done in developing a concept of rational contracting. This concept of course developed while large segments of society were in fact still feudal, and of course actual human beings are not in fact fully rational. These realities have not prevented the contractual relation from being taken as paradigmatic.

Furthermore, it may well be that the concept of the mother/child relation that I shall develop is somewhat historically specific. But perhaps no concept can avoid being that. My aim is only to have the conception I shall try to develop capable of being considered an alternative to the conception of economic man in contractual relations, that is, of being no more historically limited, and contextually dependent, than that. To the extent that the mother/child relation will be an idealization, I hope it will not be more severely idealized than the relation between rational contractors that it is to replace; for the purposes of my exploration, it does not need to be less of an idealization.

I Women and Family

A first point to note in trying to imagine society from the point of view of women is that the contractual model was hardly ever applied, as either description or ideal, to women or to relations within the family. The family was imagined to be 'outside' the polis and 'outside' the market in a 'private' domain. This private domain was contrasted with the public domain, and with what, by the time of Hobbes and Locke, was thought of as the contractual domain of citizen and state and tradesman and market. Although women have always worked, and although both women and children were later pressed into work in factories, they were still thought of as outside the domain in which the contractual models of 'equal men' were developed. Women were not expected to demand equal rights either in the public domain or at home. Women were not expected to be 'economic men.' And children were simply excluded from the realm of what was being interpreted in contractual terms as distinctively human.

The clearest example of the extraordinary bias to which such views can lead can be seen in the writings of Rousseau. Moral principles were to be applied to men and to women in ways thoroughly inconsistent with each other. Rousseau argued that in the polity no man should surrender his freedom. He thought that government could be based on a social contract in which citizens under law will be as free as in the state of nature because they will give the law to themselves.[9] But, he argued, within the household, the man must rule and the woman must submit to this rule.[10] Rousseau maintained that women must be trained from the beginning to serve and to submit to men. Since the essence of being fully human was for Rousseau being free from submission to the will of another, women were to be denied the essential condition for being fully human. And he thought that if women were accorded equality with men in the

---

9 J.-J. Rousseau, *The Social Contract*

10 J.-J. Rousseau, *Emile*, trans. B. Foxley (New York: Dutton 1911)

household (which was the only domain to be open to them) this would bring about the dissolution of society. Human society, Rousseau thought, was incompatible with extending the principles of contractual society to women and the family.

The contrast, in this view, is total: complete freedom and equality in the exclusively male polity; absolute male authority and female submission in the household. And Rousseau seems not to have considered the implications of such a view. If one really believes that two persons in a household, with ties of affection and time for discussion, can never reach decisions by consensus, or by taking turns at deciding, but must always have one person in full authority to have the final word, what hope could there possibly be for the larger democratic, participatory, consensual political life Rousseau so eloquently advocated? On the other hand, if decisions in the political realm *can* be arrived at in such a way that the will of no man needs to be overpowered, as Rousseau thought, why cannot such concern for avoiding coercion be extended to relations between men and women in the family?

One way in which the dominant patterns of thought have managed to overlook such inconsistencies has been to see women as primarily mothers, and mothering as a primarily biological function. Then it has been supposed that while contracting is a specifically human activity, women are engaged in an activity which is not specifically human. Women have accordingly been thought to be closer to nature than men, to be enmeshed in a biological function involving processes more like those in which other animals are involved than like the rational contracting of distinctively human 'economic man.' The total or relative exclusion of women from the domain of voluntary contracting has then been thought to be either inevitable or appropriate.

The view that women are more governed by biology than are men is still prevalent. It is as questionable as many other traditional misinterpretations of women's experience. Human mothering is an extremely different activity from the mothering engaged in by other animals. It is as different from the mothering of other animals as is the work and speech of men different from the 'work' and 'speech' of other animals. Since humans are also animals, one should not exaggerate the differences between humans and other animals. But to whatever extent it is appropriate to recognize a difference between 'man' and other animals, so would it be appropriate to recognize a comparable difference between human mothering and the mothering of other animals.

Human mothering shapes language and culture, and forms human social personhood. Human mothering develops morality, it does not merely transmit techniques of survival; impressive as the latter can be, they do not have built into them the aims of morality. Human mothering teaches consideration for others based on moral concern; it does not merely follow and bring the child to follow instinctive tendency. Human mothering creates autonomous persons; it does not merely propagate a species. It can be fully as creative an activity as most other human activities; to create *new* persons, and new types of *persons*, is surely as creative as to make new objects, products, or institutions. Human mothering is no more 'natural' than any other human activity. It may include many dull and repetitive tasks, as does farming, industrial production, banking, and work in a laboratory. But degree of dullness has nothing to do with degree of 'naturalness.' In sum, human mothering is as different from animal mothering as humans are from animals.

On a variety of grounds there are good reasons to have mothering become activity performed by men as well as by women.[11] We may wish to continue to use the term 'mothering' to designate the activity, in recognition of the fact that it has been overwhelmingly women who have engaged in this activity,[12] and because for the foreseeable future it is the point of view of women, including women engaged in mothering, which should be called on to provide a contrast with the point of view of men. A time may come when a term such as 'the nurturing of children' would be preferable to 'mothering.'[13]

---

11 See especially Nancy Chodorow, *The Reproduction of Mothering: Psychoanalysis and the Sociology of Gender* (Berkeley, CA: University of California Press 1978); and Joyce Trebilcot, ed., *Mothering: Essays in Feminist Theory* (Totowa, NJ: Rowman and Allanheld 1984).

12 See e.g. Susan Peterson, 'Against "Parenting,"' in Trebilcot, *Mothering*.

13 By then 'parenting' might also be acceptable to those who find it presently misleading.

Clearly, the view that contractual relations are a model for human relations generally is especially unsuitable for considering the relations between mothering persons and children. It stretches credulity even further than most philosophers can tolerate to imagine babies as little rational calculators contracting with their mothers for care. Of course the fundamental contracts have always been thought of as hypothetical rather than real. But one cannot imagine hypothetical babies contracting either. And mothering persons, in their care of children, demonstrate hardly any of the 'trucking' or trading instinct claimed by Adam Smith to be the *most* characteristic aspect of human nature.[14] If the epitome of what it is to be human is thought to be a disposition to be a rational contractor, human persons creating other human persons through the processes of human mothering are overlooked. And human children developing human personhood are not recognized as engaged in a most obviously human activity.

David Hume, whom some admire for having moral views more compatible with 'women's moral sense' than most philosophers have had,[15] had the following to say about the passion of avarice: 'Avarice, or the desire of gain, is a universal passion which operates at all times, in all places, and upon all persons.'[16] Surely we can note that in the relation between mothering person and child, not only as it should be but often enough as it is, avarice is hard to find. One can uncover very many emotions in the relation, but the avarice that fuels the model of 'economic man' with his rational interest is not prominent among them.

There is an exchange in Charlotte Perkins Gilman's *Herland* that illustrates the contrast between the motives ascribed to rational

---

14 Adam Smith, Book I, Chap. II

15 See, e.g., Annette Baier, 'Hume: The Women's Moral Theorist?' in *Women and Moral Theory*, Eva Kittay and Diana Meyers, eds. (Totowa, NJ: Rowman and Littlefield 1986).

16 David Hume, *Essays Moral, Political, and Literary*, vol. 1, Green and T.H. Grose, eds. (London: Longmans 1898), 176

economic man building contractual society, and those central to the practice of mothering. Herland is an imaginary society composed entirely of women. They reproduce by parthenogenesis, and there are only mothers and daughters in the society. Everything is arranged to benefit the next generation and the society has existed peacefully for hundreds of years, with a high level of technological advancement but without any conception of a 'survival of the fittest' ethic. Three young men from twentieth century America manage to get to Herland. They acknowledge that in Herland there are no wars, no kings, no priests, no aristocracies, that the women are all like sisters to each other and work together not by competition but by united action. But they argue that things are much better at home. In one exchange they try to explain how important it is to have competition. One of them expounds on the advantages of competition, on how it develops fine qualities, saying that 'without it there would be "no stimulus to industry."'[17] He says competition is necessary to provide an incentive to work; 'competition,' he explains, 'is the motor power' of society.

The women of Herland are genuinely curious and good-naturedly skeptical, as they so often are in Gilman's novel. 'Do you mean,' they ask, 'that no mother would work for her children without the stimulus of competition?' In Herland, the entire, industrious society works on the strong motivation of making the society better for the children. As one women explains, 'The children in this country are the one center and focus of all our thoughts. Every step of our advance is always considered in its effects on them ... You see, we are *Mothers*.'[18]

Of course, this is an idealized picture of mothering. But I am contrasting it with an idealized picture of rationally contracting. Quite probably we would not want a society devoted entirely to mothering. But then we might not want a society devoted entirely to bet-

---

17 Charlotte Perkins Gilman, *Herland* (New York: Pantheon 1979), 60; orginally publ. 1915

18 Ibid., 66

ter bargains either. In developing these suggestions, it is instructive to see what is most seriously overlooked by a contractual view of society, and to see how important what is overlooked is.

II Family and Society

In recent years, many feminists have demanded that the principles of justice and freedom and equality on which it is claimed that democracy rests be extended to women and the family. They have demanded that women be treated as equals in the polity, in the workplace, and, finally, at home. They have demanded, in short, to be accorded full rights to enter freely the contractual relations of modern society. They have asked that these be extended to take in the family.

But some feminists are now considering whether the arguments should perhaps, instead, run the other way. Instead of importing into the household principles derived from the marketplace, perhaps we should export to the wider society the relations suitable for mothering persons and children. This approach suggests that just as relations between persons within the family should be based on concern and caring, rather than on egoistic or non-tuistic contracts, so various relations in the wider society should be characterized by more care and concern and openness and trust and human feeling than are the contractual bargains that have developed so far in political and economic life, or even than are aspired to in contractarian prescriptions. Then, the household instead of the marketplace might provide a model for society. Of course what we would mean by the household would not be the patriarchal household which was, before the rise of contractual thinking, also thought of as a model of society. We would now mean the relations between mothering persons and children *without* the patriarch. We would take our conception of the *post*-patriarchal family as a model.

The model of the social contract was certainly an improvement over that of political patriarchy. Locke's prescriptions for political order are so clearly better than Filmer's that almost no one still reads the arguments made by philosophers such as Filmer, whose views were completely dominant until replaced by those of contractualists like Locke. Filmer thought that political authority should be based on correct inheritance: God gave the world to Adam, and authority to govern was transferred from Adam through the ancient patriarchs to the legitimate monarchs of any historical period. Democracy, to Filmer, was dangerous nonsense. Of course no feminist would wish to go back to such views as Filmer's, nor to those of Aristotle if interpreted as holding that the polity should be a version on a grander scale of the patriarchal household. But to consider whether we should generalize the relation between mothering person and child to any regions beyond the home is to consider generalizing a quite different relation from that which has existed within the patriarchal household, even between mothers and children within patriarchal society. It is to explore what relations between mothering persons and children should be in non-patriarchal societies, and to consider how a transformed household might contribute to a transformed society.

These questions lead us to focus on the family as a social institution of the utmost importance. The family is a set of relations creating human persons. Societies are composed of families. And a family is a small society. The family is undergoing profound change at the present time, and the attendant upheavals in the personal lives of many persons hold out the promise of remarkable social change, quite possibly for the better.

The family is only beginning to receive the central attention from feminists that it deserves, partly because feminist theory is still in such exploratory stages, trying to understand all at once the multiplicity of forces — social, economic, political, legal, psychological, sexual, biological, and cultural — that affect women. Multiple causes shape the sex/gender structures within which human females and males develop feminine and masculine characteristics and come to occupy the roles that existing societies designate as female and male. We need to understand empirically how this happens. We also need normative theories of the family. Jane Flax, surveying recent feminist writing on the family, writes that to develop alternatives to the oppressive relations that now prevail, we need to think through

> what kinds of child care are best for parents and children; what family structures are best for persons at various stages of the life cycle...; how the state

123

and political processes should affect families; and how work and the organization of production should be transformed to support whatever family forms are preferred.[19]

It is an enormous task, but recent years have provided more new thought on these subjects than many previous decades.[20]

The major question remains: what are the possibilities of remaking society by remaking what have been thought of as 'personal' relations? Societies are composed of persons in relation to one another. The 'personal' relations among persons are the most affective and influential in many ways. But the extent to which they are central to wider social relations, or could possibly provide a model for social and political relations of a kind that has been thought of as 'public,' remains an open question.

Western liberal democratic thought has been built on the concept of the 'individual' seen as a theoretically isolatable entity. This entity can assert interests, have rights, and enter into contractual relations with other entities. But this individual is not seen as related to other individuals in inextricable or intrinsic ways. This individual is assumed to be motivated primarily by a desire to pursue his own interests, though he can recognize the need to agree to contractual restraints on the ways everyone may pursue their interests. To the extent that groups have been dealt with at all, they have been treated *as* individuals.

The difficulties of developing trust and cooperation and society itself on the sands of self-interested individuals pursuing their own gain are extreme.[21] Contractual society is society perpetually in

---

19 Jane Flax, 'The Family in Contemporary Feminist Thought: A Critical Review,' in *The Family in Political Thought*, Jean Bethke Elshtain, ed. (Amherst: The University of Massachusetts Press 1982), 252

20 The collection of readings in Barrie Thorne, ed., *Rethinking The Family* (New York: Longmans 1982) is a useful source. Joyce Trebilcot's *Mothering* is another helpful collection. And among the best sources of suggestions are feminist utopian novels, e.g. Marge Piercy's *Woman on the Edge of Time* (New York: Fawcett 1976).

21 See especially Virginia Held, *Rights and Goods*, chapter 5.

danger of breaking down. Perhaps what are needed for even adequate levels of social cohesion are persons tied together by relations of concern and caring and empathy and trust rather than merely by contracts it may be in their interests to disregard. Any enforcement mechanisms put in place to keep persons to their contracts will be as subject to disintegration as the contracts themselves; at some point contracts must be embedded in social relations that are non-contractual.

The relation between mothering person and child, hardly understandable in contractual terms, may be a more fundamental human relation, and a more promising one on which to build our recommendations for the future, than is any relation between rational contractors. Perhaps we should look to the relation between mothering person and child for suggestions of how better to describe such society as we now have. And perhaps we should look to it especially for a view of a future more fit for our chldren than a global battleground for rational, egoistic entities trying, somehow, to restrain their antagonisms by fragile contracts.

The Marxian view of the relations between human beings is in various ways more satisfactory than the contractual one and more capable of accounting for social relations in general. However, the Marxian view of our history split into classes and driven by economic forces, is hardly more capable of encompassing, and does not lend itself to reflecting, the experience of the relation between mothering person and child either. So I will continue to develop here the contrast between the relation between mothering person and child on the one hand, and the contractual exchanges of 'economic man' on the other.

III The Mother/Child Relation

Let us examine in more detail the relation between mothering person and child. A first aspect of the relation that we can note is the extent to which it is not voluntary and, for this reason among others, not contractual. The ties that bind mothering person and child are affectional and solicitous on the one hand, and emotional and dependent on the other. The degree to which bearing and caring for children has been voluntary for most mothers throughout most of history has been extremely limited; it is still quite limited for most mothering persons. The relation *should* be voluntary for the mothering person but it cannot possibly be voluntary for the young child, and it can only become, gradually, slightly more voluntary.

A woman can have decided voluntarily to have a child, but once that decision has been made, she will never again be unaffected by the fact that she has brought this particular child into existence. And even if the decision to have a child is voluntary, the decision to have this particular child, for either parent, cannot be. Technological developments can continue to reduce the uncertainties of childbirth, but unpredictable aspects are likely to remain great for most parents. Unlike that contract where buyer and seller can know what is being exchanged, and which is void if the participants cannot know what they are agreeing to, a parent cannot know what a particular child will be like. And children are totally unable to choose their parents and, for many years, any of their caretakers.

The recognition of how limited are the aspects of voluntariness in the relation between mothering person and child may help us to gain a closer approximation to reality in our understanding of most human relations, especially at a global level, than we can gain from imagining the purely voluntary trades entered into by rational economic contractors to be characteristic of human relations in other domains.

Society may impose certain reciprocal obligations: on parents to care for children when the children are young, and on children to care for parents when the parents are old. But if there is any element of a bargain in the relation between mothering person and child, it is very different from the bargain supposedly characteristic of the marketplace. If a parent thinks 'I'll take care of you now so you'll take care of me when I'm old,' it must be based, unlike the contracts of political and economic bargains, on enormous trust and on a virtual absence of enforcement.[22] And few mothering persons

---

22 In some societies, social pressures to conform with the norms of reciprocal care − of children by parents and later of parents by children − can be very great. But these societies are usually of a kind which are thought to be at a stage of development antecedent to that of contractual society.

have any such exchange in mind when they engage in the activities of mothering. At least the bargain would only be resorted to when the callousness or poverty of the society made the plight of the old person desperate. This is demonstrated in survey after survey; old persons certainly hope not to have to be a burden on their children.[23] And they prefer social arrangements that will allow them to refuse to cash in on any such bargain. So the intention and goal of mothering is to give of one's care without obtaining a return of a self-interested kind. The emotional satisfaction of a mothering person is a satisfaction in the well-being and happiness of another human being, and a satisfaction in the health of the relation between the two persons, not the gain that results from an egoistic bargain. The motive behind the activity of mothering is thus entirely different from that behind a market transaction. And so is, perhaps even more clearly, the motive behind the child's project of growth and development.

A second aspect of the contrast between market relations and relations between mothering person and child is found in the qualities of permanence and non-replaceability. The market makes of everything, even human labor and artistic expression and sexual desire, a commodity to be bought and sold, with one unit of economic value replaceable by any other of equivalent value. To the extent that political life reflects these aspects of the market, politicians are replaceable and political influence is bought and sold. Though rights may be thought of as outside the economic market, in contractual thinking they are seen as inside the wider market of the social contract, and can be traded against each other. But the ties between parents and children are permanent ties, however strained or slack they become at times. And no person within a family should be a commodity to any other. Although various persons may participate in mothering a given child, and a given person

---

23 The gerontologist Elaine Brody says about old people that 'what we hear over and over again — and I'm talking gross numbers of 80 to 90 percent in survey after survey — is "I don't want to be a burden on my children."' Interview by Lindsy Van Gelder, *Ms.* Magazine (January 1986), 48.

may mother many children, still no child and no mothering person is to the other a merely replaceable commodity. The extent to which more of our attitudes, for instance toward our society's cultural productions, should be thought of in these terms rather than in the terms of the marketplace, should be considered.

A third aspect of the relation between mothering person and child that may be of interest is the insight it provides for our notions of equality. It shows us unmistakably that equality is not equivalent to having equal legal rights. All feminists are committed to equality and to equal rights in contexts where rights are what are appropriately at issue. But in many contexts, concerns other than rights are more salient and appropriate. And the equality that is at issue in the relation between mothering person and child is the equal consideration of persons, not a legal or contractual notion of equal rights.

Parents and children should not have equal rights in the sense that what they are entitled to decide or to do or to have should be the same. A family of several small children, an adult or two, and an aged parent should not, for instance, make its decisions by majority vote in most cases.[24] But every member of a family is worthy of equal respect and consideration. Each person in a family is as important as a person as every other.

Sometimes the interests of children have been thought in some sense to count for more, justifying 'sacrificing for the children.' Certainly, the interests of mothers have often counted for less than those of either fathers or children. Increasingly, we may come to think that the interests of all should count equally, but we should recognize that this claim is appropriately invoked only if the issue should be thought of as one of interest. Often, it should not. Much of the time we can see that calculations of interest, and of equal interests, are as out of place as are determinations of equal rights. Both the rights and the interests of individuals seen as separate entities, and equality between them all, should not exhaust our moral concerns. The flourishing of shared joy, of mutual affection, of bonds of

---

24 For a different view see Howard Cohen, *Equal Rights for Children* (Totowa, NJ: Littlefield, Adams 1980)

trust and hope between mothering persons and children can illus-trate this as clearly as anything can. Harmony, love, and coopera-tion cannot be broken down into individual benefits or burdens. They are goals we ought to share and relations *between* persons. And although the degree of their intensity may be different, many and various relations *between* persons are important also at the level of communities or societies. We can consider, of a society, whether the relations between its members are trusting and mutually sup-portive, or suspicious and hostile. To focus only on contractual re-lations and the gains and losses of individuals obscures these often more important relational aspects of societies.

A fourth important feature of the relation between mothering per-son and child is that we obviously do not fulfil our obligations by merely leaving people alone. If one leaves an infant alone he will starve. If one leaves a two-year old alone she will rapidly harm her-self. The whole tradition that sees respecting others as constituted by non-interference with them is most effectively shown up as in-adequate. It assumes that people can fend for themselves and pro-vide through their own initiatives and efforts what they need. This Robinson Crusoe image of 'economic man' is false for almost every-one, but it is totally and obviously false in the case of infants and children, and recognizing this can be salutary. It can lead us to see very vividly how unsatisfactory are those prevalent political views according to which we fulfil our obligations merely by refraining from interference. We ought to acknowledge that our fellow citizens, and fellow inhabitants of the globe, have moral rights to what they need to live — to the food, shelter, and medical care that are the necessary conditions of living and growing — and that when the resources exist for honoring such rights there are few excuses for not doing so. Such rights are not rights to be left to starve unimped-ed. Seeing how unsatisfactory rights merely to be left alone are as an interpretation of the rights of children may help us to recognize a similar truth about other persons. And the arguments — though appropriately in a different form — can be repeated for interests as distinct from rights.[25]

---

25 See Virginia Held, *Rights and Goods.*

A fifth interesting feature of the relation between mothering person and child is the very different view it provides of privacy. We come to see that to be in a position where others are *not* making demands on us is a rare luxury, not a normal state. To be a mothering person is to be subjected to the continual demands and needs of others. And to be a child is to be subjected to the continual demands and expectations of others. Both mothering persons and children need to extricate themselves from the thick and heavy social fabric in which they are entwined in order to enjoy any pockets of privacy at all.

Here the picture we form of our individuality and the concept we form of a 'self' is entirely different from the one we get if we start with the self-sufficient individual of the 'state of nature.' If we begin with the picture of rational contractor entering into agreements with others, the 'natural' condition is seen as one of individuality and privacy, and the problem is the building of society and government. From the point of view of the relation between mothering person and child, on the other hand, the problem is the reverse. The starting condition is an enveloping tie, and the problem is individuating oneself. The task is to carve out a gradually increasing measure of privacy in ways appropriate to a constantly shifting interdependency. For the child, the problem is to become gradually more independent. For the mothering person, the problem is to free oneself from an all-consuming involvement. For both, the progression is from society to greater individuality rather than from self-sufficient individuality to contractual ties.

Psychology and psychoanalysis have long been interested in the process by whch children develop and individuate themselves. Especially relevant now are feminist explorations of the different development of a sense of self in boys and in girls, and of a possibly different moral sense. Philosophers are just beginning to consider the normative issues involved. And social philosophers are just beginning to consider what we should think about social relations if we take women as our starting point. That we need not start with the patriarchal family in forming our concepts of society has been recognized for several centuries, ever since Locke won out over Filmer. That it might be instructive to begin with the point of view of women, and within that with the relation between mothering person and child, to try to reconceptualize society and our goals for better societies, is a new idea. A new concept of the 'self' may be at the heart of such reconceptualizations. And we should expect that a new concept of 'self' or 'person' should have as much significance for our views of politics and society, and for our conceptualizations of the supposedly 'impersonal' and 'public' domain distinct from the supposedly 'personal' and 'private' sphere of the family, as has the concept of the self as rational calculator and the conceptualization of society as contractual. The same real 'persons' can act in and inhabit both marketplace and household contexts. It is open to them to decide what sorts of institutions to encourage for the sake of what sorts of persons.

A sixth aspect of the relation between mothering person and child which is noteworthy is the very different view of power it provides. We are accustomed to thinking of power as something that can be wielded by one person over another, as a means by which one person can bend another to his will. An ideal has been to equalize power so that agreements can be forged and conflicts defused. But consider now the very different view of power in the relation between mothering person and child. The superior power of the mothering person over the child is relatively useless for most of what the mothering person aims to achieve in bringing up the child. The mothering person seeks to *empower* the child to act responsibly, she neither wants to 'wield' power nor to defend herself against the power 'wielded' by the child. The relative powerlessness of the child is largely irrelevant to most of the project of growing up. When the child is physically weakest, as in infancy and illness, the child can 'command' the greatest amount of attention and care from the mothering person because of the seriousness of the child's needs.

The mothering person's stance is characteristically one of caring, of being vulnerable to the needs and pains of the child, and of fearing the loss of the child before the child is ready for independence. It is not characteristically a stance of domination. The child's project is one of developing, of gaining ever greater control over his or her own life, of relying on the mothering person rather than of submitting to superior strength. Of course the relation may in a degenerate form be one of domination and submission, but this only indicates that the relation is not what it should be. In a form in which the relation between mothering person and child is even adequately exemplified, the conceptions of power with which we are familiar, from Hobbes and Locke to Hegel and Marx, are of little use for understanding the aspects of power involved in the relation.[26] The power of a mothering person to empower others, to foster transformative growth, is a different sort of power than that of a stronger sword or dominant will. And the power of a child to call forth tenderness and care is perhaps more different still.

IV Mothering and Moral Theory

A final aspect of the relation between mothering person and child about which I would like to speculate is what a focus on this relation might imply for our views of morality itself, and of ethical theory itself.

Hobbes thought we could build society on the equal vulnerability of every man to the sword of his fellows. Women have never fit into that picture. We are more vulnerable to the sword. And yet the sword is powerless to create new wielders of it. Only the power of mothers can in the long run triumph. But the power of mothers is continually being eclipsed by the power of children.

The vulnerability of men may bring them to seek peace and to covenant against violence. We can hope for whatever progress can be made in curbing the murderous conflicts, tempered by truces and treaties, to which this has led, though our expectations under current conditions must realistically be very modest.

But let us speculate about a different vulnerability and a different development. Mothering persons are vulnerable to the demands and needs of children. We do not know if this is instinctive or innate, or not. Some claim that women lack a mothering instinct. Others claim that the experiences of carrying a child, of laboring and suffer-

---

26 For related discussions, see Nancy Hartsock, *Money, Sex, and Power: Toward a Feminist Historical Materialism* (New York: Longmans 1983); and Sara Ruddick, 'Maternal Thinking,' in Trebilcot, *Mothering*.

ing to give birth, of suckling, inevitably cause mothers to be especially sensitive to the cries and needs of a child. Others claim that fathers, placed in the position of being the only persons capable of responding to the needs of a child, develop similar responsiveness. Whatever the truth, one can admit that no one can become a mothering person without becoming sensitive to the needs of relatively helpless or less powerful others. And to become thus sensitive is to become vulnerable. If the vulnerability is chosen, so much the better. Mothering persons become in this way vulnerable to the claims of morality.

It is not, however, the morality of following abstract, universal rules so much as the morality of being responsive to the needs of actual, particular others in relations with us. The traditional view, reasserted in the psychological studies of Lawrence Kohlberg, that women are less likely than men to be guided by the highest forms of morality, would only be plausible if morality were no more than the abstract and rational rules of pure and perfect principle.[27] For traditional morality, increasingly recognizable as developed from a male point of view, there seems to be either the pure principle of the rational law-giver, or the self-interest of the individual contractor. There is the unreal universality of *all*, or the real *self* of individual interest.

Both views, however, lose sight of acting *for* particular others in actual contexts. Mothering persons cannot lose sight of the particularity of the child being mothered nor of the actuality of the circumstances in which the activity is taking place. Mothering persons may tend to resist harming or sacrificing those particular others for the sake of abstract principles or total faith; on the other hand, it is for the sake of *others*, or for the sake of relationships between persons, rather than to further their own interests, that such resistance

---

27 For examples of the view that women are more deficient than men in understanding morality and acting morally, see e.g. Mary Mahowald, ed., *Philosophy of Woman: Classical to Current Concepts* (Indianapolis: Hackett 1978). See also Lawrence Kohlberg, *The Philosophy of Moral Development* (San Francisco: Harper and Row 1981), and L. Kohlberg and R. Kramer, 'Continuities and Discontinuities in Child and Adult Moral Development,' *Human Development* 12 (1969) 93-120.

is presented by mothering persons. Morality, for mothering persons, must guide us in our relations with actual, particular children, enabling them to develop their own lives and commitments. For mothering persons, morality can never seem adequate if it offers no more than ideal rules for hypothetical situations: morality must connect with the actual context of real, particular others in need. At the same time, morality, for mothering persons, cannot possibly be a mere bargain between rational contractors. That morality in this context could not be based on self-interest or mutual disinterest directly is obvious; that a contractual escape is unavailable or inappropriate is clear enough.

The morality that could offer guidance for those engaged in mothering might be a superior morality to those available at present. It would be a morality based on caring and concern for actual human others, and it would have to recognize the limitations of both egoism and perfect justice.[28] When we would turn to the social and political theories that would be compatible with such a view of morality, we would see that they would have to be very different not only from the patriarchial models of pre-contractual conceptions, but also from the contractual models that so dominate current thinking. Contractual relations would not be ruled out, but they would cease to seem paradigmatic of human relations, and the regions within which they could be thought to be justified would be greatly reduced.

V The Child's Perspective

What about the point of view of the child? A most salient characteristic of the relation between mothering person and child is the child's relative powerlessness. The child cannot possibly rely on the Hobbesian safeguard of the equal vulnerability of the

---

28 For further discussion, see Virginia Held, 'Feminism and Moral Theory,' in *Women and Moral Theory*, Eva Kittay and Diana Meyers, eds. (Totowa, NJ: Rowman & Littlefield 1987)

caretaker. Not even when the caretaker is asleep is she vulnerable to the sword of the small child, and it will be years, if ever, before the child can match the caretaker in even physical strength, let alone social and economic and psychological power. Whatever claims the child makes against a mothering person must be based on something else than superior strength, and the child should come to trust the restraint of one who could but does not wish to cause the child harm.

The child in relation to the mothering person is permanently in the best possible position from which to recognize that right is *not* equivalent to might, that power, including the power to teach and enforce a given morality, is not equivalent to morality itself. Becoming a person is not so much learning a morality that is being taught as it is developing the ability to decide for oneself what morality requires of one. Children characteristically go beyond the mothering persons in their lives, becoming autonomous beings. They do not characteristically then respond to the mothering persons they leave behind with proposals for better bargains for themselves now that they have the power to enforce their terms. The relation between mothering person and child is such that disparities of power are given. Though the positions may reverse themselves, unequal power is almost everpresent. But it is often also irrelevant to the relation.

When young men are invited to enter the public realm of contractual relations they are encouraged to forget their past lack of power and to assume a position of equality or superiority. But we should probably none of us ever forget what it is like to lack power. Taking the relation between child and mothering person as the primary social relation might encourage us to remember the point of view of those who cannot rely on the power of arms to uphold their moral claims. It might remind us of the distinction between the morality that, as developed autonomous persons, we come to construct for ourselves, and the moral injunctions which those with superior force can hold us to. Though I cannot develop these suggestions further in this particular paper, *much* more needs to be felt from the point of view of children.

VI Models for Society

In an earlier paper called 'Marx, Sex, and the Transformation of Society,'[29] I looked at the relation between man and woman, if it could be transformed by love into a relation of mutual concern and respect, as a possible model for transformed relations in the wider society. It now seems to me that the relation between man and woman, especially as transformed in the way I suggested, is more special and more limited, as well as far more distant and uncertain, than the relation between mothering person and child. The latter relation seems especially worth exploring to see what implications and insights it might suggest for a transformed society.

There are good reasons to believe that a society resting on no more than bargains between self-interested or mutually disinterested individuals will not be able to withstand the forces of egoism and dissolution pulling such societies apart. Although there may be some limited domains in which rational contracts are the appropriate form of social relations, as a foundation for the fundamental ties which ought to bind human beings together, they are clearly inadequate. Perhaps we can learn from a non-patriarchal household better than from further searching in the marketplace what the sources might be for justifiable trust, cooperation, and caring.

On the first occasion when I spoke about considering the relation between mothering person and child as the primary social relation, a young man in the audience asked: but in society, by which he meant society outside the family, who are the mothers and who are the children? It was meant as a hostile question, but it is actually a very good question. The very difficulty so many persons have in imagining an answer may indicate how distorted are the traditional contractual conceptions. Such persons can imagine human society on the model of 'economic man,' society built on a contract between rationally self-interested persons, because these are the theories they have been brought up with. But they cannot imagine society

---

29 Virginia Held, 'Marx, Sex, and the Transformation of Society,' *The Philosophical Forum* 5, 1-2 (Fall-Winter 1973-74)

resembling a group of persons tied together by on-going relations of caring and trust between persons in positions such as those of mothers and children where, as adults, we would sometimes be one and sometimes the other. Suppose now we ask: in the relation between mothering person and child, who are the contractors? Where is the rational self-interest? The model of 'economic man' makes no sense in this context. Anyone in the social contract tradition who has noticed the relation of mothering person and child at all has supposed it to belong to some domain outside the realm of the 'free market' and outside the 'public' realm of politics and the law. Such theorists have supposed the context of mothering to be of much less significance for human history and of much less relevance for moral theory than the realms of trade and government, or they have imagined mothers and children as somehow outside human society altogether in a region labelled 'nature,' and engaged wholly in 'reproduction.' But mothering is at the heart of human society.

If the dynamic relation between mothering person and child is taken as the primary social relation, then it is the model of 'economic man' that can be seen to be deficient as a model for society and morality, and unsuitable for all but a special context. A domain such as law, if built on no more than contractual foundations, can then be recognized as one limited domain among others; law protects some moral rights when people are too immoral or weak to respect them without the force of law. But it is hardly a majestic edifice that can serve as a model for morality. Neither can the domain of politics, if built on no more than self-interest or mutual disinterest, provide us with a model with which to understand and improve society and morality. And neither, even more clearly, can the market itself.

When we explore the implications of these speculations we may come to realize that instead of seeing the family as an anomalous island in a sea of rational contracts composing economic and political and social life, perhaps it is instead 'economic man' who belongs on a relatively small island surrounded by social ties of a less hostile, cold, and precarious kind.

CANADIAN JOURNAL OF PHILOSOPHY
Supplementary Volume 13

Rawls and Ownership: The Forgotten Category of Reproductive Labor*

SIBYL SCHWARZENBACH
Baruch College, CUNY
New York, NY 10010
U.S.A.

A careful, theoretical clarification of gender roles has only recently begun in social and political philosophy. It is the aim of the following piece to reveal that an analysis of women's traditional position — her distinctive activities, labor and surrounding sense of 'mine' — can not only make valuable contributions towards clarifying traditional property disputes, but may even provide elements for a new conception of ownership. By way of illustration, the article focusses on the influential work of John Rawls and argues that — when Rawls's own analysis and principles of justice are supplemented by an account of what is here called 'reproductive labor' — his theory in fact tends to a form of democratic socialism. Stated somewhat differently, my aim is to shift the terms of the property debate as posed by Rawls from *within* his own position. I hope to show that

* I wish to express my thanks and appreciation to Professor John Rawls for his comments on, as well as criticisms of, an earlier draft of this paper. I am also indebted to Professor John Stopford, as well to audiences at SUNY Stoneybrook, Wellesley, Wesleyan, CUNY Graduate Center and the NYU Law and Philosophy Colloquium, for important criticisms of earlier presented versions.

the real ownership question which now emerges is no longer *whether* 'justice as fairness' countenances a private property or socialist form of democracy, but what precise *form* such a socialism should take.

I

Rawls's *A Theory of Justice* has been criticized for what many perceive as the encouragement of primarily individualistic values to the exclusion of communitarian ones.[1] In his 1975 reply 'Fairness to Goodness' Rawls counters the charge of an inherent bias toward individualism in his description of the original position, as well as in his account of the primary goods. But nowhere does Rawls deal directly with what remains perhaps the major tension between his theory and any avowedly socialist one. That is, unlike the socialist, Rawls is not committed to the view that the end of private ownership in the major means of production is a necessary condition for the realization of his two principles of justice even in the long run (TJ, 274ff). It is this lack of commitment on Rawls's part, however, which appears to underlie much of the criticism that his theory is anti-communitarian. Socialists, after all, have long argued that private ownership of natural resources and the major means of production creates a rift running throughout society. If the chasm between the haves and the have-nots is allowed to continue, insurmountable difficulties emerge for solving what may be called the 'problem of community.' In Aristotle's words, this problem addresses what it is that holds a good and just society together.

It is not the case, of course, that Rawls feels all socialist arrangements are incompatible with his own theory. In *A Theory of Justice* he distinguishes, for instance, between the allocative and distributive

---

1 See, for instance, T. Nagel's review in the *Philosophical Review* 82 (1973); A. Schwartz's 'Moral Neutrality and Primary Goods' *Ethics* (1973); and most recently M. Sandel's *Liberalism and the Limits of Justice* (Cambridge: Cambridge University Press 1982). All future references to Rawls's *A Theory of Justice* (Cambridge, MA: Harvard University Press 1971) will be indicated by (TJ,) followed by the page number unless otherwise indicated.

function of market prices.[2] The former function is connected with the use of competitive markets and prices to achieve economic efficiency, while the latter relates to their employment for the purposes of determining wealth, income or power received by individuals. It is perfectly consistent, Rawls argues, for a democratic socialist regime (where the major means of production and natural resources are publicly owned) to make use of the allocative function of prices, as indicators for an efficient schedule of economic activities, while restricting their distributive role. Democratically reached decisions, for instance, could establish an interest rate to allocate resources among investment projects, and could compute rental charges to various associations for the use of capital and scarce natural assets such as land and forests.

In such an event, there need be no private persons to whom, as owners of these assets, the monetary equivalents of these evaluations accrue (and hence capitalist profit making would not here function as a motivational force in production). Rather, the net rental income imputed to natural and collective assets accrues to the larger enterprise, community or state; that which pertains to particular individuals is determined by decision on other grounds (by the demand price of labor consistent with social expectations, for instance). Prices here have a restricted distributive function and the extent of the market is clearly limited. This distinction between allocative and distributive price functions allows us to conceive restricted 'competition' as a good *between* associations without viewing it as necessarily detrimental to what J.S. Mill called the 'noble idea of co-operation' between individual workers and citizens themselves. The concern of many that the positive effects of competition will inevitably be lost in a communist society might thus be overcome by a form of 'market socialism' of which, as Rawls notes, there are a wide range of intermediate forms.

---

2 (TJ, 273). For a fuller elaboration of this distinction see J.E. Meade's *Efficiency, Equality and the Ownership of Property* (London 1964). See also DiQuattro's 'The Market and Liberal Values,' *Political Theory* **8** (1980) for a similar distinction between what the author calls the 'aggregative' and 'distributive' function of prices upon which the theory of market socialism rests.

But although Rawls notes the compatibility of democratic, market socialist arrangements with his own theory, he does not (as already noted) believe that some form of economic democracy is a necessary condition for the realization of his two principles of justice. The reasons for this important thinker's stance are, I believe, illuminating, but to uncover them will entail a closer look at the conception of ownership underlying his difference principle. Officially speaking, the historic question of private property versus socialist democracy cannot be determined 'in advance' for Rawls. The issue in the last analysis 'depends on the traditions, institutions, and social forces of each country, and its particular historical circumstances' (TJ, 274). I shall argue, however, that Rawls cannot decide because, in addition, an uncertainty remains in regard to his (political) conception of the person which he argues is an essential aspect of his theory of primary goods.[3]

II

In order to understand — and eventually evaluate — the reasons behind Rawls's concern with socialism (at the same time as he falls short of any commitment to it), we must briefly focus one more time on his famous difference principle. This principle claims, we recall, that once the principles of equal liberty and fair equality of oppor-

---

3 I shall not here repeat, but largely presuppose, Rawls's arguments showing the dependency of his particular list of primary goods on his conception of the person (with its two moral powers). See, in particular, his 'Kantian Constructivism in Moral Theory,' *The Journal of Philosophy* 77 (1980), 524ff and 'Social Unity and Primary Goods,' in Sen and Williams, eds., *Utilitarianism and Beyond* (London 1982), 165ff. I am also granting with Rawls (and in the face of, say, Sandel's recent criticism) that Rawls's conception of the person is indeed a 'political' one (drawn from our public, post-reformational, political culture) and makes no specific metaphysical claims in regard to the nature of persons (or of personal identity) beyond this. See Rawls's 'Justice as Fairness; Political Not Metaphysical,' *Journal of Philosophy* 14 (1985). Future references to these texts will be indicated by (KC,), (SU,) and (PNM,) respectively, followed by page number.

tunity are satisfied, any social and economic inequalities must be so arranged as to be 'to the greatest benefit of the least advantaged members of society' (TJ, 75ff). The index of benefit is made in terms of a list of primary social goods: those all-purpose, institutional means (or features of social institutions) necessary for rationally pursuing a conception of the good (SU, 163). And the list includes, apart from 1) basic liberties and 2) free choice of occupation, 3) powers and perogatives of office, 4) wealth and income, and finally and most importantly, 5) the social basis of self-respect. What is of special interest in this list for our purposes is the grouping together of the good of income and wealth, on the one hand, and that of the social basis of self-respect on the other. For Rawls there is no simple, one-to-one relation between these two goods and the possibilty of their coming into conflict at times is nearly certain (SU, 162). In what follows I shall argue that essentially two different (and incompatible) interpretations of the difference principle exist depending upon whether one stresses the first or the second of these goods. My contention is that beneath the surface of the difference principle two alternative conceptions of the self and ownership operate.

I here distinguish between a private 'acquisitive' conception of the self and what I shall call a moral 'purposeful' one. (In so doing I am not claiming that on any comprehensive view of the self both aspects will not be entailed; the issue, as we shall see, regards their relative weighting.) The first, or acquisitive self, is essentially based on a naturalistic model of material, even biological, gain (and is found to a great extent in, say, Locke's theory). Not only is the urge for material appropriation here viewed as fundamental in motivating productive acts of the individual, but the self's very growth and fulfillment is perceived on the model of private acquisition. In the extreme case, even the 'higher pursuits' such as freedom, the life of the mind, science, art, etc. are viewed as exclusive possessions of the individual. Social institutions and relations, in turn, become but means to his own private (competing or at least independently given) ends.

Central to what I am calling the moral 'purposeful' self, on the other hand (more fully elaborated in the German Idealist tradition), is the notion of an embodiment of a self-conception or plan of life in a recognizably public realm. The individual's nature is here viewed as a function of the aspirations and goals it adopts and seeks to actualize; its freedom and satisfaction lie in bringing its distinctively human capacities to fruition and its goals into harmony with those of others. Such a conception of the self stresses not private consumption, but shared final ends and our responsibilities – our abilities to respond – to others. Unlike on the acquisitive model, this self is dependent not merely on co-ordinated, minimally cooperative activity of others, but on the good of reciprocity and the necessity of positive social ties (what Rawls calls 'social union') both in the bolstering of its self-respect, as well as in the development and exercise of its highest capacities.

Accompanying these two conceptions of the self, one may distinguish two respective forms of ownership. In the first, the exclusive and acquisitive moment dominates; all property is fundamentally viewed as my private property. On the second, or purposeful model, what I shall call the *ascriptive* or responsible aspect of ownership is stressed. Property here comes closer to being viewed as a form of guardianship (and it is often shared and non-private). My claim is that Rawls's difference principle is not only a curious blend of these two aspects, but that this fact even accounts for the often contradictory evaluations of his work.

Many advocates of socialism, for instance, consider Rawls's principle to be unduly concerned with private material benefit (and hence with an acquisitive conception of the self) to the exclusion of such values as community, self-realization, meaningful work, etc.[4] On a view such as Esheté's, the difference principle remains 'ideological' – it assuages the consciences of the capitalist rich insofar as it claims that their greater share of the wealth (including hierarchical control and private ownership of the means of production) is justified to the extent that the poor are 'better off' in primarily monetary terms (although in fact they may be 'worse off' given any other measure). Such a reading of the difference principle which stresses the

---

4 See, for instance, A. Esheté's 'Contractarianism and the Scope of Justice,' *Ethics* **85** (1978). Also, to some extent, Sandel (1982).

acquisitive self (and its minimal duties) I shall call the 'weak interpretation.'

On the other hand, the difference principle is perceived by many as drawing attention to the responsible aspects of ownership to a degree rarely seen in the liberal tradition. For Rawls unequal ownership is, after all, *conditional* on benefiting the group as a whole, and not only in so far as my having more helps 'preserve' others in material existence (as in Locke, say), but to the extent that my greater share actually raises the social basis of their self-respect in the long term (SU, 164ff). This 'strong' reading of the difference principle tends to push Rawls towards the socialist camp; it emphasizes our duties towards others as well as the role of social union (shared final ends and activities performed for their own sake) in the general development of human capacities. Of course, this emphasis on responsibility – what I have called the ascriptive aspect of ownership – many find oppressive in Rawls's thought; it is perceived as a threat to our legitimate individual freedom.[5]

Hence the Rawlsian dilemma: the left proclaim him a capitalist ideologue, while the right even suspect him of communism. My claim is that both interpretations find validation in the texts. The acquisitive self is incorporated into the difference principle to the extent that the proper distribution of shares is viewed importantly as an *incentive* system (TJ, 126). We find, for instance, to the shock and dismay of many (see Sandel [1982], 135ff), that in a just distribution individuals are rewarded by income and the good things in life not according to their 'moral worth' (which is, for Rawls, an impractical notion and would be rejected in the original position), but in order to direct abilities to where they are needed most: to encourage learning, cover costs of training, etc.(TJ, 315). From the standpoint of distributive justice the individual receives only his 'due' or entitlement; his legitimate expectations – those thrown up and encouraged by the existing social arrangements – must be satisfied. Thus, on the one hand, Rawls views the just distribution of shares

---

5 I here have Nozick's libertarian critique of Rawls in mind. See Nozick's *Anarchy, State and Utopia* (New York 1974), Ch.4.

as a scheme of private incentives, taxes and burdens guiding men's actions hither and thither to the mutual advantage of all. And noteably, among the constituents of exchangeable 'wealth' Rawls includes scarce natural resources, means of production, as well as the rights to control them.[6] On the other hand, Rawls is well aware that an individual's 'due' or entitlement is not something given once and for all, but a derivative product of the prior form of social and economic co-operation (a point both Esheté and Sandel seem to have overlooked). To this extent his theory has incorporated the socialist insight that the rightful 'fruit' of labor will be determined and circumscribed by the background conditions (= social rules) of the type of labor to begin with. Rawls recognizes the influence of the basic structure (a common achievement) on human wants and aspirations and the economic system on the 'kind of persons' men will be (TJ, 259). Hence, to the degree these background conditions become the subject of deliberate activity or construction (which they must become if the principles of justice are to be realized), the difference principle presupposes an essentially purposeful conception of the self. This conception, we recall, entails the embodiment of a plan of life and of the individual's distinctive human capacities (including a desire for right and justice) in a public realm, a pre-requisite for which is their affirmative recognition by others. Rather than emphasizing private acquisition (and the primary good of income and wealth), this conception stresses *action ascribed to us* in a social context. Property is no longer viewed primarily as an incentive to labor, but as an instrument or background condition (often non-private) for the exercise of highest-order interests. In fact, one way of characterizing the turn from the 'early' to the 'late' work of Rawls is by noting an increasing concern with what I am calling the purposeful self, together with a change in Rawls's account of the primary goods. The primary social goods are no longer viewed as those things persons can be empirically said 'to want whatever else they want,' but are now de-

---

6 See his 'Fairness to Goodness,' *Philosophical Review* **84** (1975), 540.

fined as the 'necessary conditions for realizing the powers of moral personality' (SU,164, for instance).[7]

Any reading of the difference principle which focusses on the purposeful self will stress the primary good of public office giving 'scope to various self-governing and social capacities of the self' (SU, 166), as well as the 'social basis of self-respect' which, besides being the most important of the primary goods, presupposes the individual participate in successful social union (TJ, 440ff). We recall that for Rawls the paradigm of social union is a group of musicians; social union entails a) shared final ends and b) activity performed for its own sake. On the model of the purposeful self the development of a talent or the articulation of an opinion is not a zero-sum game; one person's gain need not be another's loss. To the contrary, the development of the capacities of another becomes a *prerequisite* for the development of my own. Individuals here reciprocally seek to protect the conditions for one another's development. Such an idea (one might say) of 'joint guardianship' leads to the 'strong' reading of the difference principle: only those inequalities benefiting the least advantaged are justified, interpreting 'benefit' now, not solely in terms of income and wealth, but in terms of those conditions which further social union, self-governing powers, and the cultivation of distinctively human capacities in all.

The crucial point is that depending on the extent to which one invokes the acquisitive or purposeful model, both the nature and the degree of social inequality the difference principle allows will *vary*. The acquisitive model, for instance, supports a far greater *qualitative* (practical or functional) inequality because only the most rudimentary needs of the least advantaged need be provided for;

---

7 What I am here calling the 'turn' to the later Rawls begins (roughly) with his 'Kantian Constructivism in Moral Theory' (1980) and is visible most recently in 'Justice as Fairness: Political not Metaphysical' (1985). In these later works, Rawls explicitly acknowledges a change in his theory of primary goods; originally a predominantly psychological or sociological thesis about what in fact motivates people (about actual empirical incentives), his 'revised' account stresses and clearly depends upon a particular moral conception of persons (see KC, 527, for instance, or PNM, 224).

the difference principle is satisfied when the worst off gain the greatest feasible measure of income and wealth. On the purposeful model, however, the imperative to such equality is far more urgent. Since 'benefit' is interpreted primarily in terms of public office and the social basis of self-respect, the worst off must participate in the major social institutions for the development of their capacities. The strong interpretation demands at the very least, for instance, that a growing portion of tax revenues be devoted to job training and self-management of the disadvantaged in contrast to simple welfare payments.

Similarly, on the acquisitive model income differentials serve as the major incentives for individuals to achieve certain skills and accept responsibilities (TJ, 151). The model can thus justify significant degrees of *quantitative* income inequality in the name of motivating economic progress. On the purposeful model, however, the added incentive of higher income diminishes in importance relative to the satisfaction of the Aristotelian Principle as a principle of motivation.[8] Economic progress could proceed with a far lower degree of income inequality. The strong reading of the difference principle is, in short, a far more demanding moral theory.

We have thus seen that beneath the surface of the difference principle two different notions of self and ownership operate. Nor are these two conceptions compatible; they offer widely different interpretations of permissible inequalities. This is not to conclude, however, that Rawls's principle is simply confused or necessarily ambiguous. Rather, in the tension between the two conceptions one perceives the movement or direction of his thought itself. That is, of the two conceptions the latter or purposeful self is clearly superior from Rawls's own perspective. This is obvious not only from his

---

8 What Rawls calls the Aristotelian Principle claims that, other things being equal, human beings enjoy the exercise of their distinctive capacities, and this enjoyment increases the more the capacity is realized, or the greater its complexity (TJ, 426). Stated somewhat differently, the claim is that human beings can be motivated by the exercise of their innate or trained abilities purely 'for their own sake.'

critique of the utilitarian 'consumer person,' while emphasizing his own view as 'Kantian,' but also from his repeated proclamations that, as conditions of civilization improve, the marginal significance of further economic advantages diminish relative to our interests in autonomy and purposeful action. Men at one point 'come to aspire to some control over the laws and rules that regulate their association' (TJ, 543). The thrust of Rawls's difference principle is to encourage the political transformation of a society of private appropriating individuals into moral purposeful ones, not through fear and punishment, but through a carefully constructed system of positive incentives.

If this is the case, however, we return to our original question of why, if not the immediate, then at least the long-term tendency of the difference principle is not towards extending social union into the economic sphere, that is, towards extending shared final ends and participatory control over the laws regulating the workplace and economy. Again, why is Rawls not *committed* to some version of economic democracy as a condition for the long-term realization of his difference principle?

From what has been said so far, there appears to be only one answer. Part Three of *A Theory of Justice* is an attempt by Rawls to demonstrate that the principles chosen in the original position are compatible with our human nature (TJ, 580). Nothing can be demanded as a matter of justice if it is in general beyond our capacities as human beings. That social union and self-government in the economic sphere are not a *requirement* of justice, must mean that Rawls remains uncertain as to whether they could be achieved without in turn too great a sacrifice − for instance, of efficiency in production.[9] That is, although the moral, purposeful self is clearly viewed as superior, Rawls remains sceptical that a majority of members in a modern industrial society − particularly in questions of labor motivation − could ever accurately be so described. In the *realm of labor*, at least, the acquisitive self appears to remain primary in

---

9 Rawls at one point voices a further (although secondary) concern: that socialist ownership may lead to a form of 'command society' (TJ, 272). See note #24 below.

Rawls's theory. We recall that Rawls claims the ownership question depends in the final analysis on the 'traditions, institutions, and social forces of each country.' And he has, at least as regards our own society, good reason to be sceptical; the nineteenth-century predictions of a Marx or Mill in regard to a free and uncoerced social union in the economic sphere have hardly come to pass, whether in capitalist or state socialist societies.

In the second half of this paper I shall argue, however, that Rawls's scepticism remains reasonable only to the degree that there exists at present (at least) one major 'tradition, institution and social force' that his theory has not taken into sufficient account. This 'social force' is the large-scale movement over the last one hundred years of women into the labor market. My claim is that an analysis of woman's traditional and distinctive labor as, among other things, *care-taker* presents us with yet a third conception of labor and ownership. And, when the implications of this third model are taken into account, the strong reading of Rawls's difference principle, which requires social union in the economic sphere, emerges as fully compatible with our nature. Hence, it can now be demanded as a matter of justice.

III

My aim in the second half of this essay is to show that because Rawls's theory remains tied to a particular view of acquisitive labor, it cannot comfortably dispense with the private conception of ownership in the economic sphere. By the 'private conception' I refer to a paradigm dominant since Locke who argued that man has a right to that with which he originally 'mixed his labor.' The metaphor grounds what one Oxford juridical philosopher has called the 'making and taking' model of ownership.[10] On this model property –

---

10 See A.M. Honoré's 'Ownership' in A.G. Guest, ed., *Oxford Essays in Jurisprudence* Vol. I (Oxford 1961) 107-47. Honoré insists this model is still the most 'morally satisfactory' as a model of original acquisition when taken together with 'consent and debt' as derivative forms. Moreover, he claims that the right

what Honoré calls the 'full, liberal' conception of ownership – includes beyond the various rights of use, management and enjoyment, the right to exclude others, as well as the right to capital, the power to alienate, consume, and even destroy the thing. The claim here is that this conception of private ownership is linked to a very specific model of labor – what I shall now call a 'craft' or 'work' model (and of commodity production at that).

By the term 'craft labor' I refer to the case whereby an individual subject confronts and labors upon a physical object. The model encompasses artisan work (Aristotle's example of sculpting a statue), individual farm labor (Locke's mixing one's labor with the soil), as well as even industrial labor (in a factory, say). These labor types all share the form of being an appropriation – a 'making one's own' – of the material, physical world. Moreover, in the modern period where commodity production is perceived as the norm, such individual labor (in contrast to that of the ancient slave or serf) ushers in a legitimate private right to the object produced (or at least to a presumed equivalent of labor expended). In Locke, for instance, this right is justified by the natural law proclamation that the individual's private need be satisfied. The individual is justified in accumulating more than he needs if a) his greater share somehow improves the lot of others, or b) in a variation such as Nozick's theory, if the greater accumulation is the result of a series of legitimate contracts. Critical to the 'making and taking' model is the assumption that the primary *motive* of labor is exclusive ownership, and it tends to presuppose what we have called an acquisitive conception of the self. In turn, private property rights are viewed as a major *incentive* to labor, an assumption which, we have seen, remains crucial still to Rawls's theory.

---

of exclusive, physical control of a thing is 'the foundation on which the whole superstructure of ownership rests' and notes that 'to exclude others from what one holds is an instinct found in babies and even ... in animals.' To point to such an 'instinct,' however, proves little. As we shall see below, one can with equal certainty point to an instinct in humans to 'include others' in what they hold.

My claim here is that this dominant paradigm of labor as an appropriation of the physical world has blinded us to a form of labor which is at least as fundamental. Socialists have long argued that the Lockean model essentially abstracts from the 'interactive' or 'social' nature of the labor process; all labor, even that performed in isolation, presupposes a prior cultural formation — an exchange of language, abilities and patterns of interaction — as backdrop against which the individual develops his aims and realizes his intentions in the first place.[11] The point I wish to make here, however, goes one step further; there exits an important form of labor (a production of use values) which is not only indirectly, but *directly* social or 'interactive.' This form I shall call 'reproductive labor.' In explicating the category, I will focus in particular on the realm in which women over the centuries have been 'mixing' their labor and effort: the realm of child-care. This is not to say, of course, that men have not always, to varying degrees, performed reproductive labor, nor that women have not also been farmers, artisans, etc. It is only to note the significant fact that, in the known societies both past and present, and but for the rarest exceptions, men *as a group* have not been the primary care-takers of young children.[12] This form of activity has traditionally been women's lot and, we may assume, it

---

11 Hegel was among the first, I believe, to make this point and it was then taken up by Marx and others. In both his *Phenomenology of Mind* and the *Philosophy of Right* Hegel argues that the relation of any subject to a given object already presupposes, or is mediated by, a particular pattern of relations *between* subjects themselves.

12 This fact appears to be a significant discovery of twentieth century anthropology. See, for instance, the collection by R. Reiter, ed., *Toward an Anthropology of Women* (London and New York 1975). Of course there are numerous exceptions, but these appear only to prove the rule. For instance, on one island off the coast of South Korea the women (for various reasons such as body-fat, etc.) are superior pearl divers to the men — pearls being the major source of the island's livelihood. Here the men as a group take care of the children, cook, clean house, etc. But we must note, it is the women who, in this case, essentially 'run' the island; they control all property, major political decisions, and so on.

has had a major influence on the formation of her distinctive personality.

My immediate aim is to develop this alternative conception of labor as child-care (which usually includes care of the husband and often the aged) in order to note its implications for the issue of ownership. I wish from the start, however, to avoid several possible misunderstandings. In elaborating the alternative model (and metaphor) I am well aware that I am performing a selective 'abstraction.'[13] Moreover, the proposed model is 'a-historical' to the degree that it pertains in particular to the division of sexual labor emergent in modern, western society. (As just noted, however, it appears no culture is altogether free from some variation or transformation of this division.) The introduction of the alternative model is to be considered here a mode of representing to ourselves structural features of the social world I believe have theoretically long been neglected. I am by no means proposing the paradigm of child-care as the norm for all human relationships! Rather, in the language of N. Goodman, presenting a new model or metaphor is a means of 'rearranging objects in the home realm'; it is a way of 'casting our nets' in order to capture what may be significant likenesses and differ-

---

13 According to a famous claim of Max Black's every metaphor is 'the tip of a submerged model.' The term 'model,' of course, is here being meant in its more ordinary sense, whereby it essentially denotes an *abstractive representation* of some object or state of affairs. (The term is thus not used in the sense intended by logicians whereby the interpretation or embodiment of a formal calculus in which the relation of isomorphism holds between the structure of the formal system and that of its interpretation.) In its more ordinary sense *anything* can be taken as a model of anything else *IFF* we can sort out the relevant respects in which one entity is like another (e.g. a grouping of ping-pong balls can model the universe). For something to be a model in this more ordinary sense it appears to suffice a) that the model as representation must be some form of abstraction; it must be less rich in the range of relevant properties than its object or reference, and b) it cannot thus be a model of itself or of something identical to it. One way of classifying models might be according to their degree of *existential commitment* – those operating at the limits of our rational belief (such as many metaphors) commanding at the same time the greatest degree of belief. See M. Wartofsky's 'The Model Muddle' in *Models* (Boston, MA: D. Reidel 1979).

ences in the world.[14] In the present instance, I aim to capture something important about human motivation in general.

To begin with, whereas the model of craft (farm or technological) labor involves a working subject confronting a given material object, the model of what I am calling (loosely 'female') reproductive labor is one in which a subject essentially confronts another subject: the child. In Aristotelian language, the 'material' as well as 'formal' cause is, in the one case, raw matter to be imposed by a form, in the other matter already informed by a human soul. Regardless of how young the child, the woman as caretaker is in the presence of another human being with elaborate needs, desires and developing rational capacities to which she is expected to respond. Her labor is essentially other-directed or 'interactive'; it pertains from the start to direct *need*-interpretation.

This fundamental difference between the two models indicates in turn a distinction in the 'final cause' of the respective activities. Whereas the immediate aim or purpose of the art, say, of shoe-making (as Socrates argued) is to produce good shoes (whether or not this is done for money), it is clear that the aim of child-care is to encourage the healthy development of the child. The ultimate 'for the sake of which' the activity is performed is to produce a mature, functioning adult. Thus, where craft labor may be said to aim *in*directly at the satisfaction of human needs ('good' shoes after all are those which produce 'happy feet'), female labor aims *directly* at it. Its end is not in the first instance a transformation of the external, physical world but rather (in the words of Habermas) its end is interactive or 'communicative'; it 'aims at the transformation of social relations' undistorted by dependency or force.[15]

---

14 See N. Goodman, *Languages of Art* (Indianapolis: Hackett Publishing 1976), 68ff, and *Ways of World-making* (Indianapolis: Hackett Publishing 1978), 129.

15 See Habermas's 'Labor and Interaction' in *Theory and Praxis* (Boston: Beacon Press 1973), as well as his *Knowledge and Human Interest* (Boston: Beacon Press 1971), ch.3. Habermas distinguishes between a) technical labor or instrumental action, and b) praxis, interactive or communicative action — a distinction which remains fundamental throughout his later works. We must note,

Another possible misunderstanding must be avoided. In pointing to the 'other-directed' nature of traditional female labor, the claim is not that women are inherently any less greedy, self-seeking, etc. than men. My point is structural, not psychological. Unless the mother (biological or otherwise) in fact looks after the child and responds to its needs (whatever her individual psychological motives), the latter will not flourish. Moreover, it is clear that the mother receives some personal 'reward' for her efforts; her work is not pure self-sacrifice. But, in noting the moment of self-interest involved in child-rearing, we must be careful not to assimilate reproductive labor to the modern category of 'human services' from which it differs in one important respect. The labor of the doctor, lawyer, etc. (to the degree their services are sold on the market) is generally felt to require some tangible reimbursement for efforts expended (usually a wage). In the case of child-rearing, on the other hand, the reward is often perceived as 'internal' to the activity. This may be explained by considering the reward in this instance as essentially the *establishment of a relationship*. As Aristotle wrote, *Philia* (a broad term covering the friendship between parents and children, siblings, lovers as well as fellow citizens) is – in its genuine form – an end-in-itself.

I now wish to stress that by 'reproductive labor' I in fact have this broader relationship in mind. The category is *not* to be confined to child-care strictly speaking (nor to traditional women's activity) but encompasses all those forms of laboring activity which bind people in friendship – which go towards establishing *Philia* in its genuine form. Reproductive labor may thus be present in numerous other types of activities to varying degrees (for instance, in teaching, ministering, artistic performances, etc.). The mother-child relationship (distinguished by the thickness of its reproductive activity) emerges as but one extreme instance; it plays the role of limit-case.

---

however, that the form of labor we are elaborating here tends to undercut the very dichotomy Habermas has established; reproductive labor does so because it is a) labor (the production of use values), and b) communicative, both at once.

In noting the different nature of the 'reward' of such labor we now turn to the central issue at hand: the alternative model's implications for the question of ownership. For centuries women have been 'mixing their labor' and efforts not for the purpose of exclusive appropriation (to dispose of the 'product' as they please), but with the ultimate aim even of 'giving' the child away as it reaches maturity (the reason one author calls such activity 'gift labor').[16] This is not to conclude, however, that women have never 'owned' anything (despite many legal appearances to the contrary). She can still say 'mine' and the children (as well as household, husband, etc.) have always been considered 'hers' in some sense. Rather, it is apparent that we are operating with an alternative paradigm of 'making something one's own,' features of which I shall next highlight. Although I call this alternative model 'female ownership' − to stress that such is the form traditionally surrounding most women − I do not mean to suggest that men have not participated in it to varying degrees.

1) *Non-exclusive ownership.* What a woman traditionally has called 'hers' − the children, husband, general houshold, etc. − are possessions essentially already *shared*. Ownership for her, whether legal or customary, has never in our tradition been equated with an absolute and exclusive control over such items, although periodically (such as at one point in Roman Law) she has herself been subject to such absolute control. The right of private property in land and goods was not granted her until the end of the nineteenth century (and even today women own exclusively only 1% of the world's property). My first claim is thus that women's situation points to important aspects of shared, communal property *maintained* in the modern period; what has been 'hers' is the result of (and constituted by) numerous intentions and collective agreements, rarely by her individual will alone.

2) *Non-economic ownership.* To the degree that women have not been the major but only supplementary bread-winners, their traditional realm (children, household, utensils, clothing, etc.) remains

---

16 L. Hyde, *The Gift* (New York: Vintage Books 1983), ch.6

an interpenetration of the economic (the useful) with interpersonal and qualitative considerations (such as religious, moral or aesthetic ones). Female ownership thus contrasts with the modern tradition's progressive reduction of the term 'property' (that which is 'properly one's own') to purely economic, and ultimately physical, quantitative terms. I stress the *narrowness* of this modern notion of 'property.' It is not only not 'prior' in any historical sense, but, I want to argue, it also emerges as conceptually far *less* fundamental. That is, it presupposes both historically and conceptually a broader conception of 'owning.'

3) *Guardianship.* Unlike the paradigm of property qua commodity, which may be acquired and disposed of at will, the children and home of the woman are clearly hers in an ascriptive not an acquisitive sense; that is, they are first and foremost her *responsibility.* Female ownership is a form accountable for the environment prior to any claim or need *exclusively* to appropriate that environment. The form emerges as fully consistent with the traditional, legal sense of the term 'possession' whereby objects are considered highly 'restricted objects' of the will. I want to suggest, moreover, that the criterion of rightful possession in this case be considered the criterion of 'care.' By 'care' is meant that specifically intelligent activity which appropriately responds to the concrete legitimate needs of others with the end of encouraging their autonomous capacities. 'Care' must here be understood in the sense of the German 'Pflege' (and not, for instance, as it is often translated by 'Sorge'). The German 'Pflege' is stressed because it, unlike its English equivalent, maintains a close etymological connection with the concept of 'Pflicht,' that is, with the concept of 'duty' itself.[17]

With its emphasis on responsibility as well as 'Pflege,' female ownership invites comparison with older, in particular medieval, forms of ownership. Scholars have long noted the absence of alienability and rights of disposal in medieval property forms, as well

---

17 According to the Duden *Deutsches Universal Woerterbuch* (1983), the term 'Pflicht' originally means no more nor less in both Old and Middle High German than 'zu pflegen.'

as emphasized the period's reigning conception of ownership as a *stewardship* of another's (God's or the community's) property.[18] The advantages of introducing the category of 'reproductive labor,' and the form of ownership accompanying it, begin to emerge. The category allows us not only to re-capture aspects of presumably long lost worlds (aspects such as 'Pflege,' guardianship, communal ownership), but it affords a fully modern and realistic interpretation of them, without committing us in the least to a medieval or religious metaphysics.

4) *Gift.* Finally, if the dominant form of property tied to the technical craft model (in the modern period) is the commodity, the form tied to reproductive labor more closely resembles the 'gift,' inviting further comparison with ownership patterns in what have come to be called 'gift cultures.'[19] A gift is something essentially 'bestowed' upon us by another; it cannot be obtained by one's own efforts or an act of will. Far more than the commodity, it remains tied to a specific set of concrete social relations; if the object qua gift is removed from these concrete relations it tends to change its 'value.' In many a fairy-tale, for instance, if the wicked child sells (or is stingy with) the loaf of bread given it to forge its way in the world, the 'spirit of the gift' flees (the bread turns to stone, etc.). This may be accounted for by viewing the 'spirit' of the genuine gift (and the reward of giving) as, again, the establishment of a relationship. The exchange of gifts thus stands in stark contrast to that of commodities where the two parties have further motives and are left relatively indifferent by the exchange.

My claim is that traditional woman is, to an astonishing degree, surrounded by such 'gift-property.' Her own child is, in most cultures, considered a 'gift' (and we speak of the 'gift of life'). But more importantly gift-exchange and the gift-labor of women in our own society — such as the female passage of food, clothing, presents,

---

18 See, for instance, A. Gurevich's 'Representations of Property during the High Middle Ages' in *Economy and Society* 6 (1977).

19 M. Mauss, *The Gift: Forms and Functions of Exchange in Archaic Societies* (New York: Newton Library 1967)

etc. within the extended family – leaves a series of interconnected relationships in its wake. This fact casts light on the problem of 'solidarity' in society. It has led one thinker to speak of women's morality as essentially 'ligational' – an activity of 'binding.'[20] Moreover, such exchange reverses the mythology of the market place where private acquisition is the mark of a substantial person. In gift exchange, or in gift labor, to 'possess' is essentially to 'give.'

The alternative model of 'making something one's own' presented here is one which by definition cannot be exclusive and private. Such 'owning' may be considered an appropriation, not of the natural physical world, but of the 'human social' one. It implies that in an important sense we in fact do make other people 'our own,' although this form must now carefully be distinguished from traditional ownership as a control or 'domination' of them. On the contrary, this form essentially entails a responsiveness to concrete need, as well as the encouragement of another's autonomous capacities. It thus emphasizes that long neglected aspect of 'ownership' as *inclusion* (participation, 'zu Hause sein') in the specifically human community. Moreover, the model clearly pre-supposes an altered conception of personality, one which now emphasizes the 'fact of continuity' with others over that of 'separateness.'[21]

Before turning to the final portion of my paper, an obvious objection arises to taking this alternative model seriously. Why not merely claim that the form of ownership belonging to women over the last few hundred years, and which retains aspects of pre-capitalist forms,

---

20 Hilda Hein, 'Woman and Morality,' *Ms* (1979)

21 One might argue that, given woman's reproductive functions (pregnancy, parturition, lactation, etc.), the suppression of the boundaries separating the body and world has been far more easily performed in her case. This is not to claim, however, that women's biology determines her 'personality,' just that it may historically have facilitated it. See Chodorow's arguments against the cruder interpretation in her *The Reproduction of Mothering* (Berkeley: University of California Press 1978). On the contrary, the relative 'ease of sliding from self to other' characteristic of so many women, appears to mark male personality in many other cultures or historical periods. See, for instance, Gurevich's (1977) discussion of the medieval personality.

only indicates the 'primitiveness' of this form? Such ownership, after all, has essentially been bound to the historical lack of independence and separateness of choice characterizing women's position.
My response is that, although historically this has undoubtedly been
the case, there exists no necessary connection between such dependence and the form of ownership here under investigation. On the
contrary, *any* society must consist of and maintain certain concrete,
bonding relations — that is, if it is going to hold itself together.

I might just add that it is not merely the liberal tradition which
has overlooked what I am calling reproductive labor, but the Marxist
one as well. For example, in predicting capitalism's inevitable down-
fall — in arguing that capitalist commodity production ultimately
'tears' a society apart — Marx apparently failed to recognize the large
portion of non-commodity labor which, precisely 'behind the scenes'
as it were (or outside the market), goes to binding relations together
again. That is, Marx not only seemed to underestimate the 'resiliency'
of capitalism (as is often claimed), but he failed to recognize the
category of reproductive labor. Part of the present system's adapta-
bility can surely be explained, however, by showing to what degree
capitalist activity actually rests on other forms of non-commodity
labor. Of course, if reproductive labor is progressively pulled into
the market — and hence subjected to its laws — who knows, the
truth of Marx's predictions may yet come to pass.

IV

We return to our discussion of Rawls's theory. We noted earlier how
the difference principle incorporates both acquisitive and ascriptive
forms of ownership. We noted further Rawls's 'scepticism' that —
given present human nature — the moral, purposeful self could ever
become primary (collectively speaking) in the realm of economic
labor. Hence the strong reading of the difference principle, which
requires social union in the economic sphere, cannot be demanded
as a matter of justice. In having turned to the domestic sphere of
women's labor, however, we have presented an alternative model
of self, labor and ownership which is at once a) one in which ascrip-

tive ownership is primary, and yet b) one which is undeniably central to our modern capitalist tradition. My claim in this final section is that Rawls's theory has not sufficiently taken the implications of such reproductive labor into account. Moreover, were his theory to do so, a novel way of conceiving an uncoerced, democratic and viable socialist ownership emerges.

It here becomes important to distinguish between a thin and a thick sense of 'ascriptive ownership.' In referring to that form of non-private, non-acquisitive ownership which essentially entails a 'responding' to the capacities of others, one may distinguish two different underlying ideals of human autonomy. These ideals reflect, it is suggested, the institutional distinction in our society between a public sphere of an ethics of principle and the familial sphere of an ethics of care.[22] The former ideal is explicitly incorporated into the difference principle; the latter (I believe) is not.

The first ideal of autonomy (essentially Kantian) may be described as taking on the standpoint of the 'generalized other' and it is crucial to what I shall call 'responsible' ownership. This form recognizes that a condition for my owning anything (developing my abilities, etc.) is that others can and will do likewise (see p. 147). This standpoint rests on the increasing capacity of the self to act upon universalistic principles of right, and requires us to view each individual as a rational being entitled to the same rights and duties we ascribe to ourselves. Rawls's original position has clearly been constructed in order to highlight this relationship to other governed by the essentially institutional norm of symmetrical reciprocity. The reigning moral categories here are right, obligation and entitlement, accompanied by moral feelings of respect, dignity and worthiness.

---

22 For the distinction between a public and private sphere of ethics I rely on such recent work in feminist theory as Gilligan's *In a Different Voice* (Cambridge: Harvard University Press 1982); Chodorow (1978); as well as Dinnerstein (1977) and Elshtain (1981). For the following distinction between the standpoint of the 'concrete' versus 'generalized other' see S. Benhabib's 'Communicative Ethics and Moral Autonomy' (Unpublished Manuscript 1982).

What S. Benhabib has called the standpoint of the 'concrete other,' on the other hand, requires us to view each rational being as an individual with a specific history, concrete identity and effective emotional constitution. This standpoint rests on the increasing capacity of the self (a capacity central to reproductive labor) to render 'inner nature' transparent — i.e. human needs, desires, drives, and so on. From this standpoint we seek to comprehend the needs of others as he (or she) comprehends himself. The governing norms here are those of reciprocal friendship, love and care; I can expect *more* in this instance than the simple assertion of my rights and duties in the face of your needs and vice versa. The accompanying moral categories are responsibility, bonding and sharing. Such an ideal of autonomy (reflecting the familial sphere) underlies what I shall now call 'responsive ownership.' This form not only entails simultaneously guarding the social conditions for the development of another's abilities, but the conditions for the possibility of genuine *Philia* as well (see pp. 155-9).

I think it is fair to claim that the standpoint of the 'concrete other' (as well as responsive ownership) has in general been little recognized in modern social and political theory. However, as women progressively as a group (and not individually one by one) move from the private sphere and enter the public, labor market, it is clear a dilemma is reached which may be met in either of at least two ways:

1) This large-scale movement of women entering the market-place can effect a transformation of the workplace. As clarity of the issues is achieved, women could demand the retention of at least certain aspects of their traditional roles, foremost among which are common activities and shared final ends (social union) in laboring activity. In turn, the requirement could emerge (one already well underway in American society) that men participate equally in the raising of small children.[23] Here we note that if men *as a group* were to participate in early child-care, this itself could effect a revolutionary trend in the workplace. Hours of work must change, for instance; they must become more flexible as well as open to discus-

---

23 See, for instance, Chodorow (1978), and Dinnerstein (1977).

sion and exchange. The private life and concerns of the individual worker (including the importance of reproductive labor) must be acknowledged to a greater degree in the public realm of labor. Moreover, such novel participation in shopfloor decisions (concerning hours, place of work, vacations, etc.) encourages a growing interest and understanding on the individual's part in regard to the ends and requirements of the business association itself; it leads in turn to a growing *capacity* on the part of each person to participate in progressively more complex and significant decisions.

My claim is that such a transformation of the workplace could quite naturally lead towards a form of 'socialist ownership': to a form of collective decision-making in regard not only to the conditions of work, but eventually (by extension) to the aims and products of the production process as well. By 'socialist ownership' I intend nothing more than that shared, final ends (social union) extend into the economic sphere and that differences in individual income, position, etc. now become conditional, not merely on bettering the financial position of all, but on actually furthering their conditions of autonomy, participation and self-governance. More specifically, I have in mind the strong interpretation of Rawls's difference principle which would now be implemented *within* the firm. That this requirement now apply inside individual firms, entails that the latter be perceived as a form of 'joint property' (with shared or at least overlapping final ends) whereby individual differences pertain, in turn, to the traditional realm of 'possession.' Considering the fact of the twentieth century women's movement (as well as our analysis of a thick ascriptive self traditionally trained to respond to, and develop the basic attributes of, other persons) this scheme of laboring on a shared property no longer appears as 'unnatural' and utopian as it once may have.

2) The opposite alternative, of course, is that as women progressively enter the labor force, rather than responsive ownership and the criterion of care going 'public,' as it were, women merely take on the traditional male personality marked by competition and private appropriation. In this instance, the model of exclusive appropriation would — for the first time in history — truly be generalized to all members of society. In the extreme case, we recall, on such an exclusive model even the higher pursuits of the mind as well as

our relations to others take on the form of private acquisitions. My claim here is that such a transformation of female activity into the traditional male role finds its inevitable limit in the fact of human reproduction. In such a case the children (as well as all relations of *Philia*) are truly left 'unattended.' That is, they would be relegated to *nothing but* wage-labor care (which would now include the labor itself of parents and friends). The suggestion here is that in such a society where there is no longer any gift-labor at all − no longer any concrete activity of bonding and sharing for its own sake − the society cannot long maintain itself. Such an alternative stands in explicit contrast to the sketch of socialist ownership given above, whereby *all* labor becomes publicly recognized as *in part* 'gift labor' − as labor done for no other reason than maintaining the social conditions for the possiblity of genuine *Philia*.

It is possible, of course (and even very likely), that a situation emerges somewhere between the above two alternatives. Our society could respond to women entering the labor force with relatively marginal adjustments (flex-time, job-sharing, guaranteed parental leaves, etc.) that only minimally effect the basic structure of ownership and corporate decision-making. The aim of this essay, however, is not to argue for any automatic and inevitable road to socialism. My aim is rather to reveal − from the standpoint of 'justice as fairness' itself − the moral superiority of a form of democratic social-

---

24 As we noted already in note #9, Rawls also expresses the further concern that socialist ownership may result in a 'command society.' Here I can only emphasize that in my discussion of Rawls's difference principle, it is to be assumed that his first principle of justice (which guarantees the various individual liberties, including freedom of occupation, etc.) is already satisfied. There is thus no question, in this instance, of a centralized state commanding the direction of labor. As I have argued elsewhere the worry that socialist property necessarily leads to a form of command society appears to derive from continuing to conceive property on the model of 'control'; 'collective ownership' then quite naturally suggests 'collective control' and, in Mill's words, 'no place left for the individual.' It is my claim, however, that with the notion of 'responsive ownership' a wedge is driven for the first time between the very notions of 'owning' and 'controlling.' See my *Towards a New Conception of Ownership* (Unpubl. diss.: Harvard 1985), ch.5.

ism once standard charges of 'utopianism' can be met (and that such can be met by recognizing the importance of reproductive labor, etc.). In the end, which of the alternative routes is in fact taken, remains up to us.

I must still, of course, address Rawls's primary worry that the proposed (market) socialist transformation of the economic sphere brings with it a reduction in economic 'efficiency.'[24] The motive of exclusive ownership has, after all, long been considered a great 'incentive' to laboring activity, and (so the familiar argument runs) only by maintaining an abundant material base can society continue to support the individual freedoms and benefits it has come to enjoy. I here offer numerous final suggestions (which at this point must necessarily remain incomplete).

First, as Mill argued long ago, if everyone is considered a part 'owner' of an enterprise (as in a worker's co-operative) the incentive to do well would seem far greater than in the case of laboring for a mere wage where the individual has 'little personal interest in his work.'[25] Second, few seem to have considered the possibility that women in particular may actually perform *less well* when they are removed from a concrete set of caring social relations and thrust into a competitive market scheme; under present working conditions their labor may thus be highly inefficient. Third, to claim that private ownership of the means of production (including the exclusive and hierarchical control over a labor force) is so strong an incentive as to outweigh these other considerations, emerges by this point as simply *too strong*. The claim presupposes a private, acquisitive conception of the self to the extreme. However, not only does Rawls's theory not rest on such an extreme version of the acquisitive self (as we have seen his view presupposes an individual capable of progressive motivation by the Aristotelian Principle), but given our previous account of women's traditional personality, the extreme acquisitive self — rather than reflecting some norm in human motivation — begins to emerge as the anomolous case.

---

25 J.S. Mill, *Principles of Political Economy* (Toronto: University of Toronto Press 1968), 204

Finally, we must note that even if there should exist in the end an irreconcilable conflict between material productive efficiency and the development of human capacities, Rawls himself believes a point is reached in a society's development where the aim of further material production *gives way* to a concern with questions of 'autonomy' (TJ, 543). Considering that responsive ownership is one which essentially encourages the autonomy of individuals (and that this at some point becomes their primary concern), a positive argument for social union in the economic sphere can now be found from within Rawls's own assumptions − that is, granting our supplementary account. Since we have shown that ascriptive ownership in the thickest sense is fully 'compatible with our human nature,' not only as it might be, but as it in fact already *is*, we may formulate our conclusion thus: Rawls's difference principle requires, as a matter of justice (at least in the long run) social union in the economic sphere. And it requires it in the name of the strong interpretation; differences in social position and wealth must benefit the 'worst off' not simply in monetary terms, but in terms of those conditions which further social union, autonomous capacities and self-governing powers in all. Another way of stating the same point is that Rawls's theory can now finally require that ownership of the major means of production be withdrawn from a part of society's private *incentive* system, and come instead to be employed as collective *instruments* for the development of distinctive human capacities. This is, of course, not to claim that other forms of private incentives (differences in material income, positions of authority, etc.) should not continue to operate.

It is possible that a thorough analysis of contemporary circumstances (of the women's movement, as well as of such significant tendencies as that an ever growing sector of the American economy is geared towards the human service factor − a sector where precisely responsive ownership may prove most 'efficient,' etc.), reveals that the difference principle demands social union in the economic sphere at present. This, however, is too much to attempt in this paper. Nor have I addressed the issue of what precise form social union in the economic sphere should take (i.e. to what degree the market should be employed, how 'participation' will proceed, and so on).[26] At the very least I hope to have revealed that John

Rawls's 'scepticism' in regard to the strong interpretations's compatibility with our human nature is no longer founded. The burden of proof shifts, in turn, towards him.

---

26 I wish to make it clear, however, that I am not arguing for 'worker sovereignty' in society. People have claims and entitlements, after all, independently of their laboring role. Instead, the suggestion here is that worker-owned enterprises be considered elements within the democratic order, rather than being viewed as society's organizational base. Thus, for instance, the control of large-scale public investment (effectively the only guarantee of a society's future) could be made available to general public deliberation, and decisions made either by a body subject to control by a legislative body, or themselves subject to direct democratic accountability. See Cohen and Rogers's *On Democracy* (New York: Penguin Books 1983), ch.6.

CANADIAN JOURNAL OF PHILOSOPHY
Supplementary Volume 13

Ethics, Ideology, and Feminine Virtue

JOHN EXDELL
Kansas State University
Manhattan, KS 66506
U.S.A.

> 'How wonderfully the ideas of virtue set afloat by
> the powerful are caught and imbibed by those un-
> der their dominion.' – Harriet Taylor Mill

In *After Virtue* Alasdair MacIntyre argues that moral argument in modern civilization is inherently ideological in character. The parties at odds present their conclusions as objective truths, but in reality each relies on premises that he or she cannot rationally justify to the other. Since moral language wraps non-rational choices in the illusion of objectivity, it is unavoidably manipulative in function. In both personal relations and political affairs we employ the language of morality in order to have our way, to get others to serve our ends.

For MacIntyre this state of affairs represents a degeneration of culture that has connected philosophical and sociological roots. Philosophical analysis reveals logical incoherence in the concepts of 'rights' and 'utility,' from which the major premises in post-Enlightenment morality are derived. We can restore 'intelligibility and rationality' to moral judgment only if we replace these 'matching fictions' with a rationally founded shared conception of the human good in which the cultivation of virtue occupies a central place. However, this can occur only in a society whose common life is comprised of 'practices' – that is, in rough terms, forms of cooperative activity that afford people the satisfaction of developing their human powers. The trouble, according to MacIntyre, is that contemporary bureaucratic and commercial civilization is founded upon the destruction of practices and the elevation of material acquisition as the dominant motive in human life. Amidst this cultural wreckage one finds the fragmentary moral philosophies of Kant and Bentham, and the axiom that what constitutes a good life must be left within the province of arbitrary individual choice.

My aim in this paper is to determine whether MacIntyre's doctrine of virtue, grounded in the idea of traditional practices, lays the foundation for genuinely non-ideological ethical judgments. To decide this we must be conscious of the connection between MacIntyre's project and Marxist social thought where the distinction between 'ideology' and 'rationality' in ethical judgment also plays a central role. Here the concept of ideology is explicitly linked to that of 'domination' and 'oppression.' An ideological ethic is one that justifies social relations which systematically sacrifice the well-being of one group to maintain the power and privileges of another. The search for a rational ethic is inseparable then from the conception of a society in which all participants relate to each other as equals — i.e., a society which requires none of its members to sacrifice important human goods in order to elevate others above them. To speak of 'ideology' in this sense implies a commitment to social equality.

MacIntyre acknowledges his debt to this tradition. His own view is intended to enlarge or supplement, not replace 'the conception of ideology of which Marx is the ancestral begetter.'[1] Yet it is by no means obvious that MacIntyre's proposal for a rational ethic is securely tied to any vision of an egalitarian social order. *After Virtue* does not have a lot to say about domination or oppression. It is market society, individualism, and bureaucracy — not social class or patriarchy — which bears the blame for the ideological abuse of moral language. MacIntyre takes pains to divorce his ideas from the politics of any contemporary feminist or socialist movement. And

---

1 *After Virtue* (Notre Dame, IN: University of Notre Dame Press 1981), 104. All references are to the 1981 edition unless otherwise noted.

he proposes medieval civilization, at least in some aspects, as an example of culture in which objective ethical judgment was once possible. It is therefore necessary that we carefully examine the conditions MacIntyre identifies as the basis for rational judgments about virtue. If in this context prevailing ideas of virtue can play an integral role in sustaining a system of class or sexual domination, then MacIntyre's theory fails to incorporate the egalitarian commitments implicit in his own distinction between ideology and rationality in ethical judgment.

To gain a vantage point for this assessment I will focus on the modern debate over the ethical status of 'feminine virtue.' Obviously MacIntyre cannot invoke liberal principles as a basis for rejecting traditional gender roles and related conceptions of masculine and feminine character. It remains to be seen then whether his philosophy gives us any alternative foundation for criticizing concepts of masculinity and femininity that have long played a clear ideological role in a culture of male domination.

The doctrine of separate virtues has an ancient lineage, entering the Western philosophical tradition with Aristotle. In the modern era its validity was first contested by Mary Wolstonecraft in her response to Rousseau's *Emile*. Then throughout the 19th century champions of women's emancipation and their romantic adversaries struggled to determine whether 'feminine virtue' should be seen as a genuine and unique ethical ideal or an ideological justification for an oppressive sexual division of labor. From the Enlightenment to the present the debate has entered the fields of sociology and natural science, as well as many great works of fiction.[2] One of the most illuminating 20th century studies on the ethical ambiguity in feminine character is found in Virginia Woolf's classic novel *To the Lighthouse*. My essay draws the connection between MacIntyre's doctrine and the views of Aristotle, Wollstonecraft, and Woolf, and assesses what his ethics of virtue can contribute to this historic controversy.

---

2 See *Women, the Family and Freedom: The Debate in Documents*, Volume I and II, Susan Groag Bell and Karen M. Offen, eds. (Stanford, CA: Stanford University Press 1983).

John Exdell

I Aristotle: The Special Virtues of Women and Slaves

MacIntyre builds his argument on what he takes to be Aristotle's central insights on the relation between virtue and the human good. Life is to be seen as an uncertain journey from an unformed state of potentiality to a condition of excellence in character. Man's final end is to become an individual who has developed perfection of soul, understood not only as the capacity to act correctly with practical wisdom, but also as a disposition to feel certain emotions and to take pleasure in certain activities. Thus for Aristotle virtue for one who has it is not a condition of self-sacrifice, but a state of fulfillment and an essential element of a happy life. Happiness of course requires a measure of life's 'external goods' — wealth, power, health, etc. But most crucially a happy man is one whose character is such that he takes pleasure in the right things, i.e., in the activities appropriate for a virtuous man.

Aristotle's idea that there is a final purpose to human life arose in a culture where individuals occupied roles with certain commonly understood social functions — e.g., craftsman, slave, soldier, architect, wife, ruler, etc. The virtues were acquired in the course of activities aimed at fulfilling the function of one's role and defined as those qualities necessary to perform those functions well (e.g., courage for a soldier). Thus Aristotle says, 'Let this be assumed about excellence, that it is the best disposition, state or capacity of anything that has some employment or function.'[3] This would suggest that virtues are entirely relative to various social functions they serve and therefore not comparable as higher and lower, superior and inferior. But this is definitely not how Aristotle saw it. Apart from the functions of particular social roles, there is a final *telos* for man himself — rational action in its most perfect form. This final end is attainable only by those men who occupy the most eminent role in society — that of ruling citizen. Their goodness is ultimate and absolute, while the virtues of all others — e.g., women and slaves —

---

3 *Eudemian Ethics*, II, 1219a, trans. Michael Woods (New York: Oxford University Press 1982)

are relative to theirs. That is, all other roles are seen to be in the service of this higher one, supplying the material conditions that enable rulers (and philosophers) to achieve these absolute forms of perfection unique to the species. The household, in which women find their special *telos*, functions to satisfy the daily recurrent needs of men engaging in the activity of citizenship.

For Aristotle it follows that there is no single set of virtues applicable to all positions in society, and in particular no standard of excellence appropriate for both men and women:

> They must all share in moral goodness, but not in the same way – each sharing only to the extent required for the discharge of his or her function. The ruler accordingly must possess moral goodness in its full or perfect form because his function demands a master-artificer, and reason is such a master artificer; but all other persons need only possess moral goodness to the extent required of them. It is thus clear that ... temperance – and similarly fortitude and justice – are not, as Socrates held, the same in a woman as they are in a man. Fortitude in the one, for example, is shown in connexion with ruling; in the other, it is shown in connexion with serving; and the same is true of the other forms of goodness....[4]

To achieve the virtues of the rulers is to realize the *telos* of the species in its 'perfect form,' by comparison with which the distinct virtues of women have an instrumental and subordinate status.

Does MacIntyre's modification of Aristotle escape this inegalitarian conclusion? To determine this, we must note that MacIntyre rejects Aristotle's 'metaphysical biology' – i.e., the idea that there is a natural, eternal 'function' for the species. Instead the virtues comprising the 'human good' must be formulated in relation to each society's traditional 'practices,' defined as 'complex forms of socially established cooperative activity.' An activity is a practice when those who participate in it aim to realize goods 'internal' to the activity itself. The game of chess is a practice. Its 'internal goods' – those for which one plays the game for its own sake – are certain qualities of mind and temperament: high analytical ability, strategic

---

4 *Politics*, I, 1260a, translated by Ernest Barker (New York: Oxford University Press 1946)

imagination, and competitive intensity. MacIntyre calls the making and sustaining of family life a practice, as well as farming, the inquiries of science, the work of the historian, painting, and music.[5] What they have in common is that people who engage in them find their main satisfaction in achieving the capacities and other qualities of excellence appropriate to the nature of the activity, with the result that their 'human powers to achieve excellence and human conceptions of the ends and goods involved, are systematically extended.'[6] A quality of character can be a *virtue* then only if it is necessary to achieve the internal goods of practices that comprise historically established social roles.

MacIntyre's analysis of the virtues in relation to practices, as defined above, does have an egalitarian thrust. To count as a virtue a quality of character must function in roles that require the development of an individual's 'human powers.' This would disqualify, for example, the qualities of slavishness and docility. We could not classify these as virtues no matter how functional they are for those occupying roles of menial service. On the contrary, one of the human powers required for exercising any genuine virtue is 'practical intelligence': knowing how to apply principles and precepts to a particular situation so that one's virtues are appropriately manifested in particular acts. Interpreting Aristotle on this point MacIntyre argues, 'The exercise of intelligence is what makes the crucial difference between a natural disposition of a certain kind and the corresponding virtue.'[7] One could then argue that to possess bonafide virtues is to exhibit qualities that, if recognized, would secure one's dignity as a human being. Conversely, the servility required of people assigned a life of mindless drudgery cannot count as a virtue. MacIntyre's adaptation of Aristotle, therefore, does not appear to give any warrant to the most blatant ideological appeals to special feminine 'virtues of submission.'

---

5 *After Virtue*, 175

6 Ibid.

7 Ibid., 145

II Mary Wollstonecraft: Human Virtues in the Domestic Sphere

The modern debate on the idea of 'feminine virtue' begins with Rousseau's *Emile* and Mary Wollstonecraft's response in *Vindication of the Rights of Women*. Like Aristotle, Rousseau held that the special virtues of women were inferior to the higher, absolute virtue attainable only by men. True virtue requires the capacity for autonomous, rational judgment – the ability to think and act independently of the customs, opinions and fashions of one's social world. However, such autonomy requires certain material conditions. It is possible, thought Rousseau, only for those who are economically independent. Those who are not must be affected by the opinions and needs of those on whom they rely for their subsistence. For this reason women as a class lack the capacity for rational virtue. Their virtues instead are defined in relation to the needs of men:

> Women and man are made for one another, but their mutual dependence is not equal. Men depend on women because of their desires; women depend on men because of both their desires and their needs. We would survive more easily without them than they would without us. For them to have what is necessary to their station, they depend on us to give it to them, to want to give it to them, to esteem them worthy of it. They depend on our sentiments, on the value we set on their merit, on the importance we attach to their charms and their virtues. By the very law of nature women are at the mercy of men's judgments, as much for their own sake as for that of their children.[8]

From this it follows that modesty, docility, guile, attention to appearance and sensitivity to the needs of men are the hallmarks of feminine excellence.

Wollstonecraft's central objective in *Vindication* is to demolish Rousseau's idea of special feminine virtues: though their duties may differ, the same virtues – the *human* virtues – apply to both sexes. Surprisingly, her argument depends less on Enlightenment ideas

---

8 *Emile, or On Education*, translated by Allan Bloom (New York: Basic Books 1979), 364

about natural rights and individual liberty than on an egalitarian adaptation of Aristotle, resembling that found in MacIntyre as interpreted above. Virtue is identified as the goal of human existence and the essential element of happiness. We are reminded repeatedly about the 'grand end of existence − the attainment of virtue,' in which 'true dignity and human happiness consists.'[9] The virtues are the qualities of character essential to the discharge of responsibilities, and 'can only be acquired by the discharge of relative duties' (aristocrats and coquettes perform no useful social function and hence lack virtue).[10] This of course involves self-discipline, the willingness to sacrifice immediate pleasure for the sake of one's obligations, through which deeper forms of satisfaction are ultimately attained: 'Necessity has been proverbially termed the mother of invention; the aphorism may be extended to virtue ... Happy is it when people have the cares of life to struggle with.'[11]

Most crucially for Wollstonecraft, virtue necessarily involves the exercise of 'understanding,' and thus cannot be regarded as something instinctive or a product of natural emotion. 'It is a farce to call any being virtuous whose virtues do not result from the exercise of its own reason,' says Wollstonecraft.[12] Indeed she is especially intent to show the necessity of reason in virtues connected with child-care and other domestic responsibilities. Emotions alone − feelings of compassion, tenderness, etc. − do not comprise a virtue. An individual's want of 'power over the feelings' make impossible 'that lofty dignified affection' essential to the education of children. Again, 'Whoever rationally means to be useful must have a plan of conduct, and in the discharge of the simplest duty, we are often obliged to act contrary to the present impulse of tenderness

---

9 *Vindication of the Rights of Women* (Harmondsworth: Penguin Books 1982), 203 and 81

10 Ibid., 252

11 Ibid., 144

12 Ibid., 103

and compassion....'[13] Hence we become virtuous through a life that demands growth and development: 'I am, indeed, persuaded that the heart, as well as the understanding, is opened by cultivation ... I am not now talking of momentary flashes of sensibility, but of affections.'[14].

On this basis Wollstonecraft justifies her thesis that there can be only *one kind* of virtue − that involving the exercise of self-discipline and rational judgment in the performance of the 'important duties of life.' Character derived from any other source − natural emotion, instinct, fear, unthinking obedience − consists of 'spurious qualities that have assumed the name.'[15] Wollstonecraft is, therefore, able to distinguish the true virtues − e.g., 'gentleness' and a capacity for 'dignified affection' − from their ideological counterfeits, docility and the servile desire to please:

> Gentleness of manners, forbearance and long suffering, are such amiable God-like qualities ... no representation of His goodness so strongly fastens on the human affections as those that represent Him abundant in mercy and willing to pardon. Gentleness, considered in this point of view, bears on its front all the characteristics of grandeur ... but what a different aspect it assumes when it is the submissive demeanor of dependence, the support of weakness that loves, because it wants protection; and is forbearing, because it must silently endure injuries, smiling under the lash at which it dare not snarl.[16]

We see in this passage how Wollstonecraft seeks to include Christian and traditionally feminine qualities − gentleness and a capacity for love and mercy − within the Aristotelian framework. If even these virtues require active intelligence, it follows for Wollstonecraft that a virtuous person deserves respect as a *rational* being.

Thus Wollstonecraft is able to link virtue with the attainment of dignity, equality, and 'independence,' by which she generally does

---

13 Ibid., 161

14 Ibid., 158

15 Ibid., 91

16 Ibid., 117

not mean (following Rousseau) economic self-sufficiency. 'Independence' signifies autonomy of mind and character, attained by one capable of making her own rational judgments about human affairs and who therefore must be listened to by those around her. She need not resort to feminine wiles (for Rousseau the only equalizing source of power for women). She need not manipulate, plead, or deceive. She can argue a case directly on its merits and will not be pressured or intimidated by a more powerful male voice:

> Besides, the woman who strengthens her body and exercises her mind will, by managing her family and practicing various virtues, become the friend, and not the humble dependent of her husband; and if she, by possessing such substantial qualities, merit his regard, she will not find it necessary to conceal her affection, nor to pretend to an unnatural coldness of constitution to excite her husband's passions.[17]

The independence of the virtuous woman is grounded then in her real capacities and in the self-confidence to which these give rise. She sees herself as a being with inherent value and not, following Rousseau, of importance relative to the pleasures of men. For Mary Wollstonecraft the virtues therefore provide the necessary and sufficient basis for social equality between men and women:

> Connected with man as daughters, wives, and mothers, their moral character may be estimated by their manner of fulfilling those simple duties; but the end, the grand end, of their exertions should be to unfold their own faculties, and acquire the dignity of conscious virtue.[18]

> Women, I allow, may have different duties to fulfil; but they are *human* duties, and the principles that should regulate the discharge of them, I sturdily maintain, must be the same ... To become respectable, the exercise of their understanding is necessary, there is no other foundation for independence of character; I mean explicitly to say that they must only bow to the authority of reason, instead of being the *modest* slaves of opinion.[19]

---

17 Ibid., 113

18 Ibid., 108-9

19 Ibid., 139

Although Wollstonecraft emphasized the importance of education for women, the passages above suggest that she saw no inconsistency between the achievement of gender equality and women's acceptance of domestic roles. To be sure, *Vindication* calls for opening the professions to women, but Wollstonecraft is careful to confine these suggestions to women of 'superior cast,' excluding those in 'the common walks of life.' Through their roles as wives and mothers the great majority of women take on 'the important duties of life'; they acquire the virtues, through which their rational powers are manifested; and thereby they establish their human dignity and equality with men.

III MacIntyre: Modernity and the Destruction of Household Practices

Mary Wollstonecraft's work serves as precedent for an Aristotelianism that avoids the inegalitarian conception of special 'women's virtues' found in Aristotle himself and later in Rousseau. However, taking MacIntyre's position in this direction poses a new difficulty: if women can gain the human virtues through their participation in the practices of domesticity, and if achieving virtue is the essential condition for 'happiness' and social equality, why have modern women so often come to regard their assignment to traditional domestic roles as a condition of confinement and oppression?[20] Wollstonecraft's analysis does not appear to offer any clear basis for such a judgment. Leaving aside the problem of the 'superior' few excluded

---

20 One finds this question posed repeatedly by 19th and 20th century commentators on 'the woman question.' Norwegian novelist Camilla Collett, for example, pondered the significance of marriage for middle class women: '... at this point they enter into the hopeless night of obscurity and insignificance. A noticeable fading characterizes this transition. Nothing is known any longer of these beings, who were once referred to as pretty so-and-sos; one scarcely notices them any longer when they show their faded selves in public. They are no longer individuals; they are Norwegian housewives' (Bell and Offen, Volume 1, 319). Originally from *Amtmadens dötre* (Christiania, 1954-55).

from the professions, dignity and equality are thought secured as long as women are permitted to cultivate the virtues necessary for success in their roles as wives and mothers. From this vantage point we cannot explain the pervasive dissatisfaction that has motivated so many women to escape confinement in domestic roles, or why women who have assumed the exclusive identity of mothers and wives have so often failed to gain the dignity and respect promised as the reward for their virtue.

MacIntyre's sociological critique of industrial society suggests an answer that avoids modern appeals to the doctrine of rights, opportunity and equal liberty: 'One of the key moments in the creation of modernity occurs when production moves outside the household ... correspondingly practices have in turn been removed to the margins of social and cultural life.'[21] The degeneration of labor as a practice occurred not only in the production line, but in the home as well, when commercial civilization stripped women of their status as direct contributors to the houshold economy. Their once essential skills – e.g., breeding poultry, caring for dairy cattle, butchering livestock, producing milk, cream, cheese, beer and cider, operating wool carders and spinning wheels, making soap and medicine, healing – were rendered redundant once these products and services were produced for the market and purchased by means of their husband's income. The new division of labor split women into two classes: 'a small group of leisured women with no work to fill the day ... and a huge group of women condemned to the drudgery of domestic service or to that of the mill or factory or to prostitution.'[22] In substance, MacIntyre's analysis suggests that when modern commercial society transferred production into the market, it also destroyed women's domestic labor *as a practice*. The reduction of women's sphere to 'homemaking,' and the rearing of young children, meant greatly reduced opportunities for realizing the various goods of self-development available to women practicing traditional productive skills. Wollstonecraft had simply failed to see the

---

21 *After Virtue*, 211

22 Ibid., 223

shape of modernity, where 'the life of the virtues is necessarily afforded a very restricted cultural and social space.'[23]

In his commentary on Jane Austen's novels MacIntyre reveals how he understands the social and ethical consequences of this transformation. The atrophy of the practice of household production *creates* the condition that Rousseau regarded as women's natural lot: one-sided dependency on men with its consequent inequality in power. 'When production was within the household the unmarried sister or aunt was a useful or valued member of the household,' but afterwards 'the woman who does not marry has to fear expulsion into drudgery as her characteristic lot. Hence to refuse a bad marriage is a great act of courage....'[24] This objective dependency is joined to the relative triviality of women's new pursuits. They become beings 'for whom occupations have to be invented − fine needlework, the reading of bad novels and organized opportunities for gossip, which are thought of by men as "essentially feminine".'[25]

Identified with the 'essentially feminine' are, we might add, certain qualities of character − weakness, passivity, and innocence − a nature in need of protection from the harsh world of business, politics, and industrial labor. More importantly 'feminine virtue' loses its connection with the Aristotelian idea of practical intelligence and appears as a *natural* disposition for self-sacrifice, an involuntary altruism. Romantics then worship women's mysterious power to love and comfort, while the more misogynistically inclined relegate feminine virtue to the nature of an animal impulse. In either case, virtue in women − once divorced from skill, education, discipline, and the exercise of practical reason − can no longer serve as a foundation for their human dignity and equality with men.[26]

---

23 Ibid., 226

24 Ibid., 223

25 Ibid.

26 For a similar analysis see Barbara Ehrenreich and Deirdre English, *For Her Own Good: 150 Years of the Experts' Advice to Women* (New York: Anchor Books 1979), especially chapters 1-3.

John Exdell

MacIntyre's position on women's roles is not systematically presented in *After Virtue*. However we definitely find the idea that the oppression of women, and the ideological use of feminine virtue, arise from the destruction of practices, rather than from the confinement of women in certain traditional roles. Left here, MacIntyre's analysis suggests that when a conception of virtue *is* defined in relation to practices, it cannot be used ideologically to induce subservience or to justify domination. Participation in practices can (1) establish one's dignity as a rational being, (2) earn one the status of an independent contributor to social life, and (3) afford opportunities for the internal satisfactions of personal development. A society founded on practices, therefore, has no room for the idea of femininity conceived of as a condition of weakness, innocence, dependency, and self-sacrifice. Indeed in such a society the phenomenon of 'domination' and 'oppression,' as modern feminists discuss it, simply would not arise.

IV Virginia Woolf: The Ideological Aspect of Feminine Virtue

Interpreted in this way MacIntyre's argument depends crucially on the premise that modern domestic life is bereft of 'practices.' Hence the qualities of character required of women assigned the duties of the household — passivity, angelic self-sacrifice, etc. — fail to qualify as bonafide virtues. The trouble with this argument is that its sociological premise is surely incorrect. Commercial society has indeed taken production out of the household, but it has by no means eliminated what MacIntyre calls 'practices' through which 'goods internal to that form of activity are realized in the course of trying to achieve those standards of excellence which are appropriate to ... that form of activity, with the result that human powers to achieve excellence, and human conceptions of the ends and goods involved, are systematically extended.'[27] MacIntyre apparently regards the 'sustaining of family life' as a practice only as once performed in

---

27 *After Virtue*, 175

pre-industrial civilization.[28] But to exclude women's domestic activities today from this category — while admitting such activities as chess, football, and architecture — risks confusing certain contemporary male perceptions of women's experience with the reality of that experience itself.

When commercial society transferred men's work from household to market, it simultaneously enlarged women's maternal role as the primary caretaker of children. Mothers acquired the day-to-day responsibility for their children's physical, emotional and intellectual development. Even with the establishment of professional medicine and public schooling women today find themselves absorbed in the tasks of healing, comforting, motivating, educating, supervising and disciplining the young. There is every reason to regard these activities as comprising a 'practice' as MacIntyre uses this term. The talents and qualities of character required by these duties are complex and, as with other skills and virtues, they are the acquired fruits of instruction, habituation and individual commitment. It is a commonplace, moreover, that those who gain and employ these capacities successfully can find in their activities deep and enduring sources of satisfaction. And surely it is still possible to say of people who nurture and educate children that their 'human powers to achieve excellence and human conceptions of the ends and goods involved, are systematically extended.'

What are the virtues we hope to find in those who raise children? Chief on the list are gentleness, sensitivity, resilient cheerfulness, patience, and perhaps a sense of humility. Philosophers from Mary Wollstonecraft to Simone Weil and Iris Murdoch have seen that these are neither natural dispositions nor simple sentiments, but capacities involving discipline and active intelligence.[29] Women have cultivated the faculty of attentiveness through which one enters a child's individual reality to gain knowledge of his or her needs. Attentiveness involves the activities of listening and watching and this in turn

---

28 Ibid., 211 and 226

29 Sara Ruddick, 'Maternal Thinking' in *Rethinking the Family: Some Feminist Questions*, Barrie Thorne and Marilyn Yalom, eds. (London: Longmans 1982), 76-94

the ability to concentrate, to screen out distracting images and self-centered desires. What Iris Murdoch aptly calls 'the patient eye of love' is thus a human power developed in many women through the practice of rearing children.[30] (To this may be added many others, for example the intelligence needed to balance and order conflicting values in the guidance of a child's conduct and sensibility.)

Moreover, the practice of 'sustaining family life' involves much more than the narrowly defined activity of 'childcare.' Parents and grandparents, brothers and sisters, cousins, friends, and lovers are connected in a complex of relationships that make up the fabric of domesticity, even in the age of the nuclear family. Simple human weakness, combined with the centrifugal forces of modern life threaten these relations in countless ways, and traditionally it has fallen on women to perform the essential duties of their preservation and repair. While men competed and achieved in the public world, it was women in the main who, as Adrienne Rich put it, did 'the invisible weaving of a frayed and threadbare family life.'[31] Here too the traditional feminine virtues of gentleness, sensitivity and resilient good humor come into play.

Commercial civilization removed production, but not practices from the domestic sphere traditionally occupied by women. If virtue is character necessary for realizing the goods of practices, then the feminine virtues are unambiguously virtues. The problem is that these same qualities are *also* ideally suited for those who are obliged to serve and obey their superiors. Indeed a capacity for gentleness, attentiveness, humility and resilient good humor are essential resources for those from whom we expect uncomplaining self-sacrifice and devotion. Thus women who cultivated such character in their roles as sustainers of family life were simultaneously equipping themselves to be the humble and obedient helpmates to their

---

30 Iris Murdoch, *The Sovereignty of Good* (London: Routledge and Kegan Paul 1970), 31-40 and 91

31 Adrienne Rich, 'Conditions for Work: The Common World of Women,' in *Working It Out*, Sara Ruddick and Pamela Daniels, eds. (New York: Pantheon 1979), xvi

husbands. It appears then that virtue alone could not provide the independence and equality expected by Mary Wollstonecraft. On the contrary, we should expect the womanly virtues also to play an ideological role in maintaining women's subservient position in a male dominated society.

This ambiguity in feminine character is one of the central themes in Virginia Woolf's novel *To the Lighthouse*. Its story begins some years prior to the first world war. Mrs. Ramsay, wife of a prominent English philosopher and mother of eight, inspires a sense of wonder even in those who do not know her well. Both physically beautiful and virtuous in the ways discussed above, she lives her life somewhat self-consciously as a model of traditional womanly excellence. We see her first giving comfort to her six year old son James, who nurtures a desire to make a boat trip to the island lighthouse within view of the Ramsay's summer home and seaside estate. For the child the contemplated journey is an adventure tinged with mystical significance, and he hopes fervently that tomorrow it finally will occur. Mrs. Ramsay suspects the weather will not permit it, but feeling the intensity of her son's desire she will not dash his hopes. Overhearing their conversation Mr. Ramsay bluntly pronounces that the weather will not be fine ('Nonsense ... there wasn't the slightest possible chance that they could go to the Lighthouse tomorrow'). For him the occasion presents itself as a lesson in realism for James. When Mrs. Ramsay persists ('But it may be fine — I expect it will be fine'), Mr. Ramsay curses her sharply ('the extraordinary irrationalty of her remark, the folly of women's minds enraged him'). Mrs. Ramsay silently responds:

> To pursue truth with such astonishing lack of consideration for other people's feelings, to rend the thin veils of civilization so wantonly, so brutally, was to her so horrible an outrage of human decency that, without replying, dazed and blinded, she bent her head as if to let the pelt of jagged hail, the drench of dirty water, bespatter her unrebuked. There was nothing to be said.[32]

---

32 *To the Lighthouse* (New York: Harcourt Brace Jovanovich 1955), 51

We see here that Mrs. Ramsay understands the fragility of human life and relationships. Her role as 'sustainer of family life' bids her to preserve and strengthen the ties that make intimacy and friendship possible. The virtues of gentleness and sensitivity are for her elemental human values. Mr. Ramsay's 'realism,' on the other hand, is a quality essential for achievement in his competitive male world and more specifically, as he sees it, for success in his lonely and relentless quest for philosophical truth. Their conflicting conceptions of proper conduct therefore reflect rival ideas of 'human flourishing,' as MacIntyre would say, each grounded in practices that yield qualitatively different, incommensurable 'internal goods.'

Significantly, Mrs. Ramsay suppresses her outrage, which is nonetheless genuine and deeply rooted in convictions that guide her daily life. It is important to see the distinct but connected motivations for her doing so. First and foremost, it is her function in the household to provide Mr. Ramsay with the emotional support he needs in his quest for recognition in the public realm. Her role is to make his home a psychic refuge from the judgmental world in which he struggles for success. To question her husband's moral character, to subject him to severe judgment in the very place where he flees to escape such scrutiny, would constitute a betrayal of a sacred trust, a gross violation of her role as devoted wife. Moreover, Mrs. Ramsay *is* a devoted wife, and what makes this possible is her elevation of Mr. Ramsay's personal worth above her own: 'Universities and people wanting him, lectures and books and their being of the highest importance ... they must know of the two he was infinitely the more important, and what she gave the world, in comparison with what he gave, negligible.'[33] Thus her doubts and resentments are simply overwhelmed by her husband's splendor, and more generally by the achievements of *men* in the public world:

> What did it all mean? To this day she had no notion. A square root? What was that? Her sons knew. She leant on them ... She let it uphold and sustain her, this admirable fabric of the masculine intelligence, which ran up and down

---

33 Ibid., 62

> and crossed this way and that, like iron girders spanning the swaying fabric,
> upholding the world, so that she could trust herself to it utterly....[34]

Mrs. Ramsay's deference to her husband is rooted in her objective dependence on him, and justified in her mind by the mystery and magnificence of his accomplishments, of male accomplishments, for which she and all women owe a duty of service.

Yet Mrs. Ramsay's deference expresses not only the social inferiority of her sex, but also the substance of her moral concerns, and therein lies the ethical ambiguity in her character. We see this clearly when, later in the same day, she must perform in her role as provider of hospitality to a number of friends and houseguests whom the Ramsays have invited to dinner. Her task is formidable, since as it happens a tangle of suspicions, resentments, and self-doubts has soured the mood of all present. Seated at the head of the table, an exhausted Mrs. Ramsay ponders her responsibility to inspire congeniality among the sullen groups to whom she mechanically ladles the soup.

> Nothing seemed to have merged. They all sat separate. And the whole of the effort of merging and flowing and creating rested on her. Again she felt, as a fact without hostility, the sterility of men, for if she did not do it nobody would do it, and so, giving herself the little shake that one gives a watch that has stopped, the old familiar pulse began beating, as the watch begins ticking — one, two, three, one, two, three.[35]

Thus Mrs. Ramsay rouses herself out of her own fatigue and depression, becomes attentive to the vanities of her male guests, and once again initiates the ceremonies of fellowship and good cheer. The effort bears fruit. Before long humor, consideration and good will prevail, and as the evening ends one of the company recites poetry in homage to Mrs. Ramsay's beauty and life-restoring powers.

All the while we see the double-aspect of Mrs. Ramsay's virtues

---

34 Ibid., 159

35 Ibid., 126

reflected through the eyes of the story's other major female character, unmarried Lily Briscoe, an aspiring artist struggling to develop
a personal vision unrestricted by the fear of male judgment. Lily
watches Mrs. Ramsay's miracle at the dinner table and is struck by
intensely ambivalent feelings. To be sure, she admires Mrs. Ramsay's resilient cheerfulness, her talent for repairing the 'thin veil of
civilization.' On the other hand, she clearly sees the mechanism by
which Mrs. Ramsay works her magic. She must be 'nice to men,'
pander to their conceits, exhaust herself in sympathetic attentions
– and thereby sustain those relations between men and women that
require her sex to consistently stifle their powers of independent
thought and expression. Lily cannot deny either the essential humanity of Mrs. Ramsay's virtues or their ideological role in a structure of male domination. Both are aspects of her being.

At the novel's end the Lighthouse itself becomes a metaphor for
the contradictory facets of Mrs. Ramsay's character. Years later
James, now a young man, is at last on his way to the Lighthouse.
However, the voyage has taken on the character of a pilgrimage,
commanded by his father, to honor the memory of the long dead
Mrs. Ramsay. As the small boat approaches, James reflects:

> "It will rain," he remembered father saying. "You won't be able to go to the
> Lighthouse." The Lighthouse was then a silvery, misty-looking tower with
> a yellow eye, that opened suddenly, and softly in the evening. Now – James
> looked at the Lighthouse. He could see the white-washed rocks; the tower,
> stark and straight, he could see that it was barred with black and white; he
> could see windows in it; he could even see washing spread on the rocks to
> dry. So that was the Lighthouse, was it? No, the other was also the Light-
> house. For nothing was simply one thing. The other Lighthouse was true
> too....[36]

Mrs. Ramsay saw herself as a beacon by which others could steer
a safe course through life's perils. Does her luster vanish too as one
approaches for a closer look? Here was a person who repressed the
expression and consciousness of her own values in order to satisfy
male needs for consolation and applause, and who therefore was

---

36 Ibid., 276-7

not fully recognized, even by herself, as a rational being. In these facts we see her oppression. Nevertheless, the other Mrs. Ramsay was also true. For the very qualities that fostered her submission were also virtues unquestionably necessary for the practice of sustaining friendship and family life.

V Shared Aims and the Quest for the Good

The example of Mrs. Ramsay challenges the idea that modernity has eradicated practices in the domestic sphere. We may wonder then whether MacIntyre's ethics is able to acknowledge and account for the ethical complexity of Mrs. Ramsay's feminine virtues. If MacIntyre may not deny that Mrs. Ramsay's character serves to realize the internal goods of the practice of sustaining family life, must he then deny the ideological character of her virtues? In other words does the Ramsey marriage actually exemplify the conditions of life MacIntyre claims to be the basis for rationally grounded judgments of virtue? If so, Virginia Woolf's rendition of Victorian gender roles does damage to MacIntyre's general conception of ethical objectivity. It reveals that his doctrine fails to sustain the egalitarian implications of his own distinction between reason and ideology.

To reach a conclusion on this issue, further exposition of MacIntyre's position is needed. Let us note to begin with that *After Virtue* emphasizes the importance of a *shared* conception of the good life as the central condition for a rational ethics.

> The application of that measure in a community whose shared aim is the realization of the human good presupposes of course a wide range of agreement in that community on goods and virtues, and it is this agreement which makes possible the kind of bond between citizens which, on Aristotle's view, constitutes a *polis*. That bond is the bond of friendship and friendship is itself a virtue. The type of friendship which Aristotle has in mind is that which embodies a shared recognition of and pursuit of a good. It is this sharing which is essential and primary to the constitution of any form of community, whether that of a household or that of a city.[37]

---

37 *After Virtue*, 146

It could be argued then that Mrs. Ramsay's position of subjection and inferiority occurs only because her values (i.e., women's values) diverge from Mr. Ramsay's, while his are pre-eminent in their society. As Virginia Woolf put the matter elsewhere, 'It is obvious that the values of women differ very often from the values of men,' yet 'it is the masculine values which prevail.'[38] Seen in this light, the drama in Woolf's novel does not truly meet the conditions MacIntyre defines as 'primary' for non-ideological judgments of virtue — 'a shared recognition of and pursuit of a good.'

The trouble with this suggestion is that the idea of 'agreement on goods and virtues' or of a 'community whose shared aim is the realization of the human good' is critically unclear. Consider again the example of Mrs. Ramsay. In one sense she and her husband do share a conception of goods and virtues. Both hold to a once widely accepted view about the practices and virtues appropriate for men and women. Men of their class take on the duties of business, medicine, law, war, science, affairs of state, etc. Their virtues are suited to achievement in these professions. Women, as noted above, specialize in those qualities needed for the practices of sustaining family life. They depend on, respect and support male accomplishments in the public sphere, and in turn men recite poetry to honor the gentle restorative powers of the feminine soul. In this respect there is agreement between the sexes that their respective labors and virtues are *complementary* in nature. Moreover, there is a concensus that Mrs. Ramsay occupies a subordinate place in this union. 'They must know of the two he was infinitely the more important,' she says, and 'what she gave the world, in comparison with what he gave, negligible.' Since her role is to make his greater achievements possible, Mrs. Ramsay is willing to defer to her husband on those occasions when their interests and values conflict. What then of their bitter clash over the relative importance of truth and kindness? Here Mrs. Ramsay can perhaps take comfort in the thought that what may seem to her to be an imperfection in her husband's character is an example of how the one-sided qualities of each sex must be balanced to create a greater harmony in their union.

---

38 *A Room of One's Own* (New York: Harcourt Brace Jovanovich 1929), 76-7

There are passages in *After Virtue* which suggest that MacIntyre would indeed count this as the kind of agreement on which rational ethical judgment is founded. As an example of 'genuine friendship' based on 'shared concern' for a common good he cites Aristotle's reference to the relationship between husband and wife in the Greek household — a relationship clearly based on separate spheres of activity, a hierarchy of command, and distinguishable forms of virtue for rulers and their wives.[39] More importantly, MacIntyre argues that *justice* can be rationally defined in a society only where there is general agreement on what its members *deserve* — based on their ranking the contributions made by the various practices and their internal goods to the more general good of their community.[40] Here again the example of Mr. and Mrs. Ramsay is troublesome, for it seems that it is such a concensus on relative desert — on the greater 'importance' of what he 'gave the world' — that justifies Mrs. Ramsay's subjection to the authority of men. A 'just woman' is therefore a deferential woman — one who knows how to uncomplainingly subordinate her interests and judgment to the standards and achievements of the masculine world. In all this one finds in *After Virtue* the elements of a conservative and impeccably Aristotelian defense of sexual hierarchy that is altogether inconsistent with the egalitarian thrust of MacIntyre's quest for an ethics beyond ideology.

However, closer examination of MacIntyre's position does not permit this interpretation. To see this we must note that to qualify as a virtue it is insufficient that a given character is needed to achieve the internal goods of a practice. This is only the first of three defining criteria. The second stipulates that a quality must also 'contribute to the good of that kind of whole human life in which the goods of particular practices are integrated in an overall pattern of goals....'[41] A quality cannot be a virtue, therefore, if it leads to a fragmented life torn by contradictory values and incompatible activities. This is why ruthlessness or relentlessness cannot be virtues, ac-

---

39 See Susan Moller Okin, *Women in Western Political Thought* (Princeton, NJ: Princeton University Press 1979), chapter 4.
40 *After Virtue*, 143 and 188
41 *After Virtue*, 1984 edition, 275

cording to MacIntyre, even when they are necessary qualities for achievement in certain practices. The practice of exploring wilderness, for example, may require an ability to be ruthless in driving others to the limits of their endurance. Nevertheless:

> Such an ability may require as a condition of its exercise the cultivation of a certain insensitivity to the feelings of others ... transpose that complex of qualities onto participation in the practice of creating and sustaining the life of a family and you have a recipe for disaster.[42]

Ruthlessness is not a virtue, says MacIntyre, because it cannot be integrated into that 'whole human life,' which for the central agents in our society involves the practice of sustaining a family.

Now the same argument would apply equally to such characteristically masculine traits as pugnacity, ambition, and aggressiveness, in that they too tend to diminish one's sensitivity to the feelings of others. If ruthlessness and relentlessness fail the second test, these qualities must also be disqualified as virtues. It follows that MacIntyre has rejected the idea that men may specialize in the 'manly virtues' while women compensate by cultivating gentleness and compassion. He cannot allow the doctrine of complementary virtues to serve as the basis of the ethical agreement that establishes 'the bond of friendship' in the household. Traditional gender specialized character is rather a 'recipe for disaster.' On the nature of the calamity MacIntyre does not elaborate. Suffice it to say that a woman who devotedly attends to the physical and emotional needs of a man who is indisposed to reciprocate is in for a rough time, and is most unlikely to experience her relationship with him as a 'friendship.' On the contrary, before long she will have reason to conclude, as did Mrs. Ramsay, that she and her husband are two very different kinds of human beings.

---

42 Ibid.

Indeed, as the incident with young James reveals, Mr. and Mrs. Ramsay are divided by a profound difference in their conception of a good human being, each grounded in distinct practices that yield divergent and potentially rival ideas of living well. 'It is the masculine values that prevail,' says Virginia Woolf. When Mr. Ramsay curses and Mrs. Ramsay bows her head, we see a discordant marriage established on terms dictated by the superior power and position of the male. Thus the second constitutive condition of true virtue reveals the absence of an appropriately shared conception of the good within a household based upon the romantic idea of masculine and feminine character.

Attention to the various goods of practices is therefore only a point of departure for rational ethical judgment in a community. When we next turn to MacIntyre's third criterion, we see directly why he cannot regard the feminine qualities of Mrs. Ramsay either as unambiguously good. Here MacIntyre argues that it is important to seek an answer to the question: What is the *best* kind of life for members of our society to lead? To pose this question is to embark on a 'quest' for 'the good for man' — i.e., some general conception of a virtuous life for those who occupy a certain set of historically created social roles. For the individual such a quest involves the existential effort 'to overcome the harms, dangers, temptations and distractions' which threaten his or her personal ethical integrity. But the hazards of a life are not merely individual in nature. They arise in characteristic ways for those who bear a certain social identity. It follows that every individual's search for his or her own good has a profound cultural and intellectual dimension. One comes to see one's individual choices in the social and historical contexts from which they arise, and in seeking the best life for oneself one is led to formulate some general conception of the best life for all those who inhabit the central roles in one's society at its present point of development. As a father or mother, husband or wife, professional, worker, citizen, etc., one sees oneself then as an actor in a larger drama determining the direction of one's community as a whole. Reflecting upon the relationship among the various practices that constitute one's social world and the qualities of character they require, one asks: How do they contribute to or undermine the achievement of a harmonious and unitary life for their participants?

The quest for the 'good for man' therefore involves a public inquiry among people in need of an historical, sociological, and philosophical understanding of their society.[43]

We can say only this much about the good for man before it is specified by a quest undertaken within a particular community: it is 'the life spent in seeking the good life for man,' comprising 'the virtues necessary for the seeking ... those which will enable us to understand what more and what else the good life for man is.'[44] Thus we arrive at MacIntyre's third criterion of virtue. A quality is a virtue only if it fosters, or at least allows, participation in a critical, self-reflective social inquiry into the nature of the good for human beings in one's community.

The flaw in Mrs. Ramsay is that aspects of her feminine character exclude her from such an inquiry. It is not that the qualities of gentleness, patience, or sensitivity *in themselves* preclude the development of critical faculties. The trouble is that Mrs. Ramsay, as wife to Mr. Ramsay, must put these qualities in the service of a relationship that stunts the growth of independent thought and expression. Mrs. Ramsay has placed herself under the protection of men. She is required to trust male intelligence as the governing authority of the social order. As noted above, this childlike submission is essential to her part as Victorian 'angel in the house,' constantly responsive to the needs of men, and revered by them in turn for her life-giving powers. As Woolf puts it:

> ... she had the whole of the other sex under her protection; for reasons she could not explain, for their chivalry and valour, for the fact that they negotiated treaties, ruled India, controlled finance; finally for an attitude towards herself which no woman could fail to feel or to find agreeable, something trustful, childlike, reverential... and woe betide the girl — pray Heaven it was none of her daughters! — who did not feel the worth of it, and all that it implied, to the marrow of her bones![45]

---

43 *After Virtue*, 203-9

44 Ibid., 204

45 *To the Lighthouse*, 13

The 'protection' Mrs. Ramsay gives to the whole of the other sex is immunity from the independent, critical judgment of women. Given this obligation, her ability to understand herself and the totality of her social world is severely limited. Tragically, her nurturing character has become an obstacle to a free, self-reflective inquiry into the nature of the good – the quest which, for MacIntyre, is an essential condition for the unqualified realization of virtue.

MacIntyre's ethics, therefore, does not lead us to deny the ideological character of Mrs. Ramsay's virtues. In another world we might praise Mrs. Ramsay's character without reservation. As it is, we are forced to recognize how such dispositions have functioned to deprive women of important human goods, and how praise itself (e.g., the poetry recited for Mrs. Ramsay) can play a role in hiding this reality from their view.

VI Summary: After Virtue and Feminism

After Virtue aims to identify the essential conditions for objective, non-ideological ethical judgments. To succeed it must set boundaries which exclude conceptions of virtue that function to justify relations of domination and subordination. Does MacIntyre's philosophy allow us then to criticize norms of masculinity and femininity that have clearly played a role in a culture of sexual inequality? I have argued it does, although not in the way that MacIntyre himself suggests.

MacIntyre proposes that modern society, by removing production from the household, eliminated the sustaining of family life as a 'practice.' If this were true, women consigned to domestic roles would lack opportunity to develop their 'human powers to achieve excellence.' In this context 'feminine virtue' becomes a counterfeit of true virtue, and could not establish women's dignity and equality with men. I have argued, using the fictional example of Mrs. Ramsay, that commercial civilization did not render the lives of mothers and wives devoid of practices in this sense. Nevertheless the new order did create oppressive conditions for women and tainted the perfection to which they aspired as mothers and wives with an ideological aspect.

With production taken from the household and reorganized according to the norms of market society, the stage was set for the division of life into public and private spheres based on antithetical values. In this context the male head of the middle-class household will generally be led to cultivate qualities suitable for professional excellence, competitive success and public acclaim, while women specialize in qualities tailored to their duties of personal service. The union of these characters fails to produce a harmony of purpose between men and women based upon a shared conception of the good. On the contrary, the resulting division in ethical perception and understanding produces conflicts that can be resolved only by superior power, rather than by the concensus on human character and purpose that MacIntyre identifies as the basis for rational judgments about right and wrong.

Moreover, we should expect that superior power will reside in the male. He is economically independent. His educational and professional experience has equipped him not with a sensitivity to the needs of others, but with a desire for leadership and a disposition to prevail in a contest of wills. On the other hand, the nurturing character of his wife — her compassion, desire to please and willingness to provide emotional support for family and friends — is easily adapted for acts of submission. To this list of handicaps we must add the homage she owes to that 'admirable fabric of masculine intelligence' which gives her husband his superior social status. All these elements combine to establish her economic, emotional and intellectual dependency. In short, her need and duty to trust in her husband's rational powers stifles the development of independent, critical faculties indispensible to a practical and philosophical inquiry into the nature of the good. Given MacIntyre's analysis, this constitutes a condition of oppression. In so far as feminine, nurturing ideals foster and legitimize this oppression, their ideological nature is then established.

For MacIntyre qualities are genuine virtues only if they 'sustain the kind of households and kind of political communities in which men and women can seek the good together and the virtues necessary for philosophical enquiry into the nature of the good.'[46] Of course, we need to ask, what will such households be like, and on what form of male-female relations will they be founded? If my interpretation of *After Virtue* is correct, MacIntyre cannot respond with 'traditionalist' or 'Aristotelian' answers. To construct 'new forms of community' consistent with MacIntyre's conception of virtue is most definitely to abandon a world in which women are dependent upon men, and in which they are defined as the primary sustainers of family and personal life while men prepare themselves for projects in the public sphere. From all that has been said it follows that MacIntyre's ethics must lead its adherents to endorse the liberation of women from their confinement in traditional domestic roles.

Nevertheless, MacIntyre's commitments are clearly distinguishable from standard liberal affirmations of equal rights and opportunity. He envisions a society guided by a collective effort to define a shared conception of what makes a good human being. But this is possible, he contends, only for people who can enjoy a 'unitary life' − i.e., the life of a person with long-term commitments acting within a network of comparatively stable personal and community relationships. Repeatedly MacIntyre defines the virtues as qualities necessary to sustain the bonds of family and community against the centrifugal forces threatening their disintegration, and by this test the 'feminine virtues' qualify without question. He cannot, therefore, advocate the integration of women into the public world − as it is now constituted − without deep feelings of ambivalence.

To begin with, women's growing self-sufficiency and independence from men clearly undermines the cohesion and permanence of marriage and family life, at least in the forms we know it today. The stability of the nuclear family depended in large part upon women's economic and social dependency.[47] The more they are able to

---

46 *After Virtue*, 204. See 1984 edition, p. 275, where MacIntyre makes it clear he is proposing this as a defining condition of *any* genuine virtue.

47 See Barbara Epstein, 'Family Politics and the New Left,' *Socialist Review* **63-64** (May-August 1982), 141-61.

support themselves, the more likely it is that wives (and husbands) will choose separation when a marriage runs into trouble. Second, we should expect that as women pursue careers in a bureaucratically organized market competition, they will come to take on the qualities we associate now with masculine character. To the extent that women become more 'like men,' they will become morally less able to provide the services that we have all come to depend on for sustaining the ties of family, friendship and local community.[48]

When MacIntyre calls for the construction of new forms of society 'within which the moral life could be sustained,'[49] he is asking us to imagine a world in which women, and men, are able to combine the intellectual and spiritual independence desired by Wollstonecraft with the gentleness and attentiveness of a Mrs. Ramsay — a world in which sexual equality and the moral resources for nurturing life are achieved together. The catch is that the present social order renders these goals incompatible. To be independent and equal, women must now assimilate into the competitive, hierarchical world of market and bureaucracy. To retain their feminine nature, they must retreat into their subordinate domestic roles. There appears to be but one ethically sound solution to the dilemma. It must become possible for both men and women to share the responsibilities of household and public life without inhabiting discordant worlds with separate virtues. For this to occur the 'womanly' values

---

48 See Carol Gilligan, *In a Different Voice: Psychological Theory and Women's Development* (Cambridge, MA: Harvard University Press 1982). Gilligan finds a distinguishable feminine ethical sensibility that is adapted to traditional women's roles. See also Virginia Woolf's *Three Guineas* (New York: Harcourt Brace Jovanovich 1938). Woolf worried about the moral effects of women's entrance into the professions, as organized and practiced by men: '... the professions have an undeniable effect upon the professors. They make the people who practice them possessive, jealous of any infringement of their rights and highly combative if anyone dares dispute them. Are we not right then in thinking that if we enter the same profession we shall acquire the same qualities?' (66)

49 *After Virtue*, 244

of caring and mutuality can no longer be confined within the boundaries of the private house, but must be extended outward as the organizing principles of the larger community. Thus MacIntyre's discourse on the social conditions for a rational ethic can also be seen as a reflection on the philosophical foundations for a radical feminist transformation of the world we experience today.

CANADIAN JOURNAL OF PHILOSOPHY
Supplementary Volume 13

Women and Moral Madness

KATHRYN PAULY MORGAN
University of Toronto
Toronto, ON
Canada M5S 1A1

In one of Marge Piercy's poems, 'For Strong Women,' we find the following verse:

> A strong woman is a woman in whose head
> a voice is repeating, I told you so,
> ugly, bad girl, bitch, nag, shrill, witch,
> ballbuster, nobody will ever love you back,
> why aren't you feminine, why aren't
> you soft, why aren't you quiet, why
> aren't you dead?[1]

Similarly, we might say that a *moral woman* is a woman in whose head a voice is repeating words like 'immature,' 'pathological,' 'inadequate,' 'immoral,' 'evil.' What I explore in this paper are various ways in which a woman's moral voice and her sense of moral integrity can be twisted and destroyed by patriarchal ideology and lived experience. I claim that, ultimately, this experience can lead to a genuine sense of confusion and a kind of moral madness which

---

1 Marge Piercy, 'For Strong Women,' *Circles on the Water: Selected Poems of Marge Piercy* (New York: Knopf 1982), 257. Reprinted in Jane Thompson, ed., *Learning Liberation: Women's Response to Men's Education* (London: Croom Helm 1983), 7.

is then cited, in a patriarchal culture, to further discredit a woman's moral subjectivity.

In accounting for this experience, at least four different maneuvers in the area of ethical theory and moral practice are worth exploring. The first classical philosophical maneuver calls into question woman's capacity for full moral agency as a result of examining the concept of human nature. The second maneuver establishes a distinction between public and private morality, consigns women to the domain of private morality, and then claims that only the public domain of morality which is lived in by men counts as genuinely moral. The third maneuver involves ingenious moral contortions which permeate the lives of women resulting from various moral double-binds and moral metamorphoses. Trying to maintain one's sense of moral balance while living out these contortions often leads to a sense of bewilderment if not outright moral insanity. And the fourth is based on the perceived invisibility of actual moral domains in women's lives so that often women don't even recognize when we are being moral. I conclude with what might boldly be called a 'Prolegomena to a Feminist Moral Heuristic.'

I Women Are Denied Full Moral Agency

Women can be denied full moral agency in at least three separate ways: first, through a process of pseudo-blind gender essentialist thinking; second, by generating theories of women's nature which claim that women and men are either different in degree or kind to such an extent that women are, necessarily, inferior to men by nature; and, third, by alleging that women's lives are marked by a kind of negative moral epiphenomenalism.

The *first way* involves *pseudo-blind gender essentialist thinking*. Put crudely, it goes something like this: Philosophy involves the search for the knowledge of essences. Whether we define this as the search for the Platonic Form, the Paradigm Case, the Nature sought after by medievalists, the elusive finite joint set of Necessary and Sufficient Conditions, or the Natural Kinds sought after by contemporary philosophers, the message coming through is virtually the same: that there is some definite description which can be given which embodies essentialist knowledge of a particular type of X (leaving aside Wittgensteinian notions of family resemblance). The particular X that is relevant here is, of course, the concept of human nature. Striving to adopt the standpoint of a detached transcendental knower, many traditional philosophers hope to define human nature in a way which is unaffected by the vicissitudes of human history, human culture, and evolutionary variability.[2] Often such definitions (particularly in western philosophical thought) claim that for X to be *human*, X must be rational, decisive, capable of exercising authority, theoretically oriented, and capable of taking the moral point of view (which usually involves adopting a posture of moral impartiality derived from commitment to universalizable moral principles). Once armed with such essentialist criteria it simply remains to discover, as a matter of empirical practice, whether any beings satisfy these criteria for being human. It is perhaps distressing or uplifting, depending upon one's perspective, to discover that at least half the members of *Homo Sapiens* fulfil these criteria, namely, males. Thus, one concludes that, as simply a matter of 'pure' empirical fact, only men are capable of full moral agency. Proponents of this maneuver claim that since the question of essence has been raised in a purely abstract fashion there can be no charge of bias or distortion vis-à-vis the real world.

I claim that this is a ruse. I am inclined to accept the existence of such reflecting transcendental egos about as much as that of the Great Pumpkin. As far as I can determine only empirical egos engage in philosophical reasoning, and empirical egos invariably walk about in gendered garb.[3] I suspect that many analogous arguments

---

2 In his recent book, aptly entitled *The View from Nowhere*, Thomas Nagel is deeply attracted to but ultimately rejects this transcendental definition of individuality as workable in science and in ethics. Nevertheless, he does suggest that saints and mystics can achieve it. Thus, it seems to function as a kind of supererogatory moral ideal. See Thomas Nagel, *The View from Nowhere* (Oxford: Oxford University Press 1986).

3 In an interesting essay, another committed Kantian theorist, Robert Paul Wolff, struggles with the aspirations of Kantian moral theory and their seeming irrelevance when juxtaposed to his actual life. See Robert Paul Wolff, 'There's

(and their attendant theories of human nature) concerning, for example, abortion or sexual perversion are generated in order to support what are already taken for granted and fallaciously referred to as *'our* moral intuitions.' Similarly, I suspect that essentialist thinking of this sort already presupposes its not terribly surprising patriarchal outcome and is generated to support widely pervasive social and political 'intuitions.'⁴ The upshot of this method of reasoning is that women are ruled out, in pseudo-a priori fashion, from the moral community.

The *second method* denies women full moral personhood by *generating theories about the nature of woman which claim that women differ from men either in degree or kind such that women are not entitled to full moral agency.*

An example of the Difference-in-Degree theory is Aristotle's. Aristotle maintains, in the *Politics*, that there are two necessary criteria for full moral agency: one must have (1) a fully developed deliberative rational faculty which is (2) capable of exercising authority. As he puts it, '... to be good a person must have the sort of understanding which issues in commands' (1143a8). Since, for a variety of reasons, woman's nature is such as to permit only a partial share in deliberative faculty so that women lack a sense of authority, the most that a woman can aspire to, from a moral point of view, is to be aligned with a fully developed man of moral integrity and to obey his commands silently (1260a4; 1260a30). The possibility of independent, self-sufficient moral integrity is ruled out for women but a life of virtue *commensurate* with a woman's essential moral limitations is not — provided that she is fortunate in her patriarchal associations.

Nobody Here But Us Persons,' in Carol Gould and Marx Wartofsky, eds., *Women and Philosophy: Toward a Theory of Liberation* (New York: G.P. Putnam's Sons 1976).

4 Virtually all of this thinking has been carried out by men in situations in which the labour of women performed under conditions of patriarchal oppression has made possible the very philosophical enterprise itself which consigns women to that labour.

This view is put starkly by Aquinas who claims that 'As regards the individual nature, woman is defective and misbegotten, for the active force in the male seed tends to the production of a perfect likeness in the masculine sex ....'[5] As a result, Aquinas maintains that '... woman is naturally subject to man, because in man the discretion of reason predominates'[6] and, as an applied corollary, that it is proper that women be denied full moral-religious personhoood as priests because '... it is not possible in the female sex to signify eminence of degree.'[7] One of the obvious consequences of the impossibility of signifying eminence of degree is that women are capable, at most, only of moral mediocrity when set against the standard established by fully developed moral men. The parallel here with the work of moral developmentalist Lawrence Kohlberg should be obvious.[8] According to Kohlberg's theory of cognitive stage moral development, women fail to advance beyond the deplorable stage of conventional morality and are thus regarded as morally immature in relation to fully developed moral men.

When patriarchal philosophers are not engaged in arguing for a Difference-in-Degree theory, they are often occupied in arguing for some sort of Difference-in-Kind theory. For example, in the *Emile*, Rousseau argues that boys should be brought up in such a way that they become self-directed, active, strong, theoretically

---

5 Aquinas, *Summa Theologica*, Part I, Question 92, Reply to Objection 1 (Westminster, MD: Christian Classics 1981)

6 Ibid., Reply to Objection 2

7 Ibid., Part III, Question 39, Reply to Objection 3

8 See, for example, Laurence Kohlberg, 'Moral Stages and Moralization: The Cognitive-Developmental Approach,' in T. Lickona, ed., *Moral Development and Behavior: Theory, Research, and Social Issues* (New York: Holt, Rinehart and Winston 1976); *The Philosophy of Moral Development* (San Francisco: Harper and Row 1981). Kohlberg's most well-known feminist critic is Carol Gilligan, *In a Different Voice: Psychological Theory and Women's Development* (Cambridge, MA: Harvard University Press 1982).

oriented, and capable of rational masterfulness.[9] Girls, on the other hand, should be raised in such a way as to be profoundly other-defined so that even a woman's own virtue must be partly constituted out of public opinion of her and not simply out of her private moral acts and intentions. According to Rousseau, women are by nature made to please, to be dominated. A woman's passivity, her weakness, her submissiveness, and her resultant reliance on guileful manipulation are taken by Rousseau to be marks of her moral virtue lived out by a woman who is obedient, loyal, and sentimental.[10] Rousseau assigns woman a different morality because, like many thinkers, he does not regard women capable of theoretical reasoning. At the same time, he claims that such rationality is a necessary precondition for a self-directed moral life.

Similarly, in the chapter 'On the Distinction of the Beautiful and the Sublime,' Kant maintains that boys and men are capable of a deep understanding, of noble virtue, and of leading a life according to rational moral principle.[11] In contrast, woman's morality should essentially be one of sentiment, governed by irrational moral feelings of aversion and beauty. To compensate for the incapacity to live according to rationally understood moral principles which are chosen autonomously, women are constructed to resonate with moral feelings, sensations, and sentiments — data of consciousness which are notorious for their episodic and variable nature. While capable of moving women to action, such feelings and sentiments are, by virtue of their intrinsic character, necessarily inferior moral 'data' when compared with the permanence provided by universalizable principles.

While Rousseau, Kant, and other philosophers of this persuasion insist that what we have here is a kind of fundamental moral equali-

---

9 Jean-Jacques Rousseau, *The* Emile *of J-J. Rousseau*, trans. William Boyd (New York: Teachers College 1962); originally published in 1779.

10 See Book V, concerning the education of Sophie.

11 See Immanuel Kant, *Observations on the Feeling of the Beautiful and Sublime*, trans. John Goldthwait (Berkeley: University of California Press 1960), 76-96

ty, it is also noteworthy that like the Difference in Degree theorists they, too, recommend patriarchal social arrangements. This shows an ideological bias at work. Such recommendations are inconsistent with these alleged claims to moral *equality*. Egalitarian complementarity would generate, at best, a heterosexual set of recommendations, *not* patriarchal ones.

In either case the message is clear: women are ruled out as full participants in the relevant moral community. At best, women can aspire to be affiliated, as a kind of moral groupie, with a man of moral integrity and partake in the goodness of his moral life.

The *third method* of denying women full moral agency is by claiming that, at best, women are *negative moral epiphenomenalists*. What I mean by this is that women's bodies are interpreted as capable of acting upon the mind so as to occlude consciousness, thought, and moral feeling. And this is assumed to be an asymmetrical process, hence the epiphenomenal characterization of the process. The mind is not regarded as capable of taking control over these processes in any rational fashion. An hysterial woman is beyond the rational pale.

Sometimes the form that this theory takes is absolute, viz. that simply by virtue of their embodiment as women, women just are closer to nature and, hence, not capable of the kind of thought that is necessary for human moral life.[12] Often the allegations concerning the afflicting nature of women's bodies are grounded in elaborate physiological theories based on an impressive array of scientific observations which war with each other in trying to decide what is the fundamental cause of the moral disorder: the uterus, the ovaries, the softness of women's musculature, female hormones, or brain development and morphology.[13] Whatever the outcome of the de-

---

12 For two feminist discussions of this notion, see Simone de Beauvoir, *The Second Sex*, trans. H.M. Parshley (New York: Vintage 1952), esp. Chs. 1 and 9 (Beauvoir discusses both the drawbacks and the potential power of such an identification), and Sherry B. Ortner, 'Is Female to Male as Nature is to Culture?' in Michelle Zimbalist Rosaldo and Louise Lamphere, eds., *Women, Culture, and Society* (Stanford, CA: Stanford University Press 1974).

13 See Brian Easlea, *Science and Sexual Oppression: Patriarchy's Confrontation with*

bates, the claim is much the same as that of Professor Holbrook who, in 1870, said that it seemed '... as if the Almighty, in creating the female sex, *had taken the uterus and built up a woman around it.*'[14]

The more interesting theories are those that support *episodic moral epiphenomenalism* by claiming that there are various normally occurring processes that occur in women's bodies which lead to a kind of moral derangement, that for given episodes of our lives we are necessarily crazy in some respect or other because of how our *healthy* womanly bodies operate. In many cultures, women who are menstruating are expected to be in some deranged and dangerous physical state. Women who are pregnant are expected to behave in peculiar sorts of ways and express bizarre preferences. In the Canadian *Criminal Code* women who have just given birth are expected to go into a period of insanity, especially if they breast-feed their infants.[15] Consequently, murder of a newborn infant by the mother is not treated like other kinds of murder even though it may occur several months after the birth. Menopause is assumed to be a state of derangement which goes on for years.[16] Similarly, postmenopausal women are expected to be permanently disordered because of the severity of the identity crises surrounding the ter-

Woman and Nature (London: Weidenfeld and Nicolson 1981), chs. 3, 5; also Marian Lowe, 'The Dialectic of Biology and Culture,' in Ruth Hubbard, Mary Sue Henifrin and Barbara Fried, eds., *The Biological Woman: The Convenient Myth* (Cambridge, MA: Schenkman 1982).

14 Barbara Ehrenreich and Deirdre English, *For Her Own Good: 150 Years of Experts' Advice to Women* (New York: Doubleday Anchor 1978), 120

15 See Martin's *Criminal Code*, 1983, Article 216: 'A female person commits infanticide when by a willful act or omission she causes the death of her newly-born child, if at the time of the act or omission she is not fully recovered from the effects of giving birth to the child and by reason thereof or of the effect of lactation consequent on the birth of the child her mind is then disturbed.'

16 In a recent judgment in British Columbia a 'Menopausal Woman' (note the use of this phrase as a kind of proper name) was removed from jury duty — one of the exercises of moral-political rationality — on the ground that she was unfit to serve because she was in menopause.

mination of reproductively-defined womanhood.[17] Now, pre-menstrual stress has been added to the list of morally disabling af-flictions and baptized with the name of 'syndrome' in order to indi-cate its prominence in virtually all women's lives. In a variety of recent court cases in Britain and in North America women are claim-ing diminished moral responsibility for an offence because they were acting during their pre-menstrual period.[18]

With all these episodic exclusions from moral life due to one's healthy embodiment as a woman, I reckon that we are left with ap-proximately 3-5 days per month during which we can act and be held fully morally responsible. But this only occurs during our child-bearing years. Once into menopause or post-menopausal, our moral eligibility disappears altogether.

In many of these contexts women are seen either as more em-bodied than men or as embodied in morally damaging ways. In either case we find the fallacious inference that, therefore, women are less capable of full moral agency than men who achieve detach-ment, transcendence, and alienated control over their bodies. We need never worry about disabling *testeria* in men. Needless to say, these theories generate intense feelings of misogynistic somatopho-bia and are often appealed to as justification of greater external con-trol and societal regulation of women than they do of men who are accorded moral autonomy.

The upshot of all these theories, then, is the disqualification of women from what is defined as a full moral life in what is regarded

---

17 See Rosaline Barnett and Grace Baruch, 'Women in the Middle Years: Con-ceptions and Misconceptions,' in Juanita Williams, ed., *Psychology of Women: Selected Readings* (New York: Norton 1979), 479-87. This article exposes patri-archal twisting of research findings on the allegedly universal 'Empty Nest Syndrome.'

18 For a critical analysis of the so-called scientific and epidemiological literature on pre-menstrual syndrome, see Anne Fausto-Sterling, *Myths of Gender* (New York: Basic Books 1985). For a critical discussion of this and similar decisions, see Hilary Allen, 'At the Mercy of Her Hormones: Premenstral Tension and the Law,' *M/F* 9 (1984).

as the community of moral persons.[19] (I return to the question of the masculinist aspect of these definitions below.)

II The Exclusion of Women from the Public Domain

Although various permutations occur in western theory, a sharp distinction is often drawn between public and private life. In some moral theories such as Plato's *Republic* or Hegel's theory of the state, the moral life of those with the greatest moral responsibility is entirely public. In the *Republic*, for example, the lives of the rulers are lives devoid of private property, private sexual relationships, and privatized familial relations. The publicizing of their lives, as it were, is rationally justified by the pivotal political role expected of them. In theories where life is not wholly public, it is still clear that participation in public life usually has pride of place.[20] Sometimes it is only the social or public domain which is accorded moral status.

However the variations occur, the distinction between the public and the private continues to play an important contributing role to women's madness. It happens like this: We begin by postulating two kinds of morality: public morality and private morality. Leaving aside Machiavellian scepticism regarding the possibility of public morality, we say that public morality is just that kind of morality that is expected in a moral public domain. It is characterized by claims to impartiality, reciprocity, universalizability, and absence of emotional distortion or bias. The proper moral agent is seen as a

---

19 For an acute theoretical discussion of this move, see Marilyn Frye, 'Male Chauvinism,' in Robert Baker and Frederick Ellison, eds., *Philosophy and Sex*, 1st edition (Buffalo, NY: Prometheus Books 1975). For an extended historical analysis of the philosophical tradition, see Genevieve Lloyd, *The Man of Reason: 'Male' and 'Female' in Western Philosophy* (Minneapolis: University of Minnesota Press 1984).

20 For two representative discussions of this distinction, see Hannah Arendt, *The Human Condition* (Chicago: University of Chicago Press 1958), and Jean Bethke Elshtain, *Public Man, Private Woman: Women in Social and Political Thought* (Princeton: Princeton University Press 1980). Also Ch. 5 of Lloyd.

detached, autonomous identityless atomic individual whose actual position is hidden behind a 'veil of ignorance.' Adopting these aims as one's moral ideals and striving to live according to them comes to be called 'taking the moral point of view.'

Private morality, then, pertains to the domain of the personal. It is immediate, situation-specific, focussed on particular individuals and relationships.[21] It is interpersonal and involves personal feelings as morally relevant factors. As a morality it is grounded in our social relatedness to other specific individuals who are friends, or family, or preferred members of a significant social group. Girls and women are socialized into, are expected to be, are praised for, and are gender-defined as experts in the domain of interpersonal feelings because of our alleged capacity for the sensitive concrete attentiveness so important in sustaining personal relations.

So far so good. What often happens at this point, however, is morally grotesque. As I noted above, the first stage of this maneuver equates public morality with morality per se. This leads to a profound devaluing of private or personal morality and often undercuts its claim to moral legitimacy altogether. The second stage generates a theory which maintains that if someone does have expertise in the area of private or personal morality this is a kind of 'default expertise.' That is, often such theories will claim that it is *because* of women's diminished rationality and congenital incapacity for a life of *principled* morality that she becomes an expert in the life of moral and psychological sentiment. This again devalues whatever moral excellences are to be found within this domain. Third, a women's moral excellences, the very nature of her allegedly moral self, are transmuted into a pitiable amoral form of agency. Her sense of relatedness and connection becomes labelled and then denounced as 'other-definition' or 'field-dependence,' and the

---

21 For a recent discussion of this distinction see the essays by Stuart Hampshire, 'Morality and Pessimism' and 'Public and Private Morality,' in *Public and Private Morality* (Cambridge: Cambridge University Press 1978). Hampshire discusses, among other things, the challenges presented to the concept of public morality by Machiavellian models of public life.

ground of her moral judgment is seen as involuntarily heteronomous rather than autonomous. Resulting from her feeble intellect,
a women's attentiveness to the concrete and the particular is seen
to disqualify her from participation in the forms of public life and
public morality.[22] Consequently, any claim to legitimate moral agency disintegrates.

Through skilful manipulation, then, of the public/private distinction not only are women obviously disqualified from full participation in the moral community. We are first told that there is a moral
domain in which we achieve excellence. Then we are told that we
can only achieve excellence in that domain. Then we are told that
this domain is not a domain in which morality operates in its most
exemplary way — if at all. And finally we are blamed for living our
moral lives in that domain while being told that we can do no other.
This must generate moral confusion if not outright madness.

III Moral Contortion: The Generation of Moral Insanity

Moral insanity can be generated in a variety of ways. In this section
I examine two such ways: (1) the metamorphoses of womanly vices
into virtues and virtues into vices, and (2) the setting up of feminine moral double-binds.

Moral Metamorphoses

Womanly vices can be turned into virtues in a variety of ways. One
way is to socialize women into illusory or distorted moral
paradigms.[23] Often these distorted paradigms are camouflaged as

---

22 Even a thinker as emancipated as John Stuart Mill succumbs to this kind of
thinking, though not as the result of an essentialist line of thinking. See J.S.
Mill, *The Subjection of Women*, reprinted in Alice Rossi, eds., *Essays on Sex Equality*
(Chicago: University of Chicago Press 1970).

23 Blum et al. discuss the notion of distorted paradigms. See L. Blum, M. Homiak, J. Houseman and N. Sheman, 'Altruism and Women's Oppression,' in
Gould and Wartofsky, eds., *Women and Philosophy*, 222-47.

moral 'vocations' calling to women in the name of destiny and womanly fulfillment and which require person-specific altruism of women as mothers, wives, and heterosexual lovers. As one examines these situations in detail what one very often uncovers is an appalling glorification of servility and consequent destruction of anything remotely resembling the kind of personal integrity (as distinct from autonomy) which must be preserved in any moral life.[24]

For example, works like *Fascinating Womanhood* and *The Total Woman* follow the Rousseauvian tradition and instruct women to dispense with an air of strength, ability, competence, and fearlessness and, instead, to cultivate the 'virtues' of submissiveness, fraility, fearfulness, guile, seduction, and economic dependence.[25] As one author puts it, the virtuous heterosexually fascinating woman should take as her moral role model the little canary![26]

The message that comes through is that the personal sense of power built into effective individual self-determination is morally bad; that powerlessness, self-abnegating self-sacrifice, and male-identified forms of dependence are what are really morally fulfilling for a good woman.

An inverted twist occurs when 'liberated' women are encouraged to adopt distorted moral paradigms of independence and self-sufficiency. As Andrea Canaan put it,

> By the time I was a woman, I had all the necessary external survival skills needed, supposedly, to protect me from rejection and humiliation projected onto me by white media, government, church, and social institutions. I had unending strength, ever-growing intellect, a heart as big as the heavens and

---

24 I distinguish moral integrity (which entails a moral and particular sense of connectedness and definition through others) from the notion of transcendent, detached, individual autonomy. I regard the latter as a form of conceptual pathology which pervades much of traditional and modern ethical theory (though the emphasis on autonomy per se is more distinctly Kantian and post-Kantian).

25 Helen B. Andelin, *Fascinating Womanhood* (New York: Bantam 1974); Marabel Morgan, *The Total Woman* (Markham, ON: Simon and Schuster 1975)

26 Andelin, 270

earth, a soul more forgiving than gods themselves, and I accepted total responsibility for myself, my own oppressed state, the oppression of the brown man, and the sin of being both brown and woman. This super-woman veneer protected me from the external world much of the time. This super-woman veneer also warded off internal self-reflection needed to assess if indeed I was strong enough to carry such heavy burdens. The ever-growing intellect was an additional burden because the ability to think allows me to look at, if not truly see, options and truth. The open heart and forgiving soul stifled my rightful indignation, gagged my rage, and forced my fear, my needs, my rage, my joys, my accomplishments, inward. The acceptance of total responsibility, real, concrete, or abstract, for myself and others became my ultimate strait jacket, the last and strongest barrier to self.[27]

I would claim that in all these cases women are socialized into and invited to participate in forms of vice masquerading as 'womanly virtues.' And vicious they are because they destroy the capacity for moral agency in the name of its very fulfillment. They do not, however, altogether shed their identity as vices in male-defined moral contexts. As a result, women are simultaneously blamed and praised for their acquisition. This can drive us crazy.

The reverse metamorphosis – virtues being turned into vices – is equally devastating in its consequences. In the first instance, 'manly' virtues are seen as vices when displayed by women. What appear to be defined, in the abstract as virtues per se often are seen as gender incongruent and blameworthy in women. As a result, a virtuous woman may be regarded as 'deviant' and her dispositions to behave labelled 'vices.' For example, if a woman is publicly described primarily as rational, strong, courageous, and decisive, she is labelled 'masculine' and seen to be lacking in *womanly* excellences. She cannot simultaneously display these moral strengths and be a woman. Or if she displays some subsets of these abilities, such as rational decisiveness and strength, she might be cast as evil. The images of Eve, of Lilith, of Pandora, of the vari-

---

27 Andrea Canaan, 'Brownness,' in Cherrie Moraga and Gloria Anzaldua, eds., *This Bridge Called My Back* (Waterton, MA: Persephone Press 1981), 233

ous active mothers and stepmothers in the western fairytales come immediately to mind.[28]

In the second instance, characteristically 'womanly' virtues are regarded as vices. Nurturing, helping, and sustaining the growth of others – the morally worthy aspects of altruism – are cited as evidence of woman's normal but pathological masochism.[29] Even though a woman's open emotional expressiveness may put her in a better epistemic position to make moral judgments than practicing postures of emotional closure and denial, this very expressiveness is cited as a disqualification for moral responsibility. Ironically, a finely developed empathetic imagination is cited as a reason for eliminating women from positions that require sensitive moral reflection on the grounds that the alleged requisite of hyper-detachment cannot be achieved. Receptivity becomes labelled 'passivity' and denounced while simultaneously encouraged. A woman's refusal to compete in situations which entail someone else's failure and to prize cooperation over domination is described as her deplorable 'fear of success.'[30]

Finally, mediating gender coding takes its toll. Classical moral theory would have us believe that certain actions or certain intentions simply are, in themselves, intrinsically moral or immoral, or, if circumstances affect this judgment, those circumstances are objectively pertaining states of affairs in the world. So goes the ideology but not the practice. Often our moral assessment is gender-dependent. Consider the following anecdote:

> Buckingham Palace has announced that 19-year old Prince Charles of England, the demure English rose and heir to the throne, has become engaged to Lady

---

28 See Andrea Dworkin, 'The Fairy Tales,' chs. 1 & 2, in *Woman Hating* (New York: E.P. Dutton 1974); Madonna Kobenschlag, *Kiss Sleeping Beauty Good-Bye* (New York: Bantam 1981).

29 For an extended analysis of this move, see Paula Caplan, 'The Myth of Masochism,' *American Psychologist* **39**, 2, (1984) 130-9.

30 For an excellent and perceptive discussion of these metamorphoses, see Jean Baker Miller, *Toward a New Psychology of Woman* (Boston: Beacon Press 1976). See especially chs. 4, 5.

Diana Spencer, the 32-year-old, worldly woman who has been seeking the "right" royal husband for ten years. (It has been stated by reliable sources that Charles is still a virgin. It is acknowledged in royal circles that Lady Diana has had several affairs over the past ten years.) When interviewed, Charles blushed sweetly over his engagement ring, and giggled happily on the TV news. The Queen had happily assented to Lady Diana's request for Charles' hand in marriage. Because of Diana's age and the fact that she is a self-proclaimed opponent of men's liberation, it is expected that the quiet prince will merge his identity with hers.[31]

At the time that the symmetrical column appeared in the press, groans of traditionalism were heard but no particular moral outrage was expressed at the thought that Diana would merge her identity with his. But this inversion of the situation does prompt such moral reactions in addition to the amusement derived from the ludicrous gender incongruence in the passage in question. But why should gender mediate our moral judgments?

Consider similar gender mediated moral assessments in an administrative context where often the identical behaviour is assessed in a praiseworthy way when the moral agent is male and in a blameworthy way when the moral agent is female. His style is praised for being aggressive and assertive; hers is denounced as pushy. He is praised for his attention to detail; she is reprimanded for her pickiness. He is seen as steadfast; she is seen as dogmatic and hard. He is valued for his firm judgments; she is deplored for her prejudices and biases. He is admired for his courageous frankness and straightforwardness; she is labelled mouthy and strident. He is seen as witty; she is experienced and blamed for being sarcastic. And so on. What are virtues in him are, invariably, vices in her. In each case, gender is mediating the judgments and personal assessments in the situation. Thus, it would appear that even if women try to emulate men who are seen as fully developed moral players in the game of morality, women will still fail because such emulation, *per impossibile*, cannot literally be seen or experienced as the *same* moral behaviour.

---

31 I am grateful to Norma Shearer and other students in my Philosophy of Feminism class for providing me with this example.

I conclude, then, that in all three types of moral metamorphoses women are put into the impossible moral position of simultaneously being moral and immoral, virtuous and vicious, for the *same* dispositions and behaviour. To try to understand this situation from the inside, to try to live out these moral prescriptions is to live not only in a situation of moral chaos but in a kind of moral madness.

Moral Double-Binds

It is clear that women can become morally insane as a result of these metamorphoses. But this is not the only pressure bearing upon us. In many societies, women are socialized to aspire to life situations which involve them in self-destroying moral double-binds. In western societies, two such situations are (1) leading a life committed to romantic love and (2) having recourse to personal manipulative power as a life defining power strategy.

(1) *Romantic Love*

The situation of romantic love is morally paradoxical and deeply threatening for women. It is morally paradoxical because it requires submission to and absorption into the identity of another in the name of one's own growth and identity realization. It is deeply threatening because, almost by definition, it entails identity destroying servility as its operating dynamic and underlying moral principle.[32]
There is a long tradition of western thought which celebrates the suggestion that loving is a woman's central vocation, that it is her highest purpose in life and that which most confirms her womanliness. What is particularly prized in this loving devotion is its unconditional character as a commitment to person-specific altruism. Whether one examines the lyrics of the familiar song 'Stand by your

---

32 For an extended analysis of this experience and ideology of love, see Simone de Beauvoir, chapter 23, 'The Woman in Love,' and my essay 'Romantic Love, Altruism, and Self-Respect,' *Hypatia* 1, 1, 117-48. This essay is reprinted in Greta Nemiroff, ed., *Woman and Man* (Toronto: Fitzhenry and Whiteside 1986).

Man' or notes Rousseau's admonitions to Sophie, the message is clear: the loving woman's moral obligation is to stay committed even in situations of manifest injustice and violence. Through loving, a woman hopes to realize her identity, stabilize her locus of value, acquire significance as a woman, integrate her eroticism, and live a life of moral self-respect gained through her commitment to her lover. One consequence of this moral commitment is that the woman comes to feel that any self-regarding intention or act is a *selfish* betrayal of her commitment to her lover. In this powerful way, then, gender and morality become inextricably intertwined for a woman in love.

Because of the totality of the commitment required women are taught to seek out a superior person to whom they will make this commitment. The commitment is honestly undertaken in the name of growth, of fulfillment, of realization of value. But the very dynamic and commitment chosen to achieve these goods rules out their realization. Ultimately, in many cases of romantic commitment, the situation degenerates into one of abject servility. As the woman in love becomes more and more aware of the vulnerability of her position, she engages in tactical behaviour which can have only a negative outcome. If she succeeds in gaining control over her lover (thereby reducing her terrifying metaphysical vulnerability), he or she loses status in her eyes and is no longer worthy of her commitment. If she fails in her maneuvers, then she is even more powerless than prior to her attempt and can only become more abject in the situation. Moreover, to the extent that romantic love is an asymmetrical identification relationship of a woman becoming absorbed into the identity of her lover, the very dynamic itself eliminates the conditions of the possibility of genuine love.

Thus we see that two moral double-binds are at work here: (1) that in attempting to create and realize her own identity in the name of moral self-determination, the woman in love enters into precisely a kind of relationship which, by its very nature, will make that moral self-determination impossible and which will likely lead to terrifying servility on her part. What promises her fulfillment ends up destroying her; and (2) that the love which is sought after, as a genuine moral good, is rendered impossible by the very dynamic which promises to create it.

(2) *Manipulative Power*

Women also experience moral double-binds with respect to the use of manipulative power. Manipulative power can be distinguished from other sorts of power such as coercion, reward power, expertise power, or positional power attached to a social role or position.[33] It differs from these because it is not publicly acknowledged and often one assumes that some covert form of management is taking place.

Women are driven to use manipulative power for a variety of reasons. First, women who exist in situations of poverty, of racial or heterosexist oppression, or who live under conditions of personal or political violence often have recourse to manipulative power because it is the only form of power available to them. Second, even when women do have access to other forms of power, we are not perceived by others or even by ourselves as genuinely having access to power. Attribution Theory in psychology documents all too easily the tendency of women to attribute our success to factors outside ourselves, e.g. luck, the position of the moon, some chance event, rather than claim it as a form of power within. Third, as women we are *expected* to be manipulative; it is gender congruent. Whether we look at the images of women in Homeric literature or the *Malleus Maleficarum* or Rousseau or the instruction books on Total Womanhood, it is clear that women are assumed to be naturally seductive, cunning, guileful, and manipulative. Such gender congruence becomes an important factor in a society such as ours where access to and practice of virtually all the other forms of power threaten to be coded as 'masculine' and labelled deviant when exercised by women. And the penalties for gender deviance are severe. Remember the line in the Piercy poem, '... bitch, nag, shrill, witch, ballbuster, nobody will ever love you back, why aren't you feminine ...?'

---

33 For a discussion of these forms of power, see the chapter 'Women and Interpersonal Power' in I. Frieze, J. Parsons, P. Johnson, D. Ruble and G. Zellman, eds., *Women and Sex Roles* (New York: Norton 1978), 301-20.

The double-binds involved in the use of manipulative power are multiple. It is generally agreed that the most effective way to exercise manipulative power is by simulating a position of weakness and vulnerability. What is problematic about this for women is that it gives actual support to a long patriarchal tradition which already regards women as 'the weaker sex' both intellectually and morally. In addition, it sustains that specific perception of the woman who is simulating weakness in order to gain power. While her manipulative tactic can gain her some immediate good, it almost invariably weakens her position in subsequent power negotiations. Moreover, role-playing is a powerful psychological mode in which, as social learning theorists point out, role-engulfment is an ever present danger. This means that the manipulative woman can, all too easily, come to see herself as weak and defenseless as well as encouraging this public perception of her. She is thereby effectively eliminated from a search for more publicly acknowledged or collective forms of power by both private and public perceptions of herself. A further difficulty with the use of manipulative power is that it is seldom cumulative. Again, a woman is encouraged and expected to behave in such a way that the very means she uses to gain power in the name of independent self-determination weaken her both publicly and privately and rule out, in principle, genuinely moral intercourse to the extent that such manipulation is covert.

To the extent, then, that women are socialized into lives of romantic love and restricted to the use of manipulative power, to that extent our lives will be filled with moral paradoxes and double-binds which contribute to our sense of moral madness.

IV The Invisibility of Moral Domains

The last factor contributing to women's moral madness is what I refer to as the invisibility of women's moral domains. What I mean by this is that very often only certain domains of human life are accorded moral status. As a result, it is difficult for women and men, literally, to *see* certain dimensions of women's lives as worthy of moral consideration. As a result, we become confused about whether what we are doing has any moral worth whatsoever and whether there are any operative moral standards. Consider the following anecdote. In a university class, the instructor asked the students to say a little bit about themselves by way of introduction to their classmates. Various interesting narratives followed but none was quite as instructive as that of a woman in her early fifties who said that 'She raised seven children and then she went back to work.' It was instructive because it highlighted two of the important domains in women's lives which are not usually accorded moral worth and significance: maternal practice, and domestic labour.

Although mothers are standardly blamed in the current clinical literature for well over 70 problems ranging from sleepwalking, ulcerative colitis, hyperactivity, peer avoidance, delusions, poor language development, and inability to deal with colour blindness, maternal practice is, nevertheless, a *morally* camouflaged process.[34] Hidden under the conceptual umbrella of 'maternal instinct,' mothering is regarded as a natural process which arises spontaneously between biological neonate and female parent between whom there is assumed to be a powerful bond which triggers mothering in normal cases. As a result, crucial questions of a social, political, and moral nature are not raised with respect to this human artifact called mothering. While some moral content must be assigned to such normative terms as 'perfect mother,' 'smothering mother,' 'bad mother' and so on, little moral subtlety is to be found.[35] And historically and theoretically, the domain of mothering and reproductive labour has been seen as, at best, a deficient and devalued moral domain involved with concerns which are individualized, private, and infantile. Often this realm is regarded as morally insignificant when compared with the transpersonal, universalizable domains of public institutional life. As a result, it is not surprising that women

---

34 See Paula Caplan and Ian Hall McCorquodale, 'Mother-Blaming in Major Clinical Journals,' *American Journal of Orthopsychiatry* (July 1985).

35 Ruddick has, of course, done much to begin to address the vacuum in this area. See Sara Ruddick, 'Maternal Thinking,' *Feminist Stuidies* 6, 2 (Summer 1980), 342-67. Reprinted in an important anthology, Joyce Trebilcot, ed., *Mothering: Essays in Feminist Theory* (Totowa, NJ: Rowman and Allenheld 1983).

not only do not accord themselves moral worth for good mothering, they describe themselves as not even engaging in morally assessible actions at all. Meanwhile they experience the agonies bound up with the absence of moral criteria for good mothering.

Similarly, domestic labour has either been ignored or been morally camouflaged as a 'labour of love' performed by an 'angel in the household.' When performed well it is, literally, unseen, as Blum et al. point out.[36] Because women are encouraged to perform domestic work and provide sexual services in disconnected and privatized ways, both their exploitative character and intrinsic connection to institutional forms of patriarchy normally remain hidden. Rather than seeing either the morally destructive dimensions of this work or the morally worthy aspect of nurturing and supporting the growth of other moral subjects, women are encouraged to describe this as 'doing nothing' while exhausting themselves in the process of trying to prove that they are gender stable 'real women.' Sometimes the domain of domestic labour becomes an area for double moral oppression when immigrant women or women of colour are employed, under exploitative conditions, to work for women who themselves exist in a situation of moral exploitation. But it is also a potential domain for moral and political revolution. As Marge Piercy puts it, 'Burning dinner is not incompetence but war.'

In this section, then, I have tried to show how complete moral domains of women's lives are rendered invisible and then ideologically removed from the sphere of human morality so that we do not even realize that we are engaged in actions capable of generating moral worth. As a result, we often feel morally worthless and empty when we might, in fact, be celebrating our moral worth. I take this to be an advanced stage of moral madness.

---

36 Blum, et al., 'Altruism and Women's Oppression'

V Prolegomena to a Heuristics for Feminist Ethics

A Prediction

I predict that there will be no Rawls, no Nozick, no 'star' of feminist moral theory. There will be no individual singled out for two reasons. One reason is that vital moral and theoretical conversations are taking place on a large dialectical scale as the feminist community struggles to develop a feminist ethic.[37] The second reason is that this community of feminist theoreticians is calling into question the very model of the individualized autonomous self presupposed by a star-centered male-dominated tradition. Thus there is a committed meta-level of shared consciousness amongst feminist moral theorists that would militate against the competitive aspiration for an individual achievement. We experience it as a common labour, a common task.

Sketch of a Heuristic: Some Central Issues

Feminist ethics must have its critical and its substantive aspects. As a moral *critique*, it is important to carry out the following tasks: It must critique any allegedly empirically grounded theories of moral human nature. It must sift out that which is true from that which is false, distorted, or compromised by skewed a priori assumptions built into the conceptual framework, the methodology, and the results. In particular, we need to exercise a vigilant deconstructionist attention to sexist, racist, heterosexist, and class presuppositions. Second, aimed at generating new moral paradigms, a feminist ethic must call into question previously accepted 'full moral paradigms' in order to identify and expose those moral paradigms which are

---

37 Some feminist theorists working in the area of feminist ethics include Kathryn Pyne Addelson, Annette Baier, Mary Daly, Marilyn Frye, Carol Gilligan, Beverley Harrison, Sarah Lucia Hoagland, Barbara Houston, Jean Baker Miller, Sheila Mullett, Nel Noddings, Adrienne Rich, Carol Robb, Sue Sherwin, and Debra Shogun. (This list is not intended to be exhaustive.)

treacherously incomplete or twisted. Third, a feminist ethic must explore and analyse moral double-binds arising in the lives of women in order to determine which ones correspond to situations of genuine moral conflict and which are spurious, resulting from patriarchal ideological camouflage and oppressive practices. A fourth, important critical task is to dis-cover and render visible the hidden moral domains of women's lives while establishing women's claim to the full human spectrum of moral action and character whether good or evil.

As a *substantive* radical moral theory, feminist ethics challenges the model of the moral subject as an autonomous, detached, rational subject, often seeing this hyper-masculinist ideal of the moral self as both psychologically and morally flawed. We can expect new models of the self, perhaps pluralistic in nature, to emerge. Whether this will call for a unitary quasi-essentialist model of the self remains to be seen; it may be that a looser, more open-textured notion of human consciousness will be necessary and that our epistemic paradigms will be similarly challenged in this process.[38] However they are described, I would expect such models literally to *incorporate* a sense of moral imagination, moral empathy, and moral feeling into an integrated, other-connected self.[39] (Whether such selves would

---

38 For a discussion of how such an epistemic shift might work, see Evelyn Fox Keller, *Reflections on Gender and Science* (New Haven: Yale University Press 1985), especially the essays 'Gender and Science,' 'Dynamic Autonomy: Objects and Subjects,' 'Dynamic Objectivity: Love, Power and Knowledge,' and 'Cognitive Repression in Contemporary Physics.'

39 The most sustained critique of the gender-labelling and devaluation of this model of the self grows out of the work of object-relations theorists such as Jane Flax and Nancy Chodorow. See, for example, Nancy Chodorow, *The Reproduction of Mothering* (Berkeley: University of California Press 1978). For an application of this work, see Nel Noddings, *Caring: A Feminine Approach to Ethics and Moral Education* (Berkeley: University of California Press 1984). This research, which emphasizes an essential sense of personal connectedness, runs through much of feminist moral theorizing. It calls into question the adequacy of Isaiah Berlin's theory of two concepts of liberty and the alleged illegitimacy of other-directness in moral agency (the 'horrible spectacle' of the craven, heteronomous moral agent). Subtler distinctions are called for here. See Isaiah Berlin, 'Two Concepts of Liberty,' in *Four Essays on Liberty* (Oxford: Oxford University Press 1969).

be, necessarily or voluntarily, gendered will continue to be a lively matter for debate, I suspect.) Correlatively, what will count as a legitimate moral 'reason' will shift.

Second, after identifying the pernicious aspects of the public/private distinction as it has been applied to women and other oppressed groups consigned to the private domain, feminist moral philosophers can be expected to blur this corrupt distinction. One way to do this is by continuing to explore the radical politicizing of the allegedly personal domain and the simultaneous personalizing of the allegedly de-personalized public domain. An important corollary of this process will be a questioning of the relationship between the moral and the political. It will be important to ask whether either set of considerations has primacy, or whether they are, necessarily, bound up in some dialectical process in relation to feminist values and collective, feminist revolutionary practice. Again, this would particularly challenge all those moral traditions and practices which have assumed that genuine moral principles are universalizable over context. Finally, feminist moral theory must identify and reclaim our genuine womanly virtues as fully human virtues, rescuing them from the odious swamp of inferiour vices. This is necessary whether virtues will come to be theoretically understood as dispositions to act or as part of a looser moral repertoire of a moral self conceptualized and experienced in some more radical way.

A Poetic Criterion of Adequacy

It would seem that any worthy moral theory must meet criteria of adequacy. I do not pretend to know what a complete set of such criteria is in the present context. It is too early to tell. Nor am I entirely convinced that the question even makes sense. Nevertheless, I have a fierce moral conviction that no moral theory is worthy of the name 'feminist' unless it can account for the following moral 'facts' of a strong woman's life. I close by citing Marge Piercy once again:

'For Strong Women'
A strong woman is a woman who loves
strongly and weeps strongly and is strongly
terrified and has strong needs. A strong woman is strong
in words, in action, in connection, in feeling;
she is not strong as a stone but as a wolf
suckling her young. Strength is not in her, but she
enacts it as the wind fills a sail.

What comforts her is others loving
her equally for the strength and for the weakness
from which it issues,...
.... Strong is what we make
each other. Until we are all strong together,
a strong woman is a woman strongly afraid.

CANADIAN JOURNAL OF PHILOSOPHY
Supplementary Volume 13

Moral Sanity or 'Who Killed Boy Staunton'

STEVEN BURNS
Dalhousie University
Halifax, NS
Canada B3H 3J5

Kathryn Morgan's paper, 'Women and Moral Madness,'[1] is a rich compound of example and analysis, which deserves to be influential in moral theory. My rejoinder can be understood as having one main point. I take her analysis of moral madness to be profoundly helpful, and I claim that it implies an understanding of the human person which can be made more precise if we also pay attention to moral sanity. My paper, then, accepts Morgan's work as fundamental, and attempts to contribute to its further development. I begin with some preliminary observations before proposing my main idea. My subtitle identifies an example which illustrates the main point, and concludes the paper.

First, there are inevitably many more phenomena which might have been invoked. I shall identify only one: Christian morality goes unmentioned by Morgan, although it has imposed profound moral conflicts on women. Jean-Luc Godard's recent 'Hail Mary' is a vivid reminder of how insistent Western morality can be that women are

---

1 'Women and Moral Madness' was read by Kathryn Pauly Morgan to the Annual Meeting of the Canadian Philosophical Association, in Winnipeg in May, 1986 and is reprinted in this volume. I shall use page numbers in parentheses to refer to the version of her paper here reprinted. The present essay is a revised version of my contribution to the symposium discussion of Morgan's paper.

to be virgin mothers. It goes without saying that women can have a hard time trying to live up to these two ideals at once. Yet in Mary the two ideals are inseparable. Christianity has also institutionalized a universal version of this ideal, in the nun who vows permanent chastity, and charity to all the children of God. Women's particular struggles to cope with this, as well as the abstract, universalized ideal itself, are both implicated in the morality which Morgan is examining.

Second, it is worth emphasis that Morgan's is not a position entirely confined to feminism. It has, as she notes, ties with the situation of oppressed minorities, and is allied to the ethical principles of various liberation struggles. There are also important alliances with earlier writing in what used to be called main-stream ethics, quasi-genderless ethics. Among the minority who challenged the contractarians and utilitarians, we should mention Elizabeth Anscombe's important paper, 'Modern Moral Philosophy,'[2] Peter Winch's inaugural lecture on moral integrity, and the case he made against universalizability,[3] the dramatic incursions into moral philosophy of the philosopher-novelist, Iris Murdoch,[4] and even the insistence of Bernard Williams on the moral significance of context, of luck, and of particular interpersonal sentiment.[5] These are British examples, but they have analogues elsewhere in anglophone philosophy.

None of these critical moments in main-stream ethics usurps the task which feminist thinkers have set for us. An important feature

---

2 G.E.M. Anscombe, 'Modern Moral Philosophy,' *Philosophy* **43** (1958)

3 'Moral Integrity' and 'The Universalizability of Moral Judgments,' among other papers in Peter Winch, *Ethics and Action* (London: Routledge and Kegan Paul 1972)

4 See, especially, Iris Murdoch, *The Sovereignty of Good* (London: Routledge and Kegan Paul 1970)

5 E.g., Bernard Williams, *Moral Luck: Philosophical Papers 1973-1980* (Cambridge: Cambridge University Press 1981). This builds on much earlier work; compare the 1965 inaugural lecture, 'Morality and the Emotions,' reprinted in Bernard Williams, *Problems of the Self* (Cambridge: Cambridge University Press 1973) 207-29.

of their analysis[6] is its account of the schizophrenic phenomenology of being female and moral. Morgan has arranged it for us in four parts: (1) That the public standards of human nature, of what it is to be a good person, do not fit you, so that you can never 'measure up.'[7] We might think, then, that Morgan would recommend a moral philosophy *without* accounts of human nature, or the female essence. But we find that she soon provides arguments *supporting* virtues and the labour said to belong to the female nature. I shall explain later why this is only an apparent contradiction. Perhaps we imagine that 'separate and equal development' is a possible ideal; female nature and male nature might support different sets of virtues and vices, for instance, without causing moral insanity. (Hume comes to mind: 'An effeminate behaviour in a man, a rough manner in a woman; these are ugly because unsuitable to each character.'[8]) But in practice this has always produced a kind of 'apartheid,' with a dominant essence making a mockery of the subordinate one.

Morgan's other points are equally complex and telling. She argues: (2) that a dichotomy between public and private spheres similarly designates a separate and inferior realm for the female, reinforcing the separation of women from the realm of rational ethics. She shows (3) that the above distinctions generate the insanity of cultivating virtues which are public vices, and despising

---

6 I am thinking, especially, of recent, unpublished papers by Sheila Mullett and Susan Sherwin, but cf. M. Hintikka and S. Harding, eds., *Discovering Reality: New Perspectives on Women and Philosophy* (Dordrecht: Reidel 1983), and C. Gould, ed., *Beyond Domination: New Perspectives on Women and Philosophy* (Totowa, NJ: Rowman and Allanheld 1984).

7 'In Western civilization the Jew is always measured on scales which do not fit him,' wrote Wittgenstein in *Culture and Value* (Oxford: Basil Blackwell 1980), 16. Rush Rhees briefly discusses the analogy with measuring women on scales which do not fit, in 'Postscript' to *Ludwig Wittgenstein: Personal Recollections*, R. Rhees, ed. (Oxford: Basil Blackwell 1981), 206. This should not be read apart from its context, 191-231.

8 *An Enquiry Concerning the Principles of Morals*, Section VIII (in the edition by L.A. Selby-Bigge [Oxford: Clarendon Press 1966] 266).

as vices what are publicly considered virtues. Both of Morgan's examples in this section require thought. Andrea Canaan writes: 'The acceptance of total responsibility ... for myself ... became ... the last and strongest barrier to self' (214). And of the 19-year-old Charles it is said to be expected, 'that the quiet prince will merge his identity with [Lady Di's]' (216). Finally (4), as if being rendered self-contradictory were not enough, you are made invisible: not productive but reproductive, not gainfully employed but wifing a house, 'raised seven children and then went back to work' (221).

My leading question is this: if these are the modes and causes of moral madness, what must moral sanity be like? If the first virtue of Morgan's paper is its exposure of the former, its second, and I think greater, virtue is that it provides prolegomena to the latter. If the mainstream of patriarchal, unsexed ethics places women in contradictions and double-binds, then empathizing, seeing it from the point-of-view of the victim, is the first prolegomenon. What may 'philosophy' learn from reversing positions? When we change positions we should find ourselves in what Morgan calls the land of the no-stars. Embodied in that prediction is a critique of the 'individualized autonomous self presupposed by a star-centred male-dominated tradition' (223). And the moral subject is misconceived if conceived as an 'autonomous, detached, rational subject' (224). These claims identify a thesis central to Morgan's feminism, and of great importance to moral philosophy in general. It is this thesis that I wish to dwell on.

Now once in the land of the no-stars, we see that we are critics of the inheritors of the rationalist, empiricist and Kantian moral philosophies. Morgan mentions their 'claims to universality, impartiality, reciprocity, universalizability, and absence of emotional distortion,' and their aspirations to 'a kind of timeless legitimacy across contexts applying to depersonalized abstract moral participants' (210). We are critics because we do not believe in the Cartesian pure consciousness. We believe that the self is not just a rational being, but is an agent. Nor is agency enough; this focus reached a certain pitch in Sartre's and de Beauvoir's too radical conception of freedom and authenticity. Nonetheless, their underlying conception of the dialectical nature of self-consciousness contains promise. The main ideas are well known.[9] The Other, whose regard momentarily fixes you, is an inescapable part of your being. The moral agent, locus of whatever authonomy and responsibility we are capable of, must also be a self-consciousness, capable of viewing herself as though she were an Other. Now we conceive the self as essentially related to other people.

Is this not a trap? Take Prince Charles, and the 32-year-old avowedly anti-masculinist Lady Diana. 'It is expected that the quiet prince will merge his identity with hers.' But is this not the very other-dependent self that we have just been growing used to? A self whose authenticity depends on recognizing and absorbing the stand-point of others? Compare Morgan's earlier passage: A woman's 'sense of relatedness and connection becomes denounced as "other-definition" or "field-dependence" and the ground of her moral judgment is seen as involuntarily heteronomous rather than autonomous' (211-12). Surely the model of someone who gets her identity only by playing moon to someone else's sun is one of the causes of moral madness? That is right; this self-smothering non-goodness must be an inadequate conception of selfhood, but there is a sterile dichotomy here. The companion notion is of the self-made man, the one with whom someone else is to merge her identity. This is, I think, a (male) self-confidence trick, a false sanity. These men, in fact, are not even superficially self-made. What could be more heteronomous than a being who is constantly being measured by coaches, by bosses, by the stock market, by research grant review panels? The purely self-constructed identity is an illusory one which will not stand scrutiny, then, either. Neither of these antitheses is the residence of moral sanity.[10]

---

9 Simone de Beauvoir, *The Ethics of Ambiguity*, tr. Bernard Frechtman (New York: Citadel Press 1964); Jean-Paul Sartre, *Being and Nothingness*, tr. Hazel Barnes (New York: Citadel Press 1964), especially III:1:iv 'The Look.'

10 In discussion, Professor Jan Narveson raised the following question: Is it not an implication of Morgan's paper that males should be less happy than females, and is there any reason to think that American males are not unhappier than their female counter-parts? American sociologists claim to have such evidence, but my reply is that Morgan's paper is not about unhappiness but about moral

Any real personal identity is under scrutiny and at the same time is a scrutiniser of both self and others, is socially constructed and at the same time a maker of self and others. This philosophical framework dictates that we spend time observing particular interactions, parent-infant, teacher-pupil, friend-friend, customer-supplier; and analysing the particular instantiations of them: *your* supplier, or *your* infants. The feminist philosopher's search for a better account than 'essence' or 'nature,' than 'public' or 'private,' coincides with the search for a dialectical account of moral sanity and self-understanding.

This then is my one idea: moral sanity is the product of this dialectical understanding of the moral self. Both the heteronomous and the autonomous self are caricatures, warped beings whose sanity is at best only apparent, who are double-bound by the myths in which they have come to believe. Not only does a proper conception of the self defuse the misleading antithesis between autonomy and heteronomy, but it also allows us to fall between the two stools of an objective, essentialist account of human nature, and a subjective, wilful and existentialist account. Those are two stools into neither of which we want to step. There is a third advantage, too. In Morgan's account, the heteronomous, other-dependent self first appears as the woman confined to her private sphere of personal relations. But as we now conceive her, the dialectical self is an inescapably *public* being. The inter-relatedness with particular others is the ideal basis on which to conceive of moral relations as neither merely public nor merely private. This brings me at last to my subtitle. I hope to give texture to these abstractions by considering a

---

madness. Narveson should ask whether there is not moral madness among males; I think that he might find analogous contradictions, double-binds, and so on. I would argue that such evidence would support, rather than undermine, the imperative to be suspicious of traditional moral theory and to pursue the issues raised in Morgan's 'prolegomena.'

I have since read Annette Baier's splendid 'Trust and Antitrust' (*Ethics* **96** [1986] 231-260), in which she characterizes what I here call the ideal of the 'self-made man' as a case of 'adolescent self-assertive individualism.' This fine rhetorical inversion of Kohlberg merely hints at the useful work she has done on the underlying conception of the morally mature self.

particularly well-detailed and dramatic incident in Canadian moral life. It is a male example, but it is one which offers support to the feminism of Morgan's project.

'Who Killed Boy Staunton'

This was, of course, a question when it was first articulated. I have written it without a question mark because I intend it to announce the answer. In Robertson Davies' Deptford trilogy the question holds one of the keys to all three books. My focus will be on the incident which ends the first novel, *Fifth Business*. Three men, who were boys together in Deptford, meet for the first time in their adult lives. They remind each other of the incident which began both the novel, and the interconnection of their lives: Boyd Staunton had thrown a snowball with a rock in it at Dunstan Ramsay. Ramsay ducked. The snowball struck a pregnant woman in the head. This caused the premature birth of Paul Dempsey (later Magnus Eisengrim), and also left his mother permanently deranged.

Ramsay had picked up the stone and saved it. This fateful evening he gives it back to Staunton, in the presence of Eisengrim. The latter two eventually leave Ramsay's together. In the morning, Staunton's body is found in his automobile, which has been driven off the end of a wharf. He has a stone in his mouth.

The two subsequent novels exploit the question, was this death a murder? a suicide? an accident?[11] Now it does not seem likely that it was an accident. The possible murderers are two, but they only play the role of Others. Staunton, to see himself as he morally is, must see himself through the eyes of some particular other person, but of course it is not just any old other who will do. The crucial other is the one whose view is unclouded, informed, and not corruptible by Staunton's attempts at deceit. In this man's life that person is Eisengrim. As I imagine it, when confronted with Eisengrim

---

11 There is also the answer of the Cabal: By the usual five, 'himself first of all, by the woman he knew, and the woman he did not know, by the man who granted his inmost wish, and the inevitable fifth, keeper of his conscience and keeper of the stone.' But what I say does not conflict with that account.

and the stone, Staunton finds that he cannot swallow it, and drives himself off the wharf.

Now it might be thought that the Other must be the Friend. (Certain people abstract this friend into Jesus of Nazareth, the personification of loving friendship who is always present in the Christian's heart. This is, of course, a conception of enormous moral influence.) In Davies' novel, however, the friend is inadequate to the task. It is a particular strength of the novel that Dunstan Ramsay, although he keeps the stone, and is keeper of the conscience, is consistently manipulated by Staunton. The scene in which Staunton shows him photos of his wife unclothed ends with the bitter challenge: Ramsay, you play Gyges to my Caudales; either you should now steal my wife away, or you should kill me. But Ramsay is impotent to express even his embarrassment and anger, so compromised is he as Staunton's 'friend.' He may harbour the desire to see Staunton brought to reckoning, but *he* will never accomplish the act.[12]

Another ploy is to insist that what is required is an Ideal Other, just, true, impartial, or behind a veil of ignorance, so that we shall see ourselves clearly only from the sort of Kantian eyes which we were fleeing. But Eisengrim is hardly that sort of other. He is magician and seer, but bearer of the truth on this occasion because his whole life has been built on the crucial truth which Staunton has spent a lifetime denying. Staunton comes to some understanding of himself — he sees his life in the new, much truer light of the archetypal action. His sense of being grander than Ramsay was founded in cheating, his national reputation rested on cowardice (he had run from the snowball scene, while Ramsay had stopped to help; he spent the war getting rich manufacturing provisions, while Ramsay lost a leg at the front). His own self-recognition is the devastating element on the evening in question.

This self-revelation can only be explained by the presence of Eisengrim. There are hints that he actually hypnotized Staunton,

---

12 In the account given by Eisengrim at the end of *World of Wonders* Staunton is deeply shaken by the discovery that Ramsay had harboured the stone and that he was never just the compromised friend which he had seemed to be.

and no doubt Staunton was mesmerized by him. But this is mis-understood if it is taken as an external force. Eisengrim did not kill him, any more than Ramsay did. We are not dealing with murder. What happened, surely, is that Staunton found himself in the presence of another consciousness whose gaze he could not evade. He could not disguise his envy with bluff generosity, or the emptiness at the heart of his marriage by keeping Ramsay as trusted friend of his wife. Eisengrim was free of these complicities, and was clairvoyant about Staunton's character. It was required for his self-recognition that Staunton see himself through *these* eyes. Thus exposed, his suicide, his complicity in his own hypnosis or whatever, his complicity in his own death makes what sense such things can.[13]

It is the dialectical nature of self-conscious moral identity which is crucial; the problem of moral sanity is the problem of what sort of other(s) you see yourself through the eyes of, as well as what sort of self you see yourself as. One of the ways to expose your moral madness is to ask the question, through whose eyes do you see yourself when you are wondering who you are or how you are doing? If, for instance, the other person is hostile or distrusting, you are already setting yourself up for paranoia. That is the kind of madness which consists in seeing others as out to get you, and yourself as victim. To take a very different sort of case, the ability to command is characteristic of the Boss, and it is through his (or her) eyes that many people get their most telling views of themselves; it is no surprise that they come to apparent self-respect through adopting facsimiles of the Boss's behaviour. The quality of the other must be as much a subject of examination, then, as the quality of the self.

Boy Staunton, who does not suffer the woman's moral madness, but who does suffer the false-confidence of the self-made man, achieves his sanity, his moral integrity only when he confronts him-

---

13 It is of further interest that according to Eisengrim's final account, Staunton casts his self-recognition in interpersonal terms; he identifies with his political hero, King Edward VIII (Duke of Windsor), so that he now sees abdication not externally as an unfortunate event, but as his own fate.

self as the particular person who can see exactly what lies hidden behind his false-confidence. I offer this case as evidence of a way of thinking about moral identity which gets us beyond the nest of contradictions which attack the person whose private virtues are public vices, whose ideals of integrity are self-destroying, whose essence is accidental, and whose relations to others are chains of dependence.

CANADIAN JOURNAL OF PHILOSOPHY
Supplementary Volume 13

Rescuing Womanly Virtues:
Some Dangers of Moral Reclamation*

BARBARA HOUSTON
Faculty of Education
The University of Western Ontario
London, ON
Canada N6G 1G7

Kathryn Morgan has introduced us to a typology of 'the ways in which women's moral voice and her sense of moral integrity are twisted and destroyed by patriarchal ideology and lived experience.'[1] She claims that this experience can induce in women 'a sense of confusion and genuine moral madness.'

I am in agreement with much of what Morgan says. However, I suspect that some others might find her case less convincing than I for the reason that she supports her claims by an appeal to classical philosophical literature and what we might loosely call 'sociological observations.' One can imagine the easy retort — 'Yes, well, it's true that Aristotle, Aquinas, Rousseau and Kant did say those silly things about women, but their remarks were mere asides and no one takes them seriously in this matter any more anyway. As for the sociological observations, well, philosophers can't be held responsible for all the gender-mediated moral assessments that the folks make. No moral philosopher today calls a moral woman "im-

---

* This paper has benefited from my discussions with Ann Diller. I thank her for astute comments and editorial assistance.

1 All quotations from Kathryn Morgan are taken from her paper, 'Women and Moral Madness.'

mature, pathological, inadequate, immoral, evil.'" It wasn't a philosopher who wrote (or sings) 'Stand By Your Man.'

Moral philosophers do not put women in the double binds that induce confusion and perhaps moral madness. No contemporary moral philosopher calls into question women's capacity for full moral agency – you don't hear moral philosophers, even those in applied ethics, claiming that women cannot be full moral agents because of 'the curse,' or because of menopause. And you'll notice that it is *Maribel Morgan* who urges women to cultivate the virtues of 'submissiveness, fearfulness, fragility, guile and seductiveness,' not Bernard Williams or Alasdair MacIntyre. No philosopher since Nietzsche has suggested that women's womanly virtues are 'pathological' and show a 'slavish mentality.' And we all know that Nietzsche was probably already demented from syphilis when he said that. Moral philosophers today do not make these gender-dependent moral assessments. 'Pernicious societal judgments' are to blame, not moral philosophy. As John Stuart Mill said, combine any moral theory with human idiocy and you'll get bad results.[2]

Such thoughts are to the point. But I think we make a serious mistake if we, as philosophers, take them to be sufficient grounds for dismissing Morgan's worries, or for thinking that contemporary moral philosophy does not contribute to moral madness in women. I share Morgan's concerns about the ways in which women's moral integrity is jeopardized, and I do think it is jeopardized as much by current moral theories as by what the folks say and do in their social practices.

Specifically, I think Morgan is correct in claiming that contemporary moral philosophy contributes to women's moral madness to the extent that moral theories:

    (a) recognize *only* the so-called public domain of morality, which is lived in and shared by men, as genuinely moral;

---

    2 John Stuart Mill, *Utilitarianism* (New York: The Liberal Arts Press, 2nd Revised Edition 1957), 30-1

(b) continue to render invisible the actual moral domains in women's lives; and

(c) assert that the circumstances affecting moral judgment are objectively pertaining states in the world ignoring the fact that we live in a culture characterized by a practice of gender-dependent moral assessments.

It is, however, beyond the scope of this paper to defend our shared agreement about the culpability of contemporary moral philosophy. For an elaborate defense of this claim, I refer the reader to the increasingly large body of literature dealing with this matter and to Annette Baier's recent careful work which summarizes a good deal of feminist criticism of contemporary moral theory.[3]

What should moral philosophers make of the fact that women's moral experiences are ignored, their thinking devalued? Suppose everything Morgan says about gender-mediated moral assessments of women's characteristics and activities is true? What follows for moral theorists? Kathryn Morgan tells us, indirectly, in her heuristic for a future feminist ethics. Any future feminist ethics, or we might say, any socially responsible moral theory, must undertake to generate new paradigms, discover and render visible women's hidden moral lives, explore and analyze moral double binds arising in the lives of women to see if they involve genuine moral conflicts or spurious ones. Substantively we should expect a new feminist ethics to offer us a new conception of self and to blur the private-public distinction. Finally, she says, we would want such an ethic to 'identify and reclaim our womanly virtues as virtues, rescuing them from the odious swamp of inferior vices.' Nurturing, helping, sustaining the growth of other moral subjects and the dispositions and psychological competencies required for this virtuous activity

---

3 Annette Baier, *Postures of the Mind: Essays on Mind and Morals* (Minneapolis, MN: University of Minnesota Press 1985). See especially 'Doing without Moral Theory?' and 'Poisoning the Wells.' See also her two most recently published articles on the subject: 'What Do Women Want in a Moral Theory?' *Nous* **19**, 1 (March 1985), 53-63 and 'Trust and Antitrust,' *Ethics* **96** (1986), 231-60.

should not be seen, as Morgan claims they often are, as pathological masochism, fear of success, passivity or as involving an empathetic imagination or emotional expressiveness that inhibits or prevents rational reflection. Again, I am wholly in agreement with Morgan on this. However, the attempt to reclaim our womanly virtues as virtues is not an easy task.

Carol Gilligan, a psychologist, has offered us perhaps the most noteworthy and systematic recent empirical effort to articulate women's voice in the moral domain.[4] She has been joined in her efforts by several women philosophers who are beginning to sketch for us the ethical differences that emerge when we attend specifically to women's moral experience. Nel Noddings, Virginia Held, Sara Ruddick and others have begun for us the complex task of theorizing about women's moral experience and womanly virtures.[5]

Given our long history of sexism and misogyny, it will take considerable persistence to not only articulate women's morality but to also rescue the womanly virtues *as virtues* in the face of those who would ignore, dismiss or devalue them. However, the Politics of Persistence may not be the only politics we shall need in this task of moral reclamation.

John Broughton has argued that the distinctive woman's morality described by Gilligan is one which 'perpetuates the status quo, affirms the established division of labor, and forecloses on the possibility of a radical transformation.'[6] The charge, if true, could not be grounds for dismissing Gilligan's work as an accurate account of (some) women's morality, nor, as I have argued, contra Broughton, as grounds for claiming that the women involved were self-

---

4 Carol Gilligan, *In a Different Voice: Psychological Theories and Women's Development* (Cambridge, MA: Harvard University Press 1982)

5 Nel Noddings, *Caring* (Berkeley, CA: The University of California Press 1984); Virginia Held, *Rights and Goods: Justifying Social Action* (New York: The Free Press 1984). Sara Ruddick's papers are listed below.

6 John Broughton, 'Women's Rationality and Men's Virtues,' *Social Research* **50**, 3 (Autumn, 1983), 626

deceptive.[7] Nevertheless, this observation of Broughton's presses on us the need to consider just how we might address the question of the *worthiness* of any purported uniquely female moral character or distinctive morality. In response to Kohlberg and others who would dismiss the allegedly distinctive moral concerns of women as 'personal' and secondary, I have elsewhere argued for their social importance.[8] But more is needed than a general endorsement of the universal significance of women's concerns. We might agree that we all like, perhaps even need, caring, along with motherhood and apple pie, but particular concoctions of it may not be to our liking, or may even be harmful. Thus, many would argue that in addition to a politics of persistence we also need a feminist politics to both deconstruct the feminine and to reconstruct women's moral experience into a worthy ethics.

To illustrate the difficulties associated with reclaiming womanly virtues as virtues, I want to consider the work of two other writers besides Gilligan who have made brave attempts at the task: Sara Ruddick and Joan Ringelheim.

A concrete description of the womanly virtues is given in the following passage from Adrienne Rich's 'The Conditions for Work: The Common World of Women.' Rich is here commenting on how

---

7 Barbara Houston, 'Gilligan and the Politics of a Distinctive Women's Morality,' in Lorraine Code, Sheila Mullett, and Christine Overall, eds., *Feminist Perspectives: Philosophical Essays on Methods and Morals* (Toronto: University of Toronto Press forthcoming)

8 Lawrence Kohlberg's most fully considered response to Gilligan's work appears in L. Kohlberg, C. Levine, and A. Hewar, *Moral Stages: A Current Formulation and Response to Critics* (New York: Karger 1983), especially ch. 3. Kohlberg here accepts the view most clearly expressed by Gertrude Nunner-Winkler that it is more appropriate to see the care orientation as Gilligan describes it as part of women's ego development, part of women's personal development. See Kohlberg, above citation, 22-7 and 141. See also Gertrude Nunner-Winkler, 'Two Moralities? A Critical Discussion of an Ethic of Care and Responsibility Versus and Ethic of Rights and Justice' in William Kartines and Jacob Gerwitz, eds., *Morality, Moral Behavior and Moral Development* (New York: John Wiley & Sons 1984), 358. John Broughton also makes this same criticism.

women have not been described as 'working' when we create the essential conditions for the work of men. She speaks of

> *Every effort that left no trace...* The efforts of women in labor, giving birth to stillborn children, children who must die of plague or by infanticide; the efforts of women to keep filth and decay at bay, children decently clothed, to produce the clean shirt in which the man walks out daily into the common world of men, the efforts to raise children against the attritions of racist and sexist schooling, drugs, sexual exploitation, the brutalization and killing of barely grown boys in war.[9]

In Rich's terms women's work has been the work of 'world-protection, world-preservation, and world-repair.' It involves what she calls, 'the invisible weaving of a frayed and threadbare family life.'[10]

A similar recognition of the invisibility and devaluation of women's labour has led Sara Ruddick to give a detailed analysis of a different voice in the special work of women, mothering. Ruddick develops a positive thesis concerning the distinctive ethical potential in women's experience which she argues has public uses and important political implications.[11]

Ruddick claims that there is a distinctive thinking which grows out of the activity of caring for children, a form of thinking which she calls 'maternal thinking.' Maternal caring, as it revolves around the preservation of the child's physical, psychological and moral well-being in an indifferent and hostile world gives rise to a form of attention which Ruddick calls 'preservative love.' This love is not a feeling, but 'an *activity* of caring for or treasuring creatures whose

---

9 Adrienne Rich, 'The Conditions for Work: The Common World of Women,' in *On Lies, Secrets, and Silence* (New York: W. W. Norton 1977), 206

10 Ibid., 205

11 Sara Ruddick, 'Maternal Thinking,' and 'Preservative Love and Military Destruction: Some Reflections on Mothering and Peace,' both in Joyce Treblicot, ed., *Mothering: Essays in Feminist Theory* (Totowa, NJ: Rowman & Allanheld 1984), 213-63

well-being is at risk.'[12] Such caring gives rise to an attitude to human nature called holding. Holding is characterized by 'the priority given to keeping over acquiring, to reconciling difference, to conserving the fragile, to maintaining the minimal harmony and material conditions necessary to a child's life.'[13] Maternal thinking, as Ruddick describes it, is a conception of an achievement and it identifies virtues which are, in effect, strengths appropriate to the taking care of people at risk.[14]

Ruddick further argues that peacefulness is one of the goods which mothers have conceptualized and realized in distinctive ways. In women's maternal thinking peacefulness, she tells us, is characterized by 'a commitment to avoid battle whenever possible; to fight necessary battles nonviolently, and to take the aim of (unavoidable) battle to be the reconciliation between opponents and the restoration of connection and community.'[15] Maternal thinking, she argues, articulates a theory of conflict consonant with the aims of maternal life. It is a theory which is noticeably like that of pacifists such as Gandhi which should not be surprising since Gandhi himself claimed to have learned his theory of conflict from women.

Ruddick draws our attention to some noteworthy facts: mothers remain peaceful in conditions in which they are powerful (with respect to children) and in which violence is a common temptation. Of course, as Ruddick recognizes, not all mothers are nonviolent in these situations. Maternal peacefulness is, as Ruddick says, 'a truth to be made.' Nevertheless, she argues, the resources lie in maternal thinking.[16]

Although Adrienne Rich and Sara Ruddick write of the virtue and value of women's work, Hannah Arendt reminds us that what we recognize as women's work 'bears little resemblance to heroic

---

12 Ruddick, 'Preservative Love and Military Destruction,' 240

13 Ibid., 240

14 Ibid., 237; see also 'Maternal Thinking,' 225.

15 Ibid., 239

16 Ibid., 244

deeds,'[17] deeds which have a grandeur because they are recognized as 'requiring great strength and courage and performed in a fighting spirit'[18] against overwhelming odds. Arendt notes, '...the endurance it needs to repair every day anew the waste of yesterday is not courage, and what makes the effort painful is not danger but its relentless repetition.'[19]

Perhaps it was passages such as this from Arendt that prompted Joan Ringelheim to look for conditions in which we might well be able to recognize women's traditional skills as virtues — conditions in which their efforts could without question be taken to be heroic. In her article 'Women and the Holocaust: A Reconsideration of Research,'[20] Ringelheim provides us first with an account of her empirical research on women's experiences in the Holocaust and then with a painfully honest reappraisal of it from a feminist point of view. It is her reappraisal of her research which raises the questions that I want to take up.

In brief summary, Ringelheim's work was designed to correct some of the deficiencies in the available studies of the Holocaust experience. In these studies Ringelheim noticed that the experiences and perceptions of Jewish women had been obscured or absorbed into men's lives. In undertaking her own research Ringelheim assumed that 'gender must have accounted for something and that focusing on women's experience would yield new questions and new data.'[21] She wanted to know whether women's experiences in the Holocaust were different from men's in some respects. In her interviews with women who were survivors of the Holocaust, her aim was to try to establish women's sense of their own particular

---

17 This phrase is quoted in Adrienne Rich, *On Lies, Secrets and Silence*, 203. See Hannah Arendt, *The Human Condition* (Chicago: University of Chicago 1958), 55.

18 Arendt, 55

19 Ibid.

20 Joan Ringelheim, 'Women and the Holocaust: A Reconsideration of Research,' *Signs: Journal of Women in Culture and Society* 10, 4 (1985), 741-61

21 Ibid., 742

experience within the Holocaust; 'what was done to them (their vulnerabilities) and what they did (their resources).'[22]

Ringelheim reports that women did have special vulnerabilities
created by sexism, such as rape, forms of sexual humiliation,
molestation and sexual exchange. She claims women also had special resources. Carefully noting that at best we still only have speculations and impressions and more questions, she reports that, 'A
number of the observers had the impression that women tended
to outlive men, at least in comparable situations,'[23] it would seem,
because of women's special resources. She says:

> Some of the differences perceived do appear as transformations related to
> gender: starving transformed into communal sharing of recipe stories; sex into
> food, rather than the reverse; rags into clothes; isolation into relationships
> or surrogate "families." Women were able to transform their habits of raising
> children or their experience of nurturing into the care of nonbiological family.
> Men, when they lost their role in the protection of their own families, seemed
> less able to transform this habit into the protection of others. Men did not
> remain or become fathers as readily as women became mothers or nurturers.[24]

Echoing Adrienne Rich's poetic observations and empirically
verifying Sara Ruddick's claims about the preservative ethic inherent in women's mothering practice, Ringelheim concludes from her
research that:

> Because of the different material conditions and social relations that charac-
> terize their lives, women are able to create or recreate "families" and so pro-
> vide networks for maintenance that may be related to survival rates.[25]

In short we might say that the 'early Ringelheim' makes a case for
women's special virtues.

---

22 Ibid., 743

23 Ibid., 746

24 Ibid., 747

25 Ibid.

However, upon reflection, Ringelheim later takes note of what she sees as 'a problematic and troubling direction' in her own research on women. She detects in her work a hidden framework, an unwitting one, which 'informed the assumptions posited, hypotheses created, and the conclusions reached.'[26] And she is insistent that this perspective be changed.

'Cultural feminism' is the name Ringelheim gives to the hidden framework she thinks structured her own research. It may also underlie other research on women's values. Without elaboration we can briefly characterize cultural feminism as 'the belief that women have a distinctive culture by virtue of being women and that women become liberated through the conscious articulation and development of this culture.'[27] But as soon as she articulates this implicit assumption, Ringelheim recognizes the need to raise a more fundamental question: '[C]an values, ways of life and skills be reclaimed as if they have not arisen within an oppressive situation? And do they become free of oppression or of its effects simply because we would like them to be so?'[28]

The later Ringelheim's point is not about asserting or denying differences in the way women and men relate to social institutions or their values. Her point is that we must question the political import of such differences. In assessing the political import of the differences she discovered, Ringelheim makes some tough observations and asks herself different, more difficult questions. She notes: 'My at-

---

26 Ibid., 253

27 Although I cannot find the source of this direct quotation, it is very close to that first offered by Brooke in 'Retreat to Cultural Feminism' in *Feminist Revolution: Redstockings of the Women's Liberation Movement* (New York: Random House 1975), 79. Brooke says, 'Cultural feminism is the belief that women will be freed via an alternate women's culture.' The definition I offer is taken from Brooke and an early version of Ringelheim's paper which was read at the American Philosophical Association Meetings, New York, December 1984. The reader is urged to consult Ringelheim's discussion of cultural feminism which draws out political features of this position and its links with Liberalism much more fully than I can discuss in this paper.

28 Ringelheim, 756

tempt... to emphasize friendships among women in the camps gives a false or misleading impression that oppression is only external and not internal as well.'[29] She thinks she imposed upon herself a silence about the possible internalized oppression of Jewish women survivors. Looking anew at her research she says:

> I seemed to be saying that in spite of rape, abuse, and murder of babies; in spite of starvation, separations, losses, terror, and violence; in spite of everything ugly and disgusting, women bonded, loved each other. Rose said: "That's what was holding the women together." Must we not ask, How many women? At what cost? For how long? Under what conditions?[30]

Ringelheim proceeds to ask the difficult questions which might reveal that the friendship and family stories cover a 'deeper, and more troubled story of intrigue, bitterness, hurt, pain, and brutality.'[31] She asks, 'Are these groups more like a form of tribalism than a form of friendship — exclusive, competitive, damaging to self and others? How much depends on context, position, class, language? How much exploitation is there in these groups?...to what extent did families — surrogate and biological — hamper women in the camps?[32]

Ringelheim presses on us her new questions: questions designed to nullify the effects of a hidden cultural feminism that might influence any research on women's morality.

> Is women's culture liberating? How can it be if it was nourished in oppression? Can we ever forget the price we pay as oppressed women? Should we? If we glorify the feminine from a presumably feminist perspective, how do we avoid valorizing oppression in order to criticize and organize against it? Are we unwilling to confront the damage of oppression — how has it killed us? How do we kill each other?...How break this dangerous allegiance be-

---

29 Ibid., 757

30 Ibid.

31 Ibid., 758

32 Ibid., 759

tween trying to understand oppression and needing to mythologize our strengths in oppression or in spite of it?[33]

In summarizing her critical reflection on her own work Ringelheim says: 'Certain values described as feminine virtues may get some women through but they do not seem to offer most women the resources for fighting the enemy – for genuine resistance. They do not, that is, push one to "cripple" or "damage" or stop the enemy...or at least to try.'[34]

Thus, in her own work, Ringelheim comes to the conclusion that it is likely that our attention is focussed wrongly when we try to rescue womanly virtues as virtues without asking the difficult questions: Do these virtues stop the enemy or try to? Do they win our liberation? Her point is the obvious one: for feminists, the moral and the political are necessarily bound to each other.

The Holocaust affords us examples of moral experience at the outermost edges of possible moral experience. Because the conditions are so extreme, it is difficult to know what we can make of such examples. But when we return to ordinary life, similar questions about the moral experiences of women that Gilligan and Ruddick describe are raised by feminists.

Claudia Card asks, 'Is Gilligan picking up on something Nietzsche identified as a "slave morality"?'[35] She acknowledges that Gilligan's description of women's morality is distinctive inasmuch as Gilligan is describing the responsibilities we have which are not correlated with rights. Card herself thinks that there are two contexts in which such responsibilities exist: (1) friendship and (2) the acceptance of

---

33 Ibid.

34 Ibid., 760

35 Claudia Card, 'Virtues and Moral Luck,' Working Series I, No. 4, November 1985, Institute for Legal Studies, University of Wisconsin, Madison, Law School. This question, as I state it, is not a direct quotation from Card's paper. She says, 'Or, is she [Gilligan] picking up on something in women's voices genuinely analogous to what Nietzsche heard, or thought he heard, in Christianity – something *he* identified as a "slave morality"?' (6)

benefactions. This leads her to suggest that: 'Gilligan may have mistaken for practical wisdom about friendship a certain misplaced sense of gratitude in women who have accepted a "benefaction" they felt they could not refuse.'[36]

Attending to the sexual politics of contemporary society, she notes that the social structures are such that women are coerced into economic dependence upon and (sexual) affiliation with men as protectors. Card elaborates:

> When people are affiliated with "protectors" their affirmation of those affiliations have little to do with love, though the language of love be the language of discourse. Women's caretaking is often simply unpaid or underpaid labor performed from a variety of motives. More likely to be mistaken for a caring virtue is the misplaced gratitude they have felt toward men for taking less than full advantage of their power to abuse or for singling them out for the privilege of service in return for "protection." Women may assume caretaking responsibility as a debt of gratitude for such "benefactions."[37]

Card thinks that 'misplaced gratitude' is only one form of moral damage women have suffered in their oppression. She suggests that other forms of moral damage may be named in our reputation for 'lying, cunning, deceit and manipulation.' But these, Card notes, Gilligan does not address.[38]

But can lying, cunning, deceit and manipulation be vices if they are needed for defense? Card is at least certain that, 'They are surely not virtues, even if we are justified in them from the point of view of justice.'[39] She urges: 'One who tells just the right lies to the right people on the right occasion may have a useful and needed skill. But it is not conducive to human good, even if needed for survival under oppressive conditions. Human good may not be realizable under such conditions.'[40]

---

36 Ibid., 23
37 Ibid.
38 Ibid.
39 Ibid., 24
40 Ibid.

This seems reasonable enough, but Sara Ruddick, who is also mindful of women's frequent state of powerlessness, does seem to regard these same skills, when used by women, as virtues. On Ruddick's account, what Card describes as women's lying, cunning, deceit and manipulation, become the nonviolent strategies of 'persuasion, appeasement, self-suffering, psychological manipulation, negotiation, and bribery'[41] which women use as 'powerless combatants.'[42] As forms of nonviolence, when chosen as alternatives to violence, they are not justified or excused but are nevertheless conceptualized as contributions to a distinctive human good — peacefulness.

The lesson Ruddick and some others would have us draw is that the distinctive ethical potential in women's experience is that of living, morally, with vulnerability, one's own and those for whom one is responsible. Nel Noddings, Ruddick and Gilligan all point out that so-called real politics aside, we all do live in this condition of vulnerability and so women's moral experience holds special lessons for us. Nel Noddings and Ruddick both recognize as a distinctive feature of women's moral morality the responsibility to nurture the moral goodness or moral well-being of others. With this in mind they suggest that one's own vulnerability can be read not as powerlessness, but as the empowerment of others to become morally good.

But the tensions introduced by Ringelheim's reappraisal of her own work and Claudia Card's queries of Gilligan's account of women's morality are heightened when we consider Jeffner Allen's analysis of women's characteristic nonviolent approach to the resolution of conflicts. Just as Ringelheim rethinks women's virtues, Jeffner Allen renames them. She calls women's nonviolence a 'heterosexual virtue.'[43]

---

41 Ruddick, 'Preservative Love and Military Destruction,' 243

42 Ibid., 243

43 Jeffner Allen, *Lesbian Philosophy: Explorations* (Palo Alto, CA: Institute of Lesbian Studies 1986), 35

> The ideology of heterosexual virtue forms the cornerstone of the designation of women as nonviolent. The ideology of heterosexual virtue charges women to be "moral," virtuously nonviolent in the face of the "political," the violent male defined world. The ideology of heterosexual virtue entitles men to terrorize – possess, humiliate, violate, objectify – women and forecloses the possibility of women's active response to men's sexual terrorization. Women, constrained to nonviolence, are precluded from claiming and creating a self, a world.[44]

Allen notes that in the special appeal made to women's maternal relations, 'Disregarded in full is the ineffectiveness of motherly virtue and nonviolence.'[45] 'Ignored,' she says, 'are the implications of situations such as the Irish Women's Peace Movement where, precisely because no attempt is made by movement leaders to involve women "in any other terms than as mothers of families," the women routinely and futilely "take themselves into the street, say prayers, sing hymns and go home again."'[46] Completely dismissed also is the history of women's nurturance 'in which women give freely, expect nothing in return, and remain powerless while partaking in unsatisfactory relationships.'[47] Not mentioned also are the terrifying facts that in Canada, every six minutes a woman is sexually assaulted; and one woman in ten married or living with a man is so severely beaten by her husband as to require medical attention. In the United States, every three seconds a woman is raped, every 18 seconds a woman is beaten by her husband severely enough to require hospitalization; and in the single State of Massachusetts, every 22 days a woman is murdered by her husband or by a heterosexual lover.[48]

---

44 Ibid., 35

45 Ibid., 36

46 Ibid., 36-7

47 Ibid., 36

48 These statistics are taken from Robin Morgan, ed., *Sisterhood is Global* (Garden City, NY: Anchor Press/Doubleday 1984). The Canadian information occurs in an article by Greta Hoffman Nemiroff and the United States statistics occur

What are we to make of the challenges posed to women's morality by Ringelheim, Allen and Card? I'm not entirely sure. At times, I think they afford us a perfect illustration of what Kathryn Morgan would call an advanced case of women's moral madness — in place of a sense of moral worth we find suspicion. Other times, I think there are important lessons in these examples.

I am repeatedly struck by the observation that what is described as women's distinctive morality or uniquely female character is good, when it is an ethics exercised in our relations with children or those dependent upon us. Nel Noddings' able phenomenological descriptions of caring and Gilligan's reports of her subjects' attempts to use the method of inclusion stir a certain gender pride in me, especially when they are offered as women's alternatives to the traditional ethical theories which seem to be, as Annette Baier describes them, 'traffic rules for self-asserters.'[49]

However, I am equally impressed by the observation that women's distinctive morality is self-defeating, or highly dubious, when exercised in our relations with men, with those more powerful than ourselves, or when exercised in conditions in which the social structures are likely to deform our caring or disguise it as a form of consent to the status quo.

Those who hold this latter observation clearly in front of them while they assess women's distinctive morality, or unique moral character, recognize that there are some serious problems to be dealt with. In their criticisms of the ethics they locate the problem in quite different places.

Some locate the problems squarely within the ethics of care itself, claiming that there is, within the ethics, nothing that asserts

---

in an article by Rayna Green. The statistics on rape and battery are generally conservative given the difficulty in estimating unreported incidents. The statistic for women killed by an abusive partner in the State of Massachussets is from the Massachussets Department of Public Health and is reported in an article entitled 'Critics Fault Police Unit in Hub Murder,' *The Boston Globe* (June 29, 1987), 1.

49 Annette Baier, 'What Do Women Want in a Moral Theory?' *Nous* **19**, 1 (1985), 62

the worth of the one-caring, although the worth of the cared-for is clearly recognized.[50] It is also argued that the ethics of care, especially as it is articulated by Noddings and Ruddick, fails to note that the mother-child relation or a dyadic caring relation cannot be taken as the paradigmatic moral relation.[51] Granted such relations have been largely ignored in traditional moral theories, still, they have their limitations as models for other moral relationships between adults which may be characterized by asymmetries of power, responsibility, equality and different needs.

Others locate the problem in those who use the ethics, pointing out that women are a damaged people because of their social position. Oppression, they remind us, is not only external, it is also internal. Because women are maimed by their history of being devalued, of being subordinate, they are susceptible to a pathological use of the ethics which may further entrench their subordination.[52]

Still others locate the problem in the social structures, pointing out the ways in which women's altruism is twisted and deformed by the existing social structures so that women's caring activity becomes damaging to the cared-for and the one-caring.[53]

---

50 Barbara Houston, 'Prolegomena to Future Caring,' paper delivered to the Association for Moral Education, Toronto, November 1985.

51 Ibid. See also Jean Grimshaw, *Philosophy and Feminist Thinking* (Minneapolis, MN: University of Minnesota Press 1986), especially ch. 7 and 8. Virginia Held also recognizes some limitations to the mother-child relation as *the* paradigmatic moral relation; nevertheless, she thinks it worthwhile to hold that criticism in abeyance long enough to fully explore the mother-child relation as *a* paradigmatic relation. She develops some insightful reflections on this moral relationship in a paper delivered to the University of Cincinnati Philosophy Colloquium, Feminist Moral, Social and Legal Theory, University of Cincinnati, November 22, 1986.

52 Many feminist writers show a sensitivity to this point. See Houston, 'Prolegomena to Future Caring'; Joan Ringelheim; Claudia Card; and Adrienne Rich, *On Lies, Secrets, and Silence* (New York: W. W. Norton 1979) and *Blood, Bread and Poetry* (New York: W. W. Norton 1986).

53 One of the best discussions of this point is found in Larry Blum, Marcia Nomiak, Judy Housman, and Naomi Scheman, 'Altruism and Women's Oppression,' in Carol Gould and Marv Wartofsky, eds., *Women and Philosophy* (New York: Putnam's 1976).

These different sorts of criticisms, at least the ones I have referred to, all arise out of feminist ethics. An examination of them reveals at least three different facets of feminist ethics: (a) a philosophical analysis of the ethical domain by feminist philosophers; (b) an account of women's moral experience or agency; and (c) the basis for a feminist political movement.[54]

The first set of criticisms which locate the problems within the ethics itself arise from feminist philosophers using standard philosophical categories and criteria of adequacy but motivated by a knowledge of women's experience and a concern for women. The second kind of criticism, noting the possible pathological use of the ethics, arises from attention to women's moral agency. But different dimensions of women's experience and agency are noted. Women's moral fragility is the focus. This is not typically the focus of Gilligan, Noddings, or Ruddick. The final type of criticism arises most obviously from a feminist ethics that forms the basis of a political movement to change the social/political situation of women.

All criticisms implicitly propose criteria of adequacy for any proposed distinctive women's morality. For example, three of the criteria of adequacy suggested by feminists doing philosophical analysis of the ethical domain might be construed somewhat neutrally as follows:

(1) the ethics must be able to recognize as moral problems, what are clearly, nontheoretically identified as moral problems;

(2) the ethics must be able to solve as large a range of moral problems as competing theories;

(3) the ethics must not presuppose unrealistic conceptions of the self as moral agent.

Feminist ethics construed as an account of women's moral agency or as a basis for the political movement for women's liberation

---

54 Debra Shogun, 'What Is "Feminist Ethics"?' paper presented to the Canadian Women's Studies Learned Society Meeting, at Winnipeg, Manitoba (June 6, 1986), 1.

might describe the criteria implicit in its criticisms differently; they might insist on using a political measure of the adequacy of women's distinctive morality. Any and all of the following criteria of the worth of women's morality are suggested by these criticisms:

(1) the morality should be successful in winning the liberation of women;

(2) the morality should make the subordination of women a primary moral concern that is a matter of primary moral attention;

(3) the morality should make the subordination of women a recognizable moral problem as opposed to a nonmoral matter;

(4) the morality should at least challenge the status quo with respect to women's social political position;

(5) the adoption of a morality, by women, in the present social context, should not further their oppression.

How does one construct a feminist ethics that recognizes womanly virtues as virtues but does not fall into the traps that Ringelheim and others are worried about? For it is very clear, as Walker reminded us, that one can end up with the unhappy consequence that 'women become the obligated bearer of certain moral values, regardless of whether they are treated equally or are oppressed as a result or more likely as a cause.'[55]

The dilemma described by Walker is a real danger if in the process of moral reclamation we endorse, jointly, the following three claims: the womanly virtues are virtues which only women can have; women's moral values have intrinsic worth; and they are the only values which have intrinsic worth.[56] Unfortunately, there is considerable

---

55 James Walker, 'In A Different Voice: Cryptoseparatist Analysis of Female Moral Development,' in *Social Research* **50**, 3 (1983), 690.

56 Walker himself thinks the problem follows from holding only the first two

pressure in the social political context that would tempt those engaged in the task to assert the conjunction of all three claims.

Those who have ventured into 'the swamp of odious vices'[57] to rescue womanly virtues have learned of some dangers. First, one must watch out for gender essentialism of both a biological and cultural sort. That is, in identifying womanly virtues as womanly, one has to avoid asserting or implying that these are virtues which only women can have, or virtues which all women have, even if they are now the virtues that only women do have. It is my unfortunate experience, however, that usually when it is acknowledged that the virtues are not essentially women's virtues, then they are not thought to be distinct in some interesting way and they seem to lose the value of the peculiar. Caring and nurturance are subsumed under the general heading of beneficence which Sidgwick, and even Kant, talked about and their distinctiveness is forgotten or ignored. So while we must not assert gender essentialism, we must also not ignore the fact that many moral virtues still continue to bear their gender related history and for that reason some risk devaluation or invisibility.

In addition to the quicksand of gender essentialism one also has to avoid the illusory safe ground of moral essentialism. One must heed Ringelheim's and Allen's warning and avoid implying that the values are intrinsically good, good independent of any special context in which they occur. After her own consideration of women's dubious attachments and caring relations, Claudia Card suggests that: 'To sustain the view that the capacity for love is part of moral

---

claims but I have argued elsewhere that he is mistaken in this and that the dilemma arises only if we hold all three claims conjointly. The monistic claim is one Walker *assumes* in his argumentation and fails to make it clear as a premise of his argument. For a detailed discussion of Walker's criticisms of Gilligan, see Barbara Houston, 'Gilligan and the Politics of A Distinctive Women's Morality.' To my knowledge, no feminist moral theorist holds the conjunction of all three claims; no theorist holds the female essentialist claim though some *appear* to hold to the moral essentialist claim (e.g., Gilligan and Noddings) and some the monistic claim (e.g., Noddings).

57 The phrase is Kathryn Morgan's.

personality, we need an understanding of this capacity comparable in sophistication to Kant's understanding of the capacity for acting on principle.'[58] Noting that Kant looked for an attachment to principle which was valuable in itself, Card urges that 'we do not need to be deterred by the charge of ill-founded attachments from recognizing the absolute value of some.'[59]

I myself doubt that the solution to the problems will be found in this way. We do of course need to clarify more precisely what caring means, and how to distinguish worthy from unworthy forms of it. However, we should not be misled into attempting to find *the* valuable form of caring, the one which is valuable independently of those who are doing the caring and independently of the contexts in which the activity occurs. This invites a dangerous kind of abstraction. Morality is a guide to conduct, for persons, in their social contexts. Any ethics which refuses to pay attention to the moral selves which might use the ethics is mistaken. Any ethics which asserts the value of actions prescribed by the ethics in abstraction from the social conditions in which they occur is wrongheaded.

We must also avoid the danger of moral monism, something which moral essentialism seems to foster. We must remember, as Ringelheim and Allen remind us, that caring is not the only value: freedom is important too. Again, however, a caution is in order. There is a strong temptation to commit these always and only fallacies because if one fails to assert that the womanly virtues have intrinsic value they easily become rejected as part of women's oppression simply because they are associated with it. Or, if one doesn't overemphasize their significance, perhaps assert that only caring is valuable, it is suggested that while these may be 'pretty virtues' there are others, like justice, which are primary. Once again, this usually leads to the unfortunate consequence that they are neglected. So while we must avoid moral essentialism and moral monism, we must also struggle to avoid thinking that womanly virtues have little or no value.

---

58 Card, 22

59 Ibid.

But we cannot leave matters here. I want to suggest that in addition to learning of some dangers associated with the enterprise of articulating and defending women's morality there is a further lesson to be learned.

The criticisms I have been discussing are suggestive of a basic question that lies behind this inquiry: what is the standpoint from which we are to assess women's morality or moral character? If one is a feminist, the controversy I have discussed can be painful as well as puzzling. In the current state of sexual politics, one is bound to have gloomy intimations that whichever perspective one takes, women are likely to end up the losers. This is not, I think, an unduly pessimistic sense of the dilemma.

In the works I have cited we have at least two distinct feminist viewpoints articulated which appear to be in tension. The first, represented by Gilligan, Noddings, Ruddick and the early Ringelheim, assume that women, by virtue of their position in the world vis-à-vis men, and by virtue of their special labor, have experienced a distinctive form of moral labor that (roughly) parallels the sexual division of labor. Women's moral labor gives rise to a different ethics, a distinctive morality, a set of womanly virtues. Although none of these theorists, with the possible exception of Ruddick, articulate this particular notion of a feminist standpoint arising out of women's different labor, very clearly, it is at the heart of their outlook. They attend carefully to women's moral experience, to women's moral agency and describe the different ethics they see manifested in women's practice. This perspective focusses on women's distinctive moral experience and on women's moral agency.[60]

The second feminist perspective is represented in the criticisms of the purported distinctive women's morality described by Gilligan et al., by the later Ringelheim, Claudia Card and Jeffner Allen. Their feminist perspective appears to have a different focus of at-

---

60 The notion of the focus centering on women's moral agency is taken from Deborah Shogun.

tention, one which arises out of political struggles to alter the condition of women's subordination.

There are admitted difficulties with both perspectives. The first feminist standpoint, that adopted by Gilligan, Ruddick and Noddings, appears to assume a form of female essentialism. That is, despite disclaimers by each of them about the dangers of speaking for all women, there does appear to be the assumption that women's experience is similar enough for us to posit a women's ethics arising out of women's distinctive labor. However, as any number of commentators have pointed out, this perspective ignores significant differences in the experience of women. 'Can there be a women's standpoint or a feminist standpoint if women's experience is divided by race, class and culture?'[61] Women of color, poor women, women who do not mother, women of ethnic minorities and lesbian women do not present us with a uniform enough experience. 'Woman' must be deconstructed to women. Once this deconstruction takes place, it is doubtful that one will be able to describe an ethics which one can confidently claim belongs to women *as women*, without a false universalism occurring: a false universalism which we can recognize as of the very same sort which characterizes most traditional and contemporary ethical theories which posit male moral experience as human moral experience.

The further difficulty with this perspective is that it fails to take account of women's social political context and history, it fails to give us a view of the enormous damage women suffer as a result of the particular position they hold. It does not encourage us to focus on the question of how we might alter women's condition; nor does it encourage us to ask whether the allegedly uniquely female moral virtues are a cause of women's subordination.

Let us grant that there are difficulties with the perspective. But there are, I think, also serious problems with giving it up too soon. If we too readily give up the feminist standpoint that focusses on

---

61 This question has been raised by a number of feminist writers. The question and the general point made here is clearly articulated in Sandra Harding, *The Science Question in Feminism* (Ithaca, NY: Cornell University Press 1986), 26.

women's special work, a very large part of women's moral experience will again become invisible or will suffer a devaluation. We can grant that the experience of women who are not mothers, who are black, or poor, or lesbian may well differ from other women. But it is not clear to me that it differs in relevant respects when we consider the distinctive sexual division of labor that overrides other differences among women. For as Marilyn Frye notes, women of all races and classes are together in 'a ghetto of sorts.' There appears to be a women's place that is defined by function and that function is 'the service of men and men's interests as men define them, which includes the bearing and rearing of children.'[62] Of course, as Frye grants, the details and working conditions of the service vary by class and race, as do the interests of the men being served. But Frye's point still stands that there are some predictable 'constants':

> Whether in lower, middle or upper class homes or work situations, women's service work always includes personal service (the work of maids, butlers, cooks, personal secretaries), sexual service (including provision for his genital sexual needs and bearing his children, but also including "being nice," "being attractive for him," etc.) and ego service (encouragement, support, praise, attention).[63]

The second feminist perspective, that arising more obviously out of feminist politics, also seems faulty. Marilyn Persall has suggested that the question 'Is it good for women?' begins feminist ethics.[64] But Janet Radcliffe Richards is certain that what is good for women cannot be the basis of ethics because 'to say that something is good for a group only means that it is to that group's advantage.'[65] Other

---

62 Marilyn Frye, *The Politics of Reality: Essays in Feminist Theory* (Trumansburg, NY: The Crossing Press 1983), 9

63 Ibid.

64 While I am certain that this is Persall's suggestion, I cannot locate the appropriate reference.

65 Janet Radcliffe Richards, *The Skeptical Feminist* (Boston, MA: Routledge and Kegan Paul 1980), 8

critics have claimed that what must be avoided is the tacit assumption of this perspective: 'whatever will improve the experience of women is ethical.'[66] Such a perspective, it is claimed, is not properly universal. Whatever is used as moral grounds for deploring the condition of women must also be extended as moral grounds to others. With these considerations in mind, Jean Grimshaw declares, 'I do not think that there can be a viable autonomous feminist criticism which merely considers the situation of women.'[67]

Again, let us grant the point. But I think there is more to be said. In their assessment of the second feminist perspective, I think the critics misconstrue the enterprise. This perspective can be seen as positing a necessary condition for a satisfactory ethics. The tacit claim is not, if it's good for women it's sufficient as an ethical stance. Rather, the feminist political perspective is insisting that if anything is to be declared good, right, or just, it had better be demonstrably good, right, or just for women.[68]

No doubt, as I've granted, critics of these feminist perspectives do raise important considerations. However, I think we would make a serious mistake, indeed a more serious mistake, if we were to give

---

66 Debra Shogun, 2

67 Grimshaw, 225

68 This is certainly a defensible interpretation of some feminist political perspectives. Others, such as Adrienne Rich, would want to claim that the question 'What is good for women' has 'an expanding, not a constricting potential' to teach us about all oppressions. She makes these remarks specifically about 'What is good for the Jews' in 'If Not with Others, How?' in *Blood, Bread and Poetry*, 209, but all her writings attempt to draw out the expanding potential of the question, 'What is good for women?' Another interesting question that arises but which I cannot go into here is whether oppressed groups need to adopt a morality that puts their group first in order to gain their liberation and full moral agency and whether a morality which fails to do this will be self-defeating *for that group*? For a discussion of a similar question considered from a Marxist point of view, see Milton Fisk, *Ethics and Society: A Marxist Interpretation of Value* (New York: New York University Press 1980). See especially the last chapter, 'Revolutionary Ethics.'

up either perspective and try to do 'ethics as usual.'[69] Let me explain.

I agree with Frye that women's sphere may perhaps be understood at one level of description, across race and class, as 'the service sector.'[70] But most importantly we also need to acknowledge that everywhere women's work is characterized by what Frye calls the 'fatal combination of responsibility and powerlessness: we are held responsible in almost every respect though we have in almost no case power adequate to that project.'[71] It is this situation which leads to 'moral madness.' Thus, we need to have this situation articulated.

Granted there are tensions generated by these perspectives, but they are needed tensions for they give evidence of an important struggle – a struggle to keep clearly before us both women's responsibility and our relative powerlessness. We need to keep both in mind if we are to give an accurate picture of women's moral agency and also if we are to assess the worth of any ethics. The struggle we have is to articulate women's morality in the face of theories which render it invisible, to articulate women's moral worth in a culture which systematically denies it.

I think, in the end, that despite appearances, the challenges posed by Ringelheim, Card and Jeffner Allen are not evidence of moral madness. They are not evidence of the damage done to us, giving us a sense of suspicion where we ought to have a sense of worth. Rather they represent challenges we must meet if we would reconstruct women's morality into a feminist ethics. We cannot do this without first knowing women's morality as it is; neither can we do it without holding women's morality to account. We must attend assiduously to both features of women's moral situation: our responsibilities and our powerlessness. Ringelheim, Card and Allen are simply, insistently, reminding us of their own criteria for a women's morality. Whatever morality women develop or adopt, it had better be one whose virtues do not cost us our freedom.

---

69 This phrase is adapted from Sandra Harding's phrase, 'science as usual' in *The Science Question in Feminism*.

70 Marilyn Frye, *The Politics of Reality*, 9

71 Ibid.

III

Some Applications

CANADIAN JOURNAL OF PHILOSOPHY
Supplementary Volume 13

Feminist Ethics and In Vitro Fertilization[1]

SUSAN SHERWIN
Dalhousie University
Halifax, NS
Canada B3H 3J5

New technology in human reproduction has provoked wide ranging arguments about the desirability and moral justifiability of many of these efforts. Authors of biomedical ethics have ventured into the field to offer the insight of moral theory to these complex moral problems of contemporary life. I believe, however, that the moral theories most widely endorsed today are problematic and that a new approach to ethics is necessary if we are to address the concerns and perspectives identified by feminist theorists in our considerations of such topics. Hence, I propose to look at one particular technique in the growing repertoire of new reproductive technologies, in vitro fertilization (IVF), in order to consider the insight which the mainstream approaches to moral theory have offered to this debate, and to see the difference made by a feminist approach to ethics.

I have argued elsewhere that the most widely accepted moral theories of our time are inadequate for addressing many of the moral issues we encounter in our lives, since they focus entirely on such

---

1 I appreciate the helpful criticism I have received from colleagues in the Dalhousie Department of Philosophy, the Canadian Society for Women in Philosophy, and the Women's Studies program of the University of Alberta where earlier versions of this paper were read. I am particularly grateful for the careful criticism it has received from Linda Williams and Christine Overall.

abstract qualities of moral agents as autonomy or quantities of happiness, and they are addressed to agents who are conceived of as independent, non-tuistic individuals. In contrast, I claimed, we need a theory which places the locus of ethical concerns in a complex social network of interrelated persons who are involved in special sorts of relations with one another. Such a theory, as I envision it, would be influenced by the insights and concerns of feminist theory, and hence, I have called it feminist ethics.[2]

In this paper, I propose to explore the differences between a feminist approach to ethics and other, more traditional approaches in examining the propriety of developing and implementing in vitro fertilization and related technologies. This is a complicated task, since each sort of ethical theory admits of a variety of interpretations and hence of a variety of conclusions on concrete ethical issues. Nonetheless, certain themes and trends can be seen to emerge. Feminist thinking is also ambivalent in application, for feminists are quite torn about their response to this sort of technology. It is my hope that a systematic theoretic evaluation of IVF from the point of view of a feminist ethical theory will help feminists like myself sort through our uncertainty on these matters.

Let me begin with a quick description of IVF for the uninitiated. In vitro fertilization is the technology responsible for what the media likes to call 'test tube babies.' It circumvents, rather than cures, a variety of barriers to conception, primarily those of blocked fallopian tubes and low sperm counts. In vitro fertilization involves removing ova from the woman's body, collecting sperm from the man's, combining them to achieve conception in the laboratory, and, a few days later, implanting some number of the newly fertilized eggs directly into the women's womb with the hope that pregnancy will continue normally from this point on. This process requires that a variety of hormones be administered to the women — which involve profound emotional and physical changes — that her blood and urine be monitored daily, and then at 3 hour intervals, that ultra-

---

2 Susan Sherwin, 'A Feminist Approach to Ethics,' *Dalhousie Reveiw* **64**, 4 (Winter 1984-85) 704-13

sound be used to determine when ovulation occurs. In some clinics, implantation requires that she remain immobile for 48 hours (including 24 hours in the head down position). IVF is successful in about 10-15% of the cases selected as suitable, and commonly involves multiple efforts at implantation.

Let us turn now to the responses that philosophers working within the traditional approaches to ethics have offered on this subject. A review of the literature in bioethics identifies a variety of concerns with this technology. Philosophers who adopt a theological perspective tend to object that such technology is wrong because it is not 'natural' and undermines God's plan for the family. Paul Ramsey, for instance, is concerned about the artificiality of IVF and other sorts of reproductive technology with which it is potentially associated, e.g. embryo transfer, ova as well as sperm donation or sale, increased eugenic control, etc.:

> But there is as yet no discernable evidence that we are recovering a sense for man [sic] as a natural object ... toward whom a ... form of "natural piety" is appropriate ... parenthood is certainly one of those "courses of action" natural to man, which cannot without violation be disassembled and put together again.[3]

Leon Kass argues a similar line in '"Making Babies" Revisited.'[4] He worries that our conception of humanness will not survive the technological permutations before us, and that we will treat these new artificially conceived embryos more as objects than as subjects; he also fears that we will be unable to track traditional human categories of parenthood and lineage, and that this loss would cause us to loose track of important aspects of our identity. The recent position paper of the Catholic Church on reproductive technology reflects related concerns:

---

3 Paul Ramsey, 'Shall We Reproduce?' *Journal of the American Medical Association* **220** (June 12, 1972), 1484

4 Leon Kass, '"Making Babies" Revisited,' *The Public Interest* **54** (Winter 1979), 32-60

267

> It is through the secure and recognized relationship to his [sic] own parents
> that the child can discover his own identity and achieve his own proper hu-
> man development ...
> Heterologous artificial fertilization violates the rights of the child; it deprives
> him of his filial relationship with his parental origins and can hinder the matur-
> ing of his personal identity.[5]

Philosophers partial to utilitarianism prefer a more scientific approach; they treat these sorts of concerns as sheer superstition. They
carefully explain to their theological colleagues that there is no clear
sense of 'natural' and certainly no sense that demands special moral
status. All medical activity, and perhaps all human activity, can be
seen in some sense as being 'interference with nature,' but that is
hardly grounds for avoiding such action. 'Humanness,' too, is a concept that admits of many interpretations; generally, it does not provide satisfactory grounds for moral distinctions. Further, it is no
longer thought appropriate to focus too strictly on questions of lineage and strict biological parentage, and, they note, most theories
of personal identity do not rely on such matters.

Where some theologians object that 'fertilization achieved outside
the bodies of the couple remains by this very fact deprived of the
meanings of the values which are expressed in the language of the
body and in the union of human persons,'[6] utilitarians quickly dismiss the objection against reproduction without sexuality in a
properly sanctified marriage. See, for instance, Michael Bayles in
Reproductive Ethics: '... even if reproduction should occur only within a context of marital love, the point of that requirement is the
nurturance of offspring. Such nurturance does not depend on the
sexual act itself. The argument confuses the biological act with the
familial context.'[7]

---

5 Joseph Card Ratzinger and Alberto Bovone, 'Instruction on Respect for Human Life in its Origin and on the Dignity of Procreation: Replies to Certain
Questions of the Day' (Vatican City: Vatican Polyglot Press 1987), 23-4

6 Ibid., 28

7 Michael Bayles, *Reproductive Ethics* (Englewood Cliffs, NJ: Prentice-Hall 1984) 15

Another area of disagreement between theological ethicists and their philosophical critics is the significance of the wedge argument to the debate about IVF. IVF is already a complex technology involving research on superovulation, 'harvesting' of ova, fertilization, and embryo implants. It is readily adaptable to technology involving the transfer of ova and embryos, and hence their donation or sale, as well as to the 'rental of womb space'; it also contributes to an increasing ability to foster fetal growth outside of the womb and, potentially, to the development of artificial wombs covering the whole period of gestation. It is already sometimes combined with artificial insemination and is frequently used to produce surplus fertilized eggs to be frozen for later use. Theological ethicists worry that such activity, and further reproductive developments we can anticipate (such as human cloning), violate God's plan for human reproduction. They worry about the cultural shift involved in viewing reproduction as a scientific enterprise, rather than the 'miracle of love' which religious proponents prefer: '[He] cannot be desired or conceived as the product of an intervention of medical or biological techniques; that would be equivalent to reducing him to an object of scientific technology.'[8] And, worse, they note, we cannot anticipate the ultimate outcome of this rapidly expanding technology.

The where-will-it-all-end hand-wringing that comes with this sort of religious futurology is rejected by most analytical philosophers; they urge us to realize that few slopes are as slippery as the pessimists would have us believe, that scientists are moral people and quite capable of evaluating each new form of technology on its own merits, and that IVF must be judged by its own consequences and not the possible result of some future technology with which it may be linked. Samuel Gorovitz is typical:

> It is not enough to show that disaster awaits if the process is not controlled. A man walking East in Omaha will drown in the Atlantic − if he does not stop. The argument must also rest on the evidence about the likelihood that

---

8 Ratzinger and Bovone, 28

judgment and control will be exercised responsibly ... Collectively we have significant capacity to exercise judgment and control ... our record has been rather good in regard to medical treatment and research.[9]

The question of the moral status of the fertilized eggs is more controversial. Since the superovulation involved in producing eggs for collection tends to produce serveral at once, and the process of collecting eggs is so difficult, and since the odds against conception on any given attempt are so slim, several eggs are usually collected and fertilized at once. A number of these fertilized eggs will be introduced to the womb with the hope that at least one will implant and gestation will begin, but there are frequently some 'extras.' Moral problems arise as to what should be done with these surplus eggs. They can be frozen for future use (since odds are against the first attempt 'taking'), or they can be used as research material, or simply discarded. Canadian clinics get around the awkwardness of their ambivalence on the moral status of these cells by putting them all into the woman's womb. This poses the devastating threat of six or eight 'successfully' implanting, and a woman being put into the position of carrying a litter; something, we might note, her body is not constructed to do.

Those who take a hard line against abortion and argue that the embryo is a person from the moment of conception object to all these procedures, and, hence, they argue, there is no morally acceptable means of conducting IVF. To this line, utilitarians offer the standard responses. Personhood involves moral, not biological categories. A being neither sentient nor conscious is not a person in any meaningful sense. For example, Gorovitz argues, 'Surely the concept of person involves in some fundamental way the capacity for sentience, or an awareness of sensations at the very least.'[10] Bayles says, 'For fetuses to have moral status they must be capable of good or bad in their lives ... What happens to them must make

---

9 Samuel Gorovitz, *Doctors' Dilemmas: Moral Conflict and Medical Care* (New York: Oxford University Press 1982), 168

10 Ibid., 173

a difference to them. Consequently some form of awareness is necessary for moral status.'[11] (Apparently, clinicians in the field have been trying to avoid this whole issue by coining a new term in the hopes of identifying a new ontological category, that of the 'pre-embryo.')[12]

Many bioethicists have agreed here, as they have in the abortion debate, that the principal moral question of IVF is the moral status and rights of the embryo. Once they resolve that question, they can, like Englehardt, conclude that since fetuses are not persons, and since reproductive processes occurring outside a human body pose no special moral problems, 'there will be no sustainable moral arguments in principle ... against in vitro fertilization.'[13] He argues,

> in vitro fertilization and techniques that will allow us to study and control human reproduction are morally neutral instruments for the realization of profoundly important human goals, which are bound up with the realization of the good of others: children for infertile parents and greater health for the children that will be born.[14]

Moral theorists also express worries about the safety of the process, and by that they tend to mean the safety to fetuses that may result from this technique. Those fears have largely been put to rest in the years since the first IVF baby was born in 1978, for the couple of thousand infants reportedly produced by this technique to date seem no more prone to apparent birth defects than the population at large, and, in fact, there seems to be evidence that birth defects may be less common in this group — presumably because of better monitoring and pre and post natal care. (There is concern expressed, however, in some circles outside of the bioethical literature about the longterm effect of some of the hormones in-

---

11 Bayles, 66

12 I owe this observation to Linda Williams.

13 H. Tristram Englehardt, *The Foundations of Bioethics* (Oxford: Oxford University Press 1986), 237

14 Ibid., 241

volved, in light of our belated discoveries of the effect of DES usage on offspring. This concern is aggravated by the chemical similarity of clomid, one of the hormones used in IVF, to DES.)[15]

Most of the literature tends to omit comment on the uncertainties associated with the effect of drugs inducing superovulation in the woman concerned, or with the dangers posed by the general anaesthetic required for the laparoscopy procedure; the emotional costs associated with this therapy are also overlooked, even though there is evidence that it is extremely stressful in the 85-90% of the attempts that fail, and that those who succeed have difficulty in dealing with common parental feelings of anger and frustration with a child they tried so hard to get. Nonetheless, utilitarian theory could readily accommodate such concerns, should the philosophers involved think to look for them. In principle, no new moral theory is yet called for, although a widening of perspective (to include the effects on the women involved) would certainly be appropriate.

The easiest solution to the IVF question seems to be available to ethicists of a deontological orientation who are keen on autonomy and rights and free of religious prejudice. For them, IVF is simply a private matter, to be decided by the couple concerned together with a medical specialist. The desire to have and raise children is a very common one and generally thought to be a paradigm case of a purely private matter. Couples seeking this technology face medical complications that require the assistance of a third party, and it is thought, 'it would be unfair to make infertile couples pass up the joys of rearing infants or suffer the burdens of rearing handicapped children.'[16] Certainly, meeting individuals' desires/needs is the most widely accepted argument in favour of the use of this technology.

---

15 Anita Direcks, 'Has the Lesson Been Learned?' *DES Action Voice* **28** (Spring 1986), 1-4; and Nikita A. Crook, 'Clomid,' DES Action/Toronto Factsheet #442 (available from 60 Grosvenor St., Toronto, M5S 1B6)

16 Bayles, 32. Though Bayles is not a deontologist, he does concisely express a deontological concern here.

What is left, then, in the more traditional ethical discussions, is usually some hand waving about costs. This is an extremely expensive procedure; estimates range from $1500 to $6000 per attempt. Gorovitz says, for instance, 'there is the question of the distribution of costs, a question that has heightened impact if we consider the use of public funds to pay for medical treatment.'[17] Debate tends to end here in the mystery of how to balance soaring medical costs of various sorts and a comment that no new ethical problems are posed.

Feminists share many of these concerns, but they find many other moral issues involved in the development and use of such technology and note the silence of the standard moral approaches in addressing these matters. Further, feminism does not identify the issues just cited as the primary areas of moral concern. Nonetheless, IVF is a difficult issue for feminists.

On the one hand, most feminists share the concern for autonomy held by most moral theorists, and they are interested in allowing women freedom of choice in reproductive matters. This freedom is most widely discussed in connection with access to safe and effective contraception and, when necessary, to abortion services. For women who are unable to conceive because of blocked fallopian tubes, or certain fertility problems of their partners, IVF provides the technology to permit pregnancy which is otherwise impossible. Certainly most of the women seeking IVF perceive it to be technology that increases their reproductive freedom of choice. So, it would seem that feminists should support this sort of technology as part of our general concern to foster the degree of reproductive control women may have over their own bodies. Some feminists have chosen this route. But feminists must also note that IVF as practiced does not altogether satisfy the motivation of fostering individual autonomy.

It is, after all, the sort of technology that requires medical intervention, and hence it is not really controlled by the women seeking it, but rather by the medical staff providing this 'service.' IVF is not

---

17 Gorovitz, 177

available to every woman who is medically suitable, but only to those who are judged to be worthy by the medical specialists concerned. To be a candidate for this procedure, a woman must have a husband and an apparently stable marriage. She must satisfy those specialists that she and her husband have appropriate resources to support any children produced by this arrangement (in addition, of course, to the funds required to purchase the treatment in the first place), and that they generally 'deserve' this support. IVF is not available to single women, lesbian women, or women not securely placed in the middle class or beyond. Nor is it available to women whom the controlling medical practitioners judge to be deviant with respect to their norms of who makes a good mother. The supposed freedom of choice, then, is provided only to selected women who have been screened by the personal values of those administering the technology.

Further, even for these women, the record on their degree of choice is unclear. Consider, for instance, that this treatment has always been very experimental: it was introduced without the prior primate studies which are required for most new forms of medical technology, and it continues to be carried out under constantly shifting protocols, with little empirical testing, as clinics try to raise their very poor success rates. Moreover, consent forms are perceived by patients to be quite restrictive procedures and women seeking this technology are not in a particularly strong position to bargain to revise the terms; there is no alternate clinic down the street to choose if a women dislikes her treatment at some clinic, but there are usually many other women waiting for access to her place in the clinic should she choose to withdraw.

Some recent studies indicate that few of the women participating in current programs really know how low the success rates are.[18] And it is not apparent that participants are encouraged to ponder the medical unknowns associated with various aspects of the technique, such as the long term consequences of superovulation and the

---

18 Michael Soules, 'The In Vitro Fertilization Pregnancy Rate: Let's Be Honest with One Another,' *Fertility and Sterility* **43**, 4 (1985) 511-13

use of hormones chemically similar to DES. Nor is it the case that the consent procedure involves consultation on how to handle the disposal of 'surplus' zygotes. It is doubtful that the women concerned have much real choice about which procedure is followed with the eggs they will not need. These policy decisions are usually made at the level of the clinic. It should be noted here that at least one feminist argues that neither the woman, nor the doctors have the right to choose to destroy these embryos: '... because no one, not even its parents, owns the embryo/fetus, no one has the *right* to destroy it, even at a very early developmental stage ... to destroy an embryo is not an automatic entitlement held by anyone, including its genetic parents.'[19]

Moreover, some participants reflect deep seated ambivalence on the part of many women about the procedure – they indicate that their marriage and status depends on a determination to do 'whatever is possible' in pursuit of their 'natural' childbearing function – and they are not helped to work through the seeming imponderables associated with their long term well-being. Thus, IVF as practiced involves significant limits on the degree of autonomy deontologists insist on in other medical contexts, though the non-feminist literature is insensitive to this anomaly.

From the perspective of consequentialism, feminists take a long view and try to see IVF in the context of the burgeoning range of techniques in the area of human reproductive technology. While some of this technology seems to hold the potential of benefitting women generally – by leading to better understanding of conception and contraception, for instance – there is a wary suspicion that this research will help foster new techniques and products such as human cloning and the development of artificial wombs which can, in principle, make the majority of women superfluous. (This is not a wholly paranoid fear in a woman-hating culture: we can anticipate that there will be great pressure for such techniques in subsequent generations, since one of the 'successes' of reproductive tech-

19 Christine Overall, *Ethics and Human Reproduction: A Feminist Analysis* (Allen and Unwin, forthcoming), 104 ms.

nology to date has been to allow parents to control the sex of their offspring; the 'choice' now made possible clearly threatens to result in significant imbalances in the ratio of boy to girl infants. Thus, it appears, there will likely be significant shortages of women to bear children in the future, and we can anticipate pressures for further technological solutions to the 'new' problem of reproduction that will follow.)

Many authors from all traditions consider it necessary to ask why it is that some couples seek this technology so desperately. Why is it so important to so many people to produce their 'own' child? On this question, theorists in the analytic tradition seem to shift to previously rejected ground and suggest that this is a natural, or at least a proper, desire. Englehardt, for example, says, 'The use of technology in the fashioning of children is integral to the goal of rendering the world congenial to persons.'[20] Bayles more cautiously observes that 'A desire to beget for its own sake ... is probably irrational'; nonetheless, he immediately concludes, 'these techniques for fulfilling that desire have been found ethically permissible.'[21] R. G. Edwards and David Sharpe state the case most strongly: 'the desire to have children must be among the most basic of human instincts, and denying it can lead to considerable psychological and social difficulties.'[22] Interestingly, although the recent pronouncement of the Catholic Church assumes that 'the desire for a child is natural,'[23] it denies that a couple has a right to a child: 'The child is not an object to which one has a right.'[24]

Here, I believe, it becomes clear why we need a deeper sort of feminist analysis. We must look at the sort of social arrangements

---

20 Englehardt, 239

21 Bayles, 31

22 Robert G. Edwards and David J. Sharpe, 'Social Values and Research in Human Embryology,' *Nature* **231** (May 14, 1971), 87

23 Ratzinger and Bovone, 33

24 Ibid., 34

and cultural values that underlie the drive to assume such risks for the sake of biological parenthood. We find that the capitalism, racism, sexism, and elitism of our culture have combined to create a set of attitudes which views children as commodities whose value is derived from their possession of parental chromosomes. Children are valued as privatized commodities, reflecting the virility and heredity of their parents. They are also viewed as the responsibility of their parents and are not seen as the social treasure and burden that they are. Parents must tend their needs on pain of prosecution, and, in return, they get to keep complete control over them. Other adults are inhibited from having warm, stable interactions with the children of others − it is as suspect to try to hug and talk regularly with a child who is not one's own as it is to fondle and hang longingly about a car or a bicycle which belongs to someone else − so those who wish to know children well often find they must have their own.

Women are persuaded that their most important purpose in life is to bear and raise children; they are told repeatedly that their life is incomplete, that they are lacking in fulfillment if they do not have children. And, in fact, many women do face a barren existence without children. Few women have access to meaningful, satisfying jobs. Most do not find themselves in the centre of the romantic personal relationships which the culture pretends is the norm for heterosexual couples. And they have been socialized to be fearful of close friendships with others − they are taught to distrust other women, and to avoid the danger of friendship with men other than their husbands. Children remain the one hope for real intimacy and for the sense of accomplishment which comes from doing work one judges to be valuable.

To be sure, children can provide that sense of self worth, although for many women (and probably for all mothers at some times) motherhood is not the romanticized satisfaction they are led to expect. But there is something very wrong with a culture where childrearing is the only outlet available to most women in which to pursue fulfillment. Moreover, there is something wrong with the ownership theory of children that keeps other adults at a distance from children. There ought to be a variety of close relationships possible between children and adults so that we all recognize that we have a stake in the well-being of the young, and we all benefit from contact with their view of the world.

In such a world, it would not be necessary to spend the huge sums on designer children which IVF requires while millions of other children starve to death each year. Adults who enjoyed children could be involved in caring for them whether or not they produced them biologically. And, if the institution of marriage survives, women and men would marry because they wished to share their lives together, not because the men needed someone to produce heirs for them and women needed financial support for their children. That would be a world in which we might have reproductive freedom of choice. The world we now live in has so limited women's options and self-esteem, it is legitimate to question the freedom behind women's demand for this technology, for it may well be largely a reflection of constraining social perspectives.

Nonetheless, I must acknowledge that some couples today genuinely mourn their incapacity to produce children without IVF and there are very significant and unique joys which can be found in producing and raising one's own children which are not accessible to persons in infertile relationships. We must sympathize with these people. None of us shall live to see the implementation of the ideal cultural values outlined above which would make the demand for IVF less severe. It is with real concern that some feminists suggest that the personal wishes of couples with fertility difficulties may not be compatible with the overall interests of women and children.

Feminist thought, then, helps us to focus on different dimensions of the problem then do other sorts of approaches. But, with this perspective, we still have difficulty in reaching a final conclusion on whether to encourage, tolerate, modify, or restrict this sort of reproductive technology. I suggest that we turn to the developing theories of feminist ethics for guidance in resolving this question.[25]

---

25 Many authors are now working on an understanding of what feminist ethics entail. Among the Canadian papers I am familiar with, are Kathryn Morgan's 'Women and Moral Madness,' Sheila Mullett's 'Only Connect: The Place of Self-Knowledge in Ethics,' both in this volume, and Leslie Wilson's 'Is a Feminine Ethics Enough?' *Atlantis* (forthcoming).

In my view, a feminist ethics is a moral theory that focusses on relations among persons as well as on individuals. It has as a model an inter-connected social fabric, rather than the familiar one of isolated, independent atoms; and it gives primacy to bonds among people rather than to rights to independence. It is a theory that focusses on concrete situations and persons and not on free-floating abstract actions.[26] Although many details have yet to be worked out, we can see some of its implications in particular problem areas such as this.

It is a theory that is explicitly conscious of the social, political, and economic relations that exist among persons; in particular, as a feminist theory, it attends to the implications of actions or policies on the status of women. Hence, it is necessary to ask questions from the perspective of feminist ethics in addition to those which are normally asked from the perspective of mainstream ethical theories. We must view issues such as this one in the context of the social and political realities in which they arise, and resist the attempt to evaluate actions or practices in isolation (as traditional responses in biomedical ethics often do). Thus, we cannot just address the question of IVF per se without asking how IVF contributes to general patterns of women's oppression. As Kathryn Payne Addleson has argued about abortion,[27] a feminist perspective raises questions that are inadmissable within the traditional ethical frameworks, and yet, for women in a patriarchal society, they are value questions of greater urgency. In particular, a feminist ethics, in contrast to other approaches in biomedical ethics, would take seriously the concerns just reviewed which are part of the debate in the feminist literature.

A feminist ethics would also include components of theories that have been developed as 'feminine ethics,' as sketched out by the empirical work of Carol Gilligan.[28] (The best example of such a

---

26 Sherwin, 'A Feminist Approach to Ethics'

27 Kathryn Payne Addelson, 'Moral Revolution,' in Marilyn Pearsall, ed., *Women and Values* (Belmont, CA: Wadsworth 1986), 291-309

28 Carol Gilligan, *In a Different Voice* (Cambridge, MA: Harvard University Press 1982)

theory is the work of Nel Noddings in her influential book *Caring*.)[29] In other words, it would be a theory that gives primacy to interpersonal relationships and woman-centered values such as nurturing, empathy, and co-operation. Hence, in the case of IVF, we must care for the women and men who are so despairing about their infertility as to want to spend the vast sums and risk the associated physical and emotional costs of the treatment, in pursuit of 'their own children.' That is, we should, in Noddings' terms, see their reality as our own and address their very real sense of loss. In so doing, however, we must also consider the implications of this sort of solution to their difficulty. While meeting the perceived desires of some women – desires which are problematic in themselves, since they are so compatible with the values of a culture deeply oppressive to women – this technology threatens to further entrench those values which are responsible for that oppression. A larger vision suggests that the technology offered may, in reality, reduce women's freedom and, if so, it should be avoided.

A feminist ethics will not support a wholly negative response, however, for that would not address our obligation to care for those suffering from infertility; it is the responsibility of those who oppose further implementation of this technology to work towards the changes in the social arrangements that will lead to a reduction of the sense of need for this sort of solution. On the medical front, research and treatment ought to be stepped up to reduce the rates of peral sepsis and gonorrhea which often result in tubal blockage, more attention should be directed at the causes and possible cures for male infertility, and we should pursue techniques that will permit safe reversible sterilization providing women with better alternatives to tubal ligation as a means of fertility control; these sorts of technology would increase the control of many women over their own fertility and would be compatible with feminist objectives. On the social front, we must continue the social pressure to change the status of women and children in our society from that of breeder and possession respectively; hence, we must develop a vision of

---

29 Nel Noddings, *Caring* (Berkeley: University of California Press 1984)

society as community where all participants are valued members, regardless of age or gender. And we must challenge the notion that having one's wife produce a child with his own genes is sufficient cause for the wives of men with low sperm counts to be expected to undergo the physical and emotional assault such technology involves.

Further, a feminist ethics will attend to the nature of the relationships among those concerned. Annette Baier has eloquently argued for the importance of developing an ethics of trust,[30] and I believe a feminist ethics must address the question of the degree of trust appropriate to the relationships involved. Feminists have noted that women have little reason to trust the medical specialists who offer to respond to their reproductive desires, for, commonly women's interests have not come first from the medical point of view.[31] In fact, it is accurate to perceive feminist attacks on reproductive technology as expressions of the lack of trust feminists have in those who control the technology. Few feminists object to reproductive technology per se; rather they express concern about who controls it and how it can be used to further exploit women. The problem with reproductive technology is that it concentrates power in reproductive matters in the hands of those who are not directly involved in the actual bearing and rearing of the child; i.e., in men who relate to their clients in a technical, professional, authoritarian manner. It is a further step in the medicalization of pregnancy and birth which, in North America, is marked by relationships between pregnant women and their doctors which are very different from the traditional relationships between pregnant women and midwives. The latter relationships fostered an atmosphere of mutual trust which is impossible to replicate in hospital deliveries today. In fact, current approaches to pregnancy, labour, and birth tend to

---

30 Annette Baier, 'What Do Women Want in a Moral Theory?' *Nous* **19** (March 1985) 53-64, and 'Trust and Antitrust,' *Ethics* **96** (January 1986) 231-60

31 Linda Williams presents this position particularly clearly in her invaluable work 'But What Will They Mean for Women? Feminist Concerns About the New Reproductive Technologies,' No. 6 in the *Feminist Perspective* Series, CRIAW.

view the mother as a threat to the fetus who must be coerced to comply with medical procedures designed to ensure delivery of healthy babies at whatever cost necessary to the mother. Frequently, the fetus-mother relationship is medically characterized as adversarial and the physicians choose to foster a sense of alienation and passivity in the role they permit the mother. However well IVF may serve the interests of the few women with access to it, it more clearly serves the interests (be they commercial, professional, scholarly, or purely patriarchal) of those who control it.

Questions such as these are a puzzle to those engaged in the traditional approaches to ethics, for they always urge us to separate the question of evaluating the morality of various forms of reproductive technology in themselves, from questions about particular uses of that technology. From the perspective of a feminist ethics, however, no such distinction can be meaningfully made. Reproductive technology is not an abstract activity, it is an activity done in particular contexts and it is those contexts which must be addressed.

Feminist concerns cited earlier made clear the difficulties we have with some of our traditional ethical concepts; hence, feminist ethics directs us to rethink our basic ethical notions. Autonomy, or freedom of choice, is not a matter to be determined in isolated instances, as is commonly assumed in many approaches to applied ethics. Rather it is a matter that involves reflection on one's whole life situation. The freedom of choice feminists appeal to in the abortion situation is freedom to define one's status as childbearer, given the social, economic, and political significance of reproduction for women. A feminist perspective permits us to understand that reproductive freedom includes control of one's sexuality, protection against coerced sterilization (or iatrogenic sterilization, e.g. as caused by the Dalkon Shield), and the existence of a social and economic network of support for the children we may choose to bear. It is the freedom to redefine our roles in society according to our concerns and needs as women.

In contrast, the consumer freedom to purchase technology, allowed only to a few couples of the privileged classes (in traditionally approved relationships), seems to entrench further the patriarchal notions of woman's role as childbearer and of heterosexual monogamy as the only acceptable intimate relationship. In other words, this sort of choice does not seem to foster autonomy for women on the broad scale. IVF is a practice which seems to reinforce sexist, classist, and often racist assumptions of our culture; therefore, on our revised understanding of freedom, the contribution of this technology to the general autonomy of women is largely negative.

We can now see the advantage of a feminist ethics over mainstream ethical theories, for a feminist analysis explicitly accepts the need for a political component to our understanding of ethical issues. In this, it differs from traditional ethical theories and it also differs from a simply feminine ethics approach, such as the one Noddings offers, for Noddings seems to rely on individual relations exclusively and is deeply suspicious of political alliances as potential threats to the pure relation of caring. Yet, a full understanding of both the threat of IVF, and the alternative action necessary should we decide to reject IVF, is possible only if it includes a political dimension reflecting on the role of women in society.

From the point of view of feminist ethics, the primary question to consider is whether this and other forms of reproductive technology threaten to reinforce the lack of autonomy which women now experience in our culture — even as they appear, in the short run, to be increasing freedom. We must recognize that the interconnections among the social forces oppressive to women underlie feminists' mistrust of this technology which advertises itself as increasing women's autonomy.[32] The political perspective which directs us to look at how this technology fits in with general patterns of treatment for women is not readily accessible to traditional moral theories, for it involves categories of concern not accounted for in those theories — e.g. the complexity of issues which makes it inappropriate to study them in isolation from one another, the

---

32 Marilyn Frye vividly describes the phenomenon of inter-relatedness which supports sexist oppression by appeal to the metaphor of a bird cage composed of thin wires, each relatively harmless in itself, but, collectively, the wires constitute an overwhelming barrier to the inhabitant of the cage. Marilyn Frye, *The Politics of Reality: Essays in Feminist Theory* (Trumansburg, NY: The Crossing Press 1983), 4-7

role of oppression in shaping individual desires, and potential differences in moral status which are connected with differences in treatment.

It is the set of connections constituting women's continued oppression in our society which inspires feminists to resurrect the old slippery slope arguments to warn against IVF. We must recognize that women's existing lack of control in reproductive matters begins the debate on a pretty steep incline. Technology with the potential to further remove control of reproduction from women makes the slope very slippery indeed. This new technology, though offered under the guise of increasing reproductive freedom, threatens to result, in fact, in a significant decrease in freedom, especially since it is a technology that will always include the active involvement of designated specialists and will not ever be a private matter for the couple or women concerned.

Ethics ought not to direct us to evaluate individual cases without also looking at the implications of our decisions from a wide perspective. My argument is that a theory of feminist ethics provides that wider perspective, for its different sort of methodology is sensitive to both the personal and the social dimensions of issues. For that reason, I believe it is the only ethical perspective suitable for evaluating issues of this sort.

CANADIAN JOURNAL OF PHILOSOPHY
Supplementary Volume 13

Surrogate Motherhood

CHRISTINE OVERALL
Queen's University
Kingston, ON
Canada K7L 3N6

I Introduction

This paper will explore some moral and conceptual aspects of the practice of surrogate motherhood. Although I put forward a number of criticisms of existing ideas about this subject, I do not claim to offer a fully developed position. Instead what I have tried to do is to call into question what seem to be some generally accepted assumptions about surrogate motherhood, and to lend plausibility to my view that surrogate motherhood may be morally troubling for reasons not always fully recognized by other writers on this issue. These reasons go beyond the fairly obvious consequentialist concerns (already well discussed in the press) about its effects on the persons — particularly the child — involved.[1] A concern for the well

---

1 The usual approach to moral questions about the practice of surrogate motherhood is simply to list the possible problems that might arise within a surrogate motherhood arrangement. For examples of this sort of approach, see Robert T. Francoeur, *Utopian Motherhood: New Trends in Human Reproduction* (Garden City, NY: Doubleday 1970), 102-6, and Council for Science and Society, *Human Procreation: Ethical Aspects of the New Techniques* (Oxford: Oxford University Press 1984), 66-70.

being of a child produced by a surrogate is, I believe, entirely justified, but my focus in this paper will be upon the surrogate mother
herself.

Surrogate motherhood is typically resorted to when the female
member of a married couple is unable — for one of a variety of possible reasons — to bear a child. The 'commissioning couple'[2] pays
a fee to a surrogate, who is artificially inseminated with the husband's sperm, gestates the child, and surrenders it to the couple,
on payment of a fee. (I emphasize that I am interested here in the
commercial forms of surrogate motherhood, not in those far rarer
cases in which a woman bears a child for a friend or relative.) Usually
the husband's name will be listed on the infant's birth certificate;[3]
the infertile wife, however, will have to formally adopt the child
in order to become its legal mother.[4]

What does surrogate motherhood suggest about the social use of
human reproductive faculties, about women's relationship to their
bodies, and about the interrelationships of males and females? Part
of the reason for the failure to fully recognize these questions lies
in the frameworks used to discuss the practice. Hence, my general

---

2 This is the term used by Mary Warnock in *A Question of Life: The Warnock Report
  on Human Fertilisation and Embryology* (Oxford: Basil Blackwell 1985), 42.

3 Michael D. Bayles, *Reproductive Ethics* (Englewood Cliffs, NJ: Prentice-Hall 1984),
  22

4 See also John A. Robertson, 'Surrogate Mothers: Not So Novel After All,' *The
  Hastings Center Report* **13** (October 1983), 29, and Council for Science and Society, 67. There are also other forms of surrogate motherhood, for example,
  those in which the surrogate gestates an embryo which is not the product of
  her own egg, but which was produced through in vitro fertilization of another
  women's ovum, or was obtained through the process of uterine lavage. These
  raise issues comparable to those in standard surrogate motherhood cases, but
  may be complicated further by the fact that the child which is produced is
  not genetically related to the gestating mother.

aim has been to reexamine those frameworks, and to subject them to critical analysis. I want to discover what surrogate motherhood really is. And in so doing, I am not seeking some hidden essence of the practice, but rather I am wondering how we ought most reasonably to look at it.

I shall present two different points of view about surrogate motherhood, which I call the free market model and the prostitution model.[5] Of the two, the prostitution model is better. But it shares with the free market model certain assumptions about reproductive labour and reproductive choice, assumptions which, I shall show, turn out to be highly implausible, and only obscure our understanding of what surrogate motherhood really is.

II The Free Market Model

According to the free market model, surrogate motherhood is, at its best, a desirable, useful, and indeed necessary service which un-coerced women may offer for purchase by childless but fertile men and their infertile wives.

This approach is defended by lawyer John A. Robertson, who regards surrogate motherhood as one type of what he calls 'collaborative reproduction,' that is, reproduction in which '[a] third person provides a genetic or gestational factor not present in ordinary paired reproduction.'[6] Other types include adoption and the use of artificial insemination by donor [AID]. For Robertson, there are few, if any, important social or moral differences among the various forms

---

5 There are others — such as Herbert T. Krimmel's view that surrogate motherhood is immoral primarily because of the motivations of the persons involved and the effects on the children produced — which I shall not discuss here. See 'The Case Against Surrogate Parenting,' *The Hastings Center Report* **13** (October 1983), 35-9. Cf. *A Matter of Life*, 45.

6 Robertson, 28

of collaborative reproduction.[7] Indeed, in some respects resort to surrogate motherhood may be preferable to agency adoption, because it is

> an alternative to the nonmarket, agency system of allocating children for adoption, which has contributed to long queues for distributing healthy white babies. This form of independent adoption is controlled by the parties, planned before conception, involves a genetic link with one parent, and enables both the father and the mother of the adopted child to be selected in advance.[8]

Robertson lists other benefits of surrogate motherhood, such as the alleviation of suffering and satisfaction of desires of the infertile.[9] But it is clear that for Robertson, the major benefit of the use of a surrogate is that it involves the uncoerced exercise of economic choice. The commissioning couple obtains the type of child they want[10] and at the time they choose. The couple freely decides to invest their money in their preferred form of consumer good: a child. As one adoptive mother of a baby born to a surrogate said, 'My God, people spend more on a Mercedes than we spent on Alexander. It's an alternative for people who want infants.'[11]

Of course, since the cost of hiring a surrogate mother is now $22,000 to $25,000,[12] and growing, this service is not, in fact, available

---

7 Bayles also compares the issues surrounding surrogate motherhood to those in AID (23). Cf. Alan B. Rassaby, 'Surrogate Motherhood: The Position and Problems of Substitutes,' in William Walters and Peter Singer, eds., *Test-Tube Babies* (Melbourne: Oxford University Press 1982), 103, and Suzanne M. Patterson, 'Parenthood by Proxy: Legal Implications of Surrogate Birth,' *Iowa Law Review* **385** (1982), 390-1.

8 Robertson, 28

9 Cf. Rassaby, 104.

10 For example, white, not black: '[A]lmost every adopting white couple wants a healthy white baby, and the great majority of young, pregnant, white American women do not give up their babies for adoption' (Cynthia Gorney, 'For Love and Money,' *California Magazine* [October 1983], 91).

11 Ibid., 155

12 Margaret Munro, '"Rent-a-Womb" Trade Thriving Across Canada-U.S. Border,' *The Montreal Gazette* (21 January 1985) D-11

to all. Robertson calls it 'a consumption item for the middle class-es.' Its limited accessibility is not, he claims, unjust to poor couples, because it does not leave them worse off than they were before.[13] Philosopher Michael D. Bayles also uses this defence and mentions some others. He says that the price will drop if many women decide, because of the attractive fees, to become surrogates, and more children will become available for adoption. 'In general,' says Bayles, 'one should not accept limitations on otherwise permissible activities because poor people cannot afford them, but should try to raise the income of the poor or subsidize the activities so that poor people can afford them.'[14]

Furthermore, the surrogate, like the commissioning couple, also exercises free choice, according to Robertson. Equality of opportunity has been extended: like the sperm donor, a woman is now free to sell her reproductive capacities.[15] She chooses, in effect, a particular type of temporary (though by no means part-time!) job. Robertson states that surrogates 'choose the surrogate role primarily because the fee provides a better economic opportunity than alternative occupations ....'[16] Thus, Jane Doe chooses to be a surrogate mother rather than a waitress, let's say, because the pay for the former is (or appears to be) better. High school guidance counsellors take note: female students should be alerted to the existence of this new employment opportunity.

It should be remarked at this point that there might be some question as to how rewarding the payment for surrogate mothering really is. Much of the money paid by the couple goes toward lawyers' fees, medical and travel expenses, and insurance; surrogate mothers

---

13 Robertson, 29

14 Bayles, 26; cf. Rassaby, 103.

15 *A Matter of Life* also cites this claim as a possible justification for surrogacy: '[C]arrying mothers ... have a perfect right to enter into such agreements if they so wish, just as they have a right to use their own bodies in other ways, according to their own decision' (45). Cf. Council for Science and Society, 66.

16 Robertson, 29

usually receive about $10,000.[17] This means that a woman who be-
comes pregnant at the very first attempt at artificial insemination
would earn around $1.50 per hour for her full-time 24-hour-per-day
'job' as a pregnant woman.

Nevertheless, says Robertson, the payment of a fee (such as it
is) is crucial to the surrogate mothering contract, for 'few surrogates
will volunteer for altruistic reasons alone.' A ban on fees is not necessary to protect the surrogate from coercion or exploitation, since the
surrogate has made 'a considered, knowing choice, often with the
assistance of counsel, before becoming pregnant.'[18] Bayles elaborates
this suggestion. Poor women, he says, are not exploited in being
offered attractive payments to be surrogates. After all, 'other people are attracted by large fees to become lawyers or physicans.' It
is true that poor, uneducated women might not have many alternative forms of employment, but this fact is not a good reason to
ban even this form of opportunity. In fact, it would be unjust to
deprive them of the opportunity, providing their decision to become
a surrogate is an informed one.[19] Philosopher Alan Rassaby expresses this idea more bluntly. 'Given a choice between poverty and exploitation,' he says, 'many people may prefer the latter.'[20]

Robertson does not fail to recognize some potential problems in
surrogate motherhood. These problems mainly concern the possibility of psychological suffering of the parties to the contract between
the surrogate and the commissioning couple, harms to the child,
the artificial manipulation of the natural process of reproduction,
and difficulties resulting from noncompliance with the contract.
Robertson apparently regards such problems as just a manifestion
of the pains of the human condition: they are not unique to sur-

---

17 Munro, D-11

18 Robertson, 32-3

19 Bayles, 25

20 Rassaby, 103. Cf. William A. W. Walters and Peter Singer, 'Conclusions —
And Costs,' in *Test-Tube Babies*, 138.

rogate motherhood. Furthermore, they can be significantly diminished by providing good medical and legal services.

Robertson summarizes his discussion of possible problems in surrogate motherhood in a most significant statement. 'The morality of surrogate mothering,' he says, 'depends on how the duties and responsibilities of the role are carried out, rather than on the mere fact that a couple produces a child with the aid of a collaborator.'[21] For Robertson what is important is 'not what we do – but how we do it.'[22] No further analysis of 'what we do' in surrogate mothering is needed. All that is required is reasonable 'public scrutiny, through regulation of the process of drawing up the contract rather than its specific terms,'[23] of how surrogate mothering is carried out.

III The Prostitution Model

At the very least, the free market model for surrogate motherhood seems naive. Among its problems are the assumptions that the commodification of babies is morally acceptable; that the high cost to the commissioning couple, along with the low fee to the mother, is not unjust; that surrogate mothers choose freely to sell their services at a fair price and are therefore not the victims of exploitation; that the practice of surrogate motherhood requires only legal regulation in order to prevent problems; and that *what* surrogate motherhood is is in no need of further analysis.

The second point of view on surrogate motherhood, which I have called the prostitution model, is, at first sight, quite different from the first, for it calls into question at least some of the assumptions made by the free market model. It is usually advanced by feminist writers, but it is nowhere as fully expressed and developed as the

---

21 Robertson, 32

22 Ibid., 33

23 Ibid., 34

free market model. Instead, it is necessary to piece it together from a variety of rather brief commentaries.

According to this second point of view, surrogate motherhood is a type of deliberate exploitation of women's reproductive capacities, and is in that way akin to prostitution.

An outline of this sort of analysis is provided by Mary Kay Blakely, in a short paper whose very title, 'Surrogate Mothers: For Whom Are They Working?' invites us to examine our underlying assumptions about surrogate motherhood. She suggests that the practice is governed by racist and sexist beliefs.[24] Surrogate motherhood, she says, raises issues concerning ownership of children, 'the conceit of patriarchal genetics,'[25] infertility as a failing in women, and finally 'guilt and money, and how women earn both.'[26] But these comments just hint at a feminist analysis, and Blakely herself never answers the provocative question in the title of her paper.

In response to Blakely's paper, another writer[27] states that recognition of a woman's right to control her own body and to make decisions about childbearing do not imply a license to exploit one's body. Surrogate mothers may feel a sense of fulfillment at least partly

---

24 Advertisements for prospective surrogates usually make it clear that applicants should be white. And the commissioning couple may 'try again' for a boy if the pregnancy produces a female infant (Mary Kay Blakely, 'Surrogate Mothers: For Whom Are They Working?' *Ms.* **11** [March 1983], 18 and 20). She could also have added class considerations. Cf. Rosalind Pollack Petchesky, 'Reproductive Freedom: Beyond "A Woman's Right to Choose,"' in Catharine R. Stimpson and Ethel Spector Person, eds., *Women: Sex and Sexuality* (Chicago: University of Chicago Press 1980), 92-116, for a discussion of class distinctions in the availability of other reproductive services, such as abortion and contraception.

25 Susan Ince states: 'The need to continue patriarchal lineage, to make certain the child has the sperm and name of the buyer, is primary' ('Inside the Surrogate Industry,' in Rita Arditti, Renate Duelli Klein, and Shelley Minden, eds., *Test-Tube Women: What Future for Motherhood?* [London: Pandora Press 1984], 112).

26 Blakely, 20

27 Susan E. Nash, letter, *Ms.* **11** (June, 1983), 5

because childbearing has been, historically, almost the only realm for which women gain recognition.[28] Thus, while women should have a 'right to choose' in regard to surrogate motherhood, 'society's endorsement of this choice as a valid female occupation' would be a mistake, because it would serve as an affirmation of the tradition of fulfillment through childbearing.

A possible answer to the question, for whom are surrogates working, is provided by feminist Susan Ince. In her investigation of the operation of a surrogate motherhood broker, she found that the infertile wife, who is the raison d'être of the surrogate industry, is 'notably absent' from the surrogate motherhood relationship. The company investigated by Ince urged each 'girl' to find ways to include the biological father (the husband of the infertile woman) in her pregnancy and birth, for example, by sending a 'nice note' to the father after conception, and later, a tape of the baby's heartbeat.[29] Furthermore, the contract used by the company makes it clear that it is the father who is the purchaser; it is he to whom the child-product belongs, and to whom it must be delivered.[30] The preeminence of the father over his infertile wife is emphasized by the fact that her consent is not usually required for his participation in the surrogate motherhood arrangement. (This contrasts with the regular procedures governing the use of AID: consent of the husband is usually required before a woman is artificially inseminated.) Thus, Susan Ince's analysis suggests that the true employer of the surrogate is not the so-called commissioning couple, but only the male who provides the sperm.

That suggestion renders more plausible the claim that surrogate motherhood is like prostitution. The comparison is used briefly by

---

28 Some confirmation for this appears in a recent brief discussion of the motives of surrogate mothers. One woman wrote, 'When I first heard of surrogate motherhood, my immediate thoughts were, "Goodness, I could do that! I can't cook, I can't play tennis or do tapestries, but I am good at being pregnant and giving birth."' Quoted in Carl Wood and Ann Westmore, *Test-Tube Conception* (Englewood Cliffs, NJ: Prentice-Hall 1984), 113.

29 Ince, 102

30 Ibid., 112

philosopher Mary B. Mahowald, who also challenges the assumption of the free market model that women freely choose the job of surrogate mother. Expressing concern about women's right to self-determination regarding their own bodies, she writes,

> Most prostitutes are driven to their "trade" by economic and emotional pressures largely beyond their control; and surrogacy? What either practice says about society is more telling than what it says about the individual. Accordingly, we might more appropriately critique the social conditions that make these options genuine and unavoidable for individual women, than worry about the legal complaints arising from their practice.[31]

Finally, feminist Andrea Dworkin has also written about surrogate motherhood in the course of a longer discussion of prostitution. She argues that the scientific separation of sex from reproduction, and of reproduction from sex, now 'enable women to sell their wombs within the terms of the brothel model.'[32] Thus, reproduction can become the sort of commodity that sex is now. All reproductive technologies 'make the womb extractable from the woman as a whole person in the same way the vagina (or sex) is now.'[33] A surrogate mother is, Dworkin says, a 'reproductive prostitute.'[34]

IV The Two Models: Similarities and Critique

The free market model and the prostitution model of surrogate motherhood appear to be rather different. The former states that surrogate motherhood is a freely chosen arrangement between two or more human beings operating to the potential benefit of all concerned. The latter sees surrogate motherhood as akin to prostitution, a type of exploitive employment by men into which the women

---

31 Letter, *The Hastings Center Report* **14** (June, 1984), 43

32 Andrea Dworkin, *Right-Wing Women* (New York: Perigee Books 1983), 181

33 Ibid., 187

34 Ibid., 188

involved enter, not freely, but out of economic necessity or social coercion. The two viewpoints are, consequently, sharply divided as to the moral justification of the practice: the free market model regards it as acceptable, the prostitution model as morally questionable; and also as to social policy, with the free market model seeing surrogacy as in need only of legal regulation, while the prostitution model sees it as necessitating a dramatic restructuring of society so that women will not be forced into being surrogate mothers.

Nevertheless, despite these apparent differences, closer examination of the two viewpoints on surrogate mothers reveals that they share several assumptions in common. I shall discuss two items of agreement between them: the first concerns the idea of reproductive labour, which is expressed in this context by treating surrogate motherhood as a job; the second concerns the concept of reproductive choice.

a) Reproductive Labour: Surrogate Motherhood as a Job

In a very literal sense, the surrogate mother is engaging in reproductive labour: her body is doing the work necessary to produce a human being. Moreover, she is being paid for this work. Hence, surrogate motherhood appears to be, or to be like, a job. This is an assumption shared by both the free market model and the prostitution model, and even by the women themselves.[35] Just as, for example, a music teacher might sell her pedagogical services privately to individual students, or a lawyer might sell her legal services to clients, or a prostitute might sell her sexual services to customers, the surrogate mother sells her reproductive services to the commissioning couple, or, more accurately, to a man, or possibly a series of individual men.

To treat surrogate motherhood as a job appears only too consistent with other traditional uses of women's reproductive labour. For, as feminist writers have pointed out, under usual circumstances,

---

35 Munro, D-11

such labour is either a species of volunteer work, which women supposedly undertake for sheer love of it, or, in less congenial circumstances, it is a type of slavery.[36] Thus, the fee paid to the surrogate mother at least appears to put reproductive labour on a more equal footing with other forms of paid labour than it ordinarily possesses.

But *if* surrogate motherhood is to be regarded as a job, then we are forced to accept the peculiar implications which follow from it. For example, consider this: The free market model assumes that the surrogate is employed by the commissioning couple; the prostitution model suggests that she is employed by the man who provides the sperm. But closer investigation makes it at least as plausible to say that the surrogate is self-employed.

Surrogate motherhood is similar in several respects to a small-scale, owner-operated business. The woman, after all, operates out of her own home; she provides the equipment for carrying out the labour; and her earnings are controlled (or limited) by the amount of work she is willing to do (that is, by the number of babies she is willing to produce). I would even venture that if the government found out about her income, it would require her to pay taxes directly to the state.[37] The surrogate motherhood brokers who bring buyers and sellers together are not the employers of the women; they explicitly disavow any responsibility for adverse outcomes,[38] and they do not pay the woman for her services. But then, neither are the couple, or the biological father, the employer of the woman, any more than a lawyer's clients or a music teacher's pupils are their employers.

Thus, *if* surrogate motherhood is a job involving the selling of reproductive labour on a private basis, then an answer, at least as plausible as any other, to Blakely's question, for whom is the surrogate working, is: herself.

---

36 Elizabeth W. Moen, 'What Does "Control Over Our Bodies" Really Mean?', *International Journal of Women's Studies* **2** (March/April 1979), 133

37 I owe these ideas to Ted Worth.

38 Ince, 107

Now of course, I do not really want to claim that surrogate mothers are self-employed. I simply want to explore the implications that follow from treating surrogate motherhood as a job. They reveal, I think, that there is an error in seeing surrogate motherhood as being, or being like, a job involving the selling of one's reproductive services. For if the surrogate mother is self-employed, then we are led to see her as an individual whose activities must be regulated in order to protect both those who specifically hire her services, and the general public, from any potential dangers or failure of responsibility in her exercise of her vocation.[39] Indeed, legislation to govern surrogate motherhood has already been proposed which is designed to safeguard lawyers, doctors, the commissioning couple, and the potential baby, by providing legal and financial penalties to be exacted if the mother should abort, engage in negligent behaviour, or fail to surrender the child, in violation of the terms of her contract.[40] The idea that the surrogate mother is self-employed thus leads us to a concern for the licensing of surrogates; for setting appropriate fees;[41] for requisite training, qualifications, screening, advertising, insurance, and contracts. Moreover, if surrogate motherhood is a job, then it appears that our only worry, if there is one at all, for the women involved must be whether it is a good job: Our concern will be directed toward improving their working conditions, raising their income, providing insurance, perhaps even offering a pension plan, and so on.

---

39 This point of view is taken most noticeably by Bernard D. Hirsch, in 'Parenthood by Proxy,' *Journal of the American Medical Association* **249** (April 22/29 1983), 2251-2.

40 This seems to be reflected in surrogate motherhood contracts: the contract signed by the mother is often longer, and specifies more limitations, than that signed by the commissioning couple. ('Nothing Left to Chance in "Rent-A-Womb" Agreements,' *The Toronto Star* [January 13, 1985].) See also Theresa M. Mady, 'Surrogate Mothers: The Legal Issues,' *American Journal of Law and Medicine* **7** (Fall 1981), 351.

41 'One wonders ... whether fair compensation for being a surrogate mother should be determined simply by market forces,' William J. Winslade, 'Surrogate Mothers: Private Right or Public Wrong?', *Journal of Medical Ethics* **7** (1981), 154.

But all of these concerns entirely lose sight of part of what seems to be implicit in, and correct about, the feminist critique of surrogate motherhood: namely, that the surrogate mother is *herself* in need of protection from the lawyers, doctors, and infertile couples who wish to make use of her services. The assumption that surrogate motherhood is, or is like, a job essentially misrepresents the power relations which are defined by the practice. The immediate locus of power in the surrogate arrangement is in a necessarily rather wealthy man who pays the fee and provides the sperm, and in the person, usually a male lawyer, who represents him, and receives a commission for his services. But the wider network of control is constituted by the authority relations defined in patriarchy, in the context of which reproduction is usually labour done by women for men. It seems highly unlikely that in becoming a surrogate mother, a woman is invested with power and independence which she would otherwise not possess in the exercise of her reproductive capacities. As in the case of prostitution, the mere payment of a small fee in no way changes the possibility that she is a victim of exploitation, and the nature of the exploitation is not such that an increase in fees or improved working conditions will change it.

b) Reproductive Choice

But in order to give more substance to this contention, I shall now introduce some analysis of the second item on which the two models of surrogate motherhood agree. Both of them assume that individuals ought, perhaps within certain limits, to have the freedom to choose what sort of job to take up (whether, let's say, to become a secretary or a waitress, or whether to choose self-employment as a doctor or as a surrogate mother). And becoming a surrogate mother is assumed to be, at least potentially, one possible result of the exercise of that free choice, in particular, free choice concerning the use of one's reproductive capacities.

Of course, the two models disagree as to whether this freedom really exists in the case of surrogate motherhood: the free market model says it does; the prostitution model says it does not. And in this respect, the prostitution model is, I would argue, correct. A question raised by the Canadian Advisory Council on the Status of Women about prostitution applies almost verbatim to surrogate motherhood: 'Can a person of minimal education and financial well-being be said truly to choose a way of life that is stigmatized by much of society, that is physically dangerous at times, that leaves her with little control over her earning power, and that can cause her considerable legal complications?'[42]

In one of the few psychological studies so far undertaken on the characteristics of women who apply to be surrogate mothers, it was discovered that 40% of the sample were unemployed or receiving some form of financial aid, or both. Moreover, 72% of the women had an education level of high school graduation or less.[43] The researcher, Philip J. Parker, also found that a large majority of the group had been pregnant previously; when pregnant these women 'felt more content, complete, special, and adequate and often felt an inner glow; some felt more feminine and attractive and enjoyed the extra attention afforded them.'[44] In this sample, 35% of the women either had had a voluntary abortion or had relinquished a child for adoption, a fact which led Parker to surmise that these women 'felt (often unconsciously) that surrogate motherhood would help them master unresolved feelings they had regarding a previous voluntary loss of fetus or baby.'[45] Considering all of these factors, the candidates for surrogate motherhood seem not only to be motivated by very real financial need, but also to be influenced by quite traditional role expectations about the importance of pregnancy and motherhood in women's lives.[46]

---

42 Canadian Advisory Council on the Status of Women, *Prostitution in Canada* (March 1984), 84

43 Philip J. Parker, 'Motivation of Surrogate Mothers: Initial Findings,' *American Journal of Psychiatry* **140** (January 1983), 117

44 Ibid., 118

45 Ibid.

46 Cf. the findings of Darrell D. Franks, 'Psychiatric Evaluation of Women in a Surrogate Mother Program,' *American Journal of Psychiatry* **138** (October 1981) 1378-9.

It is most ironic that after uncovering this information about applicants for surrogate motherhood, Parker emphasizes the importance of ensuring that every applicant for surrogate motherhood is 'competent' and is 'voluntarily and freely making an informed choice, free of coercion and undue influence.'[47] In my view, there is a fundamental contradiction between the fact that social conditions such as those delineated in Parker's study create the demand for surrogate motherhood, and permit reproductive services to become a commodity, and the fact that the women involved are perceived as able to make a free choice.[48] Yet the free market proponents of surrogate motherhood are likely to use that alleged free choice to defend the practice, by asking, rhetorically, what right the state has to deny women the exercise of her free will in selling her reproductive capacities.[49]

Perhaps the cause of the disagreement between the two models as to whether surrogate motherhood is the result of free choice is a failure to examine what reproductive choice means. Both models appear to assume that the main moral question about reproductive choice is whether or not it exists — in this context, whether the women who become surrogate mothers freely choose this use of their reproductive capacities. But I contend that the idea of reproductive choice is in need of further analysis: It is more complex than proponents of the two models appear to realize.

Sociologist Barbara Katz Rothman has sounded some warnings about the meanings of reproductive choice. Examining the varieties of choices offered by reproductive technology — options for fetal monitoring, contraceptive use, abortion, prenatal diagnosis, and infertility treatments — Rothman argues that apparent expansions of choice often result in the loss of other choices because they become socially less acceptable, or in the existence of choices which

---

47 Philip J. Parker, 'Surrogate Motherhood: The Interaction of Litigation, Legislation and Psychiatry,' *International Journal of Law and Psychiatry* 5 (1982), 352

48 Dworkin, 182

49 Ibid., 180; cf. *Prostitution in Canada*, 69, and Ince, 99.

we are, paradoxically, forced to make.[50] Thus reproductive choice sometimes turns out to be more apparent than real.

This sort of insight can be applied to surrogate motherhood. We should be asking what options may be foreclosed for some women by the existence of the apparent choice of selling one's reproductive services. To this question I can offer only a tentative response. For individual women, the existence of surrogate motherhood as an apparent choice may tend to obscure or override other possible interpretations of their lives. Just as the overwhelming presence of the role of housewife presented itself, until recently, as the only 'choice' for women, so also surrogacy may appear to be the only possible escape route for some women with few resources and opportunities. A woman may reason, in effect, that if all else fails, she can still become a surrogate mother. If surrogate motherhood becomes a socially approved 'choice,' it will affect how women see the use of their reproductive capacities, and their relationships to their children, as well as the social construction of women's reproductive roles.

So far, what I have said about reproductive choice does not go much beyond what feminists have said about it in other contexts. However, I want to suggest a second reason to reconsider the notion of reproductive choice in the context of surrogate motherhood: it can lead to an uncritical acceptance of the many ways in which women's reproductive capacities may be used. In endorsing an uncritical freedom of reproductive choice, we may also be implicitly endorsing all conceivable alternatives that an individual might adopt; we thereby abandon the responsibility for evaluating substantive actions in favour of advocating merely formal freedom of choice.[51]

---

50 Barbara Katz Rothman, 'The Meanings of Choice in Reproductive Technology,' in *Test-Tube Women*, 23-33. Cf. Kathleen McDonnell, *Not An Easy Choice: A Feminist Re-Examines Abortion* (Toronto: The Women's Press 1984), 71-2, and Petchesky, 101, on abortion as a 'free' choice.

51 An unlimited advocacy of the further development of reproductive choice would seem to imply, for example, an unlimited 'right' to choose the sex of one's children, through selective abortion, a 'right' which appears to be potentially gynecidal. See McDonnell, 79, and Petchesky, 100.

We must think very carefully about whether surrogate motherhood is a 'choice' which we want to recognize in this way.

This brings me to a more fundamental reservation about the idea of reproductive choice in the context of surrogate motherhood: Is becoming a surrogate mother really the sort of thing one can freely choose? What I am trying to get at here could perhaps be more clearly expressed by asking whether surrogate motherhood is genuinely a part of what we ought to *mean* by the exercise of reproductive choice.

The problem is not merely that surrogate motherhood may not be freely chosen by those women who take it up. The problem is that there is a real moral danger in the sort of conceptual framework which presents surrogate motherhood as even a *possible* freely chosen alternative for women.

This becomes apparent when we consider whether the practice of surrogacy would raise fewer moral questions if only middle-class, economically advantaged women became surrogate mothers. (And in fact, some commentators have suggested that such women may be a substantial component of the applicants for surrogate motherhood.[52] A study by Darrell D. Franks of a very small sample of such applicants found that nine out of ten of the women 'were of modest to moderate means' − although in many cases this turned out to mean that they were supported by a husband or boyfriend.[53]) No woman is forced into becoming a surrogate mother at the point of a gun, and middle class women are not, apparently, forced into it by economic expediency. But the absence of these or comparable compelling conditions does not mean that it makes sense to say that a woman is therefore making a choice to be a surrogate, and is thereby exercising a type of reproductive freedom.

Surrogate motherhood is not and cannot be merely one career choice among others. It is not a real alternative. It is implausible to suppose that fond parents would want it for their daughters. We

---

52 John Robertson, 'John Robertson Replies,' *The Hastings Center Report* **14** (June 1984), 43

53 Franks, 1379

are unlikely to set up training courses for surrogate mothers. Schools holding 'career days' for their future graduates will surely not invite surrogate mothers to address the class on the advantages of their 'vocation.' And surrogate motherhood does not seem to be the sort of thing one would put on one's curriculum vitae.[54]

Surrogate motherhood is no more a real job option than selling one's blood or one's gametes or one's bodily organs can be real job options. All of these commercial transactions involve an extreme form of personal and bodily alienation. Surrogate mothering is 'at the extreme end of the spectrum of alienated labour,' for the surrogate mother must contract out of all of the 'so-called "normal" love, pride, satisfaction, and attachment in, for, and to the product of her labour.'[55] In surrogate motherhood, the woman gives up the use of her body, the product of her reproductive labour, and that reproductive labour itself, to persons who pay to make them their own.[56] In so doing, she surrenders her individuality, for becoming a surrogate mother involves receiving a fee, not for labour which is the unique expression of one's personal capacities and talents, but only for the exercise of one's reproductive capacities. As one applicant for surrogate motherhood aptly expressed it: 'I'm only an incubator.'[57]

Now, some have claimed that reproductive labour is not impersonal: that some form of personal expression enters into it by means of, for example, choices as to what is consumed during pregnancy, the type of activities one engages in, and the moods and feelings one experiences. But while these factors can indeed affect the nature

---

54 Lorraine Code, 'Commentary on "Surrogate Motherhood" by Christine Overall,' unpublished paper (February 1985), 3

55 Ibid., 4. The effects on the woman of giving up her child — effects which are at least hinted at by women who change their minds about surrendering the baby once it is born — must be counted as part of the exploitation and psychological costs to the mother of the practice of surrogate motherhood.

56 Cf. Mary O'Brien, *The Politics of Reproduction* (Boston: Routledge & Kegan Paul 1981), 58-9, on alienation and appropriation.

57 Parker, 'Motivation of Surrogate Mothers: Initial Findings,' 118

of the pregnancy and its outcome (that is, not only the health of the baby, but one's own wellbeing), for the most part the course of pregnancy and even of childbirth is outside the control of the woman involved. This is emphasized by Mary O'Brien, in a discussion of Marx's comparison of the architect and the bee.

> [M]other and architect are quite different. The woman cannot realize her visions, cannot make them come true, by virtue of the reproductive labour in which she involuntarily engages, if at all. Unlike the architect, her will does not influence the shape of her product. Unlike the bee, she knows that her product, like herself, will have a history. Like the architect, she knows what she is doing; like the bee, she cannot help what she is doing.[58]

For this reason, the woman who engages in paid reproductive labour is permitted no moral significance as an individual. In fact, as Andrea Dworkin points out, when women are defined and used as a sex class, as they are when they are paid for their reproductive or sexual services, the individual woman becomes a fiction.[59] It is clear that, within certain broadly defined limits — for example, being fertile, being white, being healthy, even being pretty — the women who work as surrogate mothers are interchangeable. Despite some superficial attention to finding the 'right' woman — and indeed, sometimes the hiring father is encouraged to choose his woman on the basis of data supplied by the lawyer or agency[60] — the women involved are defined solely as gestators, without reference to their individual characteristics or potential.[61]

Thus, surrogate motherhood is not and cannot be a freely chosen job because the practice is such that it recognizes no individual who can make the choice. The institution defines the individual woman

---

58 Ibid., 38

59 Dworkin, 182

60 Munro, D-11

61 It is worth noting that this loss of individuality will be exacerbated in the near future when embryo transfers become routine, and the surrogate mother contributes only her reproductive services to the production of the baby.

out of existence. All that is left is what the press has referred to as a 'womb for rent.' In surrogate motherhood, there can be no doubt, a commercial transaction takes place, but it is not a transaction between equals, or even between potential equals. Although the woman involved may rightly be described as being freely chosen by a man, who pays her fee and who thus exercises a special type of reproductive choice, she does not freely choose him. The man who pays the fee and provides the sperm has merely leased for nine months a part of her body, together with its reproductive capacities, and has purchased outright the egg from which the baby grows. A woman can no more choose to be a surrogate mother than a room can choose to be leased, or a pet can choose to be bought. Surrogate motherhood is no more a job than being occupied, for a fee, is a job.

IV Conclusion

Thus, a close examination of the practice of surrogate motherhood leads to the rejection of two assumptions made both by those who praise and by those who condemn it, that is, by the free market model and by the prostitution model. Surrogate motherhood is not a job. And to become a surrogate mother is not the sort of thing that we should mean by the exercise of reproductive choice.

While in no way wanting to glorify some hypothetical form of 'natural' motherhood, I nevertheless believe that this examination of what surrogate motherhood is, that is, within what framework or set of assumptions it should be understood, shows both that the commercial form of surrogate motherhood as it now exists is not the sort of social practice which should be fostered or benignly tolerated, and that it is part of a broader context of morally and conceptually dubious assumptions about women's role in reproduction.

IV

Selves and Integration

CANADIAN JOURNAL OF PHILOSOPHY
Supplementary Volume 13

Only Connect: The Place of Self-Knowledge in Ethics

SHEILA MULLETT
Concordia University
Montreal, PQ
Canada H3G 1M8

> Only connect the prose and the passion, and both
> will be exalted, and human love will be seen at its
> height. Live in fragments no longer. (E.M.Forster)

I Introduction

How important is self-knowledge in moral life? What kind of self-knowledge, if any, is necessary for full moral agency? What kinds of self-knowledge are there? What is 'full moral agency'? Despite the great proliferation of theories about the self in psychology in this century, questions like these have not been addressed very often in recent literature on ethics in the Anglo-American tradition. And, although in 1958 Anscombe recommended that we stop doing moral philosophy altogether until we have a better moral psychology[1], the main response to this suggestion has been a renewed interest in the virtues.[2] Another approach to these problems can be found in

---

1 'Modern Moral Philosophy,' *Philosophy* 33 (1959), 1-19

2 Philippa Foot, *Virtues and Vices and Other Essays in Moral Philosophy* (Berkeley and Los Angeles: University of California Press 1978); James D. Wallace, *Virtues and Vices* (Ithaca, NY: Cornell University Press 1978); Alisdair MacIntyre, *After Virtue* (Notre Dame: University of Notre Dame Press 1981).

feminist ethics, with its interest in caring relations.[3] In this paper I shall describe a few of the connections between caring and self-knowledge. I shall then compare the insights generated by this approach with the views of two authors, who work from radically opposed frameworks, Richard Brandt[4] and Charles Taylor.[5] Both have produced interesting, but completely different descriptions of self-knowledge and its place in moral life.

I assume without argument that the task of the moral philosopher is to describe and perhaps clarify what we already know at some level in our daily lived experiences of moral life.[6] What I mean by the phrase 'moral life' is not so easy to define clearly. The enormous complexity of the experience of any one individual, as well as the vast differences between people make it difficult to use the term 'moral life' with any confidence of communicating a clear sense. It is because of this complexity that philosophers are driven to produce theories to give an account of morality.[7] Because there are so many moral theories, and so few that can claim any sort of comprehensiveness,[8] I confine myself to the task of drawing attention to some aspects of moral life that seem to be overlooked, or at least relegated to the background in contemporary moral philosophy. The philosophical descriptions that follow are not intended to convince the immoralist, the skeptic or the fanatic.[9] My subject matter is more

---

3 See Lorraine Code, Sheila Mullett, Christine Overall, eds., *Shifting Perspectives: Essays on Method and Morals* (University of Toronto Press, forthcoming).

4 *A Theory of The Good and the Right* (Oxford: Oxford University Press 1979)

5 *Human Agency and Language: Philosophical Papers I*, and *Philosophy and the Human Sciences: Philosophical Papers 2* (Cambridge: Cambridge University Press 1985)

6 Jack D. Douglas, 'Aspects of Existential Sociology,' in Jack D. Douglas and John M. Johnson, eds., *Existential Sociology* (Cambridge: Cambridge University Press 1977), 22-3

7 Annette C. Baier, 'What Do Women Want In a Moral Theory?' *Nous* **19**, 1 (1985), 54

8 Ibid., 55

9 'I take it that most moral philosophers have assumed that ... a fully rational

mundane. When I talk with my students, for example, I do not begin with the assumption that they need to be convinced by rational argument to become moral agents. My assumption is that they are moral agents, that they have commitments to certain values[10] which they are trying to enact, and, finally, that these commitments and enactments always take place within the context of specific relations with others.[11]

But academic philosophical reflections, typically take place within the context of our institutionalized relations and are addressed to a far larger audience than the people with whom we construct our particular lives. Yet the context of utterance dramatically affects what can be said and what interpretations can be put on what is said. The contextual constraints on meaning in personal conversations are missing in our public philosophical contexts where entirely different constraints are in effect. It takes a great deal of time for people to get to know one another personally and to understand the motives, feelings, intentions and values which infuse their talk. What people say and do requires a lot of interpretation. I introduce you with enthusiasm to everyone I know at the conference. You are a little shy and wonder whether I am doing this out of some sense of duty, or pity. You wonder if I would rather just forget about you. It takes a fair amount of conversation for us to come to understand one another. I explain that I really love introducing a person like you around, and that I rarely act out of 'duty' and never out of pity. You explain that you are more reticent in meeting people and would be content to be integrated more slowly, although you appreciate

---

morality must be capable of evaluating the highest excellence and most unspeakable evil, and that persons of the highest excellence and the most unspeakable evil must *agree* with our moral evaluations if these evaluations are to be fully rational.... Such a conception has done to moral philosophy and to the concept of morality what the events of the modern world have done to the moral life itself: made it a matter of academic questions' (Stanley Cavell, *The Claim of Reason* [Oxford: Oxford University Press 1979], 269).

10 See John Kekes, 'Moral Sensitivity,' *Philosophy* **59** (1984), 5.

11 Ibid., 268

my gregariousness, and so on. In such discussions we sort out our feelings, our thoughts, our perceptions and our values. To have such conversations presupposes a good deal of trust as well as many common 'practices.' These are the constraints on relations between individuals. In such discussions we are talking about particular events, feelings, thoughts and values. But in an acceptable philosophical description, we are talking about feelings in general, and values in general, and so on. And, further, the norms that govern academic philosophical analyses are not the norms that operate in conversation between friends. Traditionally philosophers have been concerned with the justification of norms and values in the 'public' domain, i.e., the domain that extends beyond friendship. The emphasis has had to be on rational justification and defense of values apart from the particular constraints of personal relationships. The arguments are based upon implied universal norms of rational thought which can be appealed to in the absence of personal relationship in order to achieve resolution of conflict.[12]

In both contexts, however, we are building up shared pictures of what it is to be a person. Philosophers typically focus on contexts of justification and seek out rational moral codes. Whereas in personal contexts the important thing to be aware of is the use we make of various moral principles and abstractions and the motivation underlying our talk and action. Everything hinges on the use we make of moral principles and ideals. We can use them to rationalize and justify actions and reactions of the most insensitive sort. We can, by means of the most exalted moral perspectives, control, manipulate and alienate those around us. Thus, e.g., a person might value hard work and say that hard work is good. But that claim might be made by a person who is compulsively working and cannot stop, a 'workaholic,' and thus function as a rationalization, an avoidance of feelings or relation, or it might be a genuine expres-

---

12 This is far too large a topic to develop here, but an interesting shift in perspective is presented in Cavell's 'Knowledge and the Basis of Morality' in Cavell, 265ff. Cavell suggests that the knowledge we need in ethics is a knowledge of *persons* and that presupposes, in large part, the existence between us of personal relationships.

sion of a value held non-compulsively.[13] Or one person might say 'I'm sorry' in order to placate others while another might say the same words in an attempt to express regret at harm done and to make repairs.[14]

In our personal lives what matters most is motivation, whereas in the abstraction of academic philosophizing the emphasis shifts from motivation to justification. In personal relations holding correct, or rational moral principles which can be justified by argumentation means nothing if these principles and the supporting arguments are issued from a defensive or rationalizing consciousness. In our personal moral lives we acquire certain kinds of self-knowledge which are rarely discussed in ethics. Academic moral philosophy, focussed as it is on the justification of values in the absence of relationship, is too easily disconnected from the important kinds of insight that we sorely need in our everyday moral life, where we have to live and act on the basis of the insights we have generated in our conversations. We experience the consequences of failing to act on these shared understandings as our relationships wax and wane before our eyes. Often we find that we are not acting according to the picture we had articulated and difficulties set in. We have to resume the conversation, if the difficulties have not eliminated the conversation altogether, and restructure our moral selves all over again. The process is endless, there is no final settled account that we can take for granted, any more than we can eat or sleep once and for all and get it over with. It is within such processes that we experience our own moral agency. Whereas in the academic contexts there are different constraints on our depictions of moral life. Currently moral life is viewed as a matter of following

---

13 'Most often the anxiety-motivation of behaviour is masked, the behavior frequently being rationalized. Thus the man who has always worked compulsively at his job is likely to be unable to distinguish his behavior from that of industrious and enthusiastic but anxiety-free work.... When he asks them to describe in "plain" language how *they* approach their work, victory is his – for they have to use the very same language-forms he does' (Herbert Fingarette, 'The Ego and Mystic Selflessness,' in M.R. Stein, A.J. Vidich, & D.M. White, eds., *Identity and Anxiety* [Glencoe, IL: Free Press 1960], 563).

14 Ilham Dilman, 'Reason, Passion and the Will,' *Philosophy* **59** (1984), 201

rational moral principles or of formulating rational contracts. The emphasis is on the justification of moral beliefs. The criteria for getting it right in a philosophical theory are dramatically different from the criteria that govern our personal relations. It was this sort of thing that Kierkegaard must have had in mind when he said that philosophers build castles but live in a hovels beside them. Among the criteria for a good philosophical castle, these days at least, are such considerations as rational argumentation, universalizability of principle, and transcendence of subjective dimensions of inner life. Some experiences do not translate easily into the tradition of academic exchange of argument.

The limits upon what can be said in the academic context sometimes make it almost impossible to reproduce the considerations which we are conscious of in our on-going personal relationships.[15] For example, the kinds of sensibilities a person must have in order to be a good parent, are not easily rendered in the available language of theory because they emerge in specific contexts, they change continuously with changes in relationships and with our changing sensibilities, and they go beyond the truth conditions of empirical formulations. Truths about the inner life are far more elusive and more a matter of interpretation than empirical descriptions. Furthermore, such 'inner truths' infused with feelings and emotions are difficult to articulate at the best of times, and often depend, for their articulation upon the receptivity of our interlocutors.[16] They are often not acceptable coinage in rational philosophical analyses.

---

15 Robert Paul Wolff, 'There's Nobody Here But Us Persons,' in Carol Gould and Marx Wartofsky, eds., *Women and Philosophy: Toward a Theory of Liberation* (New York: Putnam's 1976)

16 '[N]otice ... how different is the experiencing of an individual in a relationship with another, than it is when he is alone, and also, how there are differences in his manner of experiencing in different relationships. I may say and think the same given content under these different circumstances, but my experiencing along with this content will be widely different. My sense of you, the listener, affects my experiencing as I speak, and your response partly determines my experiencing a moment later. What occurs to me, and how I live as we speak and interact, is vitally affected by every word and mo-

It is for this reason that philosophical pictures of moral agency strike the non-philosopher as odd, if not outright irrelevant. To put this another way, the picture of the self that emerges in much philosophical argument seems curiously flat and unconnected. The self-knowledge that might result from such pictures is not always congruent with the self-knowledge that we achieve so painfully from our commitments to, and passionate investments in, our relations with others. I will try to illustrate this incongruity when I examine Richard Brandt's moral theory. In the meantime I will outline four kinds of self-knowledge that emerge within the contexts of caring relationships.

II Self-Knowledge

The picture of moral life as essentially a matter of caring relationships has been presented by such feminist writers as Carol Gilligan, Nel Noddings, Jean Baker Miller, Angela Miles, Lawrence Blum and Margaret Adams, to mention a few.[17] These writers have discussed both the absence of a concern with caring among contemporary Anglo-American moral theorists and the political implications for women of being assigned the role of care-taker in a society which

---

tion you make, and by every facial expression and attitude you show' (Eugene Gendlin, *Experiencing and the Creation of Meaning* [New York: Macmillan 1962], 38).

17 Carol Gilligan, *In a Different Voice* (Cambridge, MA: Harvard University Press 1982); Nel Noddings, *Caring: A Feminine Approach to Ethics and Moral Education* (Berkeley: University of California Press 1984); Jean Baker Miller, *Toward a New Psychology of Women* (Boston: Beacon Press 1976); Angela Miles, 'Ideological Hegemony in Political Discourse: Women's Specificity and Equality,' in Angela Miles and Geraldine Finn, eds., *Feminism in Canada* (Montreal: Black Rose Press 1982); Lawrence Blum, Marcia Homiak, Judy Housman and Naomi Scheman, 'Altruism and Women's Oppression' *Philosophical Forum* 5 (1975); Margaret Adams, 'The Compassion Trap,' in Vivian Gornick and Barbara Moran, eds., *Women in Sexist Society* (New York: Basic Books 1971); and Lawrence Blum, *Friendship, Altruism and Morality* (London: Routledge & Kegan Paul 1981)

does not recognize this as a dominant value. What has been neglected thus far in philosophical discussions of caring is the fact that there are certain insights, of great significance to any moral agent, which can only be achieved through caring. It is my belief that our failure to attend to this aspect of caring is due partly to the low value we assign to caring in our culture and in our philosophizing.[18]

There are four forms of self-knowledge which emerge in a caring relation and which enhance the moral aspects of the self-in-relation. (i) The first I call the process of 'unselfing.' It can be articulated best in the Freudian language of id, ego and superego, if we do not reify these terms or worry too much about the scientific status of the theory. Freud presented the ego as that part of the self which has to deal realistically with the world and its demands. But in addition to this aspect of the self there is a whole realm of passions and another dimension of internalized maxims or directives acquired fairly early in our socialization, which exert pressure on the ego. Without falling into unnecessary reification we can use these notions to describe the struggle we have to balance these tendencies within us. All of this balancing takes place, of course, within the complex context of our relationships with others who make demands upon us and confer their favors.

We are much more conscious of our own internal struggles than we are of the internal struggles of others. And, when the balancing act gets out of hand we become obsessed with ourselves, distraught, angry, defensive against internal or external threats, or the complex combination of both. In such a situation it is a common experience to be consumed with self-concern, to be self-preoccupied. Our self-knowledge is, in such moments, distorted. We attribute too much importance to small slights and we have trouble getting a balanced view of things. We act badly. But the balance can be shifted again

---

18 See, among others, Jean Baker Miller; Kathy Ferguson, *The Feminist Case Against Bureaucracy* (Philadelphia: Temple University 1984); and Stanley Cavell, 'An Absence of Morality,' in *The Claim of Reason* (Oxford: Oxford University Press 1979), 274-91.

when we focus attention on the right sort of thing. Iris Murdoch describes this shift in perspective:

> I am looking out of my window in an anxious and resentful state of mind, oblivious of my surroundings, brooding perhaps on some damage done to my prestige. Then suddenly I observe a hovering kestrel. In a moment everything is altered. The brooding self with its hurt vanity has disappeared. There is nothing now but the kestrel. And when I return to thinking of the other matter it seems less important. And of course this is something which we may also do deliberately: give attention to nature in order to clear our minds of selfish care.
> ... Self is as hard to see justly as other things, and when clear vision has been achieved, self is a correspondingly smaller and less interesting object.[19]

There are two dimensions to the process Murdoch describes. The first is the shift of attention and the second is the effect on our sense of self resulting from that shift. The shift of attention to appreciate aspects of the world in a detached way has been variously described. Ernest Schactel calls it 'allocentric perception.' In this form of perception the focus is entirely on the thing and not on the self.

> The main differences between the autocentric and the allocentric modes of perception are these: In the autocentric mode ... the emphasis is on how and what the person feels....
> Objects are ... perceived from the perspective of how they will serve a certain need of the perceiver, or how they can be used by him for some purpose, or how they have to be avoided in order to prevent pain, displeasure, injury, or discomfort...the predominating feature of the perception is not the object in its own right, but those of its aspects which relate to the perceiver's more or less conscious feelings of the need or purpose which the object is to serve...[This] exercises a decisive influence on how the object will be perceived and, conversely, on what aspects of the object will not be perceived, what will be emphasized, what will be neglected.
> In the allocentric mode ... the emphasis is on what the object is like.... The perceiver usually approaches or turns to the object actively and either opens himself toward it receptively or, figuratively, or literally, takes hold of it, tries to "grasp" it.[20]

---

19 Iris Murdoch, *The Sovereignty of Good* (London: Routledge & Kegan Paul 1970), 84; 67-8

20 Ernest Schachtel, *Metamorphosis* (New York: Basic Books 1959), 83; 167; 83

For Schachtel this shift of perception is a matter of attitude. The effect of this form of perception on the self is what Murdoch calls 'unselfing.' There are many ways of describing the phenomenon Murdoch has called 'unselfing.' But the basic picture is of a natural inclination to be self-centered and a corresponding ability to develop a more detached and diminished view of the self. While Murdoch sees this self-obsession as a form of sin, psychoanalytically minded writers call it neurosis.[21] Either term calls attention to the processes of the self which hinder moral development and moral sensitivity. The diminished sense of self that results from this sort of shift of attention is a form of self-knowledge. For it gives us a more accurate picture of the self's place in relation to others. It liberates us, however briefly, from our feelings of anxiety, hatred, jealousy, envy and vanity, and takes us out of the confinement of our needs and desires. Allocentric perception is the first step in the process of caring. In this form of caring, which extends to the world around us and need not be focussed only upon persons, we are able to care to the extent that we can be pried away from self-obsession.[22] The loss of the acutely self-conscious focussing of attention on our feelings, our perceptions, our distinctions and our logical proofs is often experienced as a liberation.

This form of perception produces a sense of connectedness with others. This appears paradoxical, at first, since one of its main features is that it views its object with detachment. However, the detachment that Schachtel and Murdoch allude to is detachment from wanting to use the object of our perception for our own purposes:

> Great art teaches us how real things can be looked at and loved without being seized and used, without being appropriated into the greedy organism of the self. Unsentimental contemplation of nature exhibits the same quality of detachment: selfish concerns vanish, nothing exists except the things which are seen.
>
> It is in the capacity to love, that is to see, that the liberation of the soul

---

21 See Fingarette on this point.

22 Ibid, 566

from fantasy consists.... What I have called fantasy, the proliferation of blinding self-centred aims and images, is itself a powerful system of energy.[23]

So the process of righting our understanding or getting a better perspective on ourselves occurs when we are inspired or captivated, however briefly, by something worthy, noble, beautiful, precious and so on. We return to our preoccupations and the distortions in our sense of self have been modified. The capacity to shift perspectives like this is, of course, a capacity that we learn from those who have cared for us, who have distracted us, countless times in childhood, and, if we are lucky, in adulthood as well, and taught us to attach the right amount of importance to these threats to our sense of self.

(ii) What is paradoxical in this form of self-knowledge is that we acquire a truer sense of self only when we forget about the self and focus upon others with this particular attitude of interest and care for them apart from ourselves. This leads me to the second form of self-knowledge made possible by caring attention, what I call 'edification.'

[This perception] is characterized by an inexhaustible and ineffable quality, by the profoundest interest in the object, and by the enriching, refreshing, vitalizing effect which the act of perception has on the perceiver. The main reason for this difference lies in the fact that the fully allocentric perception (expecially of nature, people and great works of art) always breaks through and transcends the confines of the labelled, the familiar, and establishes a relation in which a direct encounter with the object itself ... takes place.[24]

It is ... a psychological fact that we can all receive moral help by focussing our attention upon things which are valuable: virtuous people, great art.[25]

While the first aspect of self-knowledge which emerges in caring, a diminished sense of self, or a liberation, however momentary from self-obsession, occurs with caring attention to any form of beauty

---

23 Murdoch, 58; 67

24 Schachtel, 177

25 Murdoch, 56

or value, the second aspect of the process of self-knowledge that emerges from caring is the capacity to be moved, to be inspired or to receive strength from the qualities we discern in people with whom we are in relation. We become aware of qualities in others which we can develop in ourselves. Heinz Kohut discusses this in his essay 'Forms and Transformations of Narcissism.'[26] Patients who had severe deprivation in childhood had nevertheless managed to develop qualities in themselves which had enchanted them in the very adults who had so neglected them. Appreciation of forms of goodness becomes a form of personal practice. The varieties of goodness which such a person cares for are seen not as something 'out there' separate from self, but as genuine possibilities for the self. The shift in our self-knowledge that I have labelled 'edification' represents a shift from either simply being oblivious to the presence of ethical or aesthetic properties or from envying those who have them to admiration and emulation. This shift in our awareness is an important component of moral life. Many of our conversations in daily life revolve around the admirable qualities we see in others. Such conversations serve to maintain these as desirable qualities to be encouraged and rewarded.

> [O]ur ability to act well "when the time comes" depends partly, perhaps largely, upon the quality of our habitual objects of attention, "whatsoever things are true, whatsoever things are honest, pure, lovely, of good report; if there be any virtues, and if there be any praise, think on these things."[27]

(iii) A third form of self-knowledge, which I label 'regret' is what Melanie Klein has called 'depressive conscience.'[28] She contrasts depressive conscience with that other form of conscience which Freud called 'superego.' We are familiar enough with the notion of

---

26 In *The Search for Self*, P. Ornstein, ed. (New York: International Universities Press 1978).

27 Murdoch, 56

28 Dilman, 200

the superego as a collection of thoughts and feelings which are guilt inducing, harshly critical and relatively impervious to real-world information derived from our encounters. What Klein call 'depressive conscience' is the genuine dismay we feel when we have harmed someone we care for. It is the basis for moral life. Unfortunately however, this sensitivity to the pain of others is often obviated by the harsher strictures of the superego with its emphasis on rules and its rigid blaming approach to morality. The two sorts of consciousness are radically different as they focus on entirely different experiences. The guilt of the superego expresses itself in feelings of unworthiness and in harsh judgments about oneself. These judgments and feelings can be, as most of know, very paralyzing. The focus in the case of superego is on the self and how evil it is, whereas the focus in depressive guilt is on the other, and how badly they feel. Knowing the difference between these two kinds of thought-feeling processes is a valuable form of self-knowledge, which can only come from experience. The most that philosophy can do is to draw our attention to this form of emotionally laden experience and encourage reflection upon it.

(iv) A fourth form of self-knowledge made possible by caring relationships I will call 'introspection.' We might classify this as a caring attention to self-in-relation. In this form of awareness we become aware of our motives and we learn to distinguish which of our actions and reactions are motivated by anxiety, fear, hostility, desire for control, etc. We realize when, for example, we are arguing to gain control or make others feel inferior rather than to pursue the truth. This form of awareness facilitates the self-in-relation insofar as we are able to gain insight into, and detachment from some of our baser motives. We learn to distinguish the neurotic baggage that we bring to our encounters from the genuine responses to the others with whom we are in relation. It is a very liberating form of self-awareness, which cannot be induced by theorizing but can only be attained by reflection upon ourselves within specific relationships. It is like the other forms of self-knowledge in that it is liberating, it is experiential, it enhances our capacity to be selves-in-relation, and finally it is a process which is never complete.

[T]o a very large extent, thinking about what to do involves trying to become aware of the considerations inclining one in different directions and in trying to sort out the elements composing one's mixed motives.[29]

What makes moral argument rational is not the assumption that there is in every situation one thing which ought to be done and that this may be known, not the assumption that we can always come to agreement about what ought to be done on the basis of rational methods. Its rationality lies in following the methods which lead to a knowledge of our own position, of where we stand; in short, to a knowledge and definition of ourselves.[30]

I have been describing the emergence and maintenance of a moral self in the process of relation with other moral selves which themselves also emerge and are maintained in such processes of relation. What I have described is a process in which self and other are essentially connected. Furthermore in such processes thought and emotion are intricately integrated. In fact to isolate some aspect of the process and articulate it as a thought is to abstract from the whole, just as focussing on the emotional component abstracts it from the whole. Once we have relinquished the autocentric mode of perception and have assumed the appreciative and caring regard of allocentric perception, we are able to feel joy both at the sense of connection with others and at the liberation, if only momentarily, from the anxiety-generated consciousness associated with having to defend the fragile ego from real and imaginary onslaughts.[31]

In summary: to care is to be open to transformation, and it involves a change in self-knowledge in several ways: we are liberated from self-centeredness, we gain an enhanced sense of self through the emotions associated with appreciation, and we learn our position, that is to say we learn new possibilities of being.

---

29 Kekes, 5

30 Cavell, 312

31 Fingarette, 574

III An Example: Biff Loman

In Arthur Miller's play Death of a Salesman Biff Loman goes through a process of moral development which illustrates the four kinds of self-knowledge involved in moral life: i. unselfing; ii. edification; iii. regret; and iv. introspection. Biff, the angry son of the salesman Willy Loman, achieves the resolution of a life-problem that has plagued him for fifteen years. Biff had been greatly disillusioned as a young man when he discovered that his father, whom he had worshipped, was an adulterer. From then on he saw his father as nothing more than a liar and a fake. Indeed Willy did lie and was a fake and a failure. Worse, to cope with his terrible feelings of despair Willy had delusions of grandeur and thought of himself as a great salesman who would eventually be appreciated and rewarded. Willy entertained the same delusions about Biff. In Willy's view Biff was no ordinary person, he too had 'a greatness in him.'

Biff had lived as a drifter and a bum, getting fired for theft from all the good jobs he had held. He rationalized these episodes by telling himself that no one appreciated him and that he was a great salesman. The play begins when Willy returns home. He fights continuously and bitterly with his father, but he succumbs again to his father's fantasies. He believes that the life of a salesman is a noble one which society will reward and that he has the capacity to be a great salesman. His father convinces him to return to a company he had once worked for and ask the president for a loan to start his own business. Biff acquieses in the fantasy that the president will be delighted to see him and will remember him as a great salesman, when, in fact, he had been a mere shipping clerk, and worse, had been fired for theft.

The turning point in Biff's life occurs when he gives up his delusions and fantasies, accepts himself as an ordinary person and takes responsibility for his own life. The catalyst for this moral change occurs in a crucial passage in the play when his mother, Linda, begs him to look at his father, to pay attention to him and to see him as a person who has integrity and dignity despite his obvious failure, his poverty and his delusions. Linda urges Biff to have feeling for his father.

> You've got to make up your mind now, darling, there's no leeway any more. Either he's your father and you pay him that respect, or else you're not to come here. ... I don't say he's a great man. Willy Loman never made a lot of money. His name was never in the paper. He's not the finest character that ever lived. But he's a human being, and a terrible thing is happening to him. So attention must be paid. He's not to be allowed to fall into his grave like an old dog. Attention, attention must be finally paid to such a person.[32]

Biff shifts his attention, at last, from the self with its preoccupations and delusions to another who is seen in an entirely different light, as a person who can be loved, and forgiven. He gives up the previous perspective from which he saw only his father's defects and which used to justify his own shortcomings. When he sees his father through a caring regard his attention to him is no longer self-serving. Biff's caring regard provides him with the occasion for the four kinds of self-knowledge I have described: (i) Unselfing: he gets free of his inordinate self-preoccupation and the fantasies that fed it. He accepts himself as an ordinary person and decides to work as a farmhand out West. (ii) Edification: inspired by his enhanced perception of father, he begins to think positively about the work he would like to do and can do well. He is prepared to commit himself to this kind of work, and to a life with no hope of wealth and fame. (iii) Regret: he makes a sustained, almost heroic effort, to communicate with Willy, and to convey his love for him. And he feels genuine dismay for the pain he has caused his father. (iv) Introspection: Biff achieves a realistic sense of his identity and correctly identifies the kind of work for which he is suited. He comes to know his own position once he is free of his blaming attitudes and his rationalizations.

---

32 Arthur Miller, *Death of a Salesman* (New York: Viking 1973), 56

IV Richard Brandt

I have presented a picture of moral life in which self-knowledge is central. I have suggested that these forms of self-knowledge are made possible through the attitudes associated with caring for others. I want, now, to contrast this approach to Richard Brandt's theory. Brandt puts self-knowledge at the heart of moral life as well. But this account of self-knowledge is different in two respects: first, it is not connected with the caring attitude; and second, it is based upon classical conditioning theory in psychology.

In this theory behaviour is viewed as a complex set of conditioned and unconditioned responses to stimuli. All actions are need-oriented. That is to say all behavior is understood as a response to drives or needs. Rational behavior is behavior that is based upon correct information about the environment and its effect on our needs, and upon correct inference. Thus, in this model, a person's relations with others must be understood as motivated by the desires to satisfy needs or reduce drives.

Benevolence is analyzed as a conditioned response in the following way: we begin with unconditioned stimuli (US) and unconditioned responses (UR). An example of US would be the smell of food. A UR to that stimulus would be salivation. Built upon this base there are conditioned stimuli (CS) and conditioned responses (CR). Thus, for example, Pavlov's dogs salivated (UR) when the meat powder was blown into their mouths (US). Then a buzzer sounded shortly before the appearance of food. Eventually the sound of the buzzer triggered the salivation. The sound had become a conditioned stimulus (CS), and the response of salivation to the buzzer a conditioned response (CR). In the same way when a child is hurt (US) it has unconditioned aversive responses to the pain, such as fear, autonomic changes, crying, etc. Hearing the sound of his own crying or seeing his own blood acquire the status of conditioned stimuli, i.e., stimuli which evoke the memory of the original unconditioned stimulus, the pain. Conditioned stimuli such as the sound of crying or the appearance of blood can, on future occasions elicit conditioned responses (aversion, fear, etc.). Thus, when a child, or later an adult, feels badly at the sight of someone in pain it is because the sights and sounds function as conditioned stimuli and evoke a conditioned response. A similar account can be given of sympathy.[33] Brandt bases his moral theory upon this picture of the person.

He considers the task of moral theory to be to answer questions of the following sort: what is worth wanting or working for?; what is the best thing for an agent to do from his own point of view?; what is morally right and what is morally just?[34] He claims that the best way to answer these questions is to find an answer to the question 'What is it rational for an agent to do, from his own point of view?' and, 'What kind of moral system for his society would it be rational to support?'[35]

To arrive at a rational moral code Brandt proposes a procedure for the elimination of irrational desires. Irrational desires are those desires which are based upon false or irrational beliefs. Thus, e.g., a person might have an irrational fear of dogs based upon a hasty generalization made in childhood after having been attacked by a dog rendered irate by teasing. The way to rid oneself of such beliefs is to scrutinize all the available evidence and, using the best scientific knowledge of the day, vividly reflect upon the truth conditions of the belief. Brandt calls this process 'cognitive psychotherapy,' a process of 'laundering' our beliefs. Properly done it should eliminate false beliefs and the irrational desires attendant upon them. Any beliefs and desires which remain after the wash, so to speak, will be rational. A rational person will choose a rational moral code.

> This whole process of confronting desires with relevant information, by repeatedly representing it, in an ideally vivid way, and at an appropriate time, I call cognitive psychotherapy. I call it so because the process relies simply upon reflection on available information, without influence by prestige of someone, use of evaluative language, extrinsic reward or punishment, or use of artificially induced feeling states like relaxation. It is value-free reflection.[36]

---

33 Brandt, 140-1

34 Ibid., 1

35 Ibid.

36 Ibid., 113

According to Brandt, some people are selfish and do not have much sense of sympathy or benevolence, while others are benevolent. Either way, however, it is possible for these people to come up with a rational moral code using the procedure of 'fumigating' desires to eliminate irrational beliefs. Indeed the code that a 'perfectly selfish rational person' would choose will probably turn out not too differently from that which a benevolent rational person will choose. For the selfish rational person will choose a Hobbesian moral code, i.e., one that offers protection from harm and various other considerations such as the quality of life available in a group characterized by autonomous self-restraint and mutual trust and so on.[37] Further, Brandt claims that rational persons would probably opt for some form of utilitarian moral system which would maximize the expectable happiness or welfare of some large group. The difference between a selfish moral agent and a benevolent one would come down to the size of the group whose welfare each would choose to consider.[38]

The appeal of such an account is that it seems to offer a decision-procedure for generating sound values. There appears to be nothing ambiguous or vague about the procedure of eliminating false beliefs by gathering information. There is nothing inherently open-ended about 'facts,' nothing, that is, that is subject to interpretation. Furthermore values are not mysterious properties which we must learn to discern. Values, on this view, are simply desires. Good values correspond to rational desires, and rational desires are based upon factual information and sound logic. The benefit of such a theory, according to Brandt, is that it presents moral life as a matter of reflection, as something which has the status of being rationally preferred based upon human reflection, sensitivity and debate,[39] and

37 Ibid., 205

38 Ibid., 208

39 Ibid., 194-5

moral judgment as a matter of uncriticized traditions or as a system of laws handed down from Heaven, self-evident to the wise.

As I have said, Brandt's account of moral life is very appealing. By placing desire at the basis of moral life it solves problems of motivation and by providing a method for eliminating some desires it provides an action-guide. Furthermore, it seems to put psychology back into philosophy. But these gains are illusory. There are two serious problems with Brandt's account of moral life. The first is the view that moral life consists in having a rational moral code based upon 'all the available information' and upon correct logical inference. The second problem is the centrality of desire in Brandt's picture of the moral agent.

First let us examine the claim that a rational moral code rests upon 'all the available beliefs' and correct logical infererence. Certainly Brandt is right to say that we can eradicate irrational desires or aversions by careful examination of the beliefs underlying them. A large part of growing up involves the reexamination of one's beliefs. And we've all experienced this alteration in our desires; many people no longer desire diets high in cholesterol, sedentary lives or activities which they see to be detrimental to their well-being. Being clearly apprised of the facts has helped these people to actually change their desires and enjoy lifestyles based on different desires. But moral experience, as I have explained, is more than a matter of getting correct information. It involves a radical shift in perspective from a desire-based orientation to a perception of specific others in particular relationships as they are independently of our desires or aversions. And this idea is simply not expressible in Brandt's theory.

Second, when we do manage to achieve this shift in perspective, what Schachtel calls 'allocentric' perception, we cannot be said to be acquiring new information, even though we undoubtedly do learn a lot more than we would if we maintained an autocentric mode of perception. Whereas getting information is compatible with minimal sense of connection and appreciation, moral understanding is another matter altogether. It must involve the capacity to see others apart from their utility, and the capacity to alter one's relation to oneself insofar as we can, momentarily at least, drop the egocentric perspective of need fulfillment and drive reduction so as to pay attention to the other. This almost contemplative vision of others within the context of caring or sustaining relations involves a change of attitude. So the awareness or knowledge involved cannot be presumed to be radically separate from emotion and evaluation as the term 'information' suggests.

In Brandt's system the emphasis is on attaining all the available information, while the self remains static. But we can never attain all the available information. Our libraries, our newspapers and our experiences contain vast quantities of information which it would be impossible for any one person, or any group of persons to process in any meaningful way. Furthermore, what counts as relevant information will depend entirely upon our purposes. What I am suggesting is that an information-based approach to ethics is both unworkable and beside the point.

Although gathering information and working out the logic of our inferences are not to be put aside, they cannot be the focus of moral life for these activities can be done in the absence of any emotional connection with others, i.e., in the absence of caring attitudes. They are thus completely different processes from the processes of 'unselfing' and turning toward the other with an open and receptive attitude, and being transformed in some way by that experience. Moral theories that emphasize intellect and rational decision-making obscure this feature of our moral experience. On such views of moral life many experiences become absurd and must be relegated to psychopathology. What follows is an illustration of the poverty of an information-desire based approach to a moral and psychological problem.

V An Example: Bulimia

This example illustrates the inadequacy of pictures of moral agency as a matter of rational decision-making based upon information and logic. It is derived from a paper written by a bright philosophy student, OC, describing her six year struggle with bulimia. During the entire time of her struggle with this addiction she had a solid grasp of all the relevant information and her inferences were sound.

She knew that this kind of behavior was debilitating and she attempted to use her will power to stop it, but she could not. OC became bulimic when she left home to go to university and decided to keep to a strict diet of 1000 calories per day so as to maintain an attractive and slim appearance. The ideal of consuming 1000 calories per day, although austere, is nevertheless a feasible one. But she found that she was continually breaking her resolution. She began to feel desperate in the face of these failures until she hit upon the bulimic 'solution.' Gradually she began to consume huge quantities of food, to vomit afterwards, and repeat the process until exhaustion. She began to lie and to steal to get food. She became increasingly detached from her other projects and her friendships. She had become addicted to food. During this terrible personal experience she reasoned that what she was doing was not in her best interest and almost daily she 'decided' to stop. But she could not.

OC found a way out of bulimia, but her 'solution' was not a matter of getting information, nor of correcting incorrect logic. Nor is the change to be accounted for by Utilitarian ethics. Her account illustrates some of the aspects of the shift of perspective associated with a caring attitude and an ensuing transformation in her sense of herself.

> All the while I was bulimic my conscience would tell me that something was gravely wrong with me, but I simply didn't know how to change. I figured I could will my way out of bulimia but when I tried it, I never made any positive changes. Every morning I'd get up determined not to throw-up and sure enough at some point during the day I'd be triggered into a binge.
>
> I use the word "trigger" because I've noticed that bulimia is often triggered by (1) uncomfortable emotional situations or (2) daily stresses that are not dealt with but avoided through bulimic action.... Bulimics often progress to the stage of partial or complete detachment from their feelings-worlds and hence no longer have to deal with unpleasant feelings which may arise. After about three years of being regularly bulimic, I experienced an almost complete numbing of my feelings. I talked about feelings, yes, but didn't experience them. In other words, I felt very little, i.e, was detached from my bodily feelings and somehow managed to rationalize pretty well everything.
>
> Bulimia meant for me that my personal life was safe, in a shell, with no other participants...[it] filled the time that would have otherwise been

lonely. I felt connected to no one and it occurred to me that most of my daily routine was revolving around the search for this self-gratification.

The bulimic can change from within (i.e, I used to practice caring for other people, giving things away until I felt good about it, listening to others...the list goes on) or stay bulimic. That is why one cannot WILL oneself out of bulimia. The act of willing does not necessarily involve a fundamental change in *values* nor does it involve a change in character ... it is simply a deliberate, controlled motion to change, an action. Willing does not necessarily involve transformation ... The "I" in the equation stays the same... The path out of bulimia is one that takes the individual from a self-centered existence to an other-and-self centered way of being. What I have learned from my experience is that I cannot care for others unless I first care for myself. The paradox (or Catch-22) is that learning the latter happens while one practices the former. For I am not all that I can be unless I am in relationship to others. In contrast to this, as a bulimic I was constantly comparing myself to others — seeing their achievements as my own lack of ability. I was incapable of feeling good about someone else's successes.

This is a dramatic example of moving from a condition based upon autocentric, or need-oriented perception to a mode of being which includes a caring perspective. OC's focus, when she was bulimic, was on her overpowering need. Yet her intellectual picture of moral agency was the traditional one, that the task of the moral agent is to grasp a universal principle or rational principle such as e.g., one should not devote one's entire life to eating, and then to will oneself to act accordingly. This did not work.[40] OC's behavior was a surd to herself as long as she thought of herself as primarily intellect and will, and as long as she was unable to connect reason and feeling, and to find an emotional connection between herself and others. The solution to her problem was not an intellectual one for it was not a matter of grasping moral principles or of gathering information, but rather a matter of a change

---

40 This case is reminiscent of Davidson's discussion of *akrasia* as a matter of behavior that does not fit into an intelligible pattern and is thus a 'surd' to oneself. Donald Davidson, 'How is Weakness of the Will Possible?', in Joel Feinberg, ed., *Moral Concepts* (Oxford: Oxford University Press 1969), 93ff.

in attitude and in perception. When she began to pay attention to others she began to achieve the four kinds of self-knowledge I have described. Only when she stepped out of a need-oriented existence could she find herself transformed by the experience of attention to others (edification). The transformation consisted in a drastic reduction in the power of her compulsion (unselfing), an increased sensitivity to and awareness of her own feelings (introspection), and, finally, a relinquishing of the controlling and unrealistic mode of the superego for the caring concern of what Klein calls the conscience (regret).

Any theory which analyzes benevolence as a conditioned response and which sees moral life as a matter of 'scouring desires' by means of facts and logic must reject the idea that we can transcend our desires and experience an affirming interest in the being of those around us. Insofar as it views moral life as an algorithm, i.e. a kind of problem-solving envisaged as the application of the rules of logic to correct beliefs, we cannot move away from focussing attention upon the self, for, by definition, all this information gathering and checking is focussed on our desires. Furthermore as OC observed in her reflections on bulimia, as long as she conceived of herself as primarily intellect and will she could not make any change in her condition. Rational considerations and will power could not move her out of her addiction. These strategies merely enforced her sense of isolation. This is evident in Brandt's redefinition of benevolence as a conditioned response. Benevolence, in this view, is reduced to self-concern, and cannot be seen as genuine interest in and attention to the other. Regret at harming another would be reduced to regret at having to feel a conditioned response to pain. There is a world of difference between the two experiences.

Furthermore there is, in this theory, a radical separation of reason and emotion. We have desires, these are the motivating force behind our actions and choices, and we have reason which can select among desires and beliefs. Integration of the poles by means of a shift of attention and a caring regard cannot take place in this model. Each of the forms of knowledge of self-in-relation that I have described would have to be reduced to either desire or information. Thus 'unselfing,' 'edification,' 'regret' and 'introspection,' the four forms of self-knowledge that are made possible through caring attention, would be understood either as altered desires or as new information. But these categories do not capture the status of these forms of knowledge of ourselves. 'Unselfing' is not a matter of getting new information, nor is it a matter of logical inference, although it may result in new information and in an enhanced capacity to see things clearly. Nor is it a desire, although it brings with it a change in our desires.

By making use of classical conditioning theory Brandt restricts our understanding of moral life to something essentially self-centered. Our knowledge and appreciation of others is limited to their capacity to evoke conditioned responses in us. The admiration for and care for others disappears. We are locked within the circle of our own desires. The only way out that Brandt can fix upon is the rational scrutiny of desires to eliminate those desires based upon false beliefs or faulty logic. This is not the route out of self-preoccupation; nor is it the route to close moral connection with others.

VI Charles Taylor

Charles Taylor has an account of moral agency which avoids the problems associated with Brandt's view that moral reasoning consists in the acquisition of information coupled with sound logic, and his view that moral life is based upon unconditioned and conditioned responses, i.e., desires. Neither of these categories is adequate, in Taylor's view, to capture our moral experience. Instead we need to take into account what he calls 'subject-referring properties.' These properties, which he calls 'imports,' 'are what they are only in relation to the experience of subjects.'[41] Properties such as integrity, wholeness, fulfillment, etc. are 'properties about which we can only speculate or offer controvertible interpretations.'[42] They are 'experience-dependent' in a way that other properties are not. Thus, while they are essentially connected with our emotional reactions they are not 'merely subjective responses,' for they involve

---

41 Taylor, 'Self-Interpreting Animals,' in *Human Agency and Language*, 54
42 Ibid., 55

judgments 'about the way things are which cannot simply be reduced to the way we feel about them.'[43]

> Correct ascription of imports depends on whether the import gives grounds or the basis for the feeling.
> Our direct intuitive experience of imports is through feelings. What we sense through certain feelings is valid or adequate, while others are shallow, blind, distorting or perverse.
> Beyond the question of whether I feel ashamed is the question whether the situation is really shameful, whether I am rightly or wrongly, rationally or irrationally ashamed.[44]

Whether the feeling of shame is rational or irrational will thus not be simply a matter of ascertaining facts but of interpreting feelings about 'the way things are.' While Brandt makes it seem no problem how we determine what the facts are, and which facts we shall consider to be relevant, Taylor preserves a distinction between moral and non-moral properties and argues that the former are always a matter of interpretation of feelings, i.e., a matter of self-interpretation. This self-interpretation is thus very different from Brandt's version of self-knowledge as, i.e., 'cognitive psychotherapy.' The self-knowledge that figures in Brandt's theory consists in knowing which desires we have and which of these are based upon true beliefs of a factual sort. The important part in Taylor's theory is that the moral properties which we try to discern and interpret through our feelings are not properties which exist independently defined and ready to be characterized. The characterizaton of these properties is inseparably connected with characterization of the feelings which lead us to notice the properties in the first place. The properties, when they are characterized by us, exist in the connection between our experiences and the world. The properties are not subjective, yet their characterization depends upon our subjective experiences, and they are essentially connected with our feelings, or intuitions.

---

43 Ibid.

44 Ibid., 49; 62; 55

To make this difficult distinction Taylor says that we must see that 'subject-referring' properties are not the same as 'self-referring' properties. The emotions that are connected with the former are to be distinguished from self-referring emotions. He illustrates this with an example. If we come upon someone in need of help, say someone who is wounded, and feel that we must do something, we are experiencing an import and the feeling is other-referring. We are concerned not with our own needs but with the needs of the wounded person.[45] This concern arises out of our judgment that it is good, or noble, etc. to help such a person, it is a 'strong evaluation' in contrast to 'weak evaluation' which is merely an expression of our self-referring desires.

> In "weak evalution" for something to be judged as good it is sufficient that it be desired, whereas in "strong evaluation" there is also a use of "good" or some other evaluative term for which being desired is not sufficient; indeed some desires ... can be judged as bad, base, ignoble, trivial, superficial, unworthy and so on.[46]

For Taylor the moral selection of desires will depend upon some prior sense of what is 'higher' or more worthy which is not the same as factual information in that it is always a matter of interpretation. The process of interpretation involves careful attention to the world and at the same time careful attention to those feelings which enable us to discern these properties. It will depend upon some 'given' experience of qualitative distinctions which are not merely subjective, i.e., not desire-based. This is the move that Brandt cannot make. His only way to select among desires is by appeal to empirical information, whereas Taylor's way to select among desires is by means of the difficult process of self-interpretation, a determination of which of the emotionally rendered properties really are more noble, worthier, more shameful, etc. Self-knowledge, for Taylor, is a matter of finding one's identity, and that means, discovering one's

---

45 Ibid., 57

46 Taylor, 'What is Human Agency?', 17

'fundamental evaluations.' 'I identify myself by my strong evaluations as someone who essentially has these convictions.'[47] Moral life consists, in large part, in articulating and acting upon a deep sense of the relative moral worth of actions and desires, on 'our inarticulate sense of what is important.' These are 'articulations of something of which we have as yet only fragmentary intimations.'[48]

So to determine whether an act is ignoble or base is not a matter of information but a matter of interpretation of imports. He gives the example of a man trying to free himself from an addiction to overeating. He sees two ways of viewing this problem. It can be seen either as a matter of achieving greater happiness or satisfaction, through better health, or as a matter of gaining control over one's appetites so as to cease behaving in a degrading way. His argument against naturalistic theories of ethics is that they cannot articulate the second way of viewing the problem, for they must treat the notion of something being degrading as a way of characterizing our desires; they would have to assimilate it to something like disgust which is much more closely related to our desires. One alternative to this is to treat the claim that something is degrading as a claim about the world and not about the subject.

> By a process of careful attention to the world, we can improve our moral beliefs about the world, make them more approximately true; by the same process, we can improve our practical understanding, our sensitivity to the presence of instances of the moral concepts that figure in these beliefs.[49]

What Taylor adds to this alternative is the qualification that while to say that something is degrading is to say something about the world, nevertheless it is at the same time to say something about the subject's experience of that world. It is in this sense that imports

---

47 Ibid., 34

48 Ibid., 40

49 Mark Platts, *Ways of Meaning: An Introduction to the Philosophy of Language* (London: Routledge & Kegan Paul 1979), 247

are connecting terms, and that Taylor's theory emphasizes the connection between the self and the world as well as between reason and feeling.

Taylor's account of moral life is close to the one I have outlined. But there is an important difference. This difference can be illustrated by comparing his analysis of the example of an addiction to eating. Taylor uses this example to contrast two ways that a person can think about his or her own eating addiction. In the first way the person may think of it as 'a merely quantitative question of more satisfaction ... eating too much ... ruins my health, prevents me from enjoying all sorts of other desired consumations.'[50] Or the person may think of it in these terms: a person addicted to over-eating is not an admirable person.[51] It is seen as a matter of degradation. These two ways of viewing the problem express a conflict of self-interpretations.[52] Interpreting the problem as a matter of degradation completely changes the experience. The inner struggle becomes transformed. Our articulations of the problem alter us 'for an altered description or our motivation can be inseparable from a change in this motivation.'[53]

In the example I have analyzed of addiction to over-eating, following the reflections of the person who suffered the addiction, I would constrast the two ways of interpreting the problem as (i) a matter of reason and will, or (ii) as a matter of shifting perspectives and engaging in some kind of caring attitude towards others and thereby altering one's self-knowledge in the ways I have described. The difference between my analysis and Taylor's lies in my emphasis on the effects of specific caring relations on our sense of ourselves rather than on the acquisition of 'imports.' This is not to say that we do not need moral idioms, but rather to say that important changes in moral life are matters of our experiences and changes

---

50 Taylor, 'What is Human Agency?', 22

51 Ibid., 21

52 Ibid., 22

53 Ibid., 37

in our experiences are more likely to arise out of changes in our relations with others than out of changes in our vocabulary. The changes in vocabulary *result from* the changed relations.

VII Conclusion

In this paper I have outlined an approach to ethics which puts caring relations in the foregound, along with the attitudes and feelings that these relations entail. I have contrasted this approach to ethics with the approach of two radically opposed theorists, Richard Brandt and Charles Taylor both of whom seem to give more prominence to the inner life of the moral agent than has been customary in recent moral philosophy. With regard to that inner life I have presented a view of a certain kind of morally relevant self-knowledge which is connected with caring. I have contrasted this with Brandt's view of moral self-knowledge as 'cognitive psychotherapy' and with Taylor's view of moral self-knowledge as self-interpretation of 'imports.'

CANADIAN JOURNAL OF PHILOSOPHY
Supplementary Volume 13

A Feminist Aspect Theory of the Self

ANN FERGUSON
Philosophy & Women's Studies
University of Massachusetts/Amherst
Amherst, MA 01003
U.S.A.

The contemporary Women's Movement has generated major new theories of the social construction of gender and male power. The feminist attack on the masculinist assumptions of cognitive psychology, psychoanalysis and most of the other academic disciplines has raised questions about some basic assumptions of those fields. For example, feminist economists have questioned the public/private split of much of mainstream economics, that ignores the social necessity of women's unpaid housework and childcare.[1] Feminist psychologists have challenged cognitive and psychoanalytic categories of human moral and gender development arguing that they are biased toward the development of male children rather than female

---

1 For a survey of this literature, see Natalie Sokoloff, *Between Money and Love: The Dialectics of Women's Home and Market Work* (New York: Praeger 1980). Also cf. Heidi Hartmann, 'The Unhappy Marriage of Marxism and Feminism,' in Lydia Sargent, ed., *Women and Revolution* (Boston, MA: South End Press 1981) and the responses to Hartmann in the same volume; Christine Delphy, *Close to Home: A Materialist Analysis of Women's Oppression* (Amherst, MA: University of Massachusetts Press 1984) and the articles by Jean Gardiner, 'Women's Domestic Labor,' Batya Weinbaum and Amy Bridges, 'The Other Side of the Paycheck: Monopoly Capital and the Structure of Consumption,' Heidi Hartmann, 'Capitalism, Patriarchy and Job Segregation by Sex' and Margery Davies 'Women's Place Is at the Typewriter: The Feminization of the Clerical Labor Force,' all in Zillah R. Eisenstein, ed., *Capitalist Patriarchy and the Case for Socialist-Feminism* (New York: Monthly Review Press 1979).

children.[2] Feminist anthropologists have argued that sex/gender systems, based on the male exchange of women in marriage, have socially produced gender differences in sexuality and parenting skills which have perpetuated different historical and cultural forms of male dominance.[3] Feminist philosophers and theorists have suggested that we must reject the idea of a gender-free epistemological standpoint from which to understand the world.[4] Finally radical feminists have argued that the liberal state permits a pornography industry that sexually objectifies women, thus legitimizing male violence against women.[5]

---

2 Cf. Nancy Chodorow, *The Reproduction of Mothering* (Berkeley, CA: University of California Press 1978); Carol Gilligan *In a Different Voice* (Cambridge, MA: Harvard University Press 1982); Jean Baker Miller, *Toward a New Psychology of Women* (Boston, MA: Beacon Press 1976), Jean Baker Miller, ed. *Psychoanalysis and Women* (Baltimore, MD: Penguin 1973).

3 Perhaps the most original and influential article of the new feminist anthropology is that by Gayle Rubin, 'The Traffic in Women,' in Rayna Reiter, ed., *Toward a New Anthropology of Women* (New York: Monthly Review Press 1975). Other important contributions are the rest of the articles in Reiter as well as those in Michelle Zimbalist Rosaldo and Louise Lamphere, eds., *Woman, Culture and Society* (Stanford, CA: Stanford University Press 1974). See also Peggy Reeves Sanday, *Female Power and Male Dominance: On the Origins of Sexual Inequality* (New York: Cambridge University Press 1981).

4 Cf. Nancy Hartsock, *Money, Sex and Power* (New York: Longman's 1983); Mary O'Brien, *The Politics of Reproduction* (Boston: Routledge & Kegan Paul 1981); Sandra Harding and Merrill Hintikka, eds., *Discovering Reality: Feminist Perspectives on Epistemology, Metaphysics, Methodology and Philosophy of Science* (Boston, MA: Reidel 1983); Sandra Harding, *The Science Question in Feminism* (Ithaca, NY: Cornell University Press 1987).

5 Cf. Andrea Dworkin, *Womanhating* (New York: Dutton 1974); Andrea Dworkin, *Pornography: Men Possessing Women* (New York: Perigee 1981; Kathleen Barry, *Female Sexual Slavery* (Englewood Cliffs, NJ: Prentice-Hall 1979); Susan Griffin, *Pornography and Silence* (New York: Harper 1981); Laura Lederer, ed., *Take Back the Night: Women on Pornography* (New York: Wm. Morrow 1980); Andrea Dworkin, 'Against the Male Flood: Censorship, Pornography and Equality' and Catharine A. MacKinnon, 'Pornography, Civil Rights and Speech,' in Dworkin and MacKinnon, *The Reasons Why* (Cambridge, MA: Harvard Law School 1985).

Though each of these feminist approaches to understanding the social perpetuation of male dominance is insightful, they are based on overly simplistic theories of the self and human agency. As a result they tend to give us misleading ideas of what is required for social change. For one thing, they don't allow us to understand how women who are socialized into subordinate gender roles nonetheless can develop the sense of self-respect and the personal power necessary to be strong feminists able to effectively change institutional sexism. In order to grasp what is necessary to develop a strong and powerful sense of self, we must have the correct theory of what the self is. I shall defend an Aspect theory of the self in this paper.

I Developing a Sense of Self

Most feminists would take it to be a truism that women's sense of self-worth, and consequently our personal power, has been weakened by a male dominant society which has made us internalize many demeaning images of women. Thus, part of every feminist program must involve a process of feminist education which allows women to develop − some would say, reclaim − a self-integrity and self-worth that will provide each of us with the psychological resources we need to develop full self-realization. Since individuals who lack a sense of self-worth are timid and afraid to take risks, women face the problem of contributing to our own subordination because of not even trying to achieve goals we really want, thus falling victim to the adage 'nothing ventured, nothing gained.' But how do we conceive of the process of constructing self-respect? In what follows, I am going to present three different theories of the self which feminist theories have presupposed. I shall give the answers they give to the question of how women can develop a strong sense of self, critique the first two, and defend my own view.

II The Rational Maximizer Theory of the Self

There is a view of self prevalent in American society today which derives from the views of such classical liberal philosophers as John

Locke and Thomas Jefferson. This view, characteristic of many contemporary Americans of both liberal and conservative bent, holds that the self is a unified rational thinking subject, possessed of free will and the ability to choose life goals and means to achieve them, as long as fate or external social coercion does not interfere. Examples of such social coercion include government legal restrictions against certain actions or strong social groups (e.g. large corporations or community groups) whose actions or policies restrict one from certain courses of action.

On this view of self, which I call the Rational Maximizer view of self, humans are unified selves, rational maximizers, who operate to maximize their own self-interest as defined by their goals, within the external constraints laid down by force of circumstance, government or society. Social oppression of a group, for example women or Black people, is then explained by external constraints placed in the way of individuals achieving their goals. These constraints can range from the personal prejudices of employers and potential friends and lovers to the institutional sexism involved in lesser pay for work defined socially as 'women's work'; or the fact that housework, defined as women's work, is unpaid labor, which makes the exchanges between men and women in the household economy unequal.

On the rational maximizer view of self, women do not differ from men in terms of personal identity and the human ability to choose reasonable goals and means to them. Thus, if men and women make different choices as to how to develop what economists call their 'human capital,' that is, their skills and abilities, including their degree of formal education and job training, this is due not to innate gender preferences and skills (e.g. that men are more competitive and aggressive and women more nurturant and submissive). Rather, it is a result of the realistic options that society and the individual circumstances of women provide. Thus, more men than women choose to pursue graduate studies, or careers in management and other high paying careers in business, politics and medicine because women choosing as men do would have to face much sexism and would have to work twice as hard and be twice as lucky to succeed. In a male dominant society, it is not rationally maximizing for women to make the same choices as men, especially since most women want to be wives and mothers — whether this is socialized or innate — and these goals are more difficult to combine with the typical high paying masculine career.

The explanation of women's lesser sense of self worth on this view is that women lack the skills that are highly valued in our society as well as access to the wages that are necessary to achieve status and economic independence in our society. Furthermore men, because of their comparative social and economic advantage, treat women as inferiors.

On the view that both men and women are rational maximizers, there are two social conditions necessary to develop a better sense of self for women. First is a feminist social policy that makes it less worth men's while to continue their sexist treatment of women, and second are feminist education programs which compensate women for the lack of skills society has denied them by encouraging the development of those skills necessary to compete in a man's world.

Affirmative action programs are a good example of feminist social policy that provides opportunities for qualified women to learn the skills hitherto reserved for men, in higher education and in on-the-job training. Such opportunities help those women involved to change their self-concept. Men will be persuaded to overcome their sexist attitudes when they see that women can do men's jobs as well as women, and will stop treating women as inferiors.

Another kind of training need is psychological re-training: women need consciousness-raising types of education, like assertiveness training and counselling programs which advocate the goal of economic independence for women. Such programs can provide the survival skills to replace those self-denigrating traditional skills that are characteristic of most women under patriarchy, those which involve habits of deference to men and the myriad skills of indirect manipulation which we have been taught to create the greater likelihood of 'catching a man,' and in gaining indirect power through men's favors in a patriarchal world.

Since most women want to be wives and mothers, feminists must support state legislation providing affordable, quality child care centers. At the same time, feminist education must combat the traditional prejudice against combining a career with motherhood. The most important feminist goal should be to create social structures that help women learn to become more like men — in motivations, personalities and job skills — so that we can get ahead in the system and thus achieve economic parity with men.

III Difference Theory

The second theory of the self that I want to discuss is that of those I call the Difference theorists. Unlike Rational Maximizer theory, which argues that men and women are basically the same underneath though we develop different skills and goals as means to achieving social success, this theory argues that there really are extreme personality and skills differences, between the genders. These differences, whether originally innate or socialized in early infancy, are so much a part of the identities of men and women that they cannot be changed. People's identities are not analogous to little atoms of consciousness which can, chameleon-like, take on or shed their personal properties as it is expedient. Rather, since human personal identity is essentially relational, a personal identification with one's gender is an essential characteristic of personal identity. Men and women essentially define ourselves in relation to different social standards learned in childhood. Since a man or woman's sense of self worth is essentially connected to success or failure in meeting gender-related standards, women's sense of self-worth cannot be ultimately achieved by imitating men or by adopting masculine goals and skills. Rather, women must find collective ways to socially re-valorize feminine-identified values and skills in order that individual women can reclaim a sense of self-worth denied by patriarchy.

There are two schools of thought among Difference theorists on the question of the inevitability of gender differences. One school, the biological determinists, e.g. those such as Mary Daly,[6] Mary

---

6 Mary Daly, *Gyn/Ecology: The Meta-ethics of Radical Feminism* (Boston, MA: Beacon Press 1978)

O'Brien[7] and others,[8] maintain that it is inevitable that masculine traits and inner sense of self be different from feminine ones. Testoscerene makes men more aggressive than women, while women's reproductive biology not only creates womb envy in men but makes women more nurturant and altruistic in relation to others.[9] Thus, universally, men have a motivation to dominate women and the nasty personality skills capable of doing so, while women have a motivation to relate more to children than to men (thus setting up a universal conflict in male and female motivations), as well as to each other (as like understands and empathizes better with like). Thus, given these biologically based gender conflicts, systems of compulsory heterosexuality are set up for the benefit of men to keep women from bonding with each other and children to the exclusion of men.

The social schools of Difference include feminist psychoanalytic theory as well as some radical feminist theory.[10] These theorists argue that the personality differences between men and women, though they are central to personal identity and difficult to change, are not biological. Rather, they are socially produced through the sexual division of labor, particularly in parenting. This sexual division creates in women a more altruistic and relational sense of self than men, who are produced with a more oppositional and autonomous, hence more competitive and self-interested, sense of self.

The biological determinist school of feminism tends toward a separatist solution for women. Men, after all, are incorrigible! In-

---

7 Mary O. Brien

8 Simone de Beauvoir, *The Second Sex* (New York: Bantam 1952); Laurel Holliday, *The Violent Sex: Male Psychobiology and the Evolution of Consciousness* (Guerneville, CA: Bluestocking Press 1978); Kathleen Barry

9 Alice Rossi, 'A Biosocial Perspective on Parenting' *Daedulus* **106**, 2 (Spring, 1977), 1-32; Melvin Konner 'She & He,' *Science* (Sept. 1982), 54-61; Laurel Holliday; Adrienne Rich *Of Woman Born* (New York: Norton 1976)

10 Nancy Chodorow; Juliet Mitchell, *Psychoanalysis and Feminism* (New York: Pantheon 1974); Janice Raymond, *The Transsexual Empire: The Making of the She-Male* (Boston: Beacon 1979); Carol Gilligan

deed, in her latest book, Mary Daly goes so far as to suggest that they are tantamount to a separate species from women, and consequently women owe them no personal or political obligations.[11] Women should learn to value our authentic selves by relating to each other as friends and lovers, thus dropping out of, and thereby challenging the dominant patriarchal culture by providing an example to other women of a freer life – one more in tune with women-centered values.

Not all Difference theorists believe that such an extreme separtism is the political solution for feminists. Jan Raymond, in her latest book, *A Passion for Friends*,[12] maintains that women have an authentic Self (her capital 'S') different from men's. Thus if women are to be true to themselves they must prioritize being for other women. This means that we should prioritize friendships with women rather than accept the socially constructed patterns of what she calls 'heteroreality,' all of which socialize women to define our selves and our meaning in life in relationships with men.

Though Raymond wants a certain kind of cultural separtism for women, she does not advocate a 'drop out' separtism. Rather than dropping out of the world, women must strive to change the political and economic priorities of a patriarchal society by working in careers that have hitherto involved only males and male-defined values.

It is never made clear in Raymond's book whether she thinks women's authentic Self is more like other women's than like men's for biological or for social reasons. Other Difference theorists who clearly reject the biological gender difference argument are Nancy Chodorow,[13] Dorothy Dinnerstein,[14] Carol Gilligan[15] and Sara Rud-

---

11 Mary Daly, *Pure Lust: Elemental Feminist Philosophy* (Boston: Beacon Press 1984)

12 Janice Raymond, *A Passion for Friends: Toward a Philosophy of Female Affection* (Boston, MA: Beacon Press 1986)

13 Nancy Chodorow

14 Dorothy Dinnerstein, *The Mermaid and the Minotaur: Sexual Arrangements and Human Malaise* (New York: Harper 1976)

15 Carol Gilligan

dick.[16] These thinkers argue that the psychology of women differs from that of men because women rather than men mother. By 'mothering' they do not mean childbearing, that biological function that women cannot share with men, but mothering in the social sense of the nurturing and direct physical care for infants in early childrearing. The fact that women and not men mother in this sense creates a different sense of self in little girls than in little boys. Girls have an immediate role model for what it is to be female: one who is engaged in the concrete chores involved in housework and regular nurturant interaction with children. Consequently the girl defines a sense of self that is relational or incorporative (i.e. I am like mom in these ways). Girls also must identify with, rather than absolutely oppose, that aspect of mother which is resented and feared: the fact that she can never meet all of the infant's myriad needs. This tends to make females turn anger originally directed at mother inward on themselves in ways that weaken self-esteem.

Gender identity for the boy comes out differently. Society teaches him that to be male is not to be female, and due to the relative or complete absence of his father he lacks a male role model as immediate for him as is the mother for the little girl. Thus he learns to define himself oppositionally instead of relationally (I am not-mother, I am not-female). He can thus project infantile anger not only on mother but on the class of women in general. Thus, the crosscultural constant, the asymmetrical parenting of women, explains the crosscultural male deprecation of women.

Carol Gilligan argues that women tend to have a different style of moral reasoning then men — what she calls a different 'moral voice.' When presented with hypothetical moral dilemmas, females tend to find a contextual solution while males formulate abstract principles and prioritize justifying one solution rather than the other. The idea that women have a different moral voice than men's is pursued by Sara Ruddick, who argues that the socialization for,

---

16 Sara Ruddick, 'Maternal Thinking,' *Feminist Studies* 6, 2 (Summer 1980) 342-67; reprinted in Joyce Trebilcot, ed., *Mothering: Essays in Feminist Theory* (Totowa, NJ: Rowman and Allenheld 1984)

and actual experience of, mothering creates a maternal thinking in women which prioritizes the life preservation, growth and social acceptability of the child under her care. When women generalize from the values embedded in this concrete mothering experience, they develop a more care-oriented ethic, concerned with peacemaking and concrete life preserving, than men. These latter, with their gender identity and masculine training in the abstact skills necessary to do well in competitive male groups and careers, are more likely to fall prey to the militaristic thinking of the sort that justifies war, the arms race and other life- and species-endangering activities.

Social difference theory has two conflicting tendencies within it in regard to the question of how individual women can reclaim a personal power denied by the standards of femininity built into heterosexual desires. Feminist psychoanalytic theory suggests that women should have recourse to feminist therapy to undo the damages of being denied the proper nurturance for self-autonomy in early childhood. The collective strategies of radical feminism, however, tend to reject this individual solution in favor of a collective process in which women bond with other women to re-value feminine work and values, thus allowing women's self, based as it is on the worth of the feminine itself, to gain power. Thus the importance of comparable worth campaigns and women-only peace protests which reclaim the value of maternal thinking as opposed to militaristic thinking.

The general strategy of this line of Difference thought is opposed to the strategies of those liberal feminists who assume a rational maximizer theory of self. Rather than striving to make women more like men so we have a better change of succeeding in a male dominant world, the feminist empowerment process involves affirming the socially insufficiently recognized value of the feminine. Indeed, ideally, men should become more like women by committing themselves to learn so-called feminine skills. Only by so identifying with the feminine can they cease their deprecation of women. Further, only by an individual commitment of this sort, for example, the commitment to learn mothering skills by co-parenting, can a man create the kind of love relationship with a women which will allow her the maximum opportunity of obtaining a sense of self worth.

But it is at this point that Difference theory can provide us with no clear answers on how and why men are going to be motivated to make such a dramatic change in the conception of masculinity. And even if they were, how can they be expected to succeed in learning feminine skills if these demand a permeable, or incorporative, personality as opposed to an oppositional one? And, given these problems, why and how can women who are concerned to increase their sense of self-worth work with individual men to encourage change?

IV Problems With the First Two Theories of the Self

Although both the Rational Mazimizer and Difference theories of the Self have important insights, they are inadequate in other ways. Though the first explains why women remain oppressed because of the external constraints that society places on them, it cannot explain why those few women in economically and socially privileged positions in society still defer to men. Why, if a women is independently wealthy, would she be content to be a wife and mother rather than embarking on a professional or political career which would give her an even greater social effect on the world? Why do some such women even allow themselves to be battered wives? Such behavior does not seem to rationally maximizing! Why then do these women who are economically independent continue to pursue less rewarding lives that require deferring to men? And why do many women who can afford higher education choose less well paying careers in literature, nursing and elementary school teaching rather than business, physics, medical school or engineering? In short, the Rational Maximizer theory underestimates the way in which people are not rational maximizers when it comes to their ultimate goals in life, which for most are gender-defined and socially engineered.

Though the Difference school can answer this question — women after all are constructed with essentially different senses of self, skills and desires from men — this group is overly deterministic about the static nature of this social molding. Consequently they cannot answer the historical question of how and why a Women's Movement should have arisen just now in American history. If women are so different from men, why should women now be demanding the opportunity to enter male spheres? Why should the idea of developing independence and autonomy, long considered the special purview of masculine identity, suddenly be a goal for feminists as well?

My view is at odds with both the Rational Maximizer and the Difference theorist theories. Both of them are *static* and *essentialist*. That is, they conceive of the self as a given unity with certain fixed qualities, though they disagree about what those fixed qualities are. Thus, they both have *atomistic* views of the self. Whether the self is a rational calculator or a phenomenal center that defines itself in relation to others, the self is seen as having an essence fixed by human nature or by early childhood.

Many Difference theorists maintain that there is a split between the authentic and inauthentic parts of the self. This model does suggest that radical change is possible by spurning the inauthentic self. But their claim that there is such an authentic aspect of self, and speculations as to the nature of its preferences and interests, are wildly metaphysical and unprovable. Indeed, they have seemed elitist and culture bound to some. For example, since most women continue to prefer men to women as love-mates, how can it be proved that it is more authentic for those women to prefer women, as some Difference theories maintain? How do we decide whether the authentic female self is a lesbian, heterosexual, pansexual or asexual?

V The Aspect Theory of Self

My alternative theory, which I call the Aspect theory of self, rejects the idea that the self is an unchanging, unified consciousness which has a two tiered set of properties: those that are necessary and essential, and those which are accidental. Rather, conscious selfhood is an ongoing process in which both unique individual priorities and social constraints vie in limiting and defining one's self-identity.[17]

---

17 Cf. my forthcoming book: Ann Ferguson, *Blood at the Root: Motherhood, Sexuality and Male Dominance* (Boston: Methuen/Routledge 1988) as well as Ferguson, 'Motherhood and Sexuality: Some Feminist Questions,' *Hypatia: Journal of Feminist Philosophy* 1, 2 (Fall 1986), 322.

Humans may be rational maximizers if placed in the sort of social practices which encourages such a type of thinking strategy. But that is only one aspect of a self which is more like a bundle of parts or aspects than it is like a uni-dimensional means/ends calculator. Gender differences in personality, in life choices and in moral reasoning are characteristic of only one aspect of a complicated human psyche that is often at odds with itself, and therefore, cannot be thought, comfortingly, to have only one essence.

If we think of the self as having many parts or aspects, some of which are in conflict, we can make better sense out of Gilligan's claim that there is a dicotomy of masculine and feminine moral voices. Most male and female psyches, created in standard gender-dicotomous childrearing practices, have at least one characteristic difference that is reflected by a difference in moral voices. But many adult women who engage in similar social practices with adult men, e.g. as business or professional colleagues, may also share with them the so-called masculine voice of moral reasoning. And men influenced enough by feminist women to attempt co-parenting may develop a feminine voice of moral reasoning due to this practice. These men and women will have both so-called masculine and feminine aspects of self as developed by their ongoing social practices, and while they will be likely to find these opposing perspectives incongruous, and indeed inharmonious, there is no reason to say that they are thus 'denying their essence' in the social practice in which they are doing the gender anomalous job.

If the self is seen as having many aspects, then it cannot be determined universally which are prior, more fundamental or more or less authentic. Rather, aspects of our selves are developed by participating in social practices which insist on certain skills and values. Furthermore the *contents* of masculinity and femininity vary with the social practices they are connected to. A woman defending her child against attack (for example in the movie *Cudjoe* or *Aliens*) is supposed to be showing her feminine protective maternal instinct. But a similar aggressive, perhaps violent act against a man who has made deprecating sexist remarks, is not considered feminine.

Where different social practices encourage skills and values that are in conflict, those participating in them will develop conflicting aspects of self. And where certain social practices are taken to be

paradigmatic of one's personal identity (as in self-effacing mothering activities for women in our society and self-aggrandizing aggressive or competitive activities for men) then those who develop
gender anomalous aspects of self can be disempowered by attributing the inharmonious combination of the two aspects to a personal
neurosis. Though the feminist strategy of conceiving of certain
aspects of self as inauthentic (for example, manipulative skills or
heterosexual charm) is a more empowering approach than this, it
does not follow that the view of self as having an authentic core
and inauthentic outer layers is correct. Rather, one's sense of self
and one's core values may change at different times and in different contexts. How then do we understand what it is to increase a
sense of self worth and personal power when the self is conceived
of, as the Aspect theory suggests, as an *existential process* in which
incongruities and lack of power are due to participation in conflicting social practices? Let us take a concrete example to discuss.

Professional women in the helping professions are a good example of those whose concrete social practices are in conflict. Those
in jobs in higher education, nursing and social work must develop
our ability to empathize with concrete others – students, patients
or clients – to do our job well. But since most of us work in large
bureaucratic settings where impersonal rules of the game apply to
job hiring, promotions and allocations, we must develop a competitive, impersonal meritocratic set of values and principles in self-
defense. Thus one aspect of our jobs encourages the caring ethic
connected to a contextual concern for concrete others that Gilligan
claims is typical of the feminine role, and another aspect requires
adopting the masculine ethic characterized by a universalistic
rights/justice approach. Thus we have two moral voices, both in unhappy and unharmonious juxtaposition in our consciousness. What
is alienating is not that our authentic self is thus denied, but the
psychological incongruity of having to operate with conflicting
values.

This contradiction in ways of thinking and valuing is a feature
not only of women's work in the helping professions but of the work
of those in male-dominated fields like business, politics and the law
who face the second shift problem as working mothers.

Ironically, the juggling of incorporative aspects of self in nurturant work at home with oppositional and individualistic ways of being in such careers is also a problem for some men who, in sharing housework and childcare with feminist partners, find their modus operandi different from their more conservative male colleagues at the office. Black and other minority women, no matter whether employed or not, could be expected to develop a rights/justice orientation in self-defense against the social opposition of racist whites, toward whom they cannot afford to take a simple caring orientation.

The way to understand personal empowerment of an oppressed group faced with social practices which involve conflicting values is to combine the insights of the Rational Maximizer and Difference theories of Self with a historical perspective. The traditional sexual division of labor in public and private spheres is breaking down for many women and some men. Where it is no longer clear what exactly is men's and women's work, gender identities defined in terms of the different standards of self-worth attached to men's and women's work are put in crisis. It is precisely this developing conflict in gender roles, in conjunction with the American democratic ideology of the right of equality for all based on merit, that has spawned both the Women's Movement and the possibility for greater empowerment for women. Though the initial phase of capitalist development in America perpetuated male dominance by relegating women to the private, less socially valued, dependent and relatively powerless sphere of the home, advanced capitalism and consumerist standards of living have been pulling women into part and full time labor. Though this has created the second shift problem for working mothers and the the incongruity of women, brought up to do individualized, caring work, placed in impersonal and uncaring bureaucracies and anonymous institutions, it has also allowed many women to gain economic independence from men.

An existential process of resolving this incongruity of personal identity can take many forms. The New Right women may decide that homemaking in economic and social dependency on a man is a better way to resolve the incongruity in her life than to strive for a career and economic independence from men. As Phyllis Schafley notes, most women would really rather cuddle a baby than a typewriter!

If the Aspect theory of the self is correct, the feminist cannot challenge the New Right woman's choice by claiming it is inauthentic, for there is no way to prove what the authentic female self would choose. Nonetheless, due to the social crisis in gender roles, all women in the United States today are likely to have developed rational maximizer as well as incorporative (i.e. traditionally feminine) aspects of self. This is so because when traditional life styles are no longer rigidly followed, individuals are forced to a more self-conscious means/ends calculation of what in the long run will serve their interests.

Feminists can appeal to the rational maximizer aspect of women to argue that women who take the New Right solution to the gender crisis face a high risk of failing to achieve their goals of security and well being. This is so because of the rise in divorce rates, low welfare payments, low-paid wage labor work for most women and the small amount of child support most women receive from former husbands. Thus a woman who places all her eggs in the homemaker basket is increasingly likely to end up a single mother who is one of the statistics in the feminization of poverty.

With respect to women's traditional feminine identification as nurturers, feminists can argue that the only way to really have these values be effective today is not to retreat to private motherhood but to influence public policy by gaining individual and collective power in careers and politics that will allow for a public challenge to a militarism spawned by an excessive masculine thinking. Only by gaining public power as women can we have the collective power, through unionizing women and feminist political networks, to demand that those feminine values of caring and contextual moral decision-making be incorporated into the rules of the game of our economic and government institutions. In the long run, only a more decentralized worker's (and client, patient and student) -controlled type of decision making can incorporate the caring and contextual considerations needed into the more abstract meritocratic but often inhumane rules by which our public institutions operate.

Such a feminist program will require radical structural changes in the present relation between public and private. We will need to educate the American public to the idea that the raising of children is not a private luxury but a public responsibility. Employers should thus be required to reorganize wage work so as to allow flex time jobs, with no career penalty for mothers and fathers of young children, as well as maternity and paternity leave and quality affordable child care.

Our ultimate goal must be the de-genderizing of every aspect of social life. Only this can empower women to develop our potentials as unique individuals not constrained by a social definition which sees our essential nature to be to serve men. However, we cannot achieve this goal without a collective, public process which first empowers women by creating a higher public value for feminine skills and interests. Though assertiveness training and economic independence are key for women, they must be supplemented by comparable worth, social security for homemakers and other such campaigns which set a higher value on women's traditional work.

While feminist collective networking and public feminist political campaigns can start the empowerment process that allows a woman to re-define a core sense of self that can perceive itself as valuable and able to control her life independently of men, there are many other private issues that remain to be negotiated if she is to develop full personal empowerment.

For example, should a woman cut herself off from, or just try to ignore, her parents if they are very sexist? Should she pursue motherhood, given the social costs and dangers of morherhood, indeed the likelihood of being a single mother in a sexist world? Should she give up a heterosexual life style and choose a woman lover in order to create a more equal context for love? Should she choose an alternative living arrangement with a man which does not involve marriage, to avoid the sexist social and psychological expectations that may be involved? Or should she eschew sexual love relationships altogether and prioritize platonic friendships with women (and perhaps men)?[18]

There is no general answer as to which of these paths a woman should take to personal empowerment. Only trial and error and the

---

18 For a discussion of some of these feminist ethical questions, see Ferguson, *Blood at the Root*, and the articles in Ann Ferguson, ed., 'Motherhood and Sexuality' issue, *Hypatia: Journal of Feminist Philosophy* 1, 2 (Fall 1986).

experience of juggling the various aspects of her self by trying out different private commitments can lead to what is most personally empowering to different women. The Aspect theory of the self, based as it is on the view that the self is an existential process whose integration may be different for different women, must assume an ethical pluralism on such matters of personal choice.

The position of ethical pluralism is a consequence of the rejection of the essentialist idea that all women have the same inner and authentic self which can only be empowered by the same choices. But, nonetheless, we can still draw a few important generalizations about what this empowerment process must minimally entail for women in the contemporary United States: first, collective networking with other women around feminist campaigns; and second, prioritizing friendships with other women that value personal autonomy and the elimination of self-definitions that define self-worth exclusively in terms of relationships with men, whether they be fathers, employers, sons, workmates, friends, husbands or lovers. Given the fragmented aspects of self and the general deprecation of the feminine that pervades all our social life, these steps are necessary, both to empower both the rational maximizing aspect of self, which gains when women find ways to gain material equality with men, and the incorporative aspect of self, which finds empowerment when it finds a secure yet self-affirming way to ally one's self-interests in nurturing and supportive connections to others.

CANADIAN JOURNAL OF PHILOSOPHY
Supplementary Volume 13

Second Persons

LORRAINE CODE
York University
North York, ON
Canada M3J 1P3

I Autonomy and Community

Assumptions about what it is to be human are implicit in most philosophical reflections upon ethical and epistemological issues. Although such assumptions are not usually elaborated into a comprehensive theory of human nature, they are nonetheless influential in beliefs about what kinds of problem are worthy of consideration, and in judgments about the adequacy of proposed solutions. Claims to the effect that one should not be swayed by feelings and loyalties in the making of moral decisions, for example, presuppose that human beings are creatures whose nature is amenable to guidance by reason rather than emotion and are creatures capable of living well when they act as impartially as possible. Analogously, claims to the effect that knowledge, to merit that title, should be acquired out of independent cognitive endeavour uncluttered by opinion and hearsay, suggest that human beings are creatures who can come to know their environment through their own unaided efforts. And claims to the effect that knowledge, once acquired, is timelessly and universally true depend upon assumptions about the constancy and uniformity of human nature across historical and cultural boundaries.

It is my purpose in this paper to take issue with one conception of what it is to be human that has been a shaping force in much of modern ethical and epistemological thinking. This is the conception of 'autonomous man,' conceived as an exemplar of what is best in human nature. I shall discuss the artificiality of this construct — 'autonomous man' — and argue that such a conception of personhood is inimical to feminist thought.

The second part of this project may initially seem to be ill-conceived, from a feminist perspective, in view of the fact that it has been a primary feminist preoccupation to urge women to strive for autonomy, understood both as freedom *from* patriarchal oppression, and as freedom *to* realize their own capacities and aspirations. I do not mean to deny the achievement of autonomy a central place amongst feminist goals. Nonetheless, philosophical interpretations of the value of autonomy have often tended to result in an autonomy-obsession which serves no one's purposes well. As an antidote to that obsession, I shall suggest that feminist thinkers might draw valuable inspiration from a conception of 'second personhood' elaborated by Annette Baier and (with different emphasis and terminology) by Caroline Whitbeck.

Present-day autonomous man differs significantly from the Enlightenment thinker, celebrating his freedom to trust in the power of his own reason, and ready to shed the constraints of an essentially heteronomous mode of existence. A cluster of derivative attributes and assumptions have come to attach themselves to ideas about the realization of autonomy in human life. Autonomous man is — and, it is commonly believed, should be — self-sufficient, independent, and self-reliant, a self-realizing individual whose efforts are directed toward maximizing his personal gains. His valued independence is under constant threat from other (equally self-serving) individuals: hence he derives rules to protect himself from undue intrusion. Talk of rights, rational self-interest, expediency and efficiency permeates his moral, social, and political discourse. In short, there has been a gradual alignment of autonomy with individualism. This may not have been the intent of the ideal in its Enlightenment and later formulations, but the import and the intent of such concepts are not always congruent, and it is the import of much contemporary autonomy-oriented thought that is problematic.

For the purposes of this discussion, then, I am not concerned to argue that there are philosophers who believe that human beings are, or could be, *wholly* autonomous and self-sufficient. Autonomous man is an abstraction: neither all men, nor all avowedly autonomous men, would exhibit all of the characteristics all of the time that I have attributed to him. Nor are such characteristics reserved for men alone. But autonomous man does enjoy the status of a character ideal in modern society; his mode of being is considered worthy of admiration and emulation. And the problem is that characterizations of this abstract figure lend themselves to a starkness of interpretation which constrains philosophical enquiry while, at the same time, enlisting philosophical positions in support of constraining social and political policies.

John Benson, for example, finds that autonomous man often appears in philosophical writings as a 'distant and intimidating ideal' engaged in 'self-creation and persistent radical self-questioning.'[1] Daniel Callahan writes of an assumption prevalent in medical ethics to the effect that respect for patient autonomy must override practitioner paternalism. Implicit in this assumption he finds a belief that moral obligation is binding only when it is autonomously contracted into − a belief which, in his view, both 'shrivel(s) our sense of obligation' toward one another, and impoverishes the nature of health care by taking as the norm 'physicians who, far from treating us paternalistically, treat us impersonally and distantly, respecting our autonomy *but nothing else.*'[2] And Nancy Hartsock sketches a complex picture of 'rational economic man' as an agent who is an autonomous, 'independent, frequently isolated, and presumably hostile being ... whose very humanity is based on [his] independence from the wills of others...,'[3] arguing that economic and political exchanges are often taken as a model for human relations per se. It is the fact

---

1 John Benson, 'Who is the Autonomous Man?', *Philosophy* **58** (1983), 5

2 Daniel Callahan, 'Autonomy: A Moral Good, Not a Moral Obession,' *The Hastings Center Report* **14**, 5 (1984), 41

3 Nancy Hartsock, *Money, Sex and Power* (Boston: Northeastern University Press 1986), 38

that autonomy lends itself to readings of such starkness that prompts my exploration of alternative pictures of human being.

It may be that no theorist who grants the realization and maintenance of autonomy a central place amongst moral and/or cognitive values intends to dwell upon autonomy to the exclusion of interdependence and community. But, in practice, it often seems that autonomy is the central, core, or supreme value, and that values that grow out of community are seen as intrusions upon, or threats to autonomy. Indeed, starting points and focal points shape the impact of theoretical discussion: it makes a difference whether one moves from autonomy to community, or in the opposite direction. Often theorists who take autonomy to be the most prized of human possessions seem to discern an undue tension between values of self-sufficiency and interdependence; they may assume that interdependence is to be bought at the *cost* of some measure of autonomy, or they may allow the importance of self-sufficiency to obscure that of community. Theorists (such as Baier and Whitbeck) who take communality and interdependence as their starting point seem better able to accommodate the requirements of autonomy than theorists who take autonomous existence as the 'original position' are able to accommodate the requirements of community. This may be for the purely developmental reason that human life begins in interdependence, hence that communality-based positions map more readily onto human life as it is lived, and that there is an artificiality about individualistic starting points which communality-based positions escape. My claim is that these latter positions are worth exploring, for the picture of human selfhood they yield seems to escape some of the negative consequences of autonomy-obsession, yet to have equivalent explanatory power.

In fact, the central claim advanced in Annette Baier's paper 'Cartesian Persons,' contrasts sharply with autonomy-centred thinking. Baier observes that: 'A person, perhaps, is best seen as one who was long enough dependent upon other persons to acquire the essential arts of personhood. Persons essentially are *second* persons....'[4]

---

4 'Cartesian Persons,' in Annette Baier, *Postures of the Mind: Essays on Mind and Morals* (Minneapolis: University of Minnesota Press 1985), 84. I raise some of the issues I discuss here in my review of Baier's book in *Dialogue*, forthcoming.

Some implications of this claim emerge in a number of the other essays in her book *Postures of the Mind: Essays on Mind and Morals*. They add up to a repudiation of individualism both in its ethical and its epistemological manifestations, which takes the form less of an explicit critique than of a demonstration of the communal, community-dependent nature of most aspects of moral and mental activity. Yet an endorsement of Baier's 'second persons' claim would not amount to a renunciation of individuality, so long as 'individuality' is not equated with 'individualism.' While denying nothing of personal uniqueness, creativity, expressiveness, and self-awareness, Baier shows how all of these grow out of interdependence, and continually turn back to it for affirmation and continuation.

Baier maintains that moral reflection should start from the assumption that the 'good and helpful aspects of our condition, as much as the evils, stem from the fact of interdependence.'[5] Moral reflection, she believes, ought to make it possible for human beings to live and act responsibly and well with one another: to the extent that self-realization can be declared a goal of moral life, it should be understood as an outgrowth of fundamentally interactional moral activity. Hence, with Hume, Baier questions the value of a purely intellectual morality, urging the need to educate the emotions and passions. She is less concerned with the construction of moral theories whose precepts could be universally and impartially applied than with the cultivation of an ability to reflect well upon 'human active capacities for cooperation.'[6] Such reflection should draw upon virtues teachable by word and deed, hence shareable, and constitutive of a basis for an evolving moral practice. This she finds more important than the development of a *system* of moral principles, in which the less general are derivable from the more general.

With respect to cognitive activity, Baier believes that personal knowledge requires the support of common knowledge to the extent that even the liberty to change one's mind derives from membership in a community which trains its members in conventions of

---

5 Ibid., 231

6 Ibid., 218

criticism, affirmation, and second thinking. She argues that being self-conscious means knowing oneself to be a 'person among persons';[7] and that 'Realization, if professed, is essentially shared … *Realize* is used when I speak as a member, not an outsider.'[8] The kind of cooperative moral and epistemic practice that Baier seems to envisage would be free of the defensiveness characteristic of much traditional moral thought, and implicit, if in a different guise, in much mainstream epistemological thinking.

II 'Second Persons,' Maternal Thinking and Friendship

The extent to which it is reasonable to find illumination for feminist concerns in Baier's views depends upon how one reads the notion of 'the essential arts of personhood.' Feminist thinkers are by now well aware that there are many such arts, dependent upon the *kind* of personhood deemed appropriate to emerge from the process of instruction. It is by now well known that male personhood and female personhood are by no means equivalent – and the same must also be said of the personhood deemed appropriate to particular classes, races, and cultures. But it is female and male personhood that concern me here. Not only is it clear that much of women's continued oppression can be attributed to the tenacity of stereotyped expectations about what it is to be a female person, it is also apparent from the growing body of feminist literature on child-raising that the structure of these practices, at least in Western societies, is such as inevitably to create significantly different kinds of female and male personhood. Discussion of the 'essential arts of personhood' needs to be sensitive to these points.

Reading Baier's observation as a catalyst for feminist reflection also evokes a wariness against allowing it to convey any sense that a 'completed' form of personhood, in any of its guises, is to be the product of instruction in these arts. In fact, part of the implicit value of Baier's insight lies in the way it facilitates a move away from

---

7 Ibid., 89

8 Ibid., 32

assumptions to the effect that self-sufficient, universal Man must remain the undisputed hero of philosophical discourse. It allows an exploration of some implications of the fact that interdependence is continuous throughout a person's life, hence that personhood need never be fixed — that there is no implicit *stasis*. One is always a 'second person,' open to the effects of an interdependence that is manifested as much in a propensity to be influenced as it is in a capacity to influence. Shifting patterns of interaction within human lives, and constant reassimilation and reinterpretation of one's own history, often through communication with other 'second persons,' show something of how inappropriate it would be to conceive of persons as unified, wholly self-conscious selves, whose modes of being cannot accommodate contradiction, ambiguity, and gaps in self-awareness. One is constantly learning the arts of personhood; and Baier's point might be taken to be that one's mode of being a second person, throughout one's life, bears significantly upon how well one learns and practices these arts.

I spell out these considerations only to dispel any misconceptions that might arise out of Baier's reference to the 'essential' arts of personhood, not to suggest that she herself is insensitive to them. Her point, as I understand it, is that the arts in question are essential to being a person *simpliciter*: the term is not meant to convey essentialism in any traditional sense. The heuristic value of showing just how persons *are* essentially second persons is precisely in the way it precludes endorsing the centrality of autonomy, self-sufficiency, and/or self-making long assumed to be at the core of how it is — and is best — to be human. Thinking of just how essentially one is a second person indicates something of the misguidedness of any assumption to the effect that human beings grow naturally to autonomous self-sufficiency, only then — perhaps cautiously, incidentally, or as an afterthought — to engage in close relationships. The point is that one could not grow into anything recognizably human (for all of the variations of which humanness admits) were one not a second person from earliest infancy. The example of the Wild Child of Aveyron, which I have discussed elsewhere,[9] illustrates this

---

9 See chapters 3 and 7 of my *Epistemic Responsibility* (Hanover, NH: University Press of New England/Brown University Press 1987).

point most strikingly. At the very least, autonomy and self-sufficiency must be regarded as qualities that define themselves against a background of second personhood.

Baier's discussion of the significance of being a second person focusses upon the formative nature of human developmental process. It might be read to suggest that only those who have held themselves aloof from participation in child-raising practices, or from recognition of the implications of these practices either for their own histories, or for the shape of human relations as such, could have developed autonomy-centred theories. Baier convincingly maintains that all of our understanding of personality relates to its formation in childhood, where a cultural heritage is transmitted 'ready for adolescent rejection and adult discriminating selection and contribution,' pointing out that 'Gods, if denied childhood, cannot be persons';[10] and that 'Persons are the creation of persons.'[11] When one thinks of the closeness of the relationships central to these processes, one understands something of the curiousness of the assumption that a training in the arts of personhood should be expected to mature into autonomous adulthood, manifested in one of its starkest forms in the philosophical ideal of impartial moral reasoning shared by Kantians, utilitarians, and contractarians. Yet writings about moral development and moral education often emphasize the need to structure these processes so that rational, self-conscious, morally autonomous *individuals* will indeed be their products.[12] Such a self-sufficient mode of existence is conceivable only by positing an abrupt discontinuity between human developmental process and its alleged 'products.' Not only does this make no biological sense, but it works to separate philosophical theories from pre-philosophical experience to such an extent that philosophical accounts of personhood seem to leave this experience both unacknowledged and unexamined.

---

10 Baier, 85

11 Ibid., 86

12 The work of Emile Durkheim, Lawrence Kohlberg, and Jean Piaget is typical in this respect.

While Baier's points about the extent to which persons are 'second persons' are made descriptively rather than prescriptively, I think it is in keeping with the spirit of her discussion to read it as having normative implications, particularly in view of her recommendation, cited above, that philosophers acknowledge the extent to which the good and helpful aspects of our condition, as much as the evils, stem from the fact of interdependence. The kind of human relationship signalled by thinking in terms of 'second person' interaction seems, in fact, to be qualitatively different from that implicit in third person discourse about human beings. 'Second persons,' implicitly at least, are persons who engage with one another and who may well care about the quality of that engagement. The implications of a Sartrean constitution of other persons as starkly 'Other,' as *en soi*, shows by contrast something of what I mean. In feminist literature, one finds an account of a sharp antithesis to 'second personhood' in Marilyn Frye's characterisation of the arrogant (masculine) eye, which 'gives all things meaning by connecting all things to each other by way of their references to one point — Man'; and particularly in her contention that, for most of us, a woman existing outside the field of vision of that eye 'is really inconceivable.'[13] These points are echoed in Jessica Benjamin's observation that 'The repudiation of recognition between persons and its displacement by impersonal objective forms of social intercourse is the social homologue of the male repudiation of the mother.'[14] Distanced conferral of meaning upon another person's existence, and impersonal modes of interaction, are at the furthest remove from second person relations in their (potentially) normative dimension.

The persons who would emerge as the subjects of second person moral discourse would be characterisable (following Caroline Whitbeck) as 'relational and historical being[s] whose creativity and

---

13 Marilyn Frye, *The Politics of Reality* (Trumansburg, NY: The Crossing Press 1983), 80

14 Jessica Benjamin, 'The Bonds of Love: Rational Violence and Erotic Domination,' in H. Eisenstein and A. Jardine, eds., *The Future of Difference* (New Brunswick, NJ: Rutgers University Press 1985), 64

moral integrity are both developed and realized in and through relationships and practices.'[15] Thinking in terms of relations and historical experiences (both one's own and those of one's 'community') as constitutive of what each person is as a continually evolving self shows that each life is a nexus of many other life-lines and experiences, partially separate and partially interrelated and interdependent. Thinking of creativity and integrity together shows that neither of these is a static concept, but that they, too, evolve in a constantly interactive process. Persons are never quite what they were or will be; and this fact is as much dependent upon their relationships, both social and environmental, as it is upon their 'own nature.' In the self-other relation Whitbeck envisages 'between beings who are in some respects analogous ... [where] the scope and limits of that analogy ... are something to be explored in each case,'[16] primary attention is given to possibilities of mutual understanding between and among beings who are 'distinct and different *in some respect.*'[17] Relationships are conceived neither as essentially oppositional nor polar, but are taken to develop 'through identification and differentiation, through listening and speaking with *each other*, rather than through struggles to dominate or annihilate the other,'[18] as autonomy-centred theories sometimes seem to assume. The point is to approach the fact of human interdependence so as to discern its enabling possibilities rather than to concentrate upon the constraints it might present, much as Baier, too, suggests.

---

15 Caroline Whitbeck, 'Feminist Ontology: A Different Reality,' in Carol Gould, ed., *Beyond Domination* (Totowa, NJ: Rowman & Allenheld 1983), 66

16 Ibid., 75

17 Ibid.

18 Ibid. The suggestion that autonomous individuals are engaged in struggles to annihilate one another may perhaps seem excessive. Yet the (figurative) annihilation of another individual as a competitor in a contest, sporting event, or business deal, and the (literal) annihilation of an enemy are significantly continuous concepts, as the common language used to describe such various phenomena also indicates. Clearly the same kind of 'personhood' is assumed in each area of discourse.

While I see considerable promise in this relational picture of human life, I am less convinced by Whitbeck's endorsement of Sara Ruddick's view that 'maternal thinking' can serve as a paradigm upon which this self-other relation would be modelled, and by her partial incorporation of that putative paradigm into her own approach.[19] In expressing these reservations, I do not mean to deny explanatory force to human developmental processes. I have cited Baier's views on this matter, which I find both persuasive and illuminating. Certainly any assumption that there could be a 'natural' state of separateness which needs to have infringements upon it carefully controlled looks particularly odd when one thinks of the necessarily interdependent nature of human existence in infancy and childhood. Left on their own to develop autonomous self-sufficiency, protected from interference, human infants and children would simply not survive. So there is something to the contention that it makes a considerable difference to how one thinks about selfhood and moral agency if one takes ito account the centrality of care, responsibility, and trust in early childhood development, and the extent to which that development depends upon 'second person' interaction. But these insights do not warrant granting 'maternal thinking' or its close analogues (for example, family living)[20] paradigmatic status. Indeed, I suggest that the reasons against doing so are more compelling than those that recommend it.

A serious problem with the veneration of mothering practices implicit in 'maternal thinking' is in the way it works to suppress and/or condemn ambivalences often characteristic of mother-child relationships, and to ignore the darker psychic forces that may structure these relationships – not only when one member of them is really a child, but throughout their various lifetimes. In the assumption of single-mindedness on the part of maternal caregivers implicit in this line of thought it is difficult, too, to accommodate the historically contingent nature of the 'self' of a nurturer. Yet it is by no means

---

19 The reference is to Sara Ruddick's paper 'Maternal Thinking,' in *Feminist Studies* (Summer 1980).

20 Cf. Whitbeck, 75.

clear why it should be assumed that a mother is any more integrated a being than is a growing child. When such an assumption is made, even implicitly, possibilities of developing adequately nuanced accounts of these relationships are diminished.

It is disconcerting to find in this putative *repudiation* of self-sufficiency and oppositionality a concern to present a paradigm of selfhood which is equally dependent upon taking human selves to be unified and in some sense 'complete.' It begins to look as though 'maternal thinking' might, in fact, amount to an attempt to replace one unified individual/agent with another, who differs mainly in being collectively or altruistically, rather than individualistically oriented. So although 'maternal' thinking may not posit an autonomy-based conception of human nature, it does, nonetheless, appear to posit an ideal of 'wholeness' for maternal caregivers which has prescriptive dimensions with a potential to oppress women by making them feel just as guilty as older, autonomy-prescriptive positions have done. Indeed, in suppressing the ambivalence often characteristic of the exemplary relationships it extols, 'maternal' feminism makes assumptions about human nature which, despite their difference, risk being as reductivist and essentialist as those made in autonomy-centered theories.

Still more troubling is the fact that, in generating their views out of mothering practices – and even in arguing, as both Ruddick and Whitbeck do, that the kind of thinking they advocate is not open *only* to women, *or* to mothers – 'maternal thinkers' both privilege and sanctify this culturally overladen relation which has been shown to be a decisive shaping force in the creation of 'autonomous man.'[21] If it is indeed meant to stand for a mode of caring open to all, then it is difficult to see why it should be characterised as 'maternal,' especially since that characterisation requires so many disclaimers.

---

21 See, for example, Dorothy Dinnerstein, *The Mermaid and the Minotaur* (New York: Harper & Row 1976); Nancy Chodorow, *The Reproduction of Mothering* (Berkeley: University of California Press 1979); and Isaac Balbus, *Marxism and Domination* (Princeton, NJ: Princeton University Press 1982), for discussions of the contributing influence of 'mother-dominated' child-raising in the creation of 'autonomous man.'

Some of Whitbeck's own disclaimers serve to reaffirm the value of her insights, despite her assertion that she takes the 'practice of mothering and/or family living as paradigmatic.'[22] For instance, she is not prepared to use the language of 'nurturing' because of its association with self-effacing, self-sacrificing female activity; and she explicitly dissociates herself from the practice of simply inverting patriarchal structures in order to affirm and celebrate 'the feminine.' Moreover, her observation that mothers learn from children just as children learn from mothers goes some way toward dealing with the problem of 'wholeness' as it might be expected of maternal caregivers.

Given the force of these disclaimers, it is not clear why maternal relationships, in particular, need to be granted pride of place. One can fully endorse Whitbeck's point that it is masculinist, patriarchal relations that are ordinarily modelled upon individualistic, autonomy-oriented assumptions, *and* allow that a potentially more valuable way of conceiving what it is to be a person could be derived from the 'liberation of women's relationships and practices,'[23] without taking the further step of making mothering activity the central (and essential) such practice. If the point is to ground a feminist conception of personhood in a mode of relationship best and/or most commonly practised by women, then intimate personal friendships would seem to be a better candidate, and far less culturally charged. Friendships are capable of accommodating the way in which persons are essentially (i.e., essential to their continued sense of self and well-being) 'second persons' throughout their lives. The fact that men sometimes, too, experience such friendships — if perhaps (stereotypically) infrequently — is another reason in favour of believing that insights into the possibilities of self-other relationship can be gained from them, since the prospects of developing a more widely relevant position on this basis would then be greater. That friendships do not even implicitly exclude women who do not mother, or who do not mother *well*, is a further point in their favour.

---

22 Whitbeck, 75

23 Ibid., 79

And the rarity of genuine friendship whose core is such as to foster the '(mutual) realization of people'[24] is surely no greater than that of a clear and unproblematic mothering relation such as Whitbeck (with Ruddick) admires.

Although I am not concerned to posit an essence of friendship, certain of its more common features are worth noting. In friendship at its best, a balance between separateness and appropriate interdependence is effected and maintained in a caring, trusting, mutually sustaining relationship. Established friendship tends to be able to cope, over time, with fluctuations in degrees of intimacy and levels of dependence and independence. That this is believed to be one of the finer forms of human relationship is apparent in the laudatory tone of statements to the effect that X is not just Y's mother, but also her friend; that A and B are not only lovers, or spouses, but friends. By contrast with mothering, friendship is often able to admit of degree without engendering guilt; and it can be manifested in parenting and other forms of caregiving without being essential to them, or required in them. Although such relationships will not always be characterisable as friendships, they may sometimes be, and chances are that they will be better so. Friendship can accommodate its own growth, and can contribute to the growth of its participants, often by coming to terms with ambivalences and ambiguities akin to those implicit in mother-child relations, but with the potential, at least, of being less emotionally fraught. This is a fertile locus for the development of trust, and for coming to understand the nature of trust in its manifold implications. In some ways it is a more promising locus than mother-child relationships, because in friendship there may, from the outset, be symmetrical possibilities that are unlikely to exist in quite the same way between mother and child in view of their evident inequality, at least in the early years. Although intimate friendship has long been regarded as a women's practice, and devalued accordingly, the fact that there have been such friendships between men, and between women and men, as well as between women, allows it to occupy the place claimed

---

24 Ibid., 65

for maternal thinking, with none of the accompanying rhetoric that is needed to show how men, and childless women, can also be mothers.

One of the paradoxical features of individualistic thinking, in which it contrasts sharply with 'second person' thinking, is that it has no room for specificity and individua*tion*. In those of its modes which emphasize impartiality and neutrality, persons are treated as indistinguishable and interchangeable: indeed, in the moral domain, specific claims of loyalty and affection are to be overruled in the interest of treating all 'individuals' alike. Hence, in mass society, specific and special personal interests often go unheard, and become the source of pain, discrimination, and oppression. Friends, by contrast (and this, of course, is true of children – and parents – too) are not interchangeable: one cannot substitute one friend for another and establish the same relationship. Yet there is no good reason to believe that the interests of friendship will inevitably blind a morally good human being to considerations of fairness and justice, whereas fairness and justice, impartially adjudicated, often blind one to the specific needs of particular persons. Hence, I would argue, there is no *prima facie* reason against granting moral priority to concerns about the quality of human relationships.

III Community and Ecology

In point of fact, certain features of friendship might be extended, by analogy, to serve as a shaping ideal for other kinds of human relationship, particularly if this ideal is pursued in conjunction with *ecological* thinking about the creation of social situations in which human well-being can be realized. What I have in mind, briefly, is something like this: One might think of the relationships that constitute human lives as patterns of concentric circles, many of which intersect with the relationships that constitute other lives. And one might consider whether the 'outer' circles, representing those more formal, less affectively central relationships in one's life could work on an analogy with the more central ones. This might serve to undermine the long-standing assumption that there are two distinct kinds of relationships in human lives: private, emotional, personal ones, and public, formal, impersonal ones. It tends to be assumed that such relationships belong to distinct parts of a life, and that they have relatively few features in common with respect to one's appropriate attitude to them, and mode of participation in them. Hence it is assumed that there is, and indeed should be, a split between a person's private and public 'self,' with the projects of the latter often accorded greater value.

It is often persuasively argued that, in complex mass societies, it is both desirable and necessary that some human relations be kept impersonal. But my point has, again, to do with starting points and points of focus or emphasis. I am suggesting that it makes a perceptible (if perhaps not fully specifiable) difference to the quality of human relationships whether they focus primarily upon human commonality, or upon independence and separateness. Human interaction that takes continuity rather than discontinuity between public and private spheres for granted is qualitatively different from that which assumes a dichotomy between the two. Such continuity might manifest itself, for example, in the kinds of initial approach one makes to other people: in approaches which presume that interaction will be easy and friendly (though not excessively so), contrasted with those marked by wariness and distrust. This would amount to a willingness to be more nearly one's 'private' self in 'public' encounters than many people are prepared to be; and it would need to be interpreted with care, to avoid presumptuous and inappropriately familiar behaviour. But who has mastered the arts of personhood would learn how this could best be done. And there is always the option to retreat to a more formal mode, should it become necessary.

For those accustomed to the autonomy-centered mode, dissolving the public/private dichotomy would involve a radical rethinking of their sense of self and others, whose primary manifestation, as I suggested in my discussion of Baier's work, might be in working away from defensive thinking about who one is, and about how one should act. Such a reorientation might, ideally, go some way toward creating a 'communitarian' mode of existence in the best sense of that term. The fact that those objective forms of social intercourse to which Benjamin refers are standardly believed to be most suitable to the public domain is well known, as is the fact that this is typically the male domain, defined by men, occupied (often jealously) by them, and sustained in its character by the exclusion of women, and of 'feminine' values. I am suggesting that this is a pernicious exclusion, and that thinking along *ecological* lines, in awareness of the extent to which persons are second persons, might effect something of a rapprochement between these two domains, whose distinctness is, at best, highly contrived.

Feminist thought, in some of its forms, *is* continuous with ecological thinking; and Baier's concern with the interconnectedness of human lives, captured in the notion of 'second personhood' shows an analogous continuity. Ecological thinking, as I am understanding it here, focusses upon the mutual relations of organisms with one another, and the relations between organisms and their environment. By the 'environment' I mean not just the physical environment, nor only the present environment, but the complex network of relations within which an organism realizes, or fails to realize, its potential, be those relations historical, material, geographical, social, institutional, or other. Any organism, at any moment in its history, reflects its current state of accommodation both of, and to, such relations. But this is by no means a passive reflection: ecological thinking emphasizes the participation of organisms, whose choices (where the organism is such as to *have* choices) are relationally structured, and who sometimes can themselves have a shaping effect upon relational choices.

Ecological thinking is reflection both upon the implications, for organisms, of living in certain kinds of environment, and upon the possibilities, for those organisms, of creating and sustaining an environment conducive to the realization of good ways of living. It encompasses a recognition that any claims made about what it is to be a certain kind of organism, living in certain kinds of circumstances, will be tinged with provisionality. They are, necessarily, made from a certain stance, at a certain time, and always subject to revision.

My more particular purpose in exploring the implications of the claim that persons are 'second persons' within an ecological context is to indicate the centrality of relationships in shaping the kinds of environment that contribute to human well-being, and to maintain that the moral responsibilities that attach to particular relationships are at least as important as those impartially enjoined by putatively universal moral principles. As Virginia Held aptly puts it: 'To sustain a society threatened with dissolution, we will have to pay attention before everything else to the relations between persons.'[25] In short, the quality of human relations becomes a matter of pivotal moral concern.

IV Cognitive Autonomy

There are close epistemological analogues to these claims I have made with reference to moral life. They suggest, as my quotations from Baier's work also indicate, that human beings are as essentially 'second persons' in epistemic activity as they are in moral activity. In so doing, they point to an equivalent inadequacy in the long-standing assumption that knowers, too, are autonomous, self-sufficient individuals, and in the concommitant normative view that it is best that they should be.

Whereas the autonomous *moral* agent makes his most unequivocal appearance as the hero of Kantian moral discourse, the autonomous epistemic agent is perhaps most strikingly visible as the pursuer of the Cartesian 'project of pure enquiry.'[26] A follower of Descartes' method is radically independent, pursuing the method in a process of solitary rational endeavour, and embarking upon that pursuit by freeing *him*self both from his previously accumulated beliefs and habits of mind, and from the influence of his own material being. This accomplished, he works toward a subjective, individual certainty. Construals of cognitive autonomy and self-sufficiency vary throughout the history of Western philosophy both before and after Descartes — from Plato's insistence, in the *Republic*, that the last step toward knowledge of the unhypothesized hypothesis (toward 'that which requires no assumption and is the starting point of all'[27])

---

25 Virginia Held, *Rights and Goods* (New York: Macmillan/The Free Press 1984), 84

26 The allusion is to the title of Bernard Williams' book, *Descartes: The Project of Pure Enquiry*.

27 Plato, *Republic*, 511b

must be made by each would-be knower separately and singly, through to the primacy Russell accords to knowledge-by-acquaintance. Yet assumptions that knowers can be self-sufficient, and that objects of knowledge are independent and separate from those knowers, result in a composite picture of what knowledge must be which bears the mark of this assumed cognitive autonomy.

Some might contend that Cartesianism in theory of knowledge has given way to a conception of human beings as members of a community of knowers, and of the interdependence of knowledge seekers. Certainly the present-day revived interest in pragmatism, with its affinity with Peirce's conception of a community of inquirers, stands as a strong and viable challenge to Cartesianism and its successors.[28] But such ways of thinking, although they accord well with some of the aims of feminist enquiry, could not be said to have achieved mainstream philosophical status. In point of fact, autonomy obsession is as evident in theory of knowledge as it is in ethics, particularly in the extent to which the spirit of positivism is still alive in present-day epistemological thinking. Although autonomy does not have precisely the same connotations either in its ethical and its epistemic senses, or in its Cartesian and its positivistic senses, the conception of human nature presupposed in each of these contexts is virtually identical. And the effects of these presuppositions, in theory of knowledge, are analogous to those I have described in moral thinking.

Some features of the dominant picture of human knowledge, which attest to the esteem accorded to autonomy in epistemic discourse, are worth noting. In the 'autonomy of knowledge' view,[29] it is taken for granted that knowledge is the *product* of enquiry, and that it can stand alone in the sense that the details of the process

---

28 The best known example of this revived interest in pragmatism is to be found in the work of Richard Rorty, both in his *Philosophy and the Mirror of Nature* (Princeton: Princeton University Press 1979), and, especially, in his *Consequences of Pragmatism* (Minneapolis: University of Minnesota Press 1982).

29 This phrase is from Sandra Harding's article, 'Why Has the Sex/Gender System Become Visible Only Now?', in S. Harding and M. Hintikka, eds., *Discovering Reality* (Dordrecht: Reidel 1983).

that has gone into its production are irrelevant to its shape, content, and/or evaluation. Knowledge judged worthy of that name is commonly assumed to be timelessly and placelessly true, and its objects are assumed to be independent of knowing subjects. Particularly in empirically oriented theories, perception and memory are accorded a much greater role in knowledge-acquisition than testimony. (And memory is assumed to function individually and independently, contrary to Baier's assertion of its dependence upon group memory.) Knowledge properly so-called will transcend experience, whose particularity can only sully and muddle its purity and clarity. And although *individual*, autonomous knowers are depicted as the producers of knowledge, these are clearly the same abstract individuals who are the heroes of moral discourse. Their specificity, and their cognitive 'location' count for nothing: indeed, should these threaten to intrude into epistemological discussion, such intrusion must be suppressed. So it seems to follow that such knowers, who appear as undifferentiated, constantly repeated elements of a knowing situation would be at some pains, too, to deny or suppress any suggestion that, in knowledge, they are essentially 'second persons.'

Baier moves to the notion of second personhood in her discussion of '*Cartesian* Persons' by showing that, although Descartes distrusts language as it contrasts with the certainty attainable in pure thought, nonetheless, when they move out of the theoretical mode, 'Cartesian persons and embodied Cartesian thinkers *speak*....'[30] Descartes himself would not have accorded epistemic significance to the learning processes of infancy and childhood, for from the point of view of intellectual life he sees that stage of human existence as a time which sets up the 'obstacles,' such as docility, acceptance of authority, and a preoccupation with bodily appetites, 'whose overcoming constitutes intellectual progress.'[31] But Baier argues that 'Without earlier confusion to reflect on, a Cartesian intellect would

---

30 Baier, 80

31 Ibid., 83

have no purpose. Its ends, like ours, are set by its beginnings.'[32] It is out of highlighting these under-elaborated aspects of Descartes' metaphysics of the person — reading it 'against the grain' — that she is able to show that even Cartesian persons, those most independent of knowers, are essentially second persons.

It is possible to view the composite picture of knowledge that I have sketched out from an analogous 'against the grain' perspective, and to show that it, too, is dependent for its allegedly 'hard-edged' quality as a finished product upon the cognitive activities of 'second persons.' Two implications of such a viewing that I shall explore briefly, in conclusion, bear upon a knower's membership in an epistemic community, and upon a conception of subject-object relations that this altered perspective might make possible. There are clear analogies between the kinds of epistemic thinking this might facilitate and the views of human nature that Baier and Whitbeck, variously, explore.

A lesser valuation of testimony by comparison with memory and perception as sources of knowledge, together with an exaggeratedly narrow construal of testimony as something like reliance upon other people's opinions and/or authority, tends to obscure the extent of human cognitive interdependence. As I have argued at greater length elsewhere,[33] theorists of knowledge often seem to forget just how small a portion of human knowledge is, or could be, gained by straightforwardly observational means. To a much greater extent than the examples commonly taken to illustrate epistemological points might lead one to believe, people are dependent, at a fundamental level, upon other people — parents, teachers, friends, reporters, authorities, and experts — for what they, often rightly, claim to know. Hence one of the most essential arts of personhood that must be learned before one can aspire to be a knower (and an art that one is constantly learning and modifying) is the art of dis-

---

32 Ibid., 86

33 See my 'Responsibility and the Epistemic Community: Woman's Place,' in *Social Research* (October 1983); and chapter 7 of my *Epistemic Responsibility*.

cerning whom one can trust, how one can know that someone else knows, what human sources of knowledge are trust*worthy*. Far from being autonomous in the senses discussed above, knowledge is an interpersonal product that requires communal standards of affirmation, correction, and denial for its very existence. So a study of the workings of epistemic community is as important a focus of epistemological enquiry as is an analysis of perception- and memory-based knowledge claims; and some of the workings of that community, and of the status enjoyed by cognitive authorities and by 'state of the art' knowledge, count among the conditions that make knowledge possible.[34] Thinking, then, of the ecological considerations adduced above, it is clearly of paramount importance that community standards of good cognitive practice be maintained if members of epistemic communities are to be capable of knowing well. The example of the Ik society, which I have discussed elsewhere,[35] shows, by contrast, how a community simply disintegrates when the possibility of cognitive interdependece and trust is eroded.

The impersonal, objective forms of social intercourse that Benjamin refers to have their counterparts in theory of knowledge, in two aspects which feminist thinkers have recently begun to consider: in the defensiveness that is apparent in much epistemological thinking, and in the subject/object dichotomy which construes objects of knowledge as quite separate from and independent of knowers.

Defensiveness in epistemic practice, which seems, at least in part, to be a product of the autonomy-of-knowledge persuasion, is evident most notably in an alleged need to define and defend one's own cognitive products against other knowers, with their challenges and counter-claims. In the philosophical domain it is manifested most plainly in the adversarial paradigm, whose effects in terms of limiting the scope of enquiry and of foreclosing possibilities of

---

34 This function of an epistemic community is elaborated in Thomas Kuhn's *The Structure of Scientific Revolutions* (Chicago: The University of Chicago Press 1970); and it is a central theme in the work of Michel Foucault.

35 See chapter 7 of my *Epistemic Responsibility*.

understanding Janice Moulton has documented so well.[36] It is my sense that analogues of this approach are at work in other areas of research, and that their effects are similar. Most notably, with reference to the 'second person' theme of this paper, it is clear that enquiry conducted defensively and adversarially is at some pains to deny cognitive interdependence; and it is doubtful that communication could be seen as one if its primary aims. Moulton's observation à propos of philosophy that 'The only problems recognized are those between opponents, and the only kind of reasoning considered is the certainty of deduction, directed to opposition,'[37] seems to apply, mutatis mutandis, to narrowly defined research projects within any discipline, whose primary intention is to provide a safe, unassailable solution to a closely circumscribed problem. Knowers are jealously protective of *their own* items of knowledge and territories of personal expertise.

Defensiveness in self/other relations (which contrast with what are more felicitiously characterized as self-other relations) has yet another counterpart, I think, in the cognitive tradition which works from the assumption that there is a sharp split between subject and object, and that one of the primary purposes of cognitive activity is to generate an ability to control, manipulate, and predict the behaviour of its objects. This has long been true of established scientific practice which, as Evelyn Fox Keller notes, has tended in its most hegemonic form to select for those individuals for whom an objectivist ideology, 'The promise of cool and objective remove from the object of study,'[38] provides emotional comfort (i.e., in general, men).

Keller's point in her work on gender and science is neither to deny the efficacy of scientific methodology, nor to dispute the impressiveness of scientific accomplishments. But she urges critical reflect-

---

36 See Janice Moulton, 'A Paradigm of Philosophy: The Adversary Method,' in Harding & Hintikka, *Discovering Reality*.

37 Ibid., 157

38 Evelyn Fox Keller, *Gender and Science* (New Haven: Yale University Press 1985), 124

ion upon the presumptions that sustain the hegemony of science, with the aim of understanding its location within human life, and acknowledging the importance of what it excludes, at least in its dominant ideology. The consequences of taking her suggestions seriously would not, however, be a diminished respect for scientific achievement, nor a challenge to its paradigmatic (in the Kuhnian sense) structure. Rather, her work opens the possibility of moving laterally within reflection upon science and, potentially, within scientific practice itself, still within the scope of paradigms governing 'normal' scientific activity. The effect of such lateral movement might be to facilitate concentration upon the place of specific puzzles and their solutions within a wider pattern of cognitive activity, and upon the interrelation of apparently separate and isolated areas of enquiry, both in their potential for mutual illumination, and in their possible environmental effects. This is not just a matter, though, of *adding* 'new' or 'different' areas to what is legitimately done under the influence of a paradigm, any more than feminist thought, more generally, would fulfil its purposes simply by adding women to malestream discourse. Though the paradigm would probably remain in place, its shape would likely be altered, and its boundaries rendered less distinct. One might perhaps draw an analogy with looking at the negative of a photograph, which contains all of the elements of the printed product, differently illumined. Were one to develop a practice of reading both, side by side, then it might be conjectured that different aspects of each would present themselves for consideration.

It is from Keller's discussion of the work of Barbara McClintock that one has the impression that she sees room, in science itself, for a differently conceived subject-object relation, 'premised on respect rather than domination.'[39] In her account of McClintock's approach to research, it is particularly striking to note McClintock's respect for difference in the specimens she studies. This leads her to avoid dismissing difference as aberrant, but rather to respect it and to study it, peruse it, with the aim of understanding it and of

39 Keller, 135

seeing how difference can assist her in understanding conformity. Because of its emphasis upon understanding rather than manipulation, prediction, and control, McClintock's approach is attuned to the possibility of a reciprocal subject-object relation, premised *not* on the belief that phenomena will be better known in so far as knowers achieve an appropriately objective distance from objects of investigation, but rather on the assumption that it is possible to weaken presumed boundaries between subject and object, and hence to know differently. McClintock speaks of a need to 'listen to the material,' and indicates that she knows every plant she works with – knows each one intimately – and finds it 'a great pleasure to know them.'[40] While it might be fanciful to suggest that this is a form of second person interaction with inanimate specimens, it can nonetheless reasonably be claimed that this is an ecologically oriented approach to knowledge which manifests an interest in knowing the place of the gene in the cell, and the cell in the organism as a whole.[41] It is antithetical to the distanced, objective stance I have described, variously, with respect to ethical and epistemological discussion; and it is continuous with the discourse of friendship, relationship and interdependence, if not identical with it. While it does not amount to a straightforward celebration of 'feminine' values, it does move toward making space in epistemological endeavour for suppressed considerations, practices and values which have, whether coincidentally or otherwise, often tended to be dubbed feminine.

It is too early to say what implications such a shift might have in terms of its effects upon epistemology, philosophy of science and, perhaps, scientific practice itself. Nor is it clear, as yet, just how 'second person' thinking might change moral discourse and moral practice. It does seem to be possible, though, that thinking along lines

---

40 Ibid., 164

41 Nor is it entirely fanciful to see McClintock's relationship with her specimens as one of friendship. Keller observes: 'From reading the text of nature, McClintock reaps the kind of understanding and fulfillment that others acquire from personal intimacy' (Evelyn Fox Keller, *A Feeling for the Organism: The Life and Work of Barbara McClintock* [New York: W.H. Freeman 1983], 205).

Lorraine Code

such as those I have been exploring might lead to a recognition of some of the effects on human lives of the strong autonomy-orientation, in the diverse senses I have discussed, that has long manifested itself, albeit variously, in cognitive and moral activity. One of the most essential arts of personhood, as I understand them, is the art of coming to discern how one might achieve an appropriate interplay between autonomy on the one hand, and communal solidarity on the other, both in epistemological and in moral thought and action.[42]

42 Work on this paper was made possible by a Strategic Grant from the Social Sciences and Humanities Research Council of Canada, which I held in the Department of Philosophy at the Universtiy of Waterloo; and by a Visiting Fellowship at the Humanities Research Centre of the Australian National University in Canberra. Earlier versions were read at the Women and Philosophy Conference at Monash University in Melbourne, and at the Canadian Society for Women in Philosophy Conference in Halifax.

382

Afterword: Feminist Theory – Some Twistings and Turnings

KAI NIELSEN
The University of Calgary
Calgary, AB
Canada T2N 1N4

I

Feminist philosophy, along with, and as a part of, feminist thought more generally, is rapidly developing and will, and rightly, become an increasing force in our cultural life. The essays in this rich and varied volume contribute to this.[1] They have a cluster of salient features in common that is generally characteristic of feminist philosophy and contrasts markedly with most other philosophy as presently practiced. I refer here to the fact that feminist philosophy is more receptive than more traditional modes of philosophizing to currents of thought coming from a very considerable number of often quite different sources, less defensively adversarial and more tolerant of a lack of closure in philosophical thought.

---

1 Pages, references and titles to the essays in this volume are not given. Where the author of these essays is mentioned in the text it is to be assumed, unless otherwise indicated, that the reference is to the author's essay in this volume. Other references will be given in the standard way.

I do not intend here extensively to review the arguments or probe the narratives or indeed try to sort out all of the various strands of thought to be found in this volume. I shall instead take two general themes, one arising from the philosophy of science and from the more methodological essays, the other from some of the essays on ethics. The two themes I shall discuss are, I believe, important themes, but surely not the only important themes in this volume that need further investigation and reflection. (I pass over without comment essays of equal importance to the ones I discuss which do not abut so directly on the themes I wish to pursue.)

The first theme, entering from a distinctive angle the modernity/post-modernity debate, has to do with the scope, nature and authority of a critical and emancipatory theory and the second has to do with what kind of account we should give of the moral life. I shall, in the next section, start with the second theme and then move on to the first in sections V and VI. I proceed in this way because the question about the moral life raises with some urgency questions about the nature, role and point of moral theory and its relation to moral ideology. These questions in turn raise in a focussed way problems about the design of a proper emancipatory theory which, in turn, lead us naturally to a more general consideration of the scope and proper claims to justifiability of feminist theory.

Feminist accounts of morality with their stress on caring, sensitivity to context, the social determination of our moral standpoints, the use of empathetic imagination in moral reflection, the recognition of the importance of the moral emotions and the avoidance of a severe intellectualism in thinking about morality, link quite naturally with a cluster of beliefs characteristic of feminist thinking about the philosophy of science and epistemology. Such thinking is here well represented by Lorraine Code, Sandra Harding and Alison Wylie in their critiques of foundationalist epistemology, traditional philosophy of science and in their conceptualization of the modernity/post-modernity debate. This thinking in turn lends support to feminist accounts of both morality and politics.

Feminists stress that science is through and through a social enterprise. They challenge the received ideas of objectivity and rationality and the deeply embedded belief that the scientific method is a self-corrective method. They challenge the belief that science either is or ought to be a value-free enterprise; they ferret out the way science tends to be androcentric and, as Alison Jaggar neatly concretizes, how it not infrequently has an ideological bias.

They argue that social science in particular needs to incorporate a reflective component, become sensitive to the pervasiveness of gender considerations and that it must come to recognize the need to make clear the standpoint from which it proceeds. Moreover, and connectedly, scientists need to gain a critical moral, socio-political and historical self-consciousness. This is vital if they are to overcome a variety of ideological blinkers. In coming to grips with this, as Harding makes particularly clear, we need to take to heart the post-modernist insight that our accounts cannot but be culturally specific.

Feminist theory has also reinforced the argument of critical theory — indeed I think of it as a distinctive species of critical theory — about the pervasiveness in our culture of scientistic ideology. It is one thing to appreciate the impressiveness of scientific knowledge, to acknowledge the not infrequent efficiency of scientific method and even to accept the pragmatist claim that it ought to be extended to areas where it is not presently utilized; it is, however, another thing again to accept the hegemony of science and to attempt to award to the scientific method the sole right to fix the whole range of our various and context dependent beliefs. It is this that is scientistic ideology and it is, as Herbert Marcuse and Jürgen Habermas have argued, a pervasive and beguiling ideology in our societies.

There are a number of matters related to this critique of scientistic ideology that feminists bring to the forefront. Feminist theory is anti-foundationalist. It is sceptical of autonomous claims for philosophy and of claims on the part of philosophy to timeless truth. Without taking an irrationalist or nihilist turn, it is sceptical of the Man of Reason. That is to say, it is critical of any attempt to make a sharp separation of reason and the emotions or to discount the emotions. It is critical, as well, of attempts to conceptualize rationality in utterly value-neutral terms and to articulate a substantive ideal of rationality that applies across cultures, classes and historical epochs.

II

Feminists examining and attempting to articulate a feminist account of morality tend to work from such conceptions. This is plainly exemplified in the perceptive cluster of writings in and about ethics in this volume. Again there is no purist separation of moral theory from the human and social sciences and from historical and culturally specific considerations. There is no attempt to do moral theory in the grand manner of Bentham, Kant or Sidgwick or (coming down to our time) even in the manner of Brandt or Gewirth. And there is no attempt to do a Foot or Hare meta-ethical thing. Feminist moral theorizing works with thick descriptions in integral relation to all sorts of contingent considerations: psychological, social, historical and economic. Code, for example, stresses that in thinking about morality, we need to think very carefully about the essential arts of personhood and Ann Ferguson similarly stresses the importance of gaining a more adequate conception of the self. With different theories of the self we get different conceptions of politics and different conceptions of the moral life.

There is something like a mild transvaluation of values in feminist moral theory. In traditional moral theory, particularly modern and contemporary moral theory, there is a stress on rights, autonomy, justice, impartiality and universalizability. All of these values or conceptions, if they can be justifiably held at all, are typically thought to require a rational foundation. Much of the feminist moral theory represented in this volume, and indeed feminist theory found elsewhere, resists this as being at the very least a one-sided account. Code speaks of an autonomy-obsession and the critiques of other of these conceptions in this volume would, if sound, justify speaking of a universalizability-obsession, impartiality-obsession and a rationality-obsession. Related to this is a challenge to rights-based moralities, to contractarianism, to Rawls's and Kohlberg's taking justice to be primary in delineating the moral domain and to Rawls's claim that justice is the first virtue of institutions.

Code, who criticizes what she calls the autonomy-obsession, makes it perfectly clear right at the beginning of her critique that she is not denying that the achievement of autonomy has a central place amongst feminist goals. What she is objecting to is some one-sided philosophical interpretations of autonomy and its placement in the moral domain. It is the individualism of current conceptions of autonomy she is resisting such as is found in the work of Robert Nozick or in a less crude from in David Gauthier. To be autonomous, for such individualists, is to be 'self-sufficient, independent and self-reliant, a self-realizing individual whose efforts are directed toward maximizing his personal gains.' With such an ideal of autonomy *such* autonomous individuals are constantly living under the threat of the other, i.e. other equally self-serving individuals. Where the individuals are thoroughly rational, at best we will get constrained maximization. Individuals on such a world-view are obsessed, as is Nozick, with 'boundary crossings.' 'Keep off my turf' is the watchword. Such individuals will be constantly on guard against intrusion, will be untrusting of others and will have at centre stage in their moral views conceptions of individual rights jealously defended, rational self-interest, expediency, efficiency and there will be a persistent worry about being made a sucker by free-riders. These, on such an individualistic view of the world, will be the elements that will pervade moral and political discourse. It is not, of course, true that we can become wholly autonomous, even on this conception of autonomy, but this is the character ideal: the heuristic, given such an individualism, that we should strive to approximate.

Values of community and fraternity that grow out of our interdependence and connectedness with their stress on caring are seen as at least potential intrusions upon our autonomy. Such individualism does not see that anything like a rich individuality would actually be integrally linked to our connectedness. Rather than to be so obsessed with autonomy, we should recognize, given the way we human beings have to be nurtured, that our very humanness and individuality are tied to our connectedness and interdependence. We should not only have equality and liberty but as well a non-sexist equivalent of fraternity as central values.

Annette Baier and Code both start with communality and interdependence and develop a conception of autonomy-in-interdependence as distinct from autonomy as self-sufficiency and independence. With an autonomy with interdependence we see ourselves as a community of interconnected and interdependent human beings whose very humanness is dependent on being so interdependent. But still as autonomous beings in such a community we are beings who have our own standpoints, our own say and we remain our own centres of action and conception. Autonomy is one central value in a commonwealth of values and not the supreme value. It is not even evident that it is the leading value in that commonwealth. Indeed it is doubtful if there is any one value which has such pride of place. But as autonomy properly understood is compatible with equality properly understood and indeed requires it, so autonomy properly understood is compatible with and similarly requires fraternity.

Feminist moral philosophers are also critical of the emphasis placed on impartiality and universalizability in moral theory. Arguing for justice is, no doubt, arguing for principles and practices which are to be justified on the basis of disinterested or impartial considerations. But justice is not the whole of morals. However, some think, to insist on impartiality and disinterestedness in some contexts is hurtful to the moral life. We should not, they argue, claim that it is something the moral point of view invariably requires.

This contra-impartiality claim will seem to some deeply counterintuitive. Let us have a look at its rationale. We are, as Baier and Code put it, second persons. Persons are the creation of other persons and our interdependence is continuous throughout our lives. The 'good and helpful aspects of our condition, as much as the evils, stem from the fact of interdependence.' Because of this, they claim, much of our moral life cannot properly be seen in impersonal and disinterested terms. The modes of such moral interaction can hardly be impersonal. Friendship or parent/child relationships and what these relationships require can hardly be understood in such terms. And with it come to the forefront such key moral notions as trust, caring, commitment and morally sustaining relations. But they are conceptions which cannot be understood in terms of a disinterested impartiality. Here persons cannot be treated as being indistinguishable and interchangeable as impartiality and disinterestedness seem at least to require. Code tells us that 'fairness and justice, impartially adjudicated, often blind one to the specific needs of particular persons.' Because of this, Code gives us to understand, there is no even prima facie reason to give even prima facie priority to considerations of justice and fairness over concerns about the quality of human relationships.

If this is taken to mean that concerns over the specific needs of particular persons standing in distinctive and intimate relations with one override considerations of justice and fairness, then it seems to me to be mistaken. If I know a friend wants and needs a certain scholarship and I also know there is a stranger who wants it and needs it too and I am in a position to grant the scholarship I cannot rightly give it to my friend if the stranger is clearly more qualified and equally in need.

At least in such circumstances, impartiality and considerations of fairness and justice have priority over considerations of friendship and care and concern about a particular person's needs. What needs to be faced by people who would argue as Code and Marilyn Friedman do is, where considerations of justice *collide* with considerations of a *particular* caring rooted in a knowledge of the needs of some persons standing in particular relations with one, whether the considerations of justice and fairness are not always (or at least almost always) overriding.

However, the above claims about justice being overriding is one thing and it is another thing again to say, as Sara Ruddick and Carol Gilligan (among others) have, that when women reflect on the values embedded in their experience of being primary caretakers of children that they will be led to develop a more care-oriented ethic than males who have little experience of such caretaking. Males, differently socialized than women, will, Gilligan maintains, tend to stress rights and principles. By contrast, women are more care-oriented. Whatever the truth of this psychological claim, this care-oriented part of morality is also essential to morality. Indeed it may not be an exaggeration to say that if there were not such caring, such concern with human suffering, the meeting of human needs and the establishing of certain human relationships, there would be little need for justice or for a concern for rights. But the other side of the coin is that sometimes caring is one-sided, love is blind and friendship leads to unfairness. And this in turn will lead to it being the case that others (sometimes a not inconsiderable number of others), who are not part of this web of personalized caring, will suffer or be harmed in ways that are quite unnecessary. We need a stress on a justice-perspective to keep it from being the case that we will invest care on those close to ourselves while we allow social services and the like to wither. The helping and privileging of one's friends may stand in the way of a realization of a greater human flourishing in the society at large and a greater and more extensive meeting of human needs and the like than would obtain if one were to be through and through impartial. Given the background assumption of a moral world in which there are in place caring relations, where a particular caring runs afoul of justice, are not the considerations of justice, where they are clear and pronounced, overriding? Is not the stress on impartiality, principles and disinterestedness, rooted in that recognition? Is this something a caring-perspective can justifiably set aside?

Kathryn Morgan, to shift perspective a little, has persuasively argued that the traditional relegation of morality into a 'public sphere' where the men are the principal actors and into a 'private sphere' where the women are the principal actors has the effect of upholding oppressive human relations where it is women who are clearly the oppressed and indeed oppressed by men. The relegation of women's moral competency to a sphere of a personal, emotion-based, 'private morality' rather than to the impersonal public morality rooted in (supposedly rooted in) reason is an ideological device which functions to keep women in their place.

The reflection of this sexist moral mythology is, however, compatible with continuing to believe that moral claims are universalizable. To recognize that *my* friends have a special claim on me that others do not is to recognize, for someone who understands what morality is, that *your* friends also have a similar claim on you (no matter who you are), unless there is some morally relevant and in turn universalizable difference between you, your friends or your situation and me. It also involves believing that the moral point of view at crucial junctures requires impartiality. But again such a commitment to impartiality and universalizability does not require, and indeed should not require, moral agents to seek to be, what they cannot be anyway, to wit, detached, identityless atomic individuals. And there is no justification at all for identifying morality with public morality or treating 'personal morality' as a poor country cousin.

Morgan also rightly casts scorn on the idea that morality requires a hyper-detachment and an intellectualism that would maintain that rational moral reflection capable of justifying moral claims is incompatible with a 'finely developed empathetic imagination,' the ability to connect and to be persons of extensive sympathy toward a whole range of beings human and non-human. Such moral rationalism does not realize how much sympathy is an essential ingredient of morality. But again impartiality, a certain sense of detachment and a developed sense of fairness can go perfectly well with having the ability to connect and to sympathize utilizing a finely honed ability to empathetically put one's self in another's shoes and to take their situation and aspirations to heart.

To defend the universalizability of moral claims as I have is not to claim what feminist moral theorists, with their stress on contextuality and historical specificity, are rightly keen to *deny*, namely that genuine moral principles must be *universalizable over contexts*. If an American during the Vietnam war claimed she was justified in refusing to pay that portion of her taxes that would go into the war effort she is, given my understanding of universalizability, committed to saying that any person in the relevant senses like her and in a relevantly similar situation is likewise justified in so acting, but she is not committed to saying, what would be absurd to say anyway, namely that anyone in any context is justified in refusing to pay that portion of her taxes that would be used for any war effort that might be pursued by any country for any reason. The war against Hitler was one thing as was the Soviet Union's defense of its revolution against foreign invaders. But the American invasion of Vietnam was another thing again and the American support of the Contras still another. Moral principles should be universalizable — indeed, I would argue they could not fail to be universalizable — but few if any are universalizable over all contexts. Universalizable principles are not typically universal. A commitment to impartiality and to the objectivity (reflective and informed intersubjectvity) of wide reflective equilibrium is one thing and a commitment to an absolutism or universalism where correct moral principles are taken to be principles of pure practical reason available to 'the man of reason' is another. What I have been concerned to show in my above twistings and turnings is that this feminist standpoint, including the heuristic for a radical feminist ethic given at the end of Morgan's essay, does not in reality stand in conflict with a proper reading of what a commitment to autonomy, equality, justice, universalizability and impartiality would come to. These conceptions and the feminist ones are in reality not clashing conceptions but complementary. There is no need to choose, for example, between the radical feminist ethic Morgan speaks of and a commitment to impartiality. The great value of the feminist perspective in this domain is that it fills a very big gap in our understanding of and our appreciation for the moral life that preoccupation with the traditional concerns of moral philosophers tend to blind us to.

III

There remain, the above notwithstanding, puzzling questions about the comparative weight to place, to put the matter at first crudely, on 'the care-perspective' and 'the justice-perspective.' Carol Gilligan's *In a Different Voice* has taken a very considerable discussion, much of it favorable, some hostile and a significant amount ambivalent. In this volume Baier, Code, Ferguson, Sheila Mullett, Friedman and Barbara Houston direct a considerable amount of attention to Gilligan's work. In trying to begin a sorting out of the respective weights, spheres and roles of the care-perspective and the justice-perspective respectively, I want to return to some of this discussion.

Gilligan stressed that there are two pervasive moral orientations or outlooks at least in societies such as ours. One she called a justice-perspective and the other she called a care-perspective and while we all tend to alternate between these perspectives, nonetheless with men and women, at least as they are socialized in societies such as ours, the justice-perspective is the more dominant voice for men and the care-perspective for women. As John Exdell, Friedman and Morgan stress here and as Susan Moller Okin did in an important historical essay, this may tend to work in the service of a moral ideology which strengthens male domination.[2] This notwithstanding,

---

2 Susan Moller Okin, 'Women and the Making of the Sentimental Family,'

the difference in voice appears at least, whatever the causes, to be a more dominant voice with women than with men in societies such as our own.

In opposition to the rather Kantian conception of moral maturity, found in the work of Lawrence Kohlberg, who stressed the priority of the justice-perspective and found women tending not to be as morally mature as men, Gilligan articulated a care-perspective and found in her research done from that perspective that women tended to speak in a different voice than men about morality itself and, as well, about moral maturity. As Gilligan puts it: 'Since the reality of interconnection as experienced by women is given rather than freely contracted, they arrive at an understanding of life that reflects the limits of autonomy and control. As a result, women's development delineates the path not only to a less violent life but also to a maturity.'[3]

Our first experience of society, it should be noted in this connection, is in the mini-society of a family. It is there where we learn what it is to be a human being. Any kind of adequate morality requires, as Baier puts it, that it is insured 'that each new generation is made appropriately welcome and prepared for their adult lives.' And here in contrast with the stress given by the rationalism typical of the justice-perspective, we need to cultivate the moral emotions and not just stress that reason control our unruly passions. We need (to say the obvious) to love our children and to internalize a caring orientation and move beyond just worrying that we do not violate others' rights or fail to keep our contracts duly made.

There are around the care-perspective/justice-perspective division, as Friedman points out, two issues that it is useful to keep distinct. 1) There is the gender difference issue of whether 'the care-

---

Philosophy and Public Affairs **11** (Winter 1982) 65-88. See also her *Women in Western Political Thought* (Princeton, NJ: Princeton University Press 1979) and her 'Philosopher Queens and Private Wives: Plato on Women and the Family,' *Philosophy and Public Affairs* **6** (1976) 345-69.

3 Carol Gilligan, *In a Different Voice* (Cambridge, MA: Harvard University Press 1982) 172

perspective is typically or characteristically, a woman's moral voice, while the justice-perspective is typically or characteristically a man's moral voice.' 2) There is the issue of whether 'the care-perspective is a distinct moral perspective from that which is centered on justice and rights.' I shall concentrate on the second issue. The literature about the first issue is considerable. Central facets of it, as we have seen, are characterized and interestingly assessed by Friedman. My own rather untutored hunch here is that if boys and girls were socialized in rather more similar ways than they are now, if there were extensive co-parenting, a genuinely non-sexist job market such that the sexual division of labor would be eroded, then, if these things happened, the different voices of women and men in moral matters would wither away.

Be that as it may, I set such considerations aside to consider the following related cluster of questions a) quite independently of whether they go along sexual lines, whether there really are two such distinct moral perspectives or orientations, b) to the extent there are, whether either can be thought to be a complete or adequate perspective without an incorporation of the other perspective and c) whether one or other of the perspectives (if there are such distinct or quasi-distinct perspectives) can rightly be thought to have priority.

I think several of the essays here give us good reasons for believing there are two distinct or at least quasi-distinct moral orientations. Baier's essay can be taken as paradigmatic. Robert Nozick and David Gauthier just do write and think about morality in a very different way than do Annette Baier and Iris Murdoch. If we reflect on the work of these people and others like them, it will be readily apparent that there is this difference between a Nozick-like orientation stressing rights, contracts, justice and tight argument and a Baier-like orientation stressing care, contextually given moral relations, conceptions of the good life for human beings and a narrative style.

What of the completeness or adequacy taken in themselves of either perspective? Again, I think it is evident enough from various discussions in this volume that either perspective taken by itself is radically incomplete and inadequate. Justice requires that in some fair way we answer to the needs of everyone as fully as we can. Commitments to *moral* equality — a central element in the justice-perspective — come to the belief that the life of everyone matters and matters equally.[4] A respect for rights comes to a respect for persons and their moral integrity. But without a background of caring, *empathetic* imagination and a relating specifically to particular people (not just a general caring for humanity as such but a concrete caring for specific people standing in specific relations to ourselves) little flesh can be given to the very notion of respect for persons and for as full and fair as possible an answering to their needs. Without some concrete understanding of specific people, young and old, sick and well, marginalized or mainstream, religious or secular, powerful or powerless, in their distinctive and importantly variable and changing circumstances, we can give very little substance to our belief that the life of everyone matters and matters equally.

To give substance to the justice-perspective's belief in *moral* equality some understanding of the varieties of ways of human flourishing is necessary. We also need to be caring persons ourselves and to have some understanding, as well, of the moral import of caring and with that the desire to see a world in which all human beings are cared about and a determination to bring such a world into existence, for surely this is not the world we live in now in spite of the fact that in all modernizing parts of the world there is this professed belief in moral equality. Without the sets of beliefs and commitments characterized above, a claimed belief in moral equality is little more than a pretense or ideological delusion. Kant was right in seeing that the very taking of the moral point of view requires a striving for a unity of theory and practice.[5]

However, as I have already argued, caring without justice and without respect for rights is as lopsided as Nozickianism. Much of moral relevance in a family or among friends or between colleagues

---

4 Thomas Nagel, *Mortal Questions* (Cambridge, UK: Cambridge University Press 1979) 106-27; Kai Nielsen, *Equality and Liberty* (Totowa, NJ: Rowman & Allanheld 1985) 15-35; and Kai Nielsen, 'Arguing for Equality,' *Philosophic Exchange* **17** (1986) 5-23

5 Immanuel Kant, 'Theory and Practice,' in *Kant's Political Writings*, Hans Reiss, ed., trans. H.B. Nisbet (Cambridge, UK: Cambridge University Press 1970) 62-72

should go beyond what justice requires and much has little to do with matters of justice and rights. But in a family an indiscriminate caring heedless of considerations of fairness is hardly something to be desired. Similarly, at a certain stage in a child's development a parental caring, if it were to take a very paternalistic turn, might override — and wrongly so — a child's right to privacy and, in effect, attack that child's moral integrity. These things are plainly wrong and in turn undermining of human flourishing. A parent could in certain circumstances be driven to distraction with worry about a child yet out of respect for the child's moral integrity refrain from intervention.

The relations between the caring-perspective and the justice-perspective are complicated and many faceted. What does seem tolerably evident is that both are radically incomplete without the other. Any adequate moral perspective must in some coherent way weave the two perspectives together into a single more complex perspective.

What would this look like and which, if either, perspective is to be taken to have *priority*? (Perhaps we do not need anything which has priority here anymore than we need a head of a family?) Feminist moral philosophers have generally criticized the claims made by Rawls and Kohlberg that justice should be taken as having priority. As Baier points out, feminist critics of the justice-perspective do not deny that 'justice is *a* social value of very great importance, and injustice an evil' and the Rawlsians and Kohlbergians in turn do not deny that other things matter besides justice. The issue is which, if either, has priority. Is Rawls right in claiming priority for justice? Is it the first virtue of social institutions? Baier makes effective criticisms of treating questions of the good for human beings as being 'optional' in a way that justice is not. The view she opposes claims that we can insist that people act in accordance with the principles of justice in a way that we cannot rightly insist they adhere to some conception of the good. The justice-perspective is authoritative in a way the care-perspective cannot be.

Rawls, arguing from a liberal perspective, and Chantal Mouffe, arguing from a Marxist perspective, both argue that in our complex and diversified societies with people having very different life plans and visions about how to live their lives we cannot rightly insist on a single vision of the good which would be authoritative for all human beings.[6] We can, however, have some hope that in a given civilization at a given time we can have some reasonable chance of gaining a rational conception of principles of justice which could be authoritative in that civilization and provide a minimal morality with such an authoritative presence. Baier and Friedman, in turn, will question whether that minimal morality is enough. How are we to decide, or is this one of the ambivalences Harding speaks of that we must, at least for now, just learn to live with? I am not going to try to resolve this issue here but to make a gesture at some of the difficulties and problems I see that need to be resolved if we are to do so.

It seems right on the side of the Rawlsians and some Marxists on this issue to remind ourselves that we do not agree about what constitutes human excellence and that there is not much prospect, at least in the foreseeable future, of our coming to agree about it. And we are surely not going to come to agree about the goal of human existence or about whether there is or even can be one. On the care-perspective side it could be countered that we (that is people in modernizing societies) just might come in time to attain a reflective and informed consensus about what would be necessary to secure the dignity and most basic well-being of human beings. This, it is reasonable to argue against liberalism, would, if we could get such a consensus, not be an optional matter. It would then be something we could rightly insist to obtain in our society irrespective of whether some individuals want these conditions to obtain or not. (We need not ask for unanimity here.) If we can gain such a rational consensus about the conditions necessary to secure human dignity and basic well-being, then, where they can be secured, we as a society can rightly insist on them. They can be as authoritatively insisted on as the principles of justice and they would themselves be part of the content of certain principles of justice.

---

6 This is perhaps clearest in John Rawls, 'Justice as Fairness: Political not Metaphysical,' *Philosophy and Public Affairs* **14** (Summer 1985) 223-51; see Chantal Mouffe, 'What is the Crisis of Socialism?' *Symposium of Socialist Scholars Conference* (New York, April 11 1987).

Rawlsians could in turn reply that where we can do so justice requires that we secure them for everyone as far as possible. But then it can in turn be replied that at least some of what is necessary to secure human dignity and well-being is not determined by determining what is just. Rather what is just is to secure as equally as possible that dignity and well-being for everyone.

This, if it were to be secured, would still be a minimal ethic and would not constitute an answer to what is the best form of life for humankind or even for the members of our society. Some, rejecting the claim that the justice-perspective has priority, would want to argue that any adequate moral theory needs to be able to provide a persuasive sketch of an answer to that very fundamental question about human well-being, both for our alienated condition and for feasibly altered circumstances where our social world could be such that we could plausibly escape at least some of that alienation. Whether over this issue of priority we take the Rawlsian route or the care-perspective route may turn in part on whether we think that we can gain any even approximate consensus about what would, even under optimal conditions, be the best life for human beings. Rawls, for example, is doubly skeptical here. He doubts 1) whether there will be any philosophical establishment of such a conception and 2) doubts that, even if there were, whether there would in modern diversified societies such as ours be any general (public) acceptance of what is philosophically best established such that we could take it as a part of a *public* philosophy that could be authoritatively asserted.

Let us push this a little further by noting a set of claims by Alasdair MacIntyre touched on by Exdell which would (if well-taken) count for the care-perspective. To have a good society, indeed even to have a just society, MacIntyre believes, we must have a society informed by a collective effort to define a shared conception of what makes a good human being. Moreover, for MacIntyre, 'justice can be rationally defined in a society only where there is general agreement on what its members deserve — based on their ranking the contributions made by the various practices and their internal goods to the more general good of their community.'[7] Rawlsians, arguing from the

---

7 This is Exdell's paraphrase but see Alasdair MacIntyre, *After Virtue* (Notre Dame, IN: University of Notre Dame Press 1981) 143-88.

justice-perspective, will respond that we have no even remotely objective way of determining what people deserve or merit or of knowing how to rank the contributions they make to the good of society. Moreover, even if we could that is not how we determine what is just and unjust. And most definitely, even if we can get some rational agreement on basic well-being (a thin conception of the good) we will not get agreement over what makes a good human being or the good life for human beings. Keeping our attention firmly fixed on questions of social justice (questions concerning the justice of institutions) and dropping questions about desert or merit, we nevertheless can, Rawlsians argue, gain agreement on certain principles of justice which it is necessary to agree on if we are to have any prospect of so living together so that we can, as individuals, seek, and have some prospect of attaining, what we severally, and often differently, take to be good. We need principles of justice authoritatively stationed in public life in order for us to be able effectively to seek and sometimes realize our individual conceptions of what a good life for us as individuals would be. We, in turn, need, for this to be possible, to agree on a minimum list of basic human goods (something like Rawls's primary natural and social goods) and to a certain extent on their respective weights.[8] We have some prospect of eventually, given favourable conditions, gaining consensus here but our societies being very unlike *Gemeinschaften* we have no reasonable prospect of a larger consensus on the good society or the good person. Thus, for an ethic that would actually stand a chance of successfully guiding conduct about what must be done in a world of great diversity about the ends of life and about how best to live our lives, we must stick to the minimalist ethics of a justice-perspective.

It may be that a morality of rights without, as an equal partner, a morality of caring tends to dissolve the natural bonds of society, but, that notwithstanding, under any plausible extension of con-

---

8 John Rawls, 'Social Unity and Primary Goods,' in Amartya Sen and Bernard Williams, eds., *Utilitarianism and Beyond* (Cambridge, UK: Cambridge University Press 1982) 159-85

temporary conditions the nuclear family can hardly be a *Gemeinschaft* (though those caught up with the ideology of the sentimental family will believe it to be) and it is thoroughly unrealistic to expect that in our contemporary large scale societies, let alone in our interconnected world, we can become one great big *Gemeinschaft* or a cluster of harmoniously interrelated *Gemeinschaften*.[9] Whatever our 'personal moralities,' our 'private visions of the good,' we must, in a public philosophy, Rawlsians argue, stick with the minimalist ethic of justice.

Baier and Friedman (and Exdell indirectly) counter-argue that this just isn't enough to make moral sense of our fragmented lives or to meet what we expect of a morality. We have in even the most morally impoverished societies fuller relationships with each other than the minimal relationships necessary to keep civil society going. People, as Baier puts it, whose rights are respected and to whom justice is done 'may well be lonely, driven to suicide, apathetic about their work, about participation in political processes, find their lives meaningless and have no wish to leave offspring to face the same meaningless existence. Their rights, and respect for rights, are quite compatible with very great misery, and misery whose causes are not just individual misfortunes and psychic sickness, but social and moral impoverishment.' The justice-perspective, Baier seems to believe, does little to answer to such considerations. It is here where we need, she believes, the morality of caring. To have a decent society we cannot just stop with the 'essential minimum, that is on justice and rights, and let whoever wants to go further and cultivate this more demanding ideal of responsibility and care do so on a kind of volunteer basis.' We need instead something that we culturally speaking can justifiably insist on here. We cannot just go on an individual caring trip, doing our own thing, if caring is to come to much. To have this fuller life we must have the commitment of others to engage in it and not just an agreement of non-interference

---

9 Okin, 'Women and the Making of the Sentimental Family,' 65-88, clearly reveals the ideology of the sentimental family. See also Exdell and Morgan in this volume.

with those that do. The latter would only mean that the more communally minded would be in effect exploited by the libertarian types or types tending toward libertarianism.

Even going beyond old Whiggish libertarian liberalism (Hayek's sort of thing) to a Rawlsian-Dworkinian progressive welfare state liberalism, we still do not have enough of what it is in morality, Baier claims, that 'we need to pressure *everyone* to obey.' We need, as well, 'to ensure an education that will form persons to be capable of conforming to an ethics of care and responsibility.' Baier goes on to speculate that 'the liberal morality, if unsupplemented, may *unfit* people to be anything other than its justifiying theories suppose them to be ... that is, people who have no interest in each other's interests.' But this is surely not enough for there to be in place anything like a decent morality. Someone must — from anything like a decent moral point of view must — take an interest in the very young and the very old, in future generations and in those who are powerless or are lacking in the capacity for full moral agency.

It might in turn be responded a) that none of this establishes what is centrally at issue here, namely that justice-issues do not have *priority* over purely care-issues and b) that the issues mentioned in the previous paragraph are not *both* care-issues and justice-issues. They would only get ruled out as justice issues by a narrow libertarian conception of justice. They would not get ruled out as justice issues by the richer and more adequate Rawlsian conception of justice.

Perhaps we should not try to dichotomize, as Friedman argues we should not, a justice-perspective and a care-perspective? Both perspectives are essential to morality and they are intertwined. There is little point, if indeed there is any clear sense, in trying to say which is prior. We certainly need a view which incorporates both perspectives and, as Baier puts it, will 'harmonize justice and care' and *perhaps* we need not concern ourselves with which, if either, has priority or is the first virtue of institutions. There may be no *first* virtue of institutions.[10]

---

10 Sections III and IV of Friedman's essay are particularly relevant here. She challenges the dichotomy, realizes that within the justice orientation itself there

IV

However the issues discussed in the previous section get sorted out, it is evident from discussions in this volume that issues of justice will continue to loom large in feminist contributions to moral theory. Given the pervasive and seemingly intractable domination of women and a growing consciousness of that domination in its various, sometimes subtle, sometimes not so subtle, manifestations, what would a just world be taken to be by people who recognized that and resolutely struggled against it? What would a just world look like that could finally rid itself of being sexist? Friedman claims that if we are to progress in our moral thinking there must be a movement 'toward a non-gendered, non-dichotomized unified moral framework in which all moral concerns could be expressed' and Ferguson firmly asserts that 'our ultimate goal must be the degenderizing of every aspect of social life.' Nothing less could be a perfectly just society. Social reality is, of course, quite different but the coming of a society without gender and without classes is part of our ideal about what it should become.

There is not in these pages or elsewhere, as far as I know, a worked out feminist theory of justice. However, Baier, Sibyl Schwarzenbach and Susan Moller Okin in an important article (not in our volume) 'Justice and Gender,' while seeing some unintended sexist residues in Rawls's work, acknowledge the seminal importance of Rawls in constructing a theory of justice.[11] This recognition of Rawls's central importance does not mean that any of them are contractarians. They could reject contractarianism as unequivocally as Virginia Held. The parts of Rawls they accept in a re-interpreted form do not depend on his contractarianism. But Schwarzenbach and Okin in important ways build an egalitarian genderless conception of justice on a rational reconstruction of certain major elements in Rawls.

---

are two distinct orientations, points to inadequacies in Gilligan's formulations and brings to our attention an array of considerations that still need sorting out.

11 Okin, 'Justice and Gender,' *Philosophy and Public Affairs* **16** (Winter 1987) 42-72

However, first there must be a rational reconstruction. To this end Baier briefly, and Okin in detail, show how Rawls is unwittingly trapped in rather traditionalist sexist assumptions. That, as they are certainly well aware, is not his intention but his assumption that the free and equal persons reasoning in the original position are not thought of as single individuals but as heads or representatives of households and his further assumption 'that life within the family and relations between the sexes are not properly to be regarded as part of the subject matter of a theory of social justice' in effect reflects traditional sexist thinking about the family and the need for a family to have a head, male or female.

Rawls, as progressive and deeply egalitarian as he is, never raises the question of whether the monogamous, nuclear family is a just institution in either its traditional form or in even an idealization of what Okin calls the sentimental family of companionate marriage.[12] Given Rawls's own egalitarian theory of justice it is difficult to see how the family could be just. How, for example, on his account, is it possible for the viewpoint of the less advantaged members of the family ever to get heard? Rawls, as Okin well puts it, 'fails entirely to address the gender system which — with its roots in the sex roles of the family and with its branches extending into virtually every corner of our lives — is one of the fundamental structures of our society.'[13]

However, both Okin and Schwarzenbach provide a feminist reading of Rawls which shows how with (for example) the distinctive reading that Schwarzenbach provides of the difference principle Rawls's account of justice would support a strongly egalitarian androgynous society, though this reading would also push him to defending some form of democratic socialism and would not allow his account to remain, as it now is, neutral between welfare state capitalism and democratic socialism.

---

12 Ibid., 48

13 Ibid., 65. It is interesting to note that there is a similar failure in the work of Jürgen Habermas. See Nancy Fraser, 'What's Critical about Critical Theory? The Case of Habermas and Gender,' *New German Critique* **35** (Spring/Summer 1985) 97-131.

Rawls's two assumptions — his assumption about the family and about heads of households — are hardly canonical parts of his theory and can, and indeed should, be abandoned. This can be shown if we work with and from deeply embedded elements in Rawls's own theory. Rawls allows — and it is important for him to do so — his contractors in the original position to know the general facts about society. Knowing that they would then have to know about the ubiquitousness of the gender-system and they would have to know that it is a system that leads to the domination of women. These (pace post-modernism) are general facts, not just culturally specific facts, though the form and extent of the domination is, of course, culturally specific. This being so contractors (pace Rawls) in the original position must take the relevant position of women and men into account in formulating principles of justice. Moreover, Rawls's second principle of justice requires that inequalities be to the greatest benefit of the least advantaged and must, as well, be attached to offices and positions open to all under conditions of a substantial and not merely formal equal opportunity. But, given the gender system, women are not in a position of fair equality of opportunity and the family institutions that we now have certainly do not function to the greatest benefit of the least advantaged. Women are disadvantaged in such an institution in a way that they cannot justifiably be under a system of social justice operating with the difference principle and fair equality of opportunity.

Rawlsian justice (or for that matter any plausible form of egalitarian justice) requires a genderless society to be achievable. (To say that the struggle for genderlessness would break the strains of commitment assumes that it is more difficult than it actually is to engage in co-parenting or to alter the sexual division of labour. With such resistance the tides of ideology and rationalization are running high.) In fine, Rawls's principles of justice, given our best knowledge about the general facts about human society, are inconsistent with a gender-structured society. Schwarzenbach and Okin have given us a reading of those principles in which this is seen to be so.[14]

---

14 Rawls, *A Theory of Justice*, 440, 396 and 178-9. See also Okin, 'Justice and Gender,' 67-8.

As long as we continue to view the world in gendered terms, where we cannot but have an ascriptive designation of positions and expectations of behaviour in accordance with the inborn characteristic of sex, we will not have a fully adequate set of principles of justice. As long as people continue to conceptualize things in a gendered way they cannot gain correct principles of justice and, given the social practices that go with such a conceptualization, we cannot have a just society. To make it possible for us to choose principles of justice in the impartial way Rawls's theory requires, our present gendered institutions and customs 'would have to be replaced by genderless institutions and customs.'[15]

V

Both Schwarzenbach and Okin in giving a feminist reading of Rawls's conception of justice appeal to reasonably large-scale theoretically ramified factual claims. Whether or not Rawls would accept those particular factual claims as being good approximations of the truth, Rawls believes, and I think rightly so, that such appeals are perfectly in order in the constructing and defending of an ethical theory and a social philosophy. But this takes us back, albeit circuitously, to the modernist/post-modernist issue that Wylie and Harding and, less directly, Code, discuss. Can there be anything like a feminist emancipatory social science or critical social theory that could make it plain, against post-modernist scepticism of grand theory, that factual claims — albeit interpretive factual claims — of that scope can be justifiably asserted? Jaggar's essay is a clear and forceful articulation of a modernist account as is her masterful *Feminist Politics and Human Nature*. (A modernist account need not — and indeed should not — be monocausal, reductionist or believe that there is just one thing that explains sexism or exploitation.) Such a critical theory is an account relying on (though surely developing from) the central ideals and intellectual commitments of the enlight-

---

15 Okin, 'Justice and Gender,' 71. See her argument 69-72.

enment. Harding's account, by contrast, is more wary about modernism and is concerned to face the fact that influential 'post-modern tendencies question the viability of the enlightenment projects on which feminist science critiques depend.'

What we think should be believed here is clearly very relevant to what we think about the form feminist social science and feminist thought about ethics should take. Integral, for example, to Okin's feminist modification and rational reconstruction of Rawls's autonomy-respecting egalitarian principles of justice are the following three factual claims.

1 In 'a gender-structured society, women's and men's different life experiences in fact affect their respective psychologies, modes of thinking, and patterns of moral development in significant ways.'[16]

2 The 'experience of individuation — of separating oneself from the nurturer with whom one is originally psychologically fused — is a very different experience for girls, than for boys, leaving the members of each sex with a different perception of themselves and of their relations with others.'[17]

3 The 'experience of *being* primary nurturers (and of growing up with this expectation) also affects the psychological and moral perspective of women, as does the experience of growing up in a society in which members of one's sex are in many respects subordinate to the other.'[18]

It is, however, post-modernist scepticism about grand theories (totalizing theories) that makes us *holus bolus* sceptical of claims of such scope — sceptical of any claim not just these or similar feminist claims. Yet it would appear at least to be the case that the making

---

16 Ibid., 60

17 Ibid., 70

18 Ibid.

and sustaining of some *such* claims is essential for the feminist project. Yet Wylie and Harding (as do Nancy Fraser and Linda Nicholson as well) take post-modernism very seriously indeed, but they are, that notwithstanding, as much as Jaggar and Okin, concerned to defend and develop the feminist project (if we can indeed speak of it so monolithically).[19] They all believe that feminist social science can and should be both emancipatory and give explanatory and interpretive accounts of macrostructures and institutions. They further believe that it can and should give accounts of large scale social change and of the roles of ideology in social life. Things need not be as local and practice-oriented as Jean-Francois Lyotard believes. Yet how are we to meet post-modernist scepticism here?

Let us see if in Harding's and Wylie's essays we can find a way or at least a hint at a way out of the swamp. Wylie notes that second-order philosophical reflection on the import of feminist discipline-specific critiques of a given science (e.g. sexist bias in anthropological research) has revealed that even after obvious biases were corrected for it remained the case that not infrequently 'highly competent and conscientious empirical research ... consistently failed to expose sexist bias.' It was only when a feminist critical approach was brought to bear on the topic that the bias introduced into science by social and political factors was brought out in the scientific research. Here the scientific method seemed at least not to be self-correcting.

A concomitant post-modernist worry is over the status of the new critical perspective. Is it self-correcting? How critical and how objective is that perspective and on what is its critical stance and content based? This worry is particularly acute if there is nothing of a factual sort — and thus at least potentially scientific — on which to base that critique. Ideology can be Janus-faced and Hydra-headed. Moreover, if such critiques and meta-critiques expose ideological bias in science, raise questions about the scientific enterprise itself and

---

19 Nancy Fraser and Linda Nicholson, 'Criticism Without Philosophy: An Encounter Between Feminism and Postmodernism' presented at the Eastern Division of the *American Philosophical Association* (Boston, December 1986).

the meta-critiques raise questions about both the warrantability of the first-order critiques themselves and their own status, we are left in such a circumstance in perplexity about whether Okin's theoretically ramified factual claims or any such claims could justifiably be believed to be true or approximately true or (if truth is thought to be a Holmesless Watson) warrantedly assertable. So in this way post-modernist worries about science insinuate themselves into at least some programs for a feminist ethics and for an emancipatory social theory.

Standpoint theorists (including feminist standpoint theorists) stress, as Wylie brings out, that social context and one's position in it are relevant to all science, typical or abnormal, good, bad and indifferent. Feminist theorists working from that perspective are dedicated, as Wylie puts it, in a way that fits with modernism rather than post-modernist scepticism, 'to achieving a fuller, more accurate understanding of women's experience and of women's status and roles within encompassing social contexts.' (Jaggar's work is a powerful exemplification of this.) This presupposes that there are some facts of the matter that we can come to understand more or less accurately and that is, as again Wylie puts it, 'a variant of the enlightenment ideal of producing a unitary, authoritative conception of reality.'

Post-modernist critics, including some feminist critics, have responded that a belief in such unitary objective standpoints is a myth. Women's experiences from different classes, cultures and races are too varied for it to be the case that there is a distinctive women's standpoint. We simply have no Archimedean point 'to adjudicate between knowledge claims originating in different contexts or of establishing a unitary theory that is valid across contexts.' Just as there is no significant universalizability across contexts so there is no significant truth across contexts. Justified generalizations (platitudes apart) always have a narrower scope.

To this it might in turn be responded that wherever the gender-system exists (and it is monotonously ubiquitous in all societies up to the present) there is underlying the diversity of women's experience in different situations some deeply embedded similarities that give some substance to the claim of a distinctive women's standpoint. Put crudely, it is true that in all societies women of all classes and strata are in one degree or another, and in one way or another, disadvantaged compared to their male counterparts. The life chances women have and the activities they can engage in are in all societies and among all classes disproportionately narrower than those of men and what they do and their very life roles are everywhere systematically devalued relative to the activities that males engage in in the same society. This is culturally universal. As Dorothy Smith puts it, women everywhere, everywhen find themselves in subdominant gender defined positions. This is not just a grand metanarrative of some speculative theory of culture but a rather general empirical claim whose probable truth or falsity appears to be at least weakly empirically testable in a tolerably straightforward way.

Still there are sharp conflicts between modernist critiques and post-modernist critiques and this is important for feminist theory, for, as Harding points out, the 'post-modern tendencies question the viability of the enlightenment project on which the feminist science critiques depend.' Yet, as Wylie points out, Harding, her wariness here notwithstanding, finally comes down to defending a nuanced and sophisticated enlightenment theory seeking to gain a 'unified field theory' which has both an emancipatory intent and seeks to comprehend the often conflicting experiences of individuals occupying a not inconsiderable variety of standpoints. Nonetheless, as I have remarked, there remains an acknowledged ambivalence in Harding's account. She is one with the post-modernists and earlier positivists in rejecting totalizing theories or grand theories or any belief in a 'stable, coherent "master theory."' Believing in such things, in her view, is on a par with defending foundationalism or going on the quest for certainty. She with post-modernists such as Rorty realizes there are no neutral or perspectiveless descriptions of the world and with that they give up any belief that there is or can be any one-true-story-about-reality-account of the world. However, she does not draw relativistic or Feyerabendish 'anything goes' conclusions from the acceptance of these characteristic post-modern beliefs. 'While there is not and cannot be,' as she pithily puts it, 'one true story of reality, some claims are empirically less defensible than others.' But Harding does not at all waffle about rejecting arbitrarily universalizing theories which make claims to unity, comprehensiveness and coherence beyond anything we are in a position to claim or in any way empirically corroborate.

Post-modernists make us see that there are many at least apparent incoherencies in modern thought. At times there may be incoherencies or at least apparent incoherencies we do not know how to resolve. We find ourselves in a situation where we have good reasons for holding on to both of two beliefs that we cannot at a given time see how to consistently put together. The reasonable thing to do for a time might be to just tolerate that at least apparent incoherency. It may also be the case that we may never be able to achieve an overarching theory of the scope that, say, Habermas seeks. But the implausibility of such a quasi-totalizing theory (if indeed it is implausible) does not make it the case that there cannot be gained increasingly more coherent and comprehensive theories which ever more adequately meet the test of experience and reflective examination. There do not appear to be any a priori limits here and to seek for ever more coherent and comprehensive theories is, as Wylie points out, a reasonable regulative ideal. To proceed in the way characterized above is not to be committed to a rationalism or intellectualism that is blind to the complexities of experience.

I take Harding's point that both feminist science critiques and post-modernist critiques have much to offer. For an understanding of our condition and for an understanding of what can be done and what is to be done to achieve our liberation, we need, as Harding puts it, a 'full appreciation of the tensions and contradictions between the two projects.' Yet even to speak of *our* human condition so monolithically in the face of the great diversity of life experiences of so many different peoples in so many different conditions may be a bit of romantic ethnocentrism lingering on in modernism.

All the above notwithstanding, I remain inclined to believe that things do not balance out all that evenly. Perhaps I am too much a child of the enlightenment, but it does not seem to me unreasonable to work on the assumption — the rebuttable assumption — that feminist science critiques or at least feminist critical theory, without falling prey to foundationalist or essentialist assumptions, can capture within its scope the insights of post-modernism, correct for post-modernism's overstatements and errors and present a more adequate social theory, fallibilistic and pragmatic, with a better guide for emancipatory human practice than we find in post-modernism. Moreover, it can do this without the telling of just so stories or making any claim that there is a one true view of reality.

Harding rightly alludes to the fact that the epistemological turn cannot provide foundations for a critical feminist theory. But we might very well have critical feminist theory without such philosophical foundations. Perhaps what we need is social criticism, and perhaps fairly systematic social criticism at that, without philosophy.[20] Still, it is not just Rorty and Lyotard who reject taking such an epistemological perspective but the pragmatists before them and they in some sense did philosophy, though it should not be forgotten that not a few traditional philosophers thought that whatever it was that Dewey was doing, it was not philosophy. Yet, whatever we may say about that, I think it is fair enough to say that there is no need at all for feminists 'to make the results of feminist inquiry respectable from the perspective of traditional epistemologies.' Powerful cases have been made by anti-foundationalists (including post-modernists) that such traditional epistemologies actually block inquiry, are of a problematic coherence and have no corner on what our understanding of objective inquiry and critique should come to. They are too discredited to have any authority as guardians of culture.

However, free from this 'foundationalist epistemological hold' one can see how political goals might reasonably guide inquiry and could enhance its objectivity rather than diminish it. We can say, however, that political goals can, do and should guide inquiry while remaining one with Max Weber in denying they can be used to corroborate or test the truth of the claims we make on the basis of that value-guided inquiry. Neither our goals nor our wants can determine what is the case, though what categories and conceptions we use in describing what is the case are not immune from such influences and they may not be any the worse for all of that.

At the beginning of this section, I gave three theoretically rami-

---

20 Nancy Fraser and Linda Nicholson, '"Criticism Without Philosophy:" An Encounter Between Feminism and Postmodernism.'

fied factual claims of Okin that seemed to me at least reasonable claims of very considerable interest to feminists and, as well, reasonable candidates for claims that are true or approximately true. And when we say that about them we do not mean to be claiming they are 'true for me' or 'true from a certain standpoint' (say from a woman's standpoint) but true period, though some – in some instances women – might be in a much better position to realize or appreciate that they are true than are others. (And to say this, as Rorty is fond of pointing out, requires no commitment to any particular analysis of 'truth' at all.) Exactly the same thing needs to be said of two key theoretical cum-factual claims made by Harding:

1 There is a close-to universal male dominance of human beliefs and behaviour and belief systems in all societies.

2 There are in societies such as our own false social science accounts used to justify a public policy 'that is not only sexist but usually also racist and bourgeois in the sense that it oppresses women differently and worse who are not white and/or not rich.'

I think (perhaps mistakenly) that these statements are factual statements and that they are true and I think Harding thinks that too. But when we think that we do not think they are true just from the standpoint of women or from a Marxist perspective but we think they are true *sans phrase*. Moreover, these putative truths are (if true) important truths, as are Okin's previously quoted statements. It is also of some not inconsiderable moment for feminists that these statements be reasonable approximations of the truth. That is, it is important that they be true and that (if they are) they be reasonably believed to be true and that we develop political strategies around them or at least in accordance with them.

What a good feminist theory needs to do is to assert in a perspicuous representation a cluster of factual claims, such as the three claims I have taken from Okin and the two I have taken from Harding. Then, where clarification has some practical point, it should go on to clarify them, to show, where evidence is needed, the evidence for their truth, draw inferences from them and, set them, where this is feasible, in a coherent and comprehensive theory (or some approximations thereto) which has as an integral part a normative side which makes a normative critique, argumentatively backed, on the basis of such factual claims put in their proper interpretive setting. So construed such a theory is at one and the same time descriptive, interpretive, explanatory and normative, though we need not, and indeed should not, try to run these conceptions together or try to reduce one to another. A critical theory is just internally complex in doing all these distinct jobs.

A feminist critical theory attempts to describe our human condition, including, of course, the condition of women, to explain, if possible, why it is as it is and to show how, if it can, the gender-system can be broken so that women and men can attain emancipation and gain a greater human flourishing.[21]

Can post-modernists give us compelling reasons for abandoning such an account or for modifying it? The above are indeed versions of enlightenment beliefs but so what? What reasons have we for believing that they are mistaken? There seem to be no *a priori* road blocks here. No doubt we should be wary of such claims, particularly when they have an extended scope, and look for evidence to back them up but why should we just claim, particularly prior to a sustained investigation, with a fine show of cultural pessimism, that we cannot know or justifiably believe that any such things are true or even could be true?

Harding and Wylie have pointed to the fact that it appears at least to be the case that the scientific method is not a method which is self-correcting. And this, if it turns out on further examination to be firmly so, dashes great hopes and expectations of the positivists and pragmatists and with it a very central element in their programmes would be undermined. I want to suggest that even if

---

21 Even if it is too totalizing to speak of the human condition of women or of the gender-system, we can limit our generalizations to generalizations about the condition of women across classes and strata in modernizing societies such as our own. Such generalizations limited in scope as they are could be both theoretically interesting and have an emancipatory wallop in modernizing societies.

this is so about scientific method perhaps a determined but reflective and reflexive use of what has come to be called wide reflective
equilibrium might give us a way out of the yellow wood. A central
reason why scientific method seems not to be self-correcting or (put
more minimally) sufficiently self-correcting is that it has no way of
incorporating political and other social and moral standpoints into
its account in the requisite way or of adjusting for ideological factors. Wide reflective equilibrium, by contrast, can do those things.
First articulated by Goodman and Quine (though not under that
name), utilized quite self-consciously by Rawls and by the feminist
philosophers Jane English and Marsha Hanen and extensively re-
fined and developed for ethics by Norman Daniels and recently
given a more general application by Hilary Putnam and Richard
Rorty, this method is a thoroughly coherentist, fallibilist and anti-
foundationalist way of going about things.[22] Its starting points in
considered judgments will be in varying degrees ethnocentric (what
else can they be) but it provides us with a method such that the
always provisional, always for a time, *endpoints* need not be ethnocentric or ideological. We, in the by now perhaps overused
metaphor, are constantly rebuilding the ship at sea. There neither
is nor can be a God's eye view of reality where we can escape hav-

---

22 John Rawls, *A Theory of Justice*, 19-21, 48-51, 577-87; Rawls, 'The Independence
of Moral Theory,' in *Proceedings and Addresses of the American Philosophical Association* **47** (1974/5) 7-10; Rawls, 'The Idea of an Overlapping Consensus,' *Oxford Journal of Legal Studies* **7** (1987) 1-25; Jane English, 'Ethics and Science,'
Proceedings of the XVI Congress of Philosophy; Marsha Hanen, 'Justification as
Coherence' in M.A. Stewart, ed., *Law, Morality and Rights* (Dordrecht, Nether-
lands: D. Reidel 1983), 67-92; Norman Daniels, 'Wide Reflective Equilibrium
and Theory Acceptance in Ethics,' *The Journal of Philosophy* **76** (1979); 'Some
Methods of Ethics and Linguistics,' *Philosophical Studies* **37** (1980); 'Moral Theory and the Plasticity of Persons,' *The Monist* **62** (1979); 'Reflective Equilibrium and Archimedean Points,' *Canadian Journal of Philosophy* **10** (March 1980);
'Two Approaches to Theory Acceptance in Ethics,' David Copp and David
Zimmerman, eds., *Morality, Reason and Truth* (Totowa, NJ: Rowman & Allanheld 1985); Hilary Putnam, *Realism and Reason* (Cambridge, UK: Cambridge
University Press 1983) 229-47; and Richard Rorty, 'The Priority of Democracy
to Philosophy' in Meryl Patterson and Robert Vaughan, eds., *The Virginia Statute
of Religious Freedom* (Cambridge, UK: Cambridge University Press 1987).

ing some perspective or other and just see things as they are under the one true description. But historicism and contextualism need not add up to relativism or nihilism. We can have a standpoint theory without relativism or anarchism and this, I think, is exactly what Harding and Wylie want.

Post-modernist wariness will lead us to wonder whether we are trying to get a philosophical fix here — an anti-foundationalism still hankering after what only foundationalism could provide. And such wariness is to the point. It will hardly be the first time this has happened in philosophy and it surely is true that a methodology will be just such a fix if it proceeds without scepticism, is not concerned with specific studies, concrete genealogies and narratives and does not rely repeatedly on our collective reflective good sense. (Rorty's scorn of talk of conceptual foundations is surely understandable.) But perhaps we humans will sometimes use our collective good sense and perhaps wide reflective equilibrium abstractly depicts something of what it is to do so. Perhaps it is the underlying methodology of a fallibilistic non-rationalistic modernism that has taken to heart post-modernism's salient lessons.

VI

Marsha Hanen in her introduction has pointed out rightly that feminist theory should not be construed just as a political theory guiding or attempting to guide political practice. This volume surely illustrates and confirms Hanen's claim. There are contributions to what has come to be called applied ethics, to ethical theory, to a critique of moral methodology, critical examinations of some major contemporary moral philosophers, contributions to social theory, the philosophy of science, to ideology-critique, examinations of

---

23 If that is a persuasive definition make the most of it. Not all persuasive definitions, as C.L. Stevenson well argued, need be bad. See C.L. Stevenson, *Ethics and Language* (New Haven, CT: Yale University Press 1944), Chapters IX and XIII.

epistemology and contributions to meta-philosophy. To claim that feminist theory reduces to political theory is plainly a mistake.

And yet — there is always a 'yet' in philosophy — the heart of feminist theory, the underlying rationale for its being, is broadly speaking political. As the underlying rationale for Marxist theory is its functioning as an instrument in our struggle for emancipation from class society so the *raison d'être* of feminist theory is in its capacity to serve as a guide in the struggle for women's liberation and more generally our emancipation as women and men from a gendered world. Genderlessness is to feminist theory what classlessness is to Marxist theory and they can be consistently combined in a struggle for both, though there will, of course, be questions (sometimes difficult tactical and strategic questions) about which, if either, has priority.

The activities mentioned in the first paragraph of this section are in large measure at least weapons of a theory for woman's liberation. They are part of its theoretical practice. I do not think that Hanen means to deny this or underplay it and, unless I misread their intentions, I think this is understood and assented to by the contributors to this volume. In feminist theory, even pessimistic feminist theory, there needs to be a unity of theory and practice. The point is not just to understand the condition of women but to change it, where changing it has a chance of being emancipatory, and in changing it to, at least most feminists would say, change the condition of both women and men.

A weakness of this volume — or so it seems to me — is that there is not more political writing in it, including strategic theory and whatever kind of political theory is needed in support of it. A related weakness, or at least a lacunae, is the absence of work dealing with the relation of Marxism to feminism. (It is in part compensated for by the extensive discussions of this in the literature.)

It is my view that a feminist critical theory of the scope and type characterized in the previous section would fit well with Marxism. Indeed I would think that Marxist theory and a feminist critical theory properly distancing itself from post-modernism would find themselves complementary allies and not opponents or rivals. Each makes up for the other's deficiencies. Combined they provide an impressive framework. We need, to put it crudely and oversimply, a liberation (if we can get it) from both a gendered society and a class society and, or so it seems to me, we need a reasonably unified theory to guide us in our liberation struggles. We do not theorize here just for the fun of it or just for its intrinsic interest.

Given the depth and pervasiveness of female subordination to males and by males, a critical theory in our time must be a critical feminist theory of society. (That, of course, does not mean that is all it must be.) A putatively critical theory which is not also a feminist theory simply does not have the self-consciousness to be a genuinely critical theory.

What scope our critical theory can attain cannot be determined a priori and independently of the actual nature of the problems of our age and its intellectual resources, though we can, starting from what we have, forge new intellectual resources. We will have both to see what we need and what we can get as we resolutely confront actual problems that well up in our lives (including the lives of poor and uneducated people of colour and particularly women of colour whose conditions of life are very different from most, if not all, of the people who will read this volume). If we are going to have anything like a genuinely critical theory we can rule out from the start in thinking about scope and explanatory and critical power the extremes. That is we should rule out totalizing theories that are grand speculative philosophies, à la Hegel and Spengler, of history and (at the other extreme) the limitations to the restrictive localizations of Lyotard or Derrida. But in between the field is wide open and will, I believe, be determined, if there is to be a reasonable determination, by pragmatic considerations. And these pragmatic considerations will have in part a profoundly moral and political character rooted very deeply in our hopes and sympathies, though these in turn are, where non-Quixotic, chastened by what we think is possible and what we take to be inescapable and, of course, here, as Exdell's essay poignantly shows, by what we think is likely to be, but perhaps need not be, deeply ideologically distorted. Here again, seeing the desirability of seeking a wide reflective equilibrium is vital.

In this general context, Nancy Fraser's picture of what a genuinely critical theory should be is illuminating.

A critical social theory frames its research program and its conceptual framework with an eye to the aims and activities of those oppositional social movements with which it has a partisan though not uncritical identification. The questions it asks and the models it designs are informed by that identification and interest. Thus, for example, if struggles contesting the subordination of women figured among the most significant of a given age, then a critical social theory for that time would aim, among other things, to shed light on the character and bases of such subordination. It would employ categories and explanatory models which revealed rather than occluded relations of male dominance and female subordination. And it would demystify as ideological rival approaches which obfuscated or rationalized those relations. In this situation, then, one of the standards for assessing a critical theory, once it has been subjected to all the usual tests of empirical adequacy, would be: How well does it theorize the situation and prospects of the feminist movement? To what extent does it serve the self-clarification of the struggles and wishes of contemporary women?[24]

The essays collected together here have not, as I have remarked, been of a direct political character but they are indirectly political and importantly critical. They meet, in revealing and diverse ways, Fraser's criteria for a genuinely critical theory. In this way they, taken together, make an incisive contribution to the development of feminist theory and in doing so to human emancipation. In this way they are thoroughly political. It is certainly not the intent of the critical queries I have raised about some of those essays to obscure that vital contribution: a contribution which, while being a contribution to our understanding, is not just a contribution to our understanding.[25]

---

24 Nancy Fraser, 'What's Critical About Critical Theory? The Case of Habermas and Gender,' 97

25 I am grateful to Russell Cornett and Marsha Hanen for their helpful comments on an earlier draft of this essay.

CANADIAN JOURNAL OF PHILOSOPHY
Supplementary Volume 13

Notes on Contributors

Annette Baier is a professor of philosophy at the University of Pittsburgh. She has previously taught at Carnegie-Mellon University, The University of Sydney, The University of Auckland, and The University of Aberdeen. She studied at The University of Otago and Oxford University. She has published many articles in the philosophy of mind, ethics, and the history of philosophy, some of which are collected in her recent book *Postures of the Mind* (Minneapolis: University of Minnesota Press 1985; London: Methuen Press 1986). She is also working on a book about David Hume.

Steven Burns is currently Chair of the Department of Philosophy at Dalhousie University. His interest in feminist theory has led to several publications, especially concerning Plato and Hume (e.g., in *Dialogue* [1976 and 1984]). He has recently been on leave in Vienna, trying to understand the anti-feminism of Otto Weininger.

Lorraine Code is a Canada Research Fellow with the Department of Philosophy and the Women's Studies Research Group at York University. She is the author of *Epistemic Responsibility* (University Press of New England 1987) for which she was awarded the Brown University Press First Book Prize. She is coeditor of *Changing Patterns: Women in Canada* and of *Feminist Perspectives: Philosophical Essays on Minds and Morals*. Currently, she is writing a book on Knowledge and Gender, to be published by Rowman and Littlefield. She has published numerous articles on theory of knowledge, ethics, and feminist theory.

John Exdell is Associate Professor of Philosophy at Kansas State University. His research and teaching are in the areas of Marxist and feminist social philosophy. His article in this issue was written with the benefit of an NEH Summer Seminar at Stanford University on the Woman Question in Western Thought, taught by Susan Bell and Karen Offen.

Ann Ferguson is a Professor of Philosophy and Women's Studies at the University of Massachusetts at Amherst and a faculty member in the graduate concentration in Social, Political and Recent Continental Philosophy. Her recent works have included articles in feminist theory and on the sex debate in feminism. She is currently finishing a book entitled *Blood at the Root: Motherhood, Sexuality and Male Dominance*, to be published by Routledge & Kegan Paul.

Marilyn Friedman is Director of Women's Studies and Assistant Professor of Philosophy at Bowling Green State University. Her doctorate is from the University of Western Ontario. She has published in numerous journals and anthologies on such topics as: gender and moral reasoning, autonomy, friendship, and women in poverty. A book-length manuscript entitled, 'Justice Among Friends,' is her current research project.

Marsha Hanen is Professor of Philosophy and Dean of the Faculty of General Studies at the University of Calgary, where she has developed a number of integrative interdisciplinary degree programmes, including Women's Studies. She is co-editor of *Science, Pseudo-Science and Society* (Wilfrid Laurier University Press 1980) and co-author of *Archaeology and the Methodology of Science* (University of New Mexico Press 1988). She has published widely in philosophy of science, philosophy of law and feminist theory and her current research interest is the integration of feminist theory and legal theory.

Sandra Harding is Professor of Philosophy and Director of Women's Studies at the University of Delaware. She is the author of *The Science Question in Feminism* (Cornell and Open University Presses 1986), and the editor or co-editor of *Can Theories be Refuted* (Reidel 1976), *Discovering Reality: Feminist Perspectives on Epistemology, Metaphysics, Methodology, and Philosophy of Science* (Reidel 1976), *Feminism and Methodology: Issues for Social Scientists* (Indiana 1987), and *Sex and Scientific Inquiry* (Chicago 1987).

Virginia Held is a professor of philosophy at the City University of New York (Graduate School and Hunter College). She has also taught at Barnard, Yale, Dartmouth, and UCLA. Her most recent book is *Rights and Goods: Justifying Social Action* (Free Press/Macmillan 1984). She is a co-author of *Women's Realities, Women's Choices* (Oxford 1983), and an author, editor, or co-editor of 5 other books. Her current work is in the area of feminist theory. Her article 'Feminism and Moral Theory' appears in *Women and Moral Theory*, Eva Kittay and Diana Meyers, eds. (Rowman & Littlefield 1987).

Barbara Houston is Associate Professor of Philosophy, Faculty of Education, The University of Western Ontario where she teaches philosophy and women's studies. She has published numerous articles related to the philosophy of education, theories of moral development, the ethics of care, feminist ethics and the epistemology of gender identity.

Alison M. Jaggar is Wilson Professor of Ethics and Professor of Philosophy at the University of Cincinnati. She is author of *Feminist Politics and Human Nature* (1983) and co-editor of *Feminist Frameworks* (1978, 1984) and *Feminist Reconstructions of Being and Knowing* (1988). She believes that feminist philosophy is generated and sustained by feminist activism and must remain continually responsive to political concerns. Currently, she is Chair of the American Philosophical Association's Committee on the Status of Women.

Alice Mansell is a painter and author of numerous articles on women and art, especially in the Canadian context. She was formerly Associate Dean (Research) in the Faculty of Fine Arts, The University of Calgary and is now head of the Department of Art at the University of Western Ontario.

Kathryn Morgan is Associate Professor of Philosophy and Women's Studies at the University of Toronto. She is the author of various articles on romantic love, sexuality, androgyny, feminist pedagogy, manipulative power, feminist ethical theory, and women's health. When she is not teaching or caring for her newborn son she is working on two books: *Sexuality, Human Nature, and Social Structure* and *The Metaphysical Politics of Gender: Collected Essays*.

Sheila Mullett is Associate Professor of Philosophy at Concordia University, in Montreal, where she has been teaching since 1969. She is co-editor of *Shifting Perspectives: Essays on Method and Morals* (University of Toronto Press forthcoming).

Kai Nielsen is Professor and Head of the Department of Philosophy at the University of Calgary. He has previously taught at Amherst College, New York University, Brooklyn College, the Graduate Center of the City University of New York, and the University of Ottawa. He is past president of the Canadian Philosophical Association and an executive editor of the Canadian Journal of Philosophy. His most recent book is *Equality and Liberty: A Defense of Radical Egalitarianism* (Rowman and Allanheld 1985). Two forthcoming books are his *Marxism and Sticking to the Moral Point of View* (Westview Press) and *The Just Society* (Routledge & Keagan Paul).

Christine Overall is Associate Professor of Philosophy and Queen's National Scholar at Queen's University, Kingston, Ontario. She is the author of *Ethics and Human Reproduction: A Feminist Analysis* (Allen & Unwin 1987), and co-editor, with Lorraine Code and Sheila Mullett, of *Feminist Perspectives: Philosophical Essays on Method and Morals* (University of Toronto Press forthcoming).

Sibyl Schwarzenbach is an assistant professor of philosophy at Baruch College of the City University of New York. She did her undergraduate study at Cornell, studied at the University of Heidelberg and did her Ph.D. at Harvard University where she worked with John Rawls. Her doctoral dissertation was 'Toward a New Conception of Ownership,' Harvard University 1985.

Susan Sherwin is Associate Professor of Philosophy at Dalhousie University. Her major interests are in the areas of philosophy of feminism and bioethics; in particular, she is exploring the dimensions and implications of a feminist approach to ethics.

An assistant professor in the Department of Philosophy at the University of Western Ontario, **Alison Wylie** did her graduate work in the Program for the History and Philosophy of the Social and Behavioral Sciences at SUNY-Binghamton. She works primarily in philosophy of the social and historical sciences and is co-director with Kathleen Okruhlik of a SSHRC-funded research project on 'Feminist Critiques of Science.'

Bibliography

Abel, Elizabeth, and Emily K. Abel, eds., *The Signs Reader: Women, Gender and Scholarship*. Chicago: University of Chicago Press 1983.

Allen, Jeffner, *Lesbian Philosophy: Explorations*. Palo Alto: Institute of Lesbian Studies 1986.

Allen, Sally, and Joanna Hubbs, 'Outrunning Atalanta: Feminine Destiny on Alchemical Transmutation,' *Signs* **6** (1980).

Arditti, Rita, Renate Dueli Klein and Shelley Minden, eds., *Test-Tube Women: What Future for Motherhood?* London: Pandora Press 1984.

Auerbach, J., L. Blum, V. Smith, and C. Williams, 'Commentary on Gilligan's "In a Different Voice,' " *Feminist Studies* **11**, 1 (Spring 1981).

Baier, Annette C., 'What Do Women Want in a Moral Theory?' *Nous* **19** (March 1985).

Baier, Annette C., 'Trust and Antitrust,' *Ethics* **96** (1986).

Baker, Robert, and Frederick Ellison, eds., *Philosophy and Sex*. Buffalo: Prometheus Books 1975.

Bardwick, J.M., E. Donovan, M.S. Horner and D. Gutman, *Feminine Personality and Conflict*. Belmont: Brooks/Cole 1970.

Bayles, Michael, *Reproductive Ethics*. Englewood Cliffs: Prentice-Hall 1984.

Benhabib, S., 'Communicative Ethics and Moral Autonomy,' unpublished (1982).

Benhabib, S., 'The Generalized and the Concrete Other: The Kohlberg-Gilligan Controversy and Feminist Theory,' *Praxis International* **5** (January 1986).

Blum, Lawrence, Marcia Howiak, Judy Housman and Naomi Scheman, 'Altruism and Women's Oppression,' *Philosophical Forum* **5** (1975).

Broughton, John M., 'Women's Rationality and Men's Virtues,' *Social Research* **50** (1983).

Cameron, Deborah, 'Debate on Sexist Language: Sexism and Semantics,' *Radical Philosophy* **36** (Spring 1984).

Cancian, Francesca M., 'The Feminization of Love,' *Signs* **11** (1986).

Cartledge, S., and J. Ryan, *Sex and Love: New Thoughts on Old Contradictions*. London: The Women's Press 1983.

Chodorow, Nancy, *The Reproduction of Mothering: Psychoanalysis and the Sociology of Gender*. Berkeley: University of California Press 1978.

Chodorow, Nancy, 'Feminism and Difference: Gender, Relation and Difference in Psychoanalytic Perspective,' *Socialist Review* **46** (1979).

Clark, L., and L. Lange, *The Sexism of Social and Political Theory*. Toronto: University of Toronto Press 1979.

Code, Lorraine, Sheila Mullet and Christine Overall, eds., *Feminist Perspectives: Philosophical Essays on Methods and Morals*. Toronto: University of Toronto Press forthcoming 1988.

Cohen, Cheryl H., 'The Feminist Sexuality Debate: Ethics and Politics,' *Hypatia* **1** (Fall 1986).

Culpepper, Emily, 'Female History/Myth Making,' *The Second Wave* **4**, 1 (Spring 1975).

Daly, Mary, *Gyn/Ecology: The Metaethics of Radical Feminism*. Boston: Beacon Press 1978.

Daly, Mary, *Pure Lust: Elemental Feminist Philosophy*. Boston: Beacon Press 1984.

Davis, Natalie, 'Men, Women and Violence: Some Reflections on Equality,' *Smith Alumnae Quarterly* (April 1977).

de Beauvoir, Simone, *The Second Sex*. New York: Vintage 1952.

Delman, Rosalind, 'Sexism, Capitalism and the Family,' *Radical Philosophy* **4** (Spring 1973).

Delphy, Christine, *Close to Home: A Materialist Analysis of Women's Oppression*. Amherst: University of Massachusetts Press 1984.

Diner, Helen, *Mothers and Amazons: The First Feminine History of Culture*. Trans. by John Philip Lundin. Garden City: Anchor Books 1973.

Dinnerstein, Dorothy, *The Mermaid and the Minotaur: Sexual Arrangements and Human Malaise*. New York: Harper and Row 1976.

Donchin, Anne, 'The Future of Mothering: Reproductive Technology and Feminist Theory,' *Hypatia* **1** (Fall 1986).

Dowrick, S., and S. Grundberg, *Why Children*? London: The Women's Press 1980.

Dworkin, Andrea, *Woman Hating*. New York: E.P. Dutton 1974.

Dworkin, Andrea, *Right-Wing Women*. New York: Perigee Books 1983.

Eagly, Alice H., and Valerie J. Steffen, 'Gender Stereotypes Stem From the Distribution of Women and Men Into Social Roles,' *Journal of Personality and Social Psychology* **46** (1984).

Easlea, Brian, *Science and Sexual Oppression: Patriarchy's Confrontation with Woman and Nature*. London: Weidenfeld and Nicolson 1981.

Ehrenreich, Barbara, and Deirdre English, *For Her Own Good: 150 Years of the Experts' Advice to Women*. Garden City: Anchor Press 1978.

Eisenberg, Nancy, and Roger Lennon, 'Sex Differences in Empathy and Related Capacities,' *Psychological Bulletin* **94** (1983).

Eisenstein, Hester, *The Second Sex: Thirty Years Later*. New York: Workshop 12 (September 1979).

Eisenstein, H., and A. Jardine, eds., *The Future of Difference*. New Brunswick, NJ: Rutgers University Press 1985.

Eisenstein, Zillah R., ed., *Capitalist Patriarchy and the Case for Socialist-Feminism*. New York: Monthly Review Press 1979.

Elshtain, Jean Bethke, *Public Man, Private Woman: Women in Social and Political Thought*. Princeton: Princeton University Press 1980.

Elshtain, Jean Bethke, ed., *The Family in Political Thought*. Amherst: The University of Massachusetts Press 1982.

Englehardt, H. Tristram, *The Foundations of Bioethics*. Oxford: Oxford University Press 1986.

Epstein, Barbara, 'Family Politics and the New Left,' *Socialist Review* **63-64** (May-August 1982).

Fausto-Sterling, Anne, *Myths of Gender: Biological Theories about Women and Men*. New York: Basic Books 1985.

Ferguson, Ann, 'Motherhood and Sexuality: Some Feminist Questions,' *Hypatia* **1** (Fall 1986).

Ferguson, Ann, *Blood at the Root: Motherhood, Sexuality and Male Dominance*. Boston: Methuen/Routledge forthcoming.

Ferguson, Kathy, *The Feminist Case Against Bureaucracy*. Philadelphia: Temple University 1984.

Firestone, Shulamith, *The Dialectic of Sex*. London: The Women's Press 1970.

Flanagan, Owen, 'Virtue, Sex, and Gender: Some Philosophical Reflections on the Moral Psychology Debate, *Ethics* **92** (1982).

Flax, Jane, 'The Conflict Between Nurturance and Autonomy in Mother-Daughter Relationships and Within Feminism,' *Feminist Studies* (June 1978).

Flax, Jane, 'Gender as a Social Problem: In and For Feminist Theory,' *American Studies/Amerika Studien* (1986).

Francoeur, Robert T., *Utopian Motherhood: New Trends in Human Reproduction*. New York: Doubleday 1970.

Frye, Marilyn, 'Some Reflections on Separatism and Power,' *Sinister Wisdom* (Summer 1978).

Frye, Marilyn, *The Politics of Reality: Essays in Feminist Theory*. Trumansburg: The Crossing Press 1983.

Garside, Christine, 'Can a Woman Be Good in the Same Way as a Man?' *Dialogue* **10** (1971).

Gilligan, Carol, 'Moral Development in the College Years,' in A. Chickering, ed., *The Modern American College*. San Francisco: Jossey-Bass 1981.

Gilligan, Carol, *In a Different Voice: Psychological Theory and Women's Development*. Cambridge: Harvard University Press 1982.

Gilligan, Carol, 'Reply,' *Signs* **11** (1986).

Gilligan, Carol, and John Michael Murphy, 'Development from Adolescence to Adulthood: The Philosopher and the "Dilemma of the Fact," ' in D. Kuhn, ed., *Intellectual Development Beyond Childhood*, New Directions for Child Development No. 5. San Francisco: Jossey-Bass 1979.

Gordon, Linda, *Woman's Body, Woman's Right: A Social History of Birth Control in America*. New York: Penguin Books 1977.

Gornick, Vivian, and Barbara Moran, eds., *Women in Sexist Society*. New York: Basic Books 1971.

Gorovitz, Samuel, *Doctors' Dilemmas: Moral Conflict and Medical Care*. New York: Oxford University Press 1982.

Gould, C., ed., *Beyond Domination: New Perspectives on Women and Philosophy*. Totowa: Rowman and Allanheld 1984.

Gould, Carol, and Marx Wartofsky, eds., *Women and Philosophy: Toward a Theory of Liberation*. New York: G.P. Putnam's Sons 1976.

Govier, Trudy R., 'Woman's Place,' *Philosophy* **49** (1974).

Greeno, Catherine G., and Eleanor E. Maccoby, 'How Different is the "Different Voice," ' *Signs* **11** (1986).

Grimshaw, Jean, 'Feminism: History and Morality,' *Radical Philosophy* **30** (Spring 1982).

Grimshaw, Jean, *Feminist Philosophers: Women's Perspectives on Philosophical Traditions*. Brighton: Wheatsheaf Books 1986.

Grimshaw, Jean, *Philosophy and Feminist Thinking*. Minneapolis: University of Minnesota Press 1986.

Groag Bell, Susan, and Karen M. Offen, eds., *Women, the Family and Freedom: The Debate in Documents*. Stanford: Stanford University Press 1983.

Harding, Carol, *Moral Dilemmas*. Chicago: Precedent 1986.

Harding, Sandra, 'Is Gender a Variable in Conceptions of Rationality?' *Dialectica* **36** (1982).

Harding, Sandra, *The Science Question in Feminism*. Ithaca: Cornell University Press 1986.

Harding, Sandra, *Feminism and Methodology: Issues for Social Scientists*. Bloomington: Indiana University Press 1987.

Hartsock, Nancy, *Money, Sex, and Power: Toward a Feminist Historical Materialism*. New York: Longman 1983.

Haug, Frigga, 'Morals Also Have Two Genders.' Trans. Rodney Livingstone, *New Left Review* **143** (1984).

Hein, Hilda, 'Woman and Morality,' *Ms* (1979).

Held, Virginia, 'Marx, Sex, and the Transformation of Society,' *Philosophical Forum* **5**, 1-2 (Fall-Winter 1973-74).

Held, Virginia, *Rights and Goods*. New York: The Free Press 1984.

Hintikka, M., and S. Harding, eds., *Discovering Reality: Feminist Perspectives on Epistemology, Metaphysics, Methodology, and Philosophy of Science*. Dordrecht: Reidel 1983.

Hoagland, Sarah, 'On the Status of the Concepts of Masculinity and Feminity,' Transactions of the Nebraska Academy of Sciences, Vol. 5 (August 1977).

Holstein, Constance, 'Development of Moral Judgment: A Longitudinal Study of Males and Females,' *Child Development* **47** (1976).

Hooks, B., *Ain't I a Woman? Black Women and Feminism*. London: Pluto Press 1982.

Hubbard, Ruth, Mary Sue Henifrin, and Barbara Fried, eds., *The Biological Woman: The Convenient Myth*. Cambridge: Schenkman 1982.

Jaggar, Alison, *Feminist Politics and Human Nature*. Totowa, NJ: Rowman and Allenheld 1983.

Johnstone, Jill, *Lesbian Nation: The Feminist Solution*. New York: Touchstone 1973.

Keller, Evelyn Fox, 'Women in Science: A Social Analysis,' *Harvard Magazine* (October 1974).

Keller, Evelyn Fox, 'Feminism and Science,' *Signs* **7**, 3 (1982).

Keller, Evelyn Fox, *Reflections on Gender and Science*. New Haven: Yale University Press 1985.

Keohane, Nannerl O., Michelle Z. Rosaldo, and Barbara C. Gelpi, eds., *Feminist Theory: A Critique of Ideology*. Chicago: University of Chicago Press 1982.

Kerber, Linda K., 'Some Cautionary Words for Historians,' *Signs* **11** (1986).

Kittay, Eva, and Diana Meyers, *Women and Moral Theory*. New York: Rowman and Littlefield forthcoming.

Koedt, Anne, Ellen Levine and Anita Rapone, eds., *Radical Feminism*. New York: Quadrangle 1973.

Konner, Melvin, 'She and He,' *Science* (September 1982).

Kurtines, William M. and Jacob L. Gervitz, *Morality, Moral Behaviour, and Moral Development*. New York: John Wiley and Sons 1984.

Lakoff, Robin, *Language and Woman's Place*. New York: Harper and Row 1975.

Lazaro, Reyes, 'Feminism and Motherhood: O'Brien vs. Beauvoir,' *Hypatia* **1** (Fall 1986).

Le Doeuff, Michele, 'Women and Philosophy,' *Radical Philosophy* **17** (Summer 1977).

Lloyd, Genevieve, *The Man of Reason: 'Male' and 'Female' in Western Philosophy*. Minneapolis: University of Minnesota Press 1984.

Lowe, Marion, 'The Dialectic of Biology and Culture,' Marion Lowe and Ruth Hubbard, eds., *Woman's Nature, Rationalizations of Inequality*. New York: Pergamon Press 1983.

Lugones, M., and E. Spelman, 'Have We Got a Theory for You! Feminist Theory, Cultural Imperialism, and the Demand for "The Woman's Voice," ' *Women's Studies International Forum* **6** (1983).

Maccoby, Eleanor and Carol Jacklin, eds., *The Psychology of Sex Differences*. Stanford: Stanford University Press 1974.

MacKinnon, Catherine A., 'Feminism, Marxism, Method and the State: An Agenda for Theory,' *Signs* **7** (1982).

Mattfield, J. and C. van Aiken, eds., *Women in the Scientific Professions*. Cambridge, MA: MIT Press 1965.

McDonnell, Kathleen, *Not an Easy Choice: A Feminist Reexamines Abortion*. Toronto: The Women's Press 1984.

Merchant, Carolyn, *The Death of Nature: Women, Ecology and the Scientific Revolution*. New York: Harper and Row 1980.

Meyers, Diana T., and Eva Feder Kittay, eds., *Women and Moral Theory*. Totowa: Rowman and Littlefield 1987.

Miles, Angela, and Geraldine Finn, eds., *Feminism in Canada*. Montreal: Black Rose Press 1982.

Miller, Jean Baker, ed., *Psychoanalysis and Women*. Baltimore: Penguin 1973.

Miller, Jean Baker, *Toward a New Psychology of Women*. Boston: Beacon Press 1976.

Miller, Jean Baker, 'Development of the Sense of Self in Women,' presented at the American Academy of Psychoanalysis (October 1983).

Millett, Kate, *Sexual Politics*. New York: Avon 1969.

Mitchell, Juliet, *Psychoanalysis and Feminism*. New York: Pantheon 1974.

Nemiroff, Greta, ed., *Woman and Man*. Toronto: Fitzhenry and Whiteside 1986.

Nicholson, Linda, 'Women, Morality, and History,' *Social Research* **50** (1983).

Nicholson, Linda, *Gender and History*. New York: Columbia University Press 1986.

Noddings, Nel, *Caring: A Feminine Approach to Ethics and Moral Education*. Berkeley: University of California Press 1984.

Noddings, Nel, 'In Search of the Feminine,' *Philosophy of Education: Proceedings* **41** (1985).

Nuyen, A.T., 'Sociobiology, Morality and Feminism,' *Human Studies* **8** (1985).

Nye, Andrea, 'Preparing the Way for a Feminist Praxis,' *Hypatia* **1** (Spring 1986)

O'Brien, Mary, *The Politics of Reproduction*. Boston: Routledge and Kegan Paul 1981.

Okin, Susan Moller, *Women in Western Political Thought*. Princeton: Princeton University Press 1979.

Okin, Susan Moller, 'Justice and Gender,' *Philosophy and Public Affairs* **16** (1987).

Overall, Christine, *Ethics and Human Reproduction: A Feminist Analysis*. Allen and Unwin forthcoming.

Parsons, Susan, 'Feminism and Moral Reasoning,' *Australasian Journal of Philosophy* Supplementary **64** (June 1986).

Pateman, Carol, 'The Disorder of Women: Women, Love and the Sense of Justice,' *Ethics* **91** (1980).

Pearsall, Marilyn, ed., *Women and Values*. Belmont: Wadsworth Publishing 1986.

Radcliffe Richards, Janet, *The Skeptical Feminist*. Boston: Routledge and Kegan Paul 1980.

Radical Philosophy. Special Issue on Women, Gender, and Philosophy **34** (Summer 1983).

Raymond, Janice, *The Transsexual Empire: The Making of the She-Male*. Boston: Beacon Press 1979.

Raymond, Janice, 'Female Friendship: Contra Chodorow and Dinnerstein,' *Hypatia* **1** (Fall 1986).

Raymond, Janice, *A Passion for Friends: Toward a Philosophy of Female Affection*. Boston: Beacon Press 1986.

Reed, Evelyn, *Sexism and Science*. New York: Pathfinder 1978.

Reiter, Rayna R., ed., *Toward an Anthropology of Women*. New York: Monthly Review Press 1975.

Rich, Adrienne, *Of Woman Born: Motherhood as Experience and Institution*. New York: W.W. Norton 1976.

Rich, Adrienne, *On Lies, Secrets, and Silence*. New York: W.W. Norton 1977.

Bibliography

Rich, Adrienne, 'Compulsory Heterosexuality and Lesbian Existence,' *Signs* **5** (1980).

Robertson, John A., 'Surrogate Mothers: Not So Novel After All,' The Hastings Centre Report **13** (October 1983).

Rosaldo, Michelle Zimbalist, and Louise Lamphere, eds., *Women, Culture and Society.* Stanford: Stanford University Press 1974.

Rosenberg, Rosalind, *Beyond Separate Spheres: Intellectual Roots of Modern Feminism.* New Haven: Yale University Press 1982.

Rossiter, Margaret W., *Women Scientists in America.* Baltimore: Johns Hopkins University Press 1982.

Rowbotham, Sheila, *Hidden from History: Rediscovering Women in History from the 17th Century to the Present.* New York: Random House 1974.

Rowbotham, Sheila, *Women, Resistance, and Revolution: A History of Women and Revolution in the Modern World.* New York: Vintage 1974.

Ruddick, S. 'Maternal Thinking,' *Feminist Studies* **6** (Summer 1980).

Sanday, Peggy Reeves, *Female Power and Male Dominance: On the Origins of Sexual Inequality.* New York: Cambridge University Press 1981.

Sargent, Lydia, ed., *Women and Revolution.* Boston: South End Press 1981.

Sherman, J., and E.T. Beck, eds., *The Prism of Sex: Essays in the Sociology of Knowledge.* Madison: University of Wisconsin Press 1979.

Sherwin, Susan, 'A Feminist Approach to Ethics,' *Dalhousie Review* **64** (Winter 1984-85).

Shogun, Debra, 'What is "Feminist Ethics"?' Paper presented to the Canadian Women's Studies Learned Society Meeting (Winnipeg 1986).

Simons, Margaret, 'Motherhood, Feminism and Identity,' *Hypatia* (1984).

Sokoloff, Natalie, *Between Money and Love: The Dialectics of Women's Home and Market Work.* New York: Praeger 1980.

Soules, Michael, 'The In Vitro Fertilization Pregnancy Rate: Let's Be Honest With One Another,' *Fertility and Sterility* **43**, 4 (1985).

Spender, Dale, *Man Made Language.* Boston: Routledge and Kegan Paul 1980.

432

Spender, Dale, ed., *Men's Studies Modified: The Impact of Feminism on the Academic Disciplines*. New York: Pergamon Press 1981.

Spender, Dale, *Women of Ideas (And What Men Have Done to Them)*. London: Routledge and Kegan Paul 1982.

Spender, Dale, *For the Record: The Making and Meaning of Feminist Knowledge*. London: The Women's Press 1985.

Stack, Carol B., 'The Culture of Gender: Women and Men of Colour,' *Signs* **11** (1986).

Stanley, L., and S. Wise, *Breaking Out: Feminist Consciousness and Feminist Research*. London: Routledge and Kegan Paul 1983.

Starrett, Barbara, 'I Dream in Female: The Metaphors of Evolution,' *Amazon Quarterly* **3**, 1 (November 1974).

Stimpson, Catharine R., and Ethel Spector Person, eds., *Women: Sex and Sexuality*. Chicago: University of Chicago Press 1980.

Stocker, Michael, 'The Schizophrenia of Modern Ethical Theories,' *Journal of Philosophy* **63** (1976).

Strouse, J., ed., *Women and Analysis*. New York: Dell 1975.

Thorne, Barrie, and Marilyn Yalom, eds., *Rethinking the Family: Some Feminist Questions*. New York: Longman 1982.

Traweek, Sharon, 'The Consequences of the Absence of Women in Science,' presented at MIT (March 1984).

Trebilcot, Joyce, 'Sex Roles: The Argument from Nature,' *Ethics* **85** (1975).

Trebilcot, Joyce, 'Two Forms of Androgynism,' *Journal of Social Philosophy* **8** (1977).

Trebilcot, Joyce, *Mothering: Essays in Feminist Theory*. Totowa: Rowman and Allanheld 1983.

Vetterling-Braggin, M., F. Elliston and J. English, *Feminism and Philosophy*. Totowa: Littlefield Adams 1977.

Vetterling-Braggin, M., ed., *Philosophy, Sex and Language*. Totowa: Littlefield Adams 1980.

Bibliography

Walker, James, 'In a Different Voice: Cryptoseparatist Analysis of Female Moral Development,' *Social Research* **50**, 3 (1983).

Walters, William, and Peter Singer, eds., *Test-Tube Babies*. Melbourne: Oxford University Press 1982.

Warnock, Mary, *A Question of Life: The Warnock Report on Human Fertilisation and Embryology*. Oxford: Basil Blackwell 1985.

Whitbeck, Caroline, 'Theories of Sex Differences,' *Philosophical Forum* **5** (1973-74).

Williams, Juanita, ed., *Psychology of Women: Selected Readings*. New York: W.W. Norton 1979.

Williams, Linda, 'But What Will They Mean for Women? Feminist Concerns About the New Reproductive Technologies,' *Feminist Perspective* **6**.

Wilson, Leslie, 'Is a Feminine Ethics Enough?' *Atlantis* (forthcoming).